# CLASSROOM WARS

# CLASSROOM WARS

Language, Sex, and the Making
of Modern Political Culture

Natalia Mehlman Petrzela

# OXFORD
UNIVERSITY PRESS

Oxford University Press is a department of the University of
Oxford. It furthers the University's objective of excellence in research,
scholarship, and education by publishing worldwide.

Oxford   New York
Auckland   Cape Town   Dar es Salaam   Hong Kong   Karachi
Kuala Lumpur   Madrid   Melbourne   Mexico City   Nairobi
New Delhi   Shanghai   Taipei   Toronto

With offices in
Argentina   Austria   Brazil   Chile   Czech Republic   France   Greece
Guatemala   Hungary   Italy   Japan   Poland   Portugal   Singapore
South Korea   Switzerland   Thailand   Turkey   Ukraine   Vietnam

Published in the United States of America by
Oxford University Press
198 Madison Avenue, New York, NY 10016

An earlier version of Chapter 1 was published as "Before the Federal Bilingual Education Act:
Legislation and Lived Experience," *Immigration and Education: A Special Issue of the Peabody
Journal of Education* 85, no.4 (November 2010): 406–424.

An earlier version of Chapter 6 was published as "'Sex Ed . . . and the Reds?' Reconsidering
the Anaheim Battle over Sex Education, 1962–1969," *History of Education Quarterly* 47, no. 2
(May 2007): 203–232.

Some material appears in an earlier form in "Revisiting the Rightward Turn: Max Rafferty,
Education, and Modern American Politics," *The Sixties: A Journal of History, Politics, and Culture*
6, no. 2 (2013).

Library of Congress Cataloging-in-Publication Data
Petrzela, Natalia Mehlman.

Classroom wars : language, sex, and the making of modern political culture / Natalia
Mehlman Petrzela.
    pages cm
ISBN  978–0–19–935845–8 (hardback)
1. Public schools—California—History—20th century.   2. Education, Bilingual—
California—History—20th century.   3. Sex instruction—California—History—20th century.
4. Education and state—California—History—20th century.   I. Title.
LA243.P48 2015
371.0109794—dc23
2014035885

9 8 7 6 5 4 3 2 1
Printed in the United States of America
on acid-free paper

For Michal, Tobias, and Luciana

# CONTENTS

# ACKNOWLEDGMENTS

When I first became interested in the issues this book undertakes—how schools have negotiated the challenges of teaching about sexuality and language in an age of unprecedented diversity—I was a twenty-two year old concluding a dizzying year teaching Spanish at a public school populated largely by English language learners. Several years earlier, I had graduated high school in a progressive suburban district paradoxically known both for welcoming the country's first public school Gay-Straight Alliance and for germinating the Parents' Rights Coalition, a conservative grass-roots group committed to restricting sex education through opt-in requirements and removing any references to "the homosexual agenda." The more I puzzled over the questions raised by my own life as a student and a teacher, the more I realized the answers—or at least more illuminating questions—resided in historical inquiry. I am lucky to have had the opportunity to devote my graduate studies to the scholarly exploration of these topics, and my intellectual debts over the decade this book project has spanned are tremendous.

*Classroom Wars* owes its ultimate expression to Susan Ferber of Oxford University Press, who recognized the potential of my manuscript early on and has graciously and expertly shepherded me through the process of publishing my first book. Both the details of my writing and the scope of my argument have been sharpened thanks to Susan's invaluable insights, and she places the bar very high for my future editorial collaborations.

This project, however, began as a series of graduate seminar papers, and it is my doctoral advisers to whom I am most grateful for nurturing this project, though it bears the influence of all of Stanford's Americanists. Foremost, Estelle Freedman proved an even more inspiring mentor than I could have imagined when I knew only about her pathbreaking scholarship. A model teacher and scholar, Estelle has both encouraged me to conceive of my work in the most ambitious terms and has paid painstaking attention to the details of my writing and professional development. Albert Camarillo embodies a similar standard of excellence, and he led me to engage deeply with the rich history of Latinos and the West in a way this East-coaster could not have fathomed upon arriving in California in 2002. I benefited from the generous attention of scholars at Stanford's School of Education, and I am especially grateful to Joy Ann Williamson, David Tyack, David Labaree, and Sam Wineburg. I also owe great thanks to political philosopher Rob Reich for pushing me to tackle the theoretical "big questions" about morality, multiculturalism, and civic identity not always inherent to social history.

In many ways, my book is the culmination of interests first sparked during my undergraduate years in the history department at Columbia University. Alan Brinkley's magisterial lectures first fascinated me with twentieth-century American political history and the project of constructing a narrative; Richard Bushman guided me through my first serious archival research and pushed me to think about the history of moral reform, a project I have clearly continued beyond the 1830s where I began two decades ago; Kenneth T. Jackson led me to see suburbia as far more than the backdrop of my own childhood; and Ellen Baker introduced me to a field that has shaped this book and my identity as a feminist.

The California stories this book contains were largely written up in New York City and are far more engaging for the intellectual community I have found here, thanks especially to Jon Zimmerman's vibrant network of historians of education who gather on Greene Street for a monthly writing group. Since I encountered Jon's book on culture wars as a first-quarter graduate student, I knew I unquestionably "wanted to do work like that," and I never imagined I would enjoy his detailed and thoughtful insights on my manuscript. Robert Cohen, Harold Wechsler, Ansley Erickson, Zoë Burkholder, and Joan Malczewski have all been especially helpful in framing this work. My colleagues at The New School, especially Jeremy Varon, Julia Ott, Claire Potter, and Federico Finchelstein have shaped this manuscript both in their concrete contributions and in the admirable professional examples they set.

Generous financial support from the Spencer Foundation, the Mrs. Giles Whiting Foundation, the Mellon Foundation, the Stanford Department of History, and Office of the Provost at The New School allowed me to make many archival trips and to devote myself to substantial stretches of uninterrupted writing. The opportunity to present this work at a wide range of academic conferences and seminars afforded me the expert insights of a diverse range of scholars including Bruce Schulman, Adam Laats, Matt Lassiter, Amy Farrell, Stacie Taranto, Clay Howard, Andrew Hartman, Natasha Zaretsky, Michelle Nickerson, Andrew Highsmith, Kim Phillips-Fein, Heather Lewis,

Rachel Devlin, and Judith Kafka. The patience and resourcefulness of more archivists and librarians than I can list here have contributed hugely to the scope of *Classroom Wars* and to my ability to make brief trips to far-flung archives from Sacramento to San Diego and from Cedar Rapids to Cambridge highly valuable.

This formal support is matched only by the phenomenal community that has made the journey of research and writing far more exhilarating than exhausting. My circle of devoted and accomplished friends has motivated me with their excellence in diverse endeavors, rallied me with their good humor, and asked with just the right frequency for progress updates on a very long project. Sarah Manekin, my "accountability partner," kept me productive over years of daily writing "check-ins" and mutual support sessions. Her thoughtful reflections have enriched my writing and thinking, and her friendship my life. Patricia Moreno has taught me that fitness of mind and body are inextricably intertwined, and thanks to her I have endeavored to pursue both passionately while completing this book. More recently, the wonderful virtual world of the Grafton Line Challenge has cheered me on through countless early morning writing sessions and inspired me with their collective progress to cross my own finish line.

I also owe much to my immediate family. My husband, Michal Petrzela, has been a pillar of support of my "life in the archives," even as our home has often come to resemble one. My children Toby and Lucy unwittingly assisted me with completing this book, each of their births furnishing me with the most absolute deadlines I've ever been up against. Nancy Peter's incredible generosity of spirit has enabled me not only to spend countless hours on this project, but to do so with the liberating peace of mind that my children are in capable, loving hands. Finally, I thank my parents, Alicia Borinsky and Jeffrey Mehlman, who good-naturedly encouraged me, at four years old, as I regaled them nightly with "my lectures." That each began with the phrase "In the olden days" might suggest I was a born historian, but it is thanks to my parents' encouragement, contagious passion for learning and teaching, and unflagging commitment to excellence that I developed the courage and discipline to pursue this path.

For the enormous support I have received, any imperfections this book contains are my responsibility.

Natalia Mehlman Petrzela
New York City, September 2014

CLASSROOM WARS

# INTRODUCTION

In 1980, conservative social critic Tom Bethell reflected on his trip to the White House Conference on the Family in the antiabortion journal *The Human Life Review*. Even before arriving to the conference center, Bethell found the experience thoroughly depressing. Navigating traffic in the poorer neighborhoods of the nation's capital, he lamented the "morose males standing on D.C. street corners, their nearly invisible problem that they are most likely to be living with women who are on welfare—women thus paid more by the state than the men can hope to earn."[1] This distorted arrangement and these "demoralized" young men, he continued, "account for the dangerous condition of city ghettos, and for the fractured state of families at the lower end of the socio-economic spectrum."[2] Bethell was skeptical of the federal government's ability to redress these fundamental social problems and dismissed the conference as "a veiled attempt by the White House and the bureaucracy to drum up support for more governmental involvement . . . justified as 'helping families . . . ' [which] often turns out to be harmful."

That the plaintive Bethell would find a receptive audience in 1980 is not surprising. His frustrations echo complaints among conservatives then and now: poor minorities, broken homes, welfare freeloaders, and an impoverished urban core are the fault of a wrongheaded federal government spending freely on social problems perpetuated by liberal excess. As historians have shown, throughout the 1970s and 1980s, many Americans who felt excluded or frustrated by the social revolutions of the 1960s—what Richard Nixon called "the silent majority"—found their voice, sometimes in far-right journals like *The Human Life Review*. Around the country, often in suburbs and mobilized by conservative women, these citizens organized to oppose what they perceived as a dangerous "new morality." The social transformations they bemoaned were symbolized by civil rights demonstrations, a new openness about sexuality, and the "slobbish" and antipatriotic young people who spoke out against the Vietnam War and racial inequality, rejecting with miniskirts, ripped jeans, and unkempt hair their parents' neatly tailored clothing, coifs, and Cold War political consensus.

Most disturbing to some was the apparently growing role of the federal government in institutionalizing these changes. Rather than a passing phase, it seemed that Congress and the Supreme Court were, with one measure after another, fundamentally altering the fabric of American society. Over two decades, federal mandates desegregated schools, legalized the Pill and abortion, expanded African American civil rights, narrowed the definition of obscenity, constricted prayer in school, recognized interracial marriage, and opened the gates of foreign immigration to Asia and Latin America. Until recently, histories of the 1960s were defined by these seismic shifts; lately, a narrative chronicling the "rise of the Right" in opposition to these cultural changes has become crucial to fully understanding this era in American history. Bethell's frustrations in many ways epitomize the sensibility of this brewing reaction.

But Bethell's story reveals an important dimension of this era that has gone unexplored. When he finally concluded his journey through the ghettoes of Washington, DC, he encountered a less familiar scene that *really* drove home what was amiss in America. About his arrival at the convention center, Bethell wrote, "I immediately knew I had come to the right place, because there was a sign saying: *Bienvenidos a la Conferencia de la Casa Blanca Sobre las Familias.* To Bethell, who had recently penned an inflammatory piece in *Harper's* equating bilingual education with "yanking the melting pot from the stove," this Spanish-language poster at a federal conference on American families sounded a new and urgent alarm he imagined would resonate with the readership of an expressly antiabortion journal.[3] In his view, the United States and its essential building block, the nuclear family, were endangered by what he disdainfully styled "this bilingual business." The eleven-word sign was "ultimately of the greatest importance":

> What we are witnessing, I believe, is something far less auspicious; another testament to the national demoralization. Americans who put up signs in Spanish will tell you that they have become "sensitive" to the needs of other people. What they really mean, however, is that they no longer believe in themselves. The sign I saw at the front door was our country's collective weakness and self-doubt on display.[4]

Bethell's words evince an important strand of the story this book tells: how over the course of the late 1960s and 1970s, a growing number of Americans fused conventional values about family and personal morality with an Anglo jingoism, specifically marrying concerns about sexuality and language and blurring the distinction between public and private. The "Latinization" of the United States, which transpired as a result of heavy Latin American immigration after the 1965 Hart-Celler Act and a new celebration of ethnic identity empowered by the civil rights movements of the 1960s, is much discussed today and was well underway by the early 1980s. The role of Latinos in the "rise of the Right," however, has been overlooked by historians of both Latinos and of conservatism.

To many twenty-first century Americans, these questions of morality and nationhood suffuse one another and remain as urgent as Bethell thought them when he visited the nation's capital in 1980. An apparently unremitting flow of both documented and undocumented Latin American immigrants has prompted deliberation over building an "immigration fence" along the US-Mexico border—one Republican presidential hopeful suggested in 2011 that it be electrified—and groups such as the Minutemen gain national attention for their vigilante efforts to "protect" American culture from "illegals."[5] In Texas, a state literally at the front lines of this apparent onslaught, the first principle of the Republican Party's 2012 education platform champions "American Identity Patriotism and Loyalty" and dismisses "multicultural curriculum as divisive" and as fostering "alienation among racial and ethnic groups."[6] In the same document, the Texas GOP rejects any pedagogy with "the purpose of . . . undermining parental authority," casting family and nation as the twin infallible authorities most besieged by contemporary culture.[7] Amid a major economic crisis, this impassioned discourse reveals the continued rawness of cultural tensions that emerged with particular salience a half-century earlier.

Thanks to organizations ranging from James Dobson's Focus on the Family to the gay-marriage-advocating Freedom to Marry, the family is still front and center in contemporary debates about the nation's moral health. Even as the new millennium has seen the spreading, state-by-state institutionalization of gay marriage, a divergent worldview endures. California, ever a site of political volatility, became the first state to legalize gay marriage in 2008, only to repeal it by referendum months later. Four years later, Planned Parenthood, providing reproductive health education and services for nearly a century, fought against defunding in one skirmish of a struggle that liberals have styled a Republican "war against women." The issues of schools and youth are particularly fraught arenas. One television advertisement supporting the gay-marriage ban in California featured a little girl of indeterminate ethnicity telling her mother, "Mommy, today I learned a prince can marry a prince, and I can marry a princess!"[8] An older, white male law professor interrupts to inform viewers that this nightmarish scenario "has already happened" in Massachusetts, rendering parents powerless to protect their second graders from learning that "boys can marry boys."[9]

Despite fleeting claims by some journalists in the first decade of the millennium that the culture wars—first so defined in the early 1990s and waged between "the quiet, ordinary, patriotic, religious law-abiding Many, and the noisy, elitist, amoral, disorderly, condescending Few"—constituted a "dying era of politics," the twenty-first century so far reveals the persistence of these divisions.[10] In the presidential election of 2008, a sense initially prevailed that the contest between "maverick" Republican John McCain and Democrat Barack Obama, often described as "the first post-60s candidate," would transpire in the political center. McCain's selection and the ensuing celebrity of vice-presidential candidate Sarah Palin—who prided herself on embodying the values of largely white "small-town America"—dramatically altered this perception, revealing and arguably deepening the cultural rift among the American populace. To social conservatives in the new millennium, embracing abstinence-only education, limiting access to contraception, and opposing gay marriage have come to define a truly American sexual politics, in contrast to Obama's "party of Woodstock," whose support of comprehensive sex education was branded as antifamily and thus unpatriotic.[11] By the 2012 election, marked by the ideologically opposed but equally impassioned grass-roots movements of Occupy Wall Street and the Tea Party, scholars and the popular media across the political spectrum defined the contemporary era by its intense polarization.[12]

*Classroom Wars* shows how fights in and about the schoolhouse—classroom wars—formed a crucial crucible in which the powerful political notion of "family values" was contested and constructed. This book focuses on bilingual (Spanish-language) and sex education in California in order to understand how grass-roots citizens came to define the schoolhouse and the family as politicized sites during the late 1960s and 1970s.[13] Sex education became a vital arena in the classroom wars as cultural conservatives defined the family as imperiled by morally lax progressives. In the late 1960s, a central plank of the anti-sex education argument was that discussion of sexuality in the schoolhouse eroded parental authority, leaving children vulnerable to their own desires and to the blandishments of a society undergoing profound transformations in sexual behavior and morality.[14] Though contemporary conservatives lay virtually exclusive claim to the project of defending the American family, the aim of the sexual liberals who advocated for these programs was to manage the onslaught of sexual explicitness in the broader culture rather than to encourage its more overt expression. Even as such curricula proliferated, many doubted the propriety of addressing such sensitive questions outside of the home. In 1969, at one of numerous public state hearings on sex education, a liberal San Francisco physician explained that although he tentatively accepted classroom sex education, "the home was ideally the prime place for this kind of education."[15]

While the threat sex education represented to the family—in introducing an alternate value system and bringing historically private matters into the civic realm beyond the reach of parental supervision—may be more apparent than the menace embodied by Spanish-language bilingual-bicultural programs, many conservatives in the 1960s and 1970s invoked the erosion of the American family and culture to mount opposition to both.[16] Southern Californian journalist John Steinbacher was notorious for his fulminations about sex education's pernicious effects on family cohesion and on children's morality and patriotism. He turned the same argument on the federal Department of Health, Education, and Welfare (HEW) for promoting bilingual-bicultural education, denigrating its antipatriotic "one-worldism" and support for the nefarious "plan by educationists to undo the 'poison' that the American family visits on its children."[17] According to Steinbacher, "HEW is . . . impatient with the number of American homes which still hold to Christian absolutes in rearing children, and they work through the federal agency to provide an alternative to rearing the child in the home."[18] Though Steinbacher spoke from the far Right, many came to link these and other progressive educational programs not only with threats to the family and nation but also with rising taxes, which they feared were being squandered on morally lax educators teaching ethically questionable curricula.

Erosion of family authority and the erection of an invasive, liberal state bureaucracy often appeared to reinforce one another. A pamphlet popular in conservative circles, "What is Sensitivity Training?," linked this dynamic expressly to questions of race, sexuality, and student activism. First, the anonymous pamphlet argues, "PhDs, behavioral scientists, psychologists, [and] psychiatrists" portray "parents as not having exercised their responsibility [making] it necessary for government education."[19] The two social questions that represented the greatest threat to family and individual liberty were the "race issue" and sex education. The pamphlet elaborated: "Let's take a civil rights demonstration . . . which only allows the enactment of laws which can result in greater loss of liberty." Or, it suggests, well-meaning parents horri-fied by the presence of venereal disease and sexual profligacy might naively turn to school-based sex education, only to find that such programs allow "the federal government to dictate the morals of our youth. The ultimate result is that the parent relinquishes his responsibility to nurture the moral principles, which are the prerequisite of a free society."[20]

As the public schools fell in collective esteem, the white nuclear family gov-erned by an immutable set of "parental values" became similarly hallowed as infallible. The overwhelmingly white parents and policymakers who protested sex education programs did so on the grounds that parental authority should trump that of educators. Bilingual education advocates also invoked the family to support their cause, though far less successfully. Indeed, bilingual-bicultural education supporters called upon the school to recognize the salience of native language and familial culture to the educational experience of English lan-guage learners. Yet they were most often rebuffed—at times by the same peo-ple who claimed the primacy of the family in debates over sex education—with claims that the schoolhouse was civic, neutral space, where "home" language and culture had no rightful claim. Not all such opposition came from Anglos. Among the countless testimonies of Latino immigrants who had "done just fine with a blond-haired, blue-eyed teacher," Mexican American social critic Richard Rodriguez emerged in the early 1980s as a leading critic of bilingual education. He too invoked the public-private divide, claiming that central to his success was the distinction he drew between Spanish as the language of the home and English as that of civic and academic life.[21]

In short, the educational policies of the 1970s defined an Anglo and a Latino child standing at the schoolhouse doors very differently.[22] The Anglo child brought from home a legacy to be nurtured in the public sphere, while the Latino child's cultural and social patrimony was often represented as a defi-ciency. Interestingly, while bilingualism opponents continually fortified the American "value-neutral" school against incursions by the Spanish-speaking home, detractors of sex education lambasted curricula primarily for challeng-ing family unity and parental values.

The cases of sexuality and bilingual education meaningfully nuance our understanding of contemporary "small-government" conservatism. Bilingual education earned bitter condemnation as a symbol of wasteful federal spend-ing and intrusion on local prerogative. Though sex education curricula were overwhelmingly developed locally, opponents also portrayed them (very effec-tively) as tools of socialist-style big government. These opponents appealed with equal fervor to state authorities to curb sex education and to protect parental authority, successfully securing legislation to ban materials produced by the Sexuality Information and Education Council of the United States (SIECUS) from schools and to restrict access to sex education courses. In one case, they took their fight to the United States Supreme Court. This paradox—citizens condemning an imagined threat of government intrusion at the federal level while calling upon the California bureaucracy for action—reveals anxiety about the role of the state as well as universal dependence on it. This book charts how this tension was negotiated during the 1960s and 1970s as mounting concern over educational progressivism, cultural and moral decay, and fiscal improvidence galvanized a powerful politics that engaged many Californians and ultimately many Americans.[23]

These political debates took place in suburban living rooms and packed school auditoriums, on editorial pages and in the halls of state and local governments, but at the center of all of them were K–12 classrooms. Many studies of this era pose higher education "campuses in conflict" as the most evocative sites to explain this transformative era, but *Classroom Wars* takes a different tack. While the Free Speech Movement, anti-Vietnam War protests, and stirrings of the sexual revolution surely found their earliest expression among college students, the schoolhouse merits scrutiny for different reasons. The realm of K-12 education reveals how parents, teachers, and increasingly students transmitted, and resisted, the social revolutions of the 1960s and 1970s, and thus how they explicitly endeavored to influence future generations. Countless student newspapers and other writings show that issues including bilingual and sex education, busing, flexible scheduling, dress codes, and social studies inspired students far younger than college age and their parents to articulate a worldview to define the purposes for which they perceived their education. This vitality lends a new perspective to a literature that often circumscribes "the campus" within university gates.[24]

This book explores these origins in the exceptional but nationally evocative site of California during the late 1960s and 1970s, a time when the state experienced intense demographic, social, and cultural displacements that would come to shape the United States at large. The Immigration Act of 1965 transformed California's population; by some counts, over twelve hundred new immigrants, mostly Spanish speaking, flooded the state daily. These new immigrants encountered a particularly fraught moment in race relations. Black Power militants established their stronghold in Oakland, while the Watts riots of 1965 and the assassination of civil rights advocate Robert F. Kennedy in Los Angeles all testified to the militancy of racial politics in this era.

The broader counterculture also flourished in California: the Free Speech Movement was born at the University of California, Berkeley, and the sexual revolution and antiwar movement also found powerful expression on campuses statewide. While the droves of immigrants arriving in California and soon spreading nationwide attested to the durability of a particular American dream, this fraught context also indicated that the nature of that imagined America was in flux.[25]

Conservatives and liberals both seized upon California's classrooms as symbolic of the peril and promise for the larger nation. On the one hand, this exceptionally centralized system was celebrated as a laboratory for the most cutting-edge educational innovations. A policymaker recalled with some fondness that in the 1960s, "the elapsed time between the appearance of an idea in a national education journal and its legislation into the California State Education Code averaged about three months."[26] Due at least in part to such dynamism, conservatives represented California schools as cultivating citizens of questionable character. A popular pamphlet circulating nationally used the overwhelming narcotic use of students at Northern California's Fort Bragg High School as a cautionary tale, pointing to its proximity to "that famous hippie wasteland, Mendencino [sic]," and to easy access to "those south-of-the-border mind-bending drugs."[27] Locally developed sex education programs also brought California mixed attention, as communities such as San Mateo and Anaheim introduced pathbreaking curricula that were met with as much negative attention as accolades. The San Mateo superintendent declared, "The movement to purge our schools is national in scope. [Our] materials have been the source of inquiries from Nashville, Tennessee, from Newtonville, New York, from El Paso, Texas, and on."[28] As one historian aptly claimed, "California politics since 1945 have distilled to an essence what has been at stake in the nation," and education was no exception.[29]

The most familiar images of educational conflict in the 1960s and 1970s are of black children entering desegregated schools and of whites violently resisting these incursions.[30] In California, with its especially variegated racial and political environment, every educational question reverberated within the context of the desegregation mandates that cities struggled to implement in the wake of *Brown v. Board of Education*.[31] One mother ardently opposed to sex education in her almost lily-white district trumpeted the claim that sex educators played "wild African music" and encouraged interracial sex.[32] In San Francisco, Latinos and Asians confounded the image of only racist white Southerners protesting desegregation, as these two ethnic minorities rallied to maintain critical masses of their ethnic groups in particular schools in order to secure the enrollment necessary to guarantee funding for bilingual programs.[33] Desegregation had profound policy implications for Californians and also shaped daily realities and perceptions of a range of curricular questions.

Historians of elementary and secondary schooling are beginning to consider individual curricular questions in relation to one another and the broader social context, and this book expands the purview of such scholarship to offer fresh perspectives on American political culture.[34] Though historians have treated bilingual and sex education in isolation from one another (and from other curricula), there is extensive archival evidence that policymakers and citizens alike engaged with these programs together and sometimes in surprisingly illuminating ways.[35] John Steinbacher, best known for his strident equation of sex education with perversion and anti-communism, actually crafted his staunch conservatism around what he styled "the bilingual fraud": tax-financed bilingual education programs promoted by Mexican-American and liberal activists.[36] Edwin Klotz, recognized for his crusading moralism and opposition to sex education and busing as the chair of the state's Moral Guidelines Committee, is less well known for holding an advanced degree in Hispanic Studies.[37] Rafferty, remembered as a dyed-in-the-wool opponent of "all forms of progressive education," actually pioneered several bilingual education programs early in his career.[38] S. I. Hayakawa, who by his Senate term (R-CA) in the late 1970s had distinguished himself as a leading critic of bilingual education, had been a member of the American Humanist Association, an organization despised by sex education opponents.[39] Leon Panetta, President Obama's secretary of defense, whose passion for civil rights in general and bilingual education specifically led him to defect to the Democratic party in the early 1970s, credited his mentor, Orange County Republican senator Thomas Kuchel, with cultivating these sensibilities. By the late 1970s, as the culture wars took shape and definitions of *liberal* and *conservative* hardened, these juxtapositions became untenable. *Classroom Wars'* synthetic approach lays bare some unlikely political alignments that challenge prevailing assumptions about ethnicity, race, region, and political affiliation, as well as the ascendancy of New Right conservatism.

Focusing on public education challenges another common assumption about modern politics: that social and economic issues are distinct from one another. The idea that conservative strategists employ incendiary cultural issues to distract voters from "real" economic interests is argued most energetically by social critic Thomas Frank.[40] This book challenges this dichotomy, arguing that cultural and fiscal concerns are actually intertwined and that classroom wars offer an illuminating method of parsing their relationship.

Much as historian Bethany Moreton has cast Christian antipathy to abortion and homosexuality "as part of an economic vision," this story shows how resistance to ethnic and linguistic diversity, sexual liberation, and the "new morality" of the 1960s were not only intricately connected to one another but also embedded in a rising antitax and antigovernment sensibility felt across the political spectrum by the late 1970s.[41]

As these examples suggest, the "rise of the Right" narrative insufficiently explains the politics and culture of the 1970s. Specifically, the emergence of and fights over bilingual and sex education demand a reappraisal of the late 1960s as a culmination of the liberal impulses of the preceding decade which then engendered a period of backlash in the 1970s. The story is more complex. On the one hand, the passage of the federal Bilingual Education Act in January 1968 and the walkouts staged by thousands of Latino students in East Los Angeles two months later evince the full flowering of the Great Society liberalism, as well as of the increasingly widespread ritual of youth demonstration activism. Similarly, the passion of citizens all over the state organizing against sex education, and soon after bilingual education, signal a burgeoning conservatism, a "sleeping giant" roused by perceived liberal excesses.[42] Yet Rafferty, who proudly anointed himself responsible for "killing progressive education in California," is less well known for appointing Deputy Superintendent Eugene Gonzales, the highest-ranking Mexican American appointee to state office, with whom he pioneered California's first, and relatively robust, bilingual education program. This history demonstrates the need both to reconsider modern bilingual education's purportedly leftist origins and to reassess the era's liberal and conservative politics. Similarly, by late 1968, attacking "family life and sex education" had become a plank of a strengthening conservative sensibility. It can be easy to forget that such progressive programs were created, thrived, and even nationally recognized in Southern California for several years with little incident, challenging the perception of Orange County as a fount of unadulterated conservatism.[43]

Tracing bilingual and sex education in California through the 1970s unearths an intertwined history of persistent contestation the "rise of the Right" narrative can elide. If conservatives found new voice in this era, they did so in response to cultural forces that only became *more* powerful during the 1970s until today.[44] Sex education programs that engaged openly with abortion and homosexuality were bolstered by organizations such as Planned Parenthood and proliferated during the 1970s. Parents continued to complain about sex education, but their (many fewer) letters revealed that teachers often invited homosexual speakers to class, addressed abortion, and even spoke openly about female desire in certain cases. Even in the late 1960s, the programs labeled most progressive steered clear of such topics—and still ignited intense controversy. Similarly, bilingual education gained a foothold still felt today in American schools and culture. Initially implemented largely by politically strategic white policymakers, bilingual-bicultural education became a central focus of radical young Chicanos' activism and of newly formed advocacy groups, such as the Mexican American Legal and Educational Defense Fund, both of which challenged the assimilationism of earlier programs. During the 1970s, these advocates fought not only to emphasize cultural pride as much as linguistic proficiency but also to expose Anglo children to such curricula. Today's emphasis on "multiculturalism" owes much to the innovations of this era.

In the 1960s and 1970s, an especially wide range of historical actors fought bitterly to claim public schools as their own, reflecting a shared, but fleeting, faith that "the public schools are a fundamental, enduring institution of our society," and the bodies best suited to resolve what Governor Ronald Reagan deemed "a moral crisis."[45] The classroom wars of the age proved so divisive that this faith, not to mention the willingness to finance it, faltered. In 1970, one father wrote to Rafferty to agree with Hayakawa, not yet famous for founding U.S. English, which would become the nation's preeminent antibilingual education organization, that morally lax public school teachers were encouraging students to abdicate personal responsibility; this parent advocated "returning traditional authority to parents."[46] By 1976, Howard Jarvis, who would become famous for instigating the popular tax revolt Proposition 13, spoke out in support of Hayakawa's cause.[47] This concern, as one San Francisco physician put it, that both "situational ethics" and a "relatively new concept that . . . something can be amoral" became far more offensive as Californians felt tax-supported schools imparted these troubling messages.[48] Passionate parents circulated pamphlets and wrote thousands of letters linking the cultural pluralism attendant to bilingual-bicultural education with the moral relativism associated with sex education. They blamed misguided educators for the decay of family and nation, at great economic cost.

California politics are notoriously unstable. Though Governor Ronald Reagan successfully fused concerns about rising taxes, educational permissiveness, and liberalism and tethered them to his liberal predecessor Pat Brown, Democrat Gerry Brown ultimately succeeded Reagan as governor. Even as suspicion and outright opposition to pedagogical innovation and rising taxes emerged, bilingual and sex-education programs thrived in many California districts. As bilingual education advocates organized at the grass roots, made legislative inroads at the state level, and won the landmark

*Lau v. Nichols* US Supreme Court case (1974) mandating the provision of bilingual education, and as the sexual revolution rendered futile attempts to silence sexual speech, classrooms all over the state experimented with "multicultural curricula" and engaged openly on topics such as homosexuality and masturbation that a decade earlier had been considered verboten. These undeniable gains, however, continued to galvanize opposition, as ardent defenses of family and nation coalesced in antitax rhetoric and mobilization.

In 1978, such antitax sentiment bubbled over into the Jarvis Initiative (Proposition 13), the overwhelmingly popular taxpayer revolt commonly understood to have "killed" public education in California. "Prop 13," however, remains unrecognized by scholars as having originated from concerns over classroom politics. Significantly, the citizens who rallied behind the tax revolt perceived education as one of the costliest, but crucial, social goods, yet took issue specifically with the type of education untrustworthy government bureaucrats and academics advocated. Jarvis himself was unapologetic about his belief that "13 must and should force a total reevaluation of the public school system in California."[49] Concerns about education are enmeshed with concerns about the family, and Jarvis skillfully linked the two with distrust of government that perceptions of Great Society excess and the Watergate scandal had inflamed.

By the early 1980s, the shared sense across the political spectrum that public schools were sites worthy of intense contestation began to diminish. Both funding cuts and the emerging popularity of educational solutions outside the public system, such as school vouchers and later, homeschooling and charters, shifted the attention of conservative reformers and parents away from the public schools.[50] A meaningful legacy of this transition are the liberal and progressive reforms that remain inscribed in today's classrooms, from multiculturalism to group work to yoga—despite the predominant historiographical interpretation of this era as "rightward bound." By the early 1980s, the issues of family, morality, language, and nation that had germinated at California school boards and parent-teacher association (PTA) meetings and in student newspapers came to engage not only concerned observers such as Bethell but also to preoccupy Americans about the future of their culture writ large. *Classroom Wars* chronicles how and why this history transpired in the crucible of 1960 and 1970s California and suggests how it was crucial to the making of our modern political culture.

# LANGUAGE

"We should replace bilingual education with immersion in English so people learn the common language of the country and . . . of prosperity, not the language of living in a ghetto."

These words, spoken in 2007 by conservative Republican Newt Gingrich before the National Federation of Republican Women, became the source of an evocative controversy during the presidential primaries five years later. In a Spanish-language radio ad during the 2012 presidential primaries, Mitt Romney blasted Gingrich for deriding Spanish as a ghetto language—only to be called out in the presidential debates when Gingrich, to a cheering audience, correctly pointed out that he had never uttered the word *Spanish*.[1] Nonetheless, Gingrich took to YouTube to apologize publicly for his comments—to the Latino community, and in Spanish.[2]

The widespread assumption underlying this incident—Romney accusing Gingrich of insulting Spanish speakers, and Gingrich issuing his apology in Spanish—is that the Latino community stands at the center of America's fraught politics of bilingual education. In the twenty-first century, when often-plaintive rhetoric about "the Hispanic challenge" and the "Latinization" of the United States has become familiar, this association between Latinos, the ghetto, and bilingual politics is instinctive to many. But it was not always so. Indeed, America's first forays into addressing the educational needs of linguistic minorities engaged European immigrants.

The early national period saw the establishment of the first substantial bilingual education programs in the public schools—in German. Pushed from the Fatherland by modernization and the Revolution of 1848, over five hundred thousand Germans immigrated to the United States, settling primarily in the Midwest.[3] Ohio became the first state to authorize German-English instruction at parents' request, but in multicultural states such as Texas, parents, teachers, and the emerging school system addressed the needs of various language groups—including Spanish and Czech as well as German—with locally conceived initiatives.[4]

The largest waves of European immigration arrived in the late nineteenth and early twentieth centuries and brought with them unprecedented linguistic diversity. Nearly twenty million Italians, Poles, Greeks, Russians, Czechs, and Germans arrived in the United States from the 1880s until the mid-1920s. Though certain national groups came with the intention of repatriation, many remained in the United States permanently, and all experienced the weakening of cultural and linguistic ties with their home countries an ocean away. In the Southwest, a different immigration story took shape in the wake of the 1910 Mexican Revolution. Close to one million Mexicans crossed the border into the United States in the early years of the twentieth century, many joining familial networks with deep roots in the region. Unlike European immigrants, these newcomers often came and went from their country of origin, engaging in "circular migrations" that served to solidify linguistic and cultural ties to Mexico and, as some critics have argued, hamper their integration into American society.[5]

What recently arrived linguistic minorities on both coasts shared was an encounter with their new nation's climate of unapologetic assimilationism. A "melting-pot" mentality presumed that ethnic differences were best subordinated to an American identity. Industrialists such as Henry Ford promoted an explicit Americanization curriculum for largely foreign assembly line workers, while shop foremen in many factories purposefully assigned immigrants from different countries to work beside each other in an effort to dissuade cultural maintenance and hasten productivity.[6] In California, Progressive reformers visited Mexican homes and urged mothers to learn American recipes and bear fewer children, as traditional cuisine and larger families were regarded as evidence of an un-American inattention to health and lack of restraint. Jane Addams's famed Chicago settlement houses witnessed a softer side of Americanization, as foreign women gathered to learn American ways but also to share their "immigrant gifts" in displays of folk dancing, cooking, and crafts. Some immigrants even embraced Americanization, as evinced by the diary of Russian Jew Mary Antin, a young girl who effused about the "miracle" of being wrought "into a good American."[7]

The assimilationist zeitgeist was so powerful in the late nineteenth and early twentieth centuries that there was virtually no serious discussion of allocating school resources to formally recognize the needs of linguistic minorities. Interestingly, when fraternal societies or other ethnic organizations successfully petitioned schools to offer courses about the culture or language of minority students, they often found such courses under-enrolled, as occurred with the Poles and Italians of Chicago.[8] This intellectual environment, the abolition of German-language programs as unpatriotic during World War I, the virtual stoppage of immigration after the restrictive federal acts of 1921 and 1924, and the repatriation campaigns of Mexicans in the 1930s all stalled a nationwide reckoning with the issues of linguistic minorities until the later twentieth century.

In the last half of the so-called American Century, the educational needs of linguistic minorities would again come to the fore, and Latinos would begin to define themselves as the group most associated with these efforts. By the end of World War II, southern and eastern Europeans had been sufficiently assimilated to the dominant language and culture to enjoy many benefits of Anglo white privilege, and the American racial system was in many regions best defined by a rigid "black-white dyad."[9] The Southwest continued to grapple with the linguistic challenges of its substantial Latin American and Asian populations, issues that would preoccupy the entire nation in the coming years.

The 1950s saw the arrival of tens of thousands of Puerto Ricans and Cubans, who flocked to New York and Florida. Puerto Ricans were granted full US citizenship in 1917, but it was not until the economic dislocations of the Depression and World War II and the ensuing postwar economic boom that the "great migration" of Puerto Ricans to the United States occurred. By 1960, over one million Puerto Rican residents of the United States established barrios and cultural events such as the Puerto Rican Day parade in New York City.[10] Exiles from the Cuban Revolution of 1959 sent hundreds of thousands fleeing the Communist regime of Fidel Castro to American shores. Aided by US efforts such as the Catholic Charities' Operation Pedro Pan and the federal Cuban Refugee Program, which offered over one billion dollars in direct aid to exiles, these new arrivals were often of middle- and upper-class background.

Advances in air travel helped these Spanish-speaking Caribbeans emigrate in greater numbers than ever before. The differences among these postwar newcomers, however, substantially outweighed the commonalities. Unlike previous generations of working-class immigrants, Puerto

Ricans were readily able to maintain cultural and physical connection to the island; the flight from New York City's JFK to San Juan airport is still affectionately called *la guagua aérea* (the flying bus). Dominicans, who arrived in the 1970s after the fall of the Trujillo regime, were similarly able to maintain these connections. Critics have argued that this sustained linkage, much like the porous Mexico-US border, has hampered assimilation to the dominant US culture. Most Cubans, by contrast, arrived with greater economic capital and harbored a fierce anti-communism that ingratiated them to America's Cold War consensus.[11] Each of these groups advocated for some form of recognition of their linguistic identities in local schools, but they often had little in common with each other beyond speaking quite different forms of Spanish.[12]

The 1960s transformed America's demographic and cultural context and ushered in the current era of bilingual education. The civil rights movements of the 1960s altered dominant assumptions about the desirability of assimilation; by 1968, newly commonplace phrases such as "Black is Beautiful" and "Brown Power" signaled a challenge to white, Anglo norms. The Hart-Celler Immigration Act of 1965 opened the country widely to immigrants for the first time since 1924, but the sources of newcomers had shifted from the Atlantic to the Pacific shore and to the southern border, as Latin American and Asian immigrants arrived en masse. The West Coast, which during the 1960s and 1970s welcomed almost 2.5 million Spanish-surnamed immigrants—as they were then officially categorized—became a laboratory for working out methods to integrate these ethnic and linguistic outsiders when "sink-or-swim" approaches had fallen into disfavor.[13] Latinos, who experienced high rates of academic failure—one common statistic showed 50 percent dropping out by the eighth grade—were at the center of these initiatives, sometimes by virtue of their own activism, and at other moments as the objects of politicians' and educators' policies.[14]

Especially in multiracial California, with its exceptionally centralized school system, educators and politicians experimented with what would become the three primary models of bilingual education: English as a Second Language (ESL), which prized English acquisition above all; transitional bilingual education, which used the native language to ease transition to English; and maintenance bilingual education, which aimed to maintain the home language and even to teach Anglo children a second language.[15] Each of these experiments was beset by controversy.[16] Bilingual education, and the demographic realities to which it responded, would come to preoccupy policymakers, educators, and citizens nationwide in the last quarter of the century.[17]

By the early twenty-first century, social scientists pointed to California's demographic and cultural development—particularly the contours of the Latino story—as the direction the nation would follow. *Classroom Wars* looks deep within this context, during an era when Latinos grew from 12 percent to 31 percent of California's population, to begin to comprehend this important dimension in the making of modern America.[18]

# 1

# THE BEGINNINGS OF MODERN BILINGUAL EDUCATION

On January 2, 1968, the first business day of the year, President Lyndon Baines Johnson signed the Bilingual Education Act (BEA), the first federal law codifying a national commitment to serving the needs of the growing number of children in the nation's public schools whose first language was not English. The bill addressed all linguistic minorities, but advocates for Spanish speakers had spearheaded the legislation, and the president specifically articulated the case of Latinos across the Southwest:

> Thousands of children of Latin descent, young Indians, and others will get a better start—a better chance—in school. . . . We are now giving every child in America a better chance to touch his outermost limits. . . . We have begun a campaign to unlock the full potential of every boy and girl—regardless of his race, or his religion, or his father's income.[1]

In California, where Democratic and Republican legislators alike had labored in support of this bill in reaction to startling statistics such as the frequently cited nearly 50 percent dropout rate of Spanish-speaking pupils by the eighth grade, news of the act's passage was gratefully received.

While President Johnson's liberal Great Society was defined by the elaboration of federal programs designed to redress social inequality, the BEA's promise to "treat the ability to speak in a different language as an asset" was unprecedented.[2] To legislators from the Southern California city of Reseda to those at the state capitol at Sacramento concerned about the state's hundreds of thousands of Spanish-dominant students, the landmark BEA may have felt specifically aimed at California or the Southwest. In acknowledging the burgeoning presence of Spanish speakers in American classrooms, and in committing federal monies to address their needs, the BEA introduced a new era in the national politics of diversity, schooling, and state. This phase found early and important expression—in policy and practice—in California, a state that quickly became a symbol of the problems and promise of bilingual pedagogy.

This chapter focuses on California in order to explain the act's origins and impact, in contrast to the narrative told of federal bilingual politics.[3] By the time Johnson signed the BEA (Title VII of the Elementary and Secondary Education Act of 1965) into law, California had for nearly a century been grappling with educating its linguistically diverse population. Before newly politicized Chicanos donning paramilitary attire and championing Brown Power became the public face of "the bilingual issue" in the late 1960s, local and state politicians and bureaucrats had cooperated across party lines to devise curricula and legislation to educate the growing Mexican American population. Their oft-overlooked efforts evinced an impressive degree of grass-roots and state-level innovation in an era most often characterized as one of expanded federal power. This chapter also explores how pivotal the BEA was in gaining a federal commitment to the educational achievement of limited-English-speaking (LES) children and in spurring action at the state and local level. At the same time, examining the act's development from an ambitious bill proposed by Democratic senator Ralph Yarborough of Texas in 1967 to its passage in 1968 reveals how philosophically and fiscally limited its terms actually were.

Considering the intertwined histories of bilingual education in the Golden State and the nation at large reveals more than a case study of federal legislation. The emerging legislative structure embodied by Title VII pushed districts and states to question the received attitudes about Mexican American underachievement that permeated their practice. Title VII introduced increased oversight and enforcement, often casting the districts as villains and at times supplanting earlier, locally developed programs. Throughout the 1960s, Californians, as well as national politicians and educators, engaged in an unprecedented bipartisan dialogue about bilingual education. On the state and local level, to a greater degree than appears to have been the case among federal politicians, moderates and even avowed conservatives earnestly advocated for bilingual education programs until the late 1960s.[4] The stark battle lines that would harden in the classroom wars over bilingual education began to take shape during debates over the BEA and its implementation. Just as conservatives such as Tom Bethell would find in bilingual education advocacy grist for jeremiads over the decline of American culture, so too would progressives insist upon linguistic and cultural recognition as crucial to full participation in an equitable society.

## Bilingual Education in California

Early in the twentieth century, Californians in communities with high concentrations of Spanish speakers had already faced the realities attendant to incorporating their bilingual populations. One in-house history of the Los Angeles public schools fondly recalled the San Pedro Street School celebrating both Mexican Independence Day and Washington's Birthday during the 1920s, while another account describes the school day commencing with each student asking for *"la mano, señor maestro"* before kissing the teacher's hand.[5] Tolerance was not omnipresent, however, and in 1959 the state legislature voted to alter the education code to prohibit classroom instruction in languages other than English.[6] Enacted on the heels of the National Defense of Education Act, this measure evinced Cold War attitudes, in which anything foreign, including language, was suspect.

By 1965, questions of linguistic and cultural self-determination took central importance among an increasingly organized Mexican American community. At its first annual "Issues Conference" in San Diego, the Association of Mexican American Educators reviewed an influential academic study about Mexican American employment in schools and colleges that raised what became key questions about bilingual education.[7] The researchers, from the University of California, Los Angeles, revealed that while one in every seven Californians was engaged in professional work, only one in twenty-two Spanish-surnamed citizens was similarly occupied. Spanish-surnamed teachers comprised only 2.3 percent of California educators, despite representing over 8 percent of the civilian labor force. In elementary schools—where the majority of bilingual programs was concentrated—female Spanish-surnamed teachers were "strongly underrepresented" and consistently paid less than their Anglo colleagues.[8] Despite the acknowledgment that all of these numbers and disparities "are unquestionably larger today [in 1965]" than in 1960—and worsening—the researchers advised that findings must be "interpreted with caution and do not necessarily have pejorative implications."[9]

The study underscored Latinos' underrepresentation in the teaching force, which would be marshaled as a central and problematic tautology of the bilingual education debate: lack of qualified Latino and Spanish-speaking educators led to ineffective bilingual programs, which in turn trained students inadequately for the professions, including education. Californians across party lines were swift to identify the pragmatic implications of this situation, if not to recognize its gravity. In the 1970s, for example, white teachers state-wide vehemently protested what they perceived to be the en masse hiring of unqualified teachers and personnel to serve a student body increasingly in need of bilingual services.

Californian educators also enacted curricular measures before federal and state frameworks existed to guide them. With funding from Title III of the Elementary and Secondary Education Act (ESEA), the ESL Center of California piloted programs in four districts with high concentrations of Spanish-speaking students: San Ysidro, San Diego, San Dieguito, and Carlsbad. Within just a few years, advocates of ESL would criticize this method as too conservative, yet in early 1967, the approach was considered sufficiently adventurous to merit Title III "risk money" allocated for creative educational proposals deserving further exploration.[10] The demonstration districts experimented with videotaping teachers at work, traveling to Tijuana to experience a Mexican educational environment, and embarking on small research projects to understand the culture shock Latino students faced in US schools. Though pedagogically moderate in advocating English acquisition to the exclusion of Spanish maintenance, these pilot programs aimed to "replace the old repressive punishment system of 'no Spanish on the playground'" with a less punitive approach that encouraged a practical, though decidedly "inconspicuous English."[11] Still, the programs were geared to redress the "magnitude of the ESL problem" and perpetuated the idea of Mexican American victimhood by enlisting local high school students as "barrio guides" to reveal to visitors "the unenviable lot of the unskilled Mexican-American in the affluent society."[12]

In the absence of a bilingual education infrastructure, superintendent of public instruction Max Rafferty, an outspoken social conservative, initiated and oversaw creative state and local efforts to educate LES students.[13] Rafferty traveled with a member of the Mexican Ministry of Education to Baja California schools in 1965, piloted a textbook exchange program, and introduced the possibility of a teacher exchange between the two nations.[14] Less than six months later, California school districts with high concentrations of Spanish-speaking students at the elementary school level were employing Spanish-language science and social studies textbooks for Mexican American children and Anglo students alike in neighborhoods as socioeconomically diverse as lavish Beverly Hills and rural Oxnard. Minimized as an "informal program" and a tentative "experiment in goodwill" between the neighboring countries, this program presented a version of bilingual education more ambitious than the ESL model. First, the oversight committee, comprised of local and state officials, agreed that maintaining bilingual students in a classroom with their peers was more conducive to learning than withdrawing them for special assistance. The nascent program embraced cultural education as well as language acquisition for both Spanish-speaking and Anglo pupils. Though the state and local teachers who comprised the planning committee discussed applying for both Title I and Title III funding to expand the program, at its inception this program was state and locally funded. It just happened to be spearheaded by one of the most vociferous conservatives in state politics.

This exchange plan bolstered an existing homegrown bilingual-bicultural program in Calexico, an exceptional border town that in the early 1960s was home to a balanced population of Anglos, Mexican immigrants, and bilingual Mexican-Americans, and witnessed little political conflict or Chicano radicalism. The town's mostly Anglo administrators developed a "top-down" but genuinely bicultural and bilingual program that engaged all students, regardless of their linguistic background. Calexico's Anglo superintendent Carl Varner became a national pioneer of bilingualism, and the district's innovative curriculum thrived until greater national attention to the issue, criticism of the absence of rigorous evaluation metrics for bilingual programs, and shifting demographics generated skepticism of the pluralistic program.[15]

In Calexico in particular, and in the textbook and teacher exchange program in general, the direct relationship with Mexico engendered a different cultural slant than that of later programs concerned with addressing a uniquely Mexican American identity. Students and teachers who were in contact with successful Mexican professionals and could visit thriving Mexican communities had more inspiring reference points than those who were primarily familiar with communities circumscribed by crime, racism, and low academic achievement.[16] Such beneficial links to Mexico were supplanted with a thoroughly domestic, and arguably more insular, federal bilingual education project.

These efforts marked a sea change during the 1960s. In 1967, the state legislature amended California's English-only statute to allow bilingual education "in those situations when such instruction is educationally advantageous to the pupils and to the extent that it does not interfere with . . . regular instruction of all pupils in the English language."[17] The same year, Senator Charles Lee commented that not supporting Title VII, on which Texas and California legislators were already working, seemed un-American.

The imminent passage of the BEA prompted California educators and legislators across party lines to cooperate in support of Senate Bill (SB) 53. SB 53 acknowledged the inherent benefit of Spanish fluency and recognized an inextricable link between language and culture that went unmentioned in the 1968 version of the BEA. It advocated a transitional form of bilingual education by "permitting instruction . . . in a language other than English, while a systematic, sequential and regular program planned to acquire mastery of English is administered simultaneously." Bolder than the federal measure signed into law just days later, California's SB 53 declared that "the native language of all students should be respected and utilized . . . and the bilingual ability should be viewed as a distinct asset." In fact, according to state deputy superintendent Eugene Gonzales (see figure 1.1), though "the immediate motivation for the passage of SB 53 stemmed from the recognition of the challenge California schools face in educating Americans of Mexican descent," its "long-range goals" included fostering "opportunities for both the native and non-native speakers of English to become bilingual."[18] This stance represented an evolution from California's pioneering 1960s ESL programs, which, despite claiming to cultivate the "bilingual, bicultural citizen of tomorrow," focused almost exclusively on English instruction.[19] Still, SB 53 referenced "culture" precisely to mention how culturally and linguistically sensitive instruction could ultimately serve to create for "the non-English speaking child" "a natural and effective fusion with the school and the American heritage it perpetuates."[20]

EUGENE GONZALES
. . . educationist

FIGURE 1.1 Deputy superintendent of education Eugene Gonzales was the highest-ranking Latino in California's Department of Education. Gonzales was appointed by Superintendent Max Rafferty. "S.B. Mexican C of C Sets Installation Dinner Dance," *San Bernardino County Sun*, January 12, 1966. Reprinted with permission of *San Bernardino County Sun* and by courtesy of Newspapers.com.

Fundamental obstacles to implementing equitable—or any—bilingual programming did, however, loom large. Aside from the pervasive assignment of Latino children in Educable Mentally Retarded (EMR) classes, Gonzales could think of nowhere to find "qualified, certificated employees who are bilingual except . . . foreign countries." Even then, state certification regulations would slow their hiring process.[21] Similarly, Julia Gonsalves, a foreign language consultant to the state Department of Education, felt "somewhat uneasy" in the uncharted territory of bilingual education, so much so that she felt it necessary to articulate the very basic "ground rule" that "the Mexican texts should be used only by teachers who have adequate knowledge of Spanish and who can competently use such materials."[22] Gonsalves and Gonzales hardly misjudged the cultural moment. A progress report from the Guadelupe School District in Santa Barbara County, which had been participating in a state-funded bilingual program, optimistically noted that the superintendent and principal "displayed a more positive attitude toward the Mexican-American than they had at the first meeting in October."[23] At the same time, they described matter-of-factly what sounds like a crisis situation:

> The schools do not have any Mexican-American teachers. Large classes of between 25–30 students are burdensome, especially if the teacher lacks training in problems of the minority child . . . Teachers tend to categorize students, saying that "they are hostile and act just like animals." In addition, the teachers do not live in the community but in outlying districts.[24]

This amalgam of innovation and conservatism evokes the spectrum of political sensibilities at play in the implementation of bilingual education in California before the federal act. Approaches to educating LES students ranged from expansive cross-district efforts to infuse every subject with a bilingual-bicultural component to widespread and disproportionate assignment of Latino children to non-academic tracks. In California, with its long bilingual and bicultural history, Title VII would stimulate many districts to engage more energetically with the question of how to educate Mexican-Americans. However, this legislative imperative could also prove useless in remedying existing systems of academic exclusion of LES students, or even stymie local pedagogical ingenuity that already thrived in certain communities.

## The Federal Bilingual Education Act

The BEA was, if not the watershed legislation in California scholars once imagined, still a major turning point. An amendment to the ESEA of 1965, Title VII marked the first acknowledgment of federal responsibility for the educational well-being of linguistic minorities. It signaled a shift from the notion that students should be afforded equal educational opportunity to the idea that educational policy should work to equalize academic outcomes, even if such equity required providing different learning environments. The evolution of the bilingual measure from bill to law over the course of 1967 reveals a significant narrowing of its reach and purpose. Created primarily with the advocacy of Spanish speakers in mind, Title VII came to articulate an argument for bilingual education based on the deficiencies of LES students. In part because of its measured tone, and in part due to a cultural climate in which bilingual education was not yet politicized, Title VII was developed by and gained the support of politically diverse sources.

Title VII made it the policy of the United States to fund local educational agencies "to develop and carry out new and imaginative elementary and secondary programs designed to meet the special educational needs of children of limited-English speaking ability."[25] Though the BEA authorized only $85 million in its first three years, its passage appeared to usher in a year that would mark the apex of 1960s idealism, reformism, and federal activism. Never before had there been a discussion at the federal level about ensuring equal educational opportunity to limited-English speakers. During the civil rights struggles of the 1950s and 1960s, only Native- and African-American minority groups had been acknowledged in federal legislation. In recognizing as an "urgent need" the growing numbers of linguistic minorities suffering from "serious learning difficulties," the BEA generated hitherto unmatched attention to the idea that the federal government bore responsibility for the educational well-being of the Spanish-speaking population.[26]

In fact, the civil rights advances of the preceding years were palpable in the cultural climate in Congress. As Charles Lee, the executive director of the lobbying group the Committee for Full Funding of Education Programs, commented, "elected officials are hesitant to express negative views toward programs for limited-English speakers, since these views could be interpreted as a stand against equal educational opportunities." Such opposition, Lee explained, would not be viewed as "in keeping with national values."[27] Indeed, incipient research on bilingualism and ethnicity challenged the validity of the "sink-or-swim" approach to educating LES students, as well as the notion of the "melting pot," suggesting that linguistic and cultural differences were not—and perhaps should not be—"melted" away as completely as previous generations had thought.[28] Lee's reflection suggests the exceptionalism of the historical moment in which legislators considered the question of bilingual education. In 1968, supporting bilingual education was seen by many legislators as the "American thing to do." However, a crux of the emergent opposition to such programs would be the claim that funding public school instruction in a foreign language for students of frequently dubious citizenship was anathema to American values, an argument that suggested a return to an earlier, assimilationist framework.

Title VII represented the dawning of a "new educational age," according to contemporary educator Susan Gilbert Schneider. For historian Guadelupe San Miguel, it ushered in "a new phase of ethnic and race relations in the history of American public schooling that soon polarized Americans along the lines of language, culture, ethnicity, and pedagogy."[29] Historian Adam Nelson perceived the act's greatest significance in the shift signified by its undergirding philosophy. Unlike the ethos of integration policy, which relied on the inherent similarity of black and white students and their right to an equal education, Title VII asserted the need to establish alternative curricula to serve language minorities. Bilingual education, Nelson claimed, highlighted a rising skepticism of integration, for "*total* integration seems to preclude the possibility of identifying and effectively addressing students' 'special' educational needs."[30] Though Latino leaders were certainly influenced by the black freedom struggle, at the level of federal policy the perspective Nelson describes was first articulated in legislation for LES students. Most broadly, the passage of the BEA provided the basis for the claims, increasingly contested over the last quarter of the twentieth century, that bilingual programs were legitimate recipients of federal monies and that desegregation might not be the panacea for social inequality its early advocates imagined.[31]

The passage of the BEA was also remarkable in that, despite possessing more than a century-long history of bilingual-bicultural education, the United States had been characterized at the federal and legislative level by a "clear lack of any national policy" regarding linguistic minorities.[32] Prior to 1968, the law had been silent on the specific needs of limited-English speakers, and no federal programs of bilingual-bicultural education existed. The meager federal funds spent on such programming were granted under the purview of the Migration and Refugee Program, a measure that had originated under the Indian Education Acts in the 1920s and 1930s but never had the express purpose of assisting limited-English speakers in the United States.[33] By contrast, the act's introduction as a US Senate bill in January 1967 by Democratic senator Ralph Yarborough of Texas unabashedly stated its purpose to fund "the creation of bilingual-bicultural programs, the teaching of Spanish as a native language, the teaching of English as a second language, programs designed to impart to Spanish-speaking students a knowledge and pride in their culture, efforts to attract and retain as teachers promising individuals of Mexican or Puerto Rican descent, and efforts to establish closer cooperation between the school and the home."[34] It originated from legislators' efforts to serve, or at least capture the vote of, a growing constituency—the 3,465,000 limited-English speakers comprising 12 percent of the population of the Southwest—that was making specific demands on public schools to serve its needs.[35] The final wording of the act described the state of affairs it addressed somewhat nonchalantly as merely "a perplexing educational situation," portending little of the cultural gravitas the presence of Spanish speakers and the question of their attendant linguistic and educational rights would attain in the next thirty years.

Title VII signified more than a fleeting watershed moment, and assessing the year or so between the inception and passage of the BEA is vital. In early 1967, Senator Yarborough had made an idealistic entreaty to a resistant President Johnson to acknowledge the transformative role bilingual education could play in overcoming the "poor performance in school and high dropout rates . . . and great psychological harm" caused by "English-only policies, no Spanish-speaking rules, and cultural degradation" that characterized American public schools.[36] The president did not support the bill, echoing critics who claimed that ESEA Titles I, II, and III adequately served the needs of LES children. However, that same year, the National Educational Association, activist groups of Mexican American teachers and parents, and several state and local departments of education rallied around the developing bill.[37] As chairman of the Senate Special Subcommittee on Bilingual Education, Yarborough carefully ensured passage of the bill by selecting sympathetic committee members and convening hearings in locations with large Latino populations: California, Texas, and New York.[38] Scholar Gilbert Sanchez points out that the hearings and conferences in 1967 "were major public episodes that provided the impetus for Congress to take action on the notion of bilingual education as it applied to the Spanish-speaking child."[39] Yarborough realized the import of these gatherings, deflecting resistance to the bill before a hearing in Corpus Christi, Texas, by "making sure that the Johnson people were not involved unless absolutely necessary, and then they were screened, having their prepared statements submitted in advance to the staff of the Select Subcommittee."[40] Another aide recalled that prior to the Edinburg, Texas, hearing, he phoned a suspected opponent "to [read] him the riot act."[41]

Despite Yarborough's best efforts, the scope of the bill was narrowed significantly over the course of 1967. While both power and the bulk of fiscal responsibility lay with local and state educational agencies, the act delimited its reach in certain ways. First, it specified that programs eligible for federal funding would target children between the ages of three and eight, along with existing and potential dropouts, writing off older students as a "lost cause" or "expendable."[42] In contrast to the breadth of earlier versions of the bill, its final language pointedly designated funds to be allocated uniquely for demonstration programs rather than for the establishment of permanent, federally financed programs. The reason for this restriction was also clearly spelled out: Title VII did not advocate a "philosophy of entitlement" that guaranteed all LES students bilingual-bicultural instruction, particularly not with financing from federal coffers.[43]

In its final form, the BEA certainly recognized "difference," but in the sense of redressing students' "serious learning difficulties" rather than suggesting the potential value of their background to the polity or to their own academic and civic development. The New York City hearing determined that in order to secure funding, programs had to serve populations with median annual incomes of less than three thousand dollars, the ESEA poverty threshold.[44] Although the poverty test clause resulted from the "emergency" nature of the bill, this provision painted in the public mind an image of the BEA as a program of "handouts" to the largely Latino poor. Significantly, rather than prizing the native language of LES students or allocating funds for cultural programming as Yarborough had envisioned just twelve months earlier, the act in its final form was silent on the value of LES students' home languages or cultures. Yarborough recalled in an interview that several senators resisted the inclusion of the "cultural factor," citing the unrest among French-speaking Quebecois in Canada and making clear that they opposed federal encouragement of a Hispanic subculture.[45] By 1972, the climate had changed, and acting director of the Department of Housing, Education and Welfare's (HEW) Division of Bilingual Education Albar Peña stated that "an essential ingredient in all projects is the concurrent effort to develop and maintain the child's self esteem and a legitimate pride in both cultures."[46]

In 1968, however, the act made no mention of culture, of teaching Spanish as a native language (as Yarborough had initially envisioned), or of the cultural and civic benefits that might accrue to enrolled students, who would become fully bilingual citizens. The compensatory tone of Title VII derived in part from the climate generated among policymakers by the heavily funded Title I, the first amendment to the ESEA, which focused on providing educational opportunity to children "disadvantaged" by "special educational problems," or mental and physical disabilities.[47] Title I, emerging from the War on Poverty's focus on America's "other half," dominated policy discourse at the time. Schneider acknowledges that it was a "short step" from Title I for the federal government to address the needs of limited-English speakers. Belonging to a language minority was thus cast in the 1968 law as akin to suffering a mental or physical disability. Yarborough nonetheless perceived Title VII as a "major blood transfusion" as opposed to the ad hoc "shot in the arm" Title I funds had been providing for bilingual programs.[48]

Categorization of Latinos as educationally disadvantaged arguably galvanized the passage of Title VII and continued to generate considerable associated funding compared to the meager eighty-five million dollars allocated to the BEA in its first three years. Astute bilingualism advocates, however, were perpetually wary of labeling LES students "disadvantaged." Assemblyman Peter Chacón, one of California's most devoted proponents of bilingual education, actually hedged before pursuing much-needed additional Title I funding for the state Task Force on Bilingual-Bicultural Instruction, precisely because it involved adopting the damaging designation of "compensatory education." As bilingual education became increasingly politicized in the years after the passage of Title VII, Chacón felt such a label could be more damning to the public perception of bilingual education than the infusion of funds would be a boon. Manuel V. Ceja and James Nelson of the state Bilingual-Bicultural Instruction Task Force commented in 1973 that while "politically, Assemblyman Peter Chacón does not see bilingual-bicultural education as a compensatory education program—[he] sure would like to get access to Title I funds."[49] San Miguel concurred that one of the act's enduring shortcomings was its focus on redressing "linguistic handicaps," even if, as one legislator pointed out, this framing "was simply the most feasible way of getting it passed."[50]

Juxtaposing the breadth of Yarborough's initial proposal and its network of supporters with the less ambitious prose of the act's final wording reveals the conflicting forces already at work in the realm of bilingual education as soon as it became a matter of federal interest. The federal attention to LES students that Title VII represented was certainly remarkable, but the act just as pointedly framed the lot of the nation's LES students as a "problem" to be fixed. In its expansion of the federal role in public education and its robust recognition of minority rights, Title VII remains one of the most obvious legacies of the political activism of the 1960s. And, as these debates among legislators seeped into public discourse in the 1970s, these traits led bilingual education to become shorthand in certain conservative circles for the liberal assault on "American values." One libertarian Southern California pamphleteer described an activist federal role as distinctly un-American. He emphasized his point with the rhetorical question, "Might big government have a foreign accent?"[51] While the specific accent to which he alluded may well have been Russian, it is hard to imagine that a Southern California conservative, increasingly skeptical of foreign influence and big government and living among an ever-growing Latino population, would have lent support to Title VII.

Still, this caricature overlooks the measured terms of the act's ultimate passage and its initially limited funding base as well as its complex, bipartisan origins.[52] Putatively conservative Republicans were instrumental in carrying out bilingual education at the federal level. Though quintessentially liberal Democratic President Johnson signed the act into law, he resisted to the point that Yarborough labored to have the "Johnson people" excluded from hearings on the act, lest they poison public opinion. It was Richard Nixon, a California Republican, who in an effort to court the Latino vote later safeguarded the program's federal funding sources, despite cutting many of Johnson's other Great Society measures.[53] Congress bore out this complex story as well. In 1967, at a San Antonio, Texas, conference to articulate the paths legislators would take to meet the educational needs of Mexican American students, Democratic congressman Henry B. Gonzalez, a longtime community leader who often distanced himself from more liberal politics, emerged as the most vocal opponent of the BEA. Gonzalez "disliked" even the term "Mexican American" as too heavily emphasizing Mexican identity and said as much at the Senate hearings in May of that year.[54] A year after the passage of Title VII, Californian Republican senator George Murphy introduced a bilingual education and dropout prevention plan to Congress that tripled federal funding requests. He cited California's "urgent need" for such programs and, underscoring the appeal of these programs across the political spectrum, even couched his request in the anti-communist idiom of the moment: "Russia seems to have a more enlightened [bilingual] policy than we do," he stated, because Soviet schools permitted linguistic minorities to be taught in their native tongues.[55]

At the state legislature in California as well, bilingual education was hardly the brainchild of the left that later conservative critiques—and even liberal elegies about "the rise and fall of bilingual education"—suggest.[56] Leon Panetta, who undertook enforcement of ESEA Titles VI and VII in California, credited the development of his civil rights sensibilities to his mentor Senator Thomas

Kuchel, an Orange County Republican.[57] Kuchel, one of the original seven members of the Senate subcommittee who supported the federal bilingual bill in 1967, expressed perhaps the most expansive vision of federal bilingual policy: "We must treat the ability to speak Spanish and other languages as an asset. The US can no longer pretend that it can communicate with other people with but one tongue—no matter how widely the English language is spread over the Earth."[58] Democratic congressmen Edward Roybal and George Brown of California, perhaps more probable allies of bilingual education, introduced a House bill that expanded the scope of Yarborough's original bill to address language minorities other than Mexican-Americans, but it was Republican senator George Murphy who spoke out, along with prominent Los Angeles Latino rights advocate Julian Nava, on the urgency of remedying the dropout rate.[59]

Though Title VII can understandably be conceived of as a liberal victory, reigning interpretations blur these diverse sources of support. They also underplay seeds of opposition to federal support for bilingual education already sufficiently present during the initial congressional debates of 1967 to mitigate Title VII's potential power. Indeed, the act was neither the dramatic last gasp nor the apex of a liberal impulse. Title VII was actually strengthened between 1969 and 1972 as its funding grew, and it was expanded to eliminate the poverty test and to include cultural and historical programming within its purview. Reinforced by the 1974 *Lau v. Nichols* decision, the act introduced the landmark idea that the federal government bore responsibility for the educational well-being of LES speakers, but the implementation of this bold claim was from its inception contested in ways that foreshadowed the debates of the coming decade.

Back in California, the passage of Title VII reverberated in myriad ways. Educational professionals who had always looked to California districts to learn from their bilingual programs returned to study the BEA's impact.[60] Southern California's Project Frontier, which drew many state and national visitors, was a model district in its amalgam of local and external resources, and its pedagogical innovation and community involvement. In 1969, Project Frontier, given $442, 216 of Title VII funds in its first year, was one of the most generously funded efforts in the country. The program pioneered curricula in middle and secondary schools rather than exclusively at the elementary level. It also articulated a commitment to nurturing "all youngsters by accepting them as they are, by valuing and developing biculturalism both inside and outside of class, by providing success-oriented experiences, and by exposure to and involvement in the cultural heritage of Mexico, other Spanish-speaking countries, and the United States."[61]

Project Frontier not only engaged Anglo children in its programs but also envisioned this grouping as a method of "enabling students to realize that bilingual/bicultural children have not one, but two important tools for transmitting culture and ideas."[62] According to the Project Frontier newsletter, each "unit of work" assigned to Anglo or Mexican American students would layer "subject content, bicultural concepts, and self concept" upon the curricular themes of "world cultures, western hemispheres, 'here & now,' 'my own political unit and others,' communities of the world, common needs of man, and families," with the ultimate objective of producing a "coordinate bilingual bicultural student."[63] The six directors and curriculum writers developed a unique approach to teaching culture that defied a simple assimilation or maintenance model. Rather, in their application for Title VII funds, they claimed to foster a "detachment towards the Spanish and English languages to enable the student to function in either his native or Anglo-Culture whenever he so chooses."[64] The program also forthrightly articulated goals for English-speaking children that included not only the study of Spanish as a foreign language from elementary school on but also the redesign of the K–12 social studies curriculum to engage significantly with Mexican history.[65] At the elementary level, "forming the spine of the program," were readers in both Spanish and English, and the curriculum followed a Mexican American family's experiences in multicultural California.[66]

The five districts involved in the program published all newsletters and grant materials bilingually for the whole community. A central goal of Project Frontier was to "actively involve parents of participating children." All of the parents of the children—over five thousand participated by 1970, the program's second year—were visited at home by community aides, hired specifically to "develop and maintain good home-school communication" by "interpreting the program to parents, explaining to them the purpose of parent involvement . . . seeking their view of community-school relationships . . . encouraging parents to visit the schools; arranging meetings at the school between parents and teachers . . . and identifying leaders . . . in the community.[67] Anglo and Spanish-speaking parents voluntarily enrolled their children in large numbers. At least monthly, they convened informally "to make input in positive ways" and also organized officially in five school-appointed local advisory committees dedicated to "help in decision making concerning the bilingual education program."[68]

Despite such innovations, the "compensatory tone" of the federal act deeply resonated in California. Minority children, particularly LES students, had long been misplaced in classes for the mentally retarded. This effectively thwarted their prospects for academic success.[69] In an interview with longtime Latino leader, intellectual, and bilingual education activist Ernesto Galarza, San Jose teacher Minerva Mendoza-Friedman expressed as much: "A disproportionately high number of Mexican-Americans are wrongly . . . placed in EMR classes. For all practical purposes, this marks the end of their education. The child who might have developed normally becomes an academic retardate."[70] In late 1969, Leon Panetta met with civil rights activists in San Francisco in what he described as "the most intense lobbying session of [his] life," during which parents and activists faulted unfair English-language tests for steering bilingual children into dead-end EMR classes, and thus to "drop out at an alarmingly high rate."[71] Later that year, the state Division of Instruction, under the leadership of Max Rafferty appointee Eugene Gonzales, released a study re-evaluating the effect of these placement exams on Spanish-speaking pupils and demanding revisions.[72] The researchers had employed Spanish-speaking examiners, given a Spanish-language test, and rephrased certain questions (which had been designed by Puerto Ricans) into the Mexican American dialect. Spanish-speaking children in California significantly improved their performance on the modified exam, often resulting in scores higher than the "80" that had designated them as mentally retarded.

Such evidence confronted ingrained attitudes and district practices unaltered by the passage of Title VII. A written exchange between Gonzales and the Santa Barbara County School District's coordinator of special education programs, Alton Safford, reveals the resistance among practitioners to implementing even these minor changes in the placement exams. Safford questioned the motivation of Gonzales's researchers, suggesting that "the investigators started out to 'prove' a point of view, then geared their methodologies to achieve . . . results . . . in agreement with their preconceptions." Moreover, he posited, might it not be possible that "the time spent in the EMR program was the major cause for the rise in I.Q. scores?" While Safford conceded that "the erroneous diagnosis of Mexican-American children as retarded was a problem," he balked at the report's recommendation to gear testing circumstances toward the achievement of this population.

"By giving a similar treatment to a group of Anglo, English-speaking EMR pupils (that is, by rewording certain items, substituting easier answers, and being flexible with timing standards—in short, making it an easier test to pass) might it not be expected that the mean IQ for this group of pupils would also rise? And if their individual scores rose above 80, would that mean that they were no longer mentally retarded and should be sent back to regular classes? Or would it mean only that they had been given an easier version of the test, and that as a consequence, their raw scores went up?"[73]

Gonzales corrected Safford's misconceptions about the degree to which the test was being "made easier" in the study. However, his rebuttal did not question the validity of the test overall, but rather suggested amendments to its form and administration. For instance, Gonzales defended the change from Puerto Rican to Mexican American Spanish, comparing it to the hypothetical absurdity of testing American knowledge of automobiles using the British vocabulary of "bonnet" for "hood" or "windscreen" for "windshield." Most energetically, Gonzales asserted, "I do not think a person should give the test who is *not* a sympathetic examiner," and he suggested that "should one use investigators who are not in sympathy with the problems of the Mexican-American children, there is a strong possibility that this 'bias' may extend in the opposite direction again to 'find what we seek.' "[74] This exchange reveals both the narrowness of the terms of the debate about educating Mexican-Americans at the state and local level and the context in which Title VII was enacted and implemented. Though Gonzales and Safford could weakly agree on their shared concern about "the plight of these children," Gonzales's advocacy of Mexican American interests in this situation was restricted to modifying the existing IQ test, hardly echoing the bold invocations of the early framing of Title VII or of certain locally developed programs.

Even the Mexican American members of the California School Board emphatically declared in a position paper: "I.Q. examinations must be abolished because they discriminate against Mexican-American pupils who have bilingual problems . . . condemning [them] to a disproportionate representation in mentally retarded categories that do not correspond to their actual ability." They ultimately conceded, "If I.Q. exams are used, they should be translated in the most effective language."[75] The force of Safford's rebuttal helps illuminate the restricted scope of the debate. His allusion to the advances Anglos might make if only they were given the same allowances as Mexican-Americans foreshadowed the discourse equating equal treatment for minorities with the disempowerment of white Americans that would characterize attacks on bilingual education throughout the 1970s and 1980s.

The impact of this coding of LES students as educationally disadvantaged was long-lasting and damaging to the public perception of bilingual education and also of its largest client group, Latinos. As late as 1992, Latinos in San Francisco accepted with uneasiness the hiring of Superintendent Waldemar

(Bill) Rojas from the New York City school system—despite his impeccable record of advocacy for Spanish-speaking students—due to his tenure as Director of Special Education in New York.[76] By 1969, bilingualism advocates managed to expand the scope of Title VII programs to engage "children from environments where the dominant language is English," casting the policy as an enrichment, rather than remedial, program, but "the idea of 'deficiency' continued to permeate bilingual policy and practice."[77] The flip side of this assumption that children were mentally deficient, as Galarza pointed out, was that "the educational system avoids investigating its own responsibility for educational problems." Rather, the "systematic labeling of LES children as mentally retarded took for granted theoretical assumptions which perpetuated the mainly Mexican-American children's low scholastic achievement."[78] As it were, the underlying philosophy of programs that had been born of a "genuine desire to help minority children to achieve" ostensibly ended up exacerbating the very problems of poor academic performance and attrition they were intended to redress.[79]

Bilingual education in the United States was not the product of Title VII and, in terms of students directly served, the BEA did not immediately make a dramatic impact, especially in California, which had been grappling with these questions for years. By 1972, only 100,391 students nationally—out of approximately 5,000,000 in need—were enrolled in a Title VII-funded program. By 1976, only about 250 bilingual-bicultural programs received federal monies.[80] Though certainly an improvement on the sparse offerings that received earlier federal funding, these programs were not as robust an efflorescence as advocates might have hoped for from the "little beginnings" represented by Title I-funded bilingual-bicultural efforts prior to Title VII.[81] Indeed, the Senate committee report on Title VII forthrightly stated: "The proposed legislation does not intend to prescribe the types of programs or projects that are needed. Such matters are left to the discretions or judgments of the local school districts."[82] This did little to encourage project development by foot-dragging legislatures and districts. In the opinion of policy analyst Richard Navarro, "the program was so ambiguously defined and unevenly implemented that the concept itself drew negative responses."[83]

In California, the imprecision of Title VII was apparent. Even two years after the law passed, the Office of Civil Rights (OCR) was compelled to issue a memorandum to California school districts declaring that educational provisions for LES students could not amount to "dead-end tracks."[84] Drafted by HEW assistant secretary Leon Panetta and implemented by his successor, J. Stanley Pottinger of the OCR—both liberal Republican lawyers from

California—the memorandum essentially mandated meaningful compliance with Title VII. Yet in allocating no funds for implementation, the memo reproduced the ineffectiveness of the federal legislation. It also inspired resentment for bilingual education among the state's financially strapped school districts, which scholar Gareth Davies argues the OCR treated as "disreputable bastions of prejudice and obstruction."[85] As the bureaucratic and legislative bilingual education apparatus grew at the federal and state levels throughout the 1970s, California came under more intense criticism for its failures in this realm. In turn, these attacks generated a robust discourse of resistance to bilingual education.

The 1968 BEA was unquestionably a landmark piece of legislation in that it officially condemned environments such as those in the Santa Barbara schools and articulated a federal responsibility to remedy them by funding curriculum development, teacher training, and services for LES students. Still, in the years before the proverbial battle lines were boldly drawn, pockets existed statewide in which progressive bilingual education programs, such as that in Calexico, were enacted with a degree of decentralization and creativity that greater federal oversight could actually inhibit. Project Frontier, along with its more sparsely funded counterparts, represented the template for modern, federally funded bilingual education programs in the mix of local, federal, and community prerogatives that shaped its practice. Such programs and the professionals who ran them grew quickly in response to the burgeoning need to educate the masses of Spanish-speaking children concentrated in Southwestern public schools in the 1960s, but they often built upon existing curricula. While maintaining aspects of an older, assimilationist strategy of schooling foreigners, bilingual education in California also invoked novel approaches that derived from the increased value placed on ethnic consciousness during the civil rights era. Accordingly, programs across the state could be both pluralistic but assimilationist, expansive and unevenly funded, and adventurous yet conservative. As federal bureaucrats and school districts across the country looked to California, all of these aspects influenced the shape modern bilingual education would take nationally. Since the BEA stopped short of mandating a specific path, districts and state governments were left to design and implement programs on their own, and individual communities, with all their local contexts and particularities, were expected to carry them out.

The multiple, and often unexpected, origins of bilingual-bicultural policy and practice in California and the nation at large reveal how the impetus for these programs was both top-down and bottom-up, and the result of frequently surprising political alliances.[86] Only when local groups marshaled district, state, and federal funds did programming gain traction. Moreover, bilingual-bicultural education, not just history and civics instruction, was part of the development of multicultural education.[87] As the nation watched Latino immigrants attain a permanent place in California schools and society in the 1960s, bilingual-bicultural education became a contested site for negotiating the promise and problems of education in a diverse society.

# 2 THE POLARIZATION OF BILINGUAL EDUCATION

On March 5, 1968, two months after President Lyndon Johnson signed the federal BEA into law, 2,700 of Garfield High's mostly Mexican American student body of 3,750 walked out of the East Los Angeles school during recess. By the next day, at four predominantly Latino high schools, student demonstrators carried placards claiming "¡Viva la Revolución! [Long Live the Revolution!]," and a policeman was hit with a glass bottle in the commotion.[1] Though the demonstrations were relatively nonviolent, the mainstream press wondered whether these "blowouts" marked "the start of a revolution—the Mexican-American Revolution of 1968."[2] The Brown Berets, an ethnic youth group instrumental in organizing the blowouts, dressed in paramilitary uniforms, demanded that Anglo teachers and administrators be summarily fired and replaced with Mexican Americans in Latino-majority schools, and called for students to have access to Chicano studies courses and Spanish-language instruction. Considering the unparalleled organization among Chicanos, Mexican American advocate and school board member Julian Nava commented to Los Angeles City Schools superintendent Jack Crowther in what must have been a tone of both foreboding and wonder: "This is BC and AD. You know the schools will not be the same hereafter." "Yes," Crowther replied, "I know."[3]

In the two years following the BEA's passage and the blowouts, bilingual-bicultural education evolved from a relatively uncontroversial issue that garnered significant bipartisan support to a lightning rod dividing and defining conservatives and liberals, as well as the diverse and rapidly growing Mexican American community.[4] The unprecedented two weeks of East Los Angeles protests, during which ten thousand predominantly Chicano students walked out of high schools in resistance to educational inequity, were both an engine and a symbol of this shift. Thereafter, bilingual education became yoked to the emergent and radicalizing Left, energizing the cause but also costing it the conservative and moderate support integral to its formation. Conservatives reviled with growing fervor the "Sick Sixties," defined by its ethnic rights struggles, sexual liberation, and antiwar activism.[5] The Chicano and conservative movements, whose histories are written almost entirely separately, developed in close relation to one another, finding fertile ground in bilingual education politics in California.

Early criticism of bilingual-bicultural education had come in the form of screeds from the far right, while even putative conservatives had supported the programs throughout much of the 1960s. State superintendent of public instruction Max Rafferty had been elected in 1962 on a platform that enshrined "the first duty of the schools [as] to impart the wisdom of [our] race and nation to the children," especially in the face of the Soviets, "a race of faceless, godless peasants from the steppes of Asia . . . striving to reach across our bodies for the prize of world dominion."[6] Along with associate superintendent Eugene Gonzales, the highest appointed Mexican American in the state Department of Education, the fiercely anti-communist Rafferty pioneered California's openly pluralistic bilingual education policy in the mid-1960s. By the early 1970s, however, Rafferty, Gonzales, and their vocal constituencies had all but abandoned their early commitment to such programs. By late 1968, bilingual education was gaining a foothold in an educational culture gradually opening its arms to many things multicultural, a process that would serve to embed bilingual-bicultural programs in many schools. Simultaneously, this progress would cost the movement the advocacy of political conservatives—such as Rafferty and Gonzales—who now viewed such curricula as part of a radical agenda. The successes of the very programs Rafferty and Gonzales had been instrumental in building during the early 1960s helped consolidate a conservatism grounded in patriotism, family, and, paradoxically, Anglo cultural and linguistic ascendancy.

Gonzales's role in California's bilingual education story raises important questions about how moderate and conservative Mexican Americans—as opposed to the radical Chicanos—shaped the fate of bilingual education. It also illuminates both the conservative and Latino past. The Latino community was hardly monolithic. While some Latinos explicitly invoked their ethnicity to support the bilingual programs, others claimed both their *Latinidad* (Latino identity) and their whiteness equally energetically to oppose such curricula. At the same time, Latinos in both parties were aware of their precarious place in government and society, so they often strove to bridge wide ideological chasms with tenuous alliances formed around a shared ethnic past. These complicated identity politics reveal both the contested landscape against which bilingual-bicultural education emerged and the unique place Latinos assumed in the American ethno-racial and political system. Ultimately, polarization destroyed the early consensus over bilingual education in California. The significant strides its advocates had made were eventually met with an equally vibrant opposition.

This chapter explores how during the 1960s and 1970s both the Latino and conservative movements gained political and cultural power, and in particular how California's percolating classroom wars over Spanish bilingual education proved a crucible in these two movements' often intertwined development.

## The Blowouts

Measured curricular and legislative advances from schoolhouses to Congress hardly satisfied Mexican American grass-roots activists, who in the late 1960s and early 1970s organized in neighborhoods all over California to protest the police brutality, housing discrimination, and lack of access to education that plagued their communities. The organizers were not only adults but also students. Over ten thousand teenagers and even some teachers abandoned their classes to protest educational inequities: high dropout rates, low test scores, and the absence of Chicano studies or bilingual course offerings in predominantly Chicano schools. Histories of the blowouts, as these walkouts were called, have primarily emphasized them as part of grass-roots political culture and the young movement that spoke "truth to power."[7] Yet these blowouts contributed as much to the development and implementation of bilingual programs as did legislative action.

"Cultural affirmation" was the rallying cry of East Los Angeles protestors in 1968. Despite years of pursuing reform through traditional channels, many Latino community advocates in Los Angeles felt that formal efforts had yielded few results. In 1963, the Los Angeles Unified School District (LAUSD) Board of Education had been presented with a list of recommendations to redress the inferior conditions hampering Mexican American achievement, but four years later, the district's director of compensatory education testified to the US Commission on Civil Rights that "few of those recommendations had been accepted and even fewer reached the community."[8] An early campaign to elect a Chicano, Ralph Poblano, to the LAUSD board, failed in the mid-1960s, but in 1967, the community succeeded in electing

Latino activist and Harvard Ph.D. Julian Nava.[9] Despite new attention to the specific problem of disproportionately shunting Mexican American children into classes for the mentally retarded, low expectations and hostile attitudes continued to characterize Mexican Americans' educational experiences. At a conference for Southern Californian educators, Mexican American scholar Uvaldo Palomares recalled how poorly the public schools had served him; he was first placed in a class for "the mentally retarded" and "later typecast as a future mechanic and discouraged from entertaining thoughts of a college education."[10] One city-wide task force, funded by the federal government and assembled for the purpose of motivating Mexican American students, articulated in a workshop its circumscribed aims: "It is important that [the students] understand that not all youngsters are expected to receive a college education. They should aspire to the highest level of education they can attain."[11] Days later, at Garfield High School—where students and teachers had participated in this very workshop—2,700 students walked out of their classes.

Students at Wilson High first walked out in response to the cancellation of their school production of the decidedly uncontroversial play *Barefoot in the Park*. The blowouts that spread across multiple campuses, however, resulted from mounting frustration with longstanding educational inequities and the politicization of a specific group of Chicano high school and college students. A number of the students had met through the Mexican American Youth Leadership Conference, a series of weekend retreats to Malibu sponsored by the Los Angeles County Committee on Human Relations. Though the conference emphasized pursuing leadership through traditional channels, such as running for student government, excelling academically, and attending college, future blowout leaders credited the retreats with sparking their first "feelings of group consciousness" and "opening their eyes" to systemic inequities facing their community in the schoolhouse and in the agricultural fields in which some of their parents worked.[12] Out of the conference emerged the group that later evolved into the Brown Berets, who helped organize the blowouts and whose paramilitary clothing and radicalism made the protests appear especially threatening. Disenchanted with traditional avenues of reform, these students connected with radical campus organizations such as United Mexican American Students (UMAS) and Mexican American Students Association (MASA) and communicated through two high school and college newspapers, *Inside Eastside* and *La Raza*. As early as December 1967, a student comment in *La Raza* portended the changing tactics to improve Chicano education: "It is now apparent that our voices are not being heard. So to hell with it. Merry Christmas, brother. 1968 will be different. One way or another, our voices will be heard."[13]

The Wilson High students had been planning the walkouts for weeks, and the student newspaper described the atmosphere as electric: "The word had been around . . . The bell rang to go to lunch. Practically half the school was mobbed together in the halls . . . encouraging others to walk out."[14] Ultimately, 2,700 of the 3,750 students at Garfield High School, and 700 of 1,900 students at largely African American Jefferson High School boycotted class. The following day, hundreds of students from Roosevelt High School abandoned school for a gathering in nearby Evergreen Park, while over 500 Lincoln High students marched to the LAUSD offices to meet with two district superintendents to voice their demands.[15] Hundreds of the protesting students convened in Hazard Park, where they were met by board members Julian Nava and Ralph Richardson, as well as US representative Edward Roybal—the first Mexican American elected to Congress in Los Angeles—who had flown in from Washington, DC.[16] (See Figure 2.1.)

FIGURE 2.1 During the East Los Angeles walkouts in March 1968, thousands of Chicano students and their allies took to the streets in protest of educational inequities, spawning countless protests all over the country. Here, East LA students take to the streets again in February 1969, demanding "school not prison." Devra Weber, *Chicano Student Movement* newsletter, February 1969, Los Angeles, California. Reprinted with permission from Devra Weber and by courtesy of the Chicano Studies Research Center, University of California, Los Angeles.

The LAUSD treated students and teachers involved in the blowouts as a unified group, but the experiences at the five schools varied during the ten days of walkouts. Most schools attempted to deal with the protests internally, though the police were eventually involved on all campuses. One Roosevelt High student participant recalled years later that the police "treated us as if we were rioting and tearing things up, which we weren't. All of a sudden [the riot squad] started whacking people . . . badly beating them up." When administrators attempted to usher students back into the building, police warned them "to mind their business."[17] Another Roosevelt student recalled being called a "motherfucking Chicano" by the police officers.[18] Even at Wilson High's relatively small demonstration, administrators squared off against both protesting students and an overzealous police force. One student recounted that those students who remained indoors "demonstrated by throwing fruit, books, malts, and even a trash can over the gate . . . Mr. Williamson was ordering students out of this area and was thrown an egg at." At the same time, however, administrators such as the principal, Mr. Skinner, resisted policemen "who wanted to use tear gas on us."[19] Across the city, Mexican American protests of educational inequity were met with force, auguring the intensifying activism and attendant reaction.

The blowouts were singular in the central role played by secondary and even junior-high students. Newly radicalized college students such as Vickie Castro helped organize the protests by returning to their alma maters, but the youngest generation successfully led. A *Los Angeles Times* article expressed older Latinos' amazement at the politicization of Chicano youth: "Surprisingly to some, stunningly to others, the community backed [the protestors] up . . . the men and women of the once-conservative older generation jammed school board and civic meetings, shouting their approval of what their children had done."[20] The day after the board conceded to convene a special meeting to address the issues students raised, a Garfield High teacher commented on the week's events with both shame and awe: "We feel disturbed and ashamed that these kids are carrying out our fight. . . . We should have been fighting for these things as teachers and as a community. Apparently we have been using the wrong weapons. These kids found a new weapon—a new monster—the walkout."[21]

For all of their radicalism, however, the blowouts bore marks of their planners' adolescence and precocity. Along with entreaties to hire minority administrators and to redesign the curriculum to engage Chicano historical narratives and the Spanish language, students also demanded lounges with jukeboxes and the right to wear miniskirts and long hair in school.[22] One editorialist simultaneously poked fun at the demonstrators' age—"the Mexican American Students Association [said] that it would be so well-organized that 'ladies with sweetbread would be waiting for kids when they walked out' "— and expressed admiration for their comportment in a potentially explosive situation: "The kids were met by armed guards instead. They kept it from being a really seriously violent event."[23] Indeed, many students strove to contrast their movement with increasingly stock images of militant, long-haired youths violently flouting authority. Floyd Benton, a Jefferson High student, criticized the media depictions of the students as "unruly or violent . . . instead of dealing with causes. . . . We were very orderly." His classmate agreed, "Some of the students here worked very hard to make sure no trouble started."[24] In his sympathetic study of the blowouts, Juan Inda acknowledges, "The [Brown] Berets received a disproportionate amount of media coverage because of their military uniforms and militant outlook. Overnight, they were considered to be the Chicano equivalent of the Black Panthers, but in reality they were just a small group of high school students."[25]

Other students, however, embraced the mantle of radicalism. In contrast to the measured formality of the student presentation to the board, a student publication, *Chicano Student News: Mano a Mano*, took a more fervent tone. Just three days after the special board session during which students requested the transfer of "any teachers and administrators who show any form of prejudice toward students" and demanded that the "curriculum should be revised to allow Mexican contributions to society," *Mano a Mano* more shrilly declared, "HOW CAN THEY EXPECT TO TEACH US IF THEY DO NOT KNOW US? . . . We want the textbooks revised to make us aware of the injustices that we, Chicanos, as a people, have suffered in a *gabacho*-dominated society."[26] One Chicano student angrily retorted to the board's excuse that it had "no money": "Do you know why they have no money for us. Because of a war in Vietnam 10,000 miles away, that is killing Mexican-American boys—and for WHAT? We can't read, but we can die. Why?"[27] Another student was amazed that Anglos clearly aligned their struggle with other civil rights struggles and mimicked Chicano students' methods: "The Anglo kids asking the Chicanos how to organize! Imagine that! Should've told them, 'Ask your dads how they organized to oppress us all these years.'"[28]

Teachers and administrators at the schools involved in the blowouts were quick to distance their own students from the troubling protests and from the larger social transformations occurring beyond the public schools. Roosevelt High's principal blamed "the student demands and the idea of the boycotts" on the "urging of outsiders, including members of the Brown Berets."[29] The appeal of such a rationale must have been even greater for Principal Robert Bosanko of largely Anglo Venice High, where less than one-sixth of the student body was Mexican American and where the walkouts began late but ended in violence. Despite the board's district-wide pardon, Bosanko suspended forty students and blamed the physical environment: "The campus is not enclosed and outsiders can walk in without difficulty . . . a group of militants from the outside sparked the disturbances."[30] Similarly, when Los Angeles assistant district attorney Evelle J. Younger announced his re-election campaign, he assured the electorate that his office would issue complaints against "outside agitators who went too far" in fomenting the walkouts, suggesting that voters did not want to see the blowouts as generated from within the schools.[31] A *Los Angeles Times* editorial the following week reinforced this "us versus them" perspective: "Efforts by outside agitators to stir sympathy walkouts in high schools throughout the city generally fizzled. Most Los Angeles youngsters were too level-headed to be caught in the 'student power' trap which could ultimately lead to destruction of the educational system." The editorial emphasized that "these young Mexican Americans themselves are crying for the education tools that will keep them from becoming the victims of a kind of apartheid via language," but contradicted the *Times'* extensive reporting of the thousands who did participate in the boycotts, claiming that "even on the east side, only a minority of students actually joined the 'strike.' Most stayed in the classroom, aired their grievances through normal channels."[32] Clearly, the Los Angeles establishment—school administrators, the school board, and the city's paper of record—was invested in portraying community youth as upstanding, law-abiding citizens only ephemerally influenced by ill-intentioned outsiders.

Curiously, Julian Nava, the school board's most vocal advocate for the protestors, also dealt with this sea change in ethnic-youth politics by articulating an "us versus them" dichotomy when apportioning blame for the blowouts.[33] "I still think this thing is fully controllable and is positive and constructive," Nava opined of the blowouts. "These students are resisting the efforts of outsiders to become influential . . . things should remain all right."[34] The board refused to meet protestors officially, but Nava and fellow board member Ralph Richardson assured students congregating in Hazard Park that the entire board would hear their concerns.[35] Nava effectively made his sympathetic perspective that of the board in stark contrast to that of the state administration, embodied by Gonzales's unflinching and very public claim that "without pickets, demonstrations, walkouts, or walk-ins . . . we will win this battle to adequately educate Americans of Mexican descent!"[36] The intensity and suddenness of the walkouts, however, highlighted tensions within the alliance between Nava, a Latino working within the system, and some demonstrators, who radically rejected the establishment. A *Chicano Student News* editorial directly targeted the board member: "Dr. Nava came to 'LOOK' over our school, took one look at our gym, and reported the gym was beautiful. But did our Dr. Nava look at all our school? Did he notice our crowded classrooms, lousy food, closed restrooms?"[37] To many students, the walkouts were an expression of their own organic educational advocacy, echoing and inspiring the campus radicals nationwide who spurned the reformist liberalism that had spawned many of their movements.

After a special three-hour school board meeting held on March 11 before two hundred students and parents, with three hundred more listening on loudspeakers set up outside, the students began to lower their "Chicano Power" and *"Viva la Raza"* signs and return to class under police watch. The LAUSD board exhibited measured sympathy to the protestors, unanimously granting the involved students amnesty and claiming agreement with, but inability to fund, 99 percent of the students' thirty-eight demands, all of which centered on enhancing the educational experience of Latinos by improving school property and expanding bilingual and bicultural programming.[38] Concretely, the board satisfied the demand for more minority administrators by enabling fifteen black and Mexican American teachers from mid-city schools to complete internships that would accelerate their eligibility for higher-paying administrative jobs. It also appointed three African American administrators to Jefferson High School. These steps calmed many of the campuses.[39]

Two weeks later, at a board meeting demanded by the Blowout Committee and attended by 1,200 people, board president Georgiana Hardy was similarly sympathetic. She opened the floor to public comments and specifically invited Sal Castro, faculty advisor to the radical Eastside Democratic Club, to speak.[40] The board agreed to pursue proactively any teachers and administrators who had harassed students participating in the walkouts, unanimously voted to cease disciplinary action against involved students and faculty, and advised, albeit fruitlessly, the Los Angeles Police Department (LAPD) to do the same.[41] As the commitment of the police department and school administrators to discipline participants became more apparent, board members moved the urban affairs office from under the direct jurisdiction of the superintendent to the Board of Education in order to mitigate retaliation.[42] The call to redress the educational disadvantages in the Latino community had never been articulated so coherently and vehemently, nor been met with such public and official, though halting, recognition. Even this measured sympathy is noteworthy considering the negative reactions that "minority programs" in general, and bilingual education in particular, would elicit in coming years.[43]

The community was soon disappointed again. The meeting may have mitigated punishments for the protestors, but it yielded only vague directives such as "encourage fluency in Spanish." By May, thirteen organizers of the blowouts were arrested for conspiracy, most notably Sal Castro, who was only reinstated after an eight-day sit-in by supporters that October.[44] National political leaders voiced support for the East Los Angeles Chicanos in the months following the blowouts and during the repeatedly delayed trials of the "LA 13." Diverse public figures and organizations, such as civil rights champion Senator Robert Kennedy, Chicano labor organizer César Chávez, African American activists Stokely Carmichael and Maulana Karenga, the campus group Students for a Democratic Society, and the radical African American Black Panthers spoke out, and on June 2, over two thousand supporters filled the steps of the Central Police Station. The American Civil Liberties Union and the NAACP Legal Defense Fund joined the Chicano Legal Defense Committee, giving the cause of bilingual-bicultural education greater exposure and linking it with the broader freedom struggles of the era.

Some activists were quick to express concern over bilingual education's new association with radicalism. Uvaldo Palomares pled with fellow educators to "try to get away from Black Power and violence. Think about yourself. Somehow you have failed their trust . . . You can't make these people disappear."[45] This impulse, however, was gaining power far beyond the high schools of East Los Angeles. In 1969, a year after the blowouts, a radical movement grew in San Francisco in defense of seven Latino youths facing the death penalty for shooting a police officer. "*Los siete de la Raza*," as the youths' defenders called them, were being unfairly judged in part because they were the product of an insensitive school system that demanded children "learn English immediately and instantly or 'we teach you nothing.'"[46] The academic failure and criminality of *los siete* and countless other Latino children was described as the tragic result of hopeful Latin American immigrants enrolling their once intellectually curious children in American public schools, only to "gradually and painfully discover . . . the children were not learning anything and their teachers didn't care. The children dropped out."[47] *Los siete*, the account went, were the casualties of schools defined by "the knowledge that the child has no future."[48] Defenders of *los siete* echoed the East LA students in demanding a restructuring of the unjust educational system and thus allied the activist teenagers with a broader movement.

As the *Los Angeles Times* began to use the term "Brown Power" on a daily basis, many citizens bristled at these impassioned calls for reform, especially considering the cost they exacted on Anglo Californians. One irate teacher reflected in the *Los Angeles Times* on the fast-track program for minority administrators implemented in response to the blowouts: "There is no question that we need minority group administrators. However . . . this program is grossly unfair . . . a direct threat to our present promotional policies . . . and [many teachers] fear it could open the door to other questionable practices. . . . There is little doubt that it will further lower teacher morale and make recruitment more difficult."[49] Some Californians felt that as these reforms gained traction, allowances for minority students and educators would corrupt the schoolhouse and divide the polity. The blowouts thrust onto the public stage bilingual education and a host of educational and political issues important to the burgeoning Chicano movement, but such successes engendered similarly powerful opposition. This teacher's plaintive claim would soon be echoed by many.[50]

The two most powerful educational policymakers in California, Max Rafferty and Eugene Gonzales, were already distancing themselves from the bilingual-bicultural education programs they had once so actively supported. Rafferty publicly advocated brandishing a "hickory stick" against the students involved. A well-known disciplinarian known for celebrating "alert police and tough courts" as the "happy combination" integral to a community's educational prosperity, Rafferty condemned students "leaving classes for any reason except illness" and disparagingly redefined the walkout as "the easy and lazy way out."[51] Just months earlier, Rafferty had agreed with the protestors that the educational underachievement of Spanish-speaking youth was "the state's most pressing problem," and he had organized California's first Conference on the Education of the Mexican American.[52]

Less than a month after the blowouts, however, Rafferty's associate superintendent and chief of the Division of Instruction, Mexican American Eugene Gonzales, articulated the administration's philosophy on educating "the Spanish-speaking child." Obliquely rejecting the aims and methods of the protestors in East Los Angeles as an "attempt to justify actions in contrast to personal responsibility," Gonzales claimed that teachers needed to fulfill their "main purpose as educators . . . to aid students to become learned" rather than succumb to "vocal if not militant groups not at all worried about whether Juanito or Jane receive instruction commensurate with ability or potential."[53] Disavowing ethnic particularism, Gonzales emphasized the "degree of embarrassment" he would suffer "should Spanish-surnamed educators spend all their time interested only in one ethnic group."[54] With two months left in the academic year, policymakers, teachers, students, and parents on the Right and Left had identified the education of the Spanish-speaking child as a central and inescapable responsibility of the state educational system. In April 1968, however, how and for what purpose to educate this growing population was less clear.

## Moderates, Conservatives, and "The Bilingual Business"

Though two-term incumbent superintendent Rafferty would soon suffer a surprising loss to liberal African American Wilson Riles in early 1970, he waxed hopeful about the decade stretching before him: "I believe the Seventies will NOT bring Black or Brown or Yellow Power schools supported by public tax money but run by various minority groups. . . . Speaking as both an educator and an individual, I have been impatiently waiting for the Seventies to get here."[55] How the conservatism of Rafferty and much of the polity hardened in the late 1960s is closely intertwined with increased Latino self-determination. Mexican immigrants flooded California upon the passage of the Hart-Celler Act of 1965, and the problems of agricultural labor and the inequalities attendant to educational marginalization galvanized the movement for civil rights and recognition. Simultaneously, many California conservatives and moderates were moving right. In 1964, the Los Angeles County Young Republicans cast out moderate Republican Thomas Kuchel for his allegedly "leftist, socialistic views," and fiercely libertarian Barry Goldwater and openly racist George Wallace enjoyed substantial support among Southern California conservatives in their 1964 and 1968 presidential campaigns, respectively.

These political trends took place throughout the 1960s in a region concurrently known for nurturing both the seedbeds of *La Raza* and "the origins of the new right."[56] The anti-communism which led Orange County politico Walter Knott to contend that "big government has a foreign accent," and others to declare that the most terrifying consequences of "socialistic" educational policy was the cultivation of a "one-world child" devoid of allegiance to God or country, found a new target in bilingual-bicultural education.[57] The global cultural pluralism foundational to the curricula espoused by bilingual-bicultural advocates unsurprisingly jarred proponents—Anglo and Latino—of an increasingly robust, even jingoistic, Americanism. As perspectives on bilingual-bicultural education radicalized both the political Right and Left, moderate support for these pedagogies was strained, and California's Latinos evinced a range of reactions to programs. By the early 1970s, it was apparent that, on this question, the once vital and care-fully constructed center could not hold.

Since the early 1960s, Latino educational rights activists and cultural and political conservatives had locked horns. A series of cartoons and editorials in ¿Que Tal?, San Jose State University's Chicano campus newspaper, revealed nearly a decade of tension between Chicanos and the Young Americans for Freedom (YAF), the nation's leading conservative campus organization. In April 1971, an editorial in this Chicano paper brushed off the YAF presi-dent Martha O'Connell's claims that the Chicanos had threatened campus violence, maintaining that the "YAF'ers'" efforts "to arouse, instigate, and psychologically annihilate a people's positive cultural concept and national pride" were a far more insidious form of aggression.[58] Not only did these two movements emerge simultaneously on the San Jose State campus, but the editorial also credits the YAF with defining Chicanos as the "irrational, ani-malistic and brutal" counterpoint to the YAF's self-styled "intelligent, pure, and infallible" nature.[59] To Chicano activists, the YAF represented uninspired traditionalism. One cartoon depicted O'Connell as an elderly lady fruitlessly waving an issue of ¿Que Tal? at an inattentive policeman, pleading, "But look what those Chicanos are writing about me!" By contrast, the editorial asked, "As for Chicanos? They'll be around a long time! ¡Que viva la causa!"[60]

Southern Californians, who experienced the influx of Latino immigrants and the upsurge in conservative mobilization most acutely, lived these simul-taneous historical trends vividly. Journalist John Steinbacher, best known for his offensive against sex education and his ardent support of Goldwater in 1964, attacked Chicano activism generally and bilingual education in particu-lar as an example of how government-funded educational pluralism defiled American culture. His 1970 book Bitter Harvest excoriated identity politics, especially as manifested in the public schools. The chapter "Bilingual Fraud" described a "newly created being, the Mexican-American," engineered by anon-ymous "managers" and "mind benders," "where only [good] Americans were before," a construct necessary to uphold the bilingual education programs' philosophy, and, most concretely, the jobs to perpetuate it.[61] To Steinbacher, this theorized Mexican American was a hapless victim manipulated by "flotsam . . . disgorged by the jungles of the cities" such as Los Angeles and perceived liberal strongholds of San Francisco and Berkeley.

In discussing the United Farm Workers' strike of 1965, for example, Steinbacher barely mentioned the Delano grape pickers themselves but graph-ically depicted their supporters as "strangers" who belonged to the Student Nonviolent Coordinating Committee (SNCC): a woman "who listed herself as a civil rights worker and student" living "in a housing tract for people on welfare just north of the Golden Gate Bridge"; an associate of "the bearded Los Angeles head of the American Civil Liberties Union, an organization started mostly by Communists"; and a "tough-talking professional" woman "who doesn't seem to call any place home for very long."[62] Each evoked precise threats: women identifying more energetically as professionals than as homemakers, protestors of racial inequality, and skeptics of the cultural and political status quo—all of whom congregated in morally suspect urban or campus environments.[63] While Johnson's Great Society programs inspired a reactionary discourse that vilified blacks and excoriated a creeping Soviet influence on American sensibilities, in Southern California it was inevitable that the institutionalization of Latino immigrants' presence in tax-supported public schools would be particularly odious to the anti-interventionist, patriotic Americanism of many citizens.

As the legislative advances and grass-roots mobilization of the late 1960s gave rise to a more robust apparatus of professional organizations and advocacy groups supporting bilingual education, the programs became more obvious targets of cultural and fiscal conservatives. Most notably, the important legislative support that California Republicans had initially supplied waned precipitously. Ronald Reagan, for one, embodied this shift. In 1967, Governor Reagan had signed the pro-bilingual Senate Bill 53 into law, but in 1971, he vetoed a state bill that would have funded such programs, thus garnering "Lord Reagan" vilification as a sworn enemy of bilingual education and Chicano rights.[64] In a special issue devoted to education, *¿Que Tal?* ran a parable lambasting Reagan and the state Republican leadership. Entitled "What Does it Mean?," the story described schoolboy Juanito, usually glad to "spend all weekends working and studying," tormented by questions "flashing in his head. . . . Was it true? Were all his hopes lost? Had he worked so hard for nothing?" Panicked by press reports of state budget cuts for bilingual education, Juanito sought solace from his teacher, Mr. Alvarez, who was usually "very busy helping parents in the community," but who he luckily found "still sitting at his desk preparing lessons for all his children." Sounding remarkably like Steinbacher, though from the opposing ideological perspective, Alvarez explained that "he and all the Chicano Educators and Community Leaders" had been long aware that " 'Leaders' in Sacramento were deliberately trying to hurt their people because of the success *La Raza* had had in exposing their various methods of oppression." Alvarez assured Juanito, however, that though the nebulously defined "they" attempted "to make us fail by cutting the budget," "we will not fail."

Instead, Alvarez explained, this resistance was a reaction to Chicano success and a catalyst for future action. "We are as capable and competent as any of them. They fear us, Juanito, because they know we are a determined people . . . to receive our education . . . to take our rightful place in society . . . [and] stop the oppression of our people." The specific issue at hand was bilingual education, but the implications were far broader: "They know we refuse to walk with our heads bent to the ground and that we have means of fighting."[65] By 1971, the newsletter tarred the state budget cuts as overtly hostile toward Latinos—a "boulder that they have placed in our path so that we may trip"—unlike the prevalent depiction of the LAUSD as passive and noncommittal in reaction to the walkouts just three years earlier. Only when a heartened Juanito threw the offending newspaper into the trash did the reader see the headline that had sparked the exchange: "REAGAN PROPOSES CUTTING EOP."[66] Reagan, who had initially appointed Rafferty (and who had only switched from the Democratic to the Republican Party in 1962), thus came to symbolize the diffuse and menacing network of "leaders" and "politicians" intent on thwarting Latino progress.

To fully appreciate how this stark polarity emerged, it is vital to remember the active and consistent role conservatives and moderates played in the development of bilingual programs in California and to examine how their perspectives, and the course of bilingual education in California, changed in the wake of the blowouts. Eugene Gonzales, appointed by Rafferty to steer the state's bilingual education policy, embodied this shift, and his leadership also highlights the tensions Mexican American moderates negotiated in this fraught climate. Within weeks of the blowouts, Gonzales publicly impugned the protestors for shirking "personal responsibility" and claimed for the educational bureaucracy—rather than the populace—the responsibility of resolving the educational problems of the "ghetto and barrio student." Leadership, he argued, should derive from a "consolidation of viewpoints" within the Department of Instruction, not from "cadres of followers of different philosophies."[67] During a May address to the Department of Instruction, Gonzales explained with apparent reluctance that "we can't escape the inevitable": demands for change from parents who "not too long ago were indifferent about their children's education" and from "[parents and students] without 'the credentials' we hold so dear [who] were formerly labeled 'undesirables.'"[68] In addition to the department's fundamental purpose of teaching children "basic subject matter" and "engendering love of country," Gonzales conceded that "if [the Department] is to maintain, continue and assume even more leadership in education, it had 'no choice' but to honor this new and unrelenting "wailing" for recognition of students' "backgrounds, cultural attributes and self-perceptions." Critical, however, was that the department embark on this new path soberly, with "well developed programs accompanied by carefully stated and documented procedures and techniques for implementation" rather than allowing "experts and ad hoc groups . . . to exercise direction."[69]

Still, the early sympathy Gonzales exhibited toward bilingual-bicultural programs was not immediately extinguished by the blowouts. During the 1968 Nuevas Vistas conference, the second annual gathering of educators interested in Mexican American education, Gonzales rallied teachers to abandon their "do-nothing" attitude and defensiveness in the face of "senseless . . . pickets, demonstrations, and walkouts" and to focus on educating "the mythical tortilla eater, the sleepy giant now flexing his muscles and gaining attention," as a "real person, as a new resource to be developed as beneficial to the nation."[70] Speaking to the still more liberal Mexican American Youth Association (MAYA) just two weeks later, Gonzales sounded more aggressive, dismissing " 'studies' " of Mexican Americans as rarely delving any deeper than "the first veneer, or coating of enchiladas and frijoles." Gonzales excoriated the prevailing social treatment of Mexican Americans as a kind of serfdom, resembling "the feudal system of long ago" in which the majority of Anglos held tenaciously to the "old tattered concept" that an entire ethnic group could be "relegated to back-breaking manual labor . . . ignorant of opportunities . . . in no need of education . . . [and] possessing a language not socially acceptable."

In far more energetic language than he employed when addressing his state Department of Instruction colleagues, Gonzales decried the underrepresentation of Mexican Americans in the teaching force, their disproportionate presence in special education classes, and the preposterous expectation among some benighted educators that "the Spanish-surnamed child be 100 percent English-speaking and totally Anglicized."[71] Like any savvy politician negotiating the vagaries of an unfamiliar bureaucracy and a fickle public, Gonzales shifted the tenor of his comments in these diverse contexts, but his message remained consistent. The injustices a racist society visited upon Mexican Americans were surmountable, if teachers embraced Spanish as a transitional tool to English mastery and recognized and resisted "apathy on the part of school authorities, the existence of *de facto* segregated schools, poor and inferior facilities and equipment, ill-prepared teachers, and inadequately trained school administrators."[72]

Gonzales's defense of bilingual education was arguably strategic, relying on shifting definitions of Mexican Americans' qualification as "true" Americans. On the one hand, Gonzales faulted Mexican Americans for having, "by choice,

in many respects, clung to [their] past traditions of family-clan unity, of dog-
matic adherence to certain morals, of steadfastness to a language different
from that of the majority."[73] However, he argued, schools must adapt to serve
this population, in part because public pressure threatened to bring about
change in a far more disruptive and radical fashion, but also for apparently
paradoxical reasons. "The schools of California must make similar promises
to our children" as those inscribed on the Statue of Liberty made to a previous generation's "tired . . . poor . . . huddled masses yearning to breathe
free."[74] Thus, Mexican Americans were owed the same charity that European
immigrants were afforded—at least in the rhetoric of the age—at the turn
of the century. At the same time, Gonzales painted Mexican Americans as
so unequivocally American that denying them the opportunity to fulfill their
academic potential amounted to disloyalty. Not only did they belong to "an
identified ethnic group that preceded the early Californian," but "a very large
proportion, 80 percent, was born in the United States or its territories or pos-
sessions."[75] Gonzales concluded his speech to the young activists with an
apparently peculiar digression about the Congressional Medal of Honor:

> More Mexican-American servicemen during World War II received
> this award than members of any other single ethnic or minority
> group in the nation. . . . During the Korean conflict, I know of no
> Mexican-American who betrayed his country under communist pres-
> sure and psychological warfare. . . . Both Indians and Spaniards, from
> whom Mexican-Americans are descended, loved their land, their home,
> their country. This was their legacy; this is the Mexican-American's
> inheritance.[76]

Gonzales's concluding point, however, was neither contradictory nor tan-
gential. In the aggressive and politicized climate of spring 1968, there was
no way that the state educational bureaucracy could avoid responding to
mounting protests that challenged American society as a whole. In response,
Gonzales invoked every example he could to show the young students he
addressed that Mexican Americans were thoroughly American and valiant
patriots, no less fully entitled to all the rights of citizenship. If alluding to the
generation of European immigrants who had so legendarily assimilated to
American culture seemed at odds with the image of a decorated military ser-
viceman, they were both patriotic archetypes. Addressing a group of students
constantly barraged with entreaties to embrace *la Raza* and to denounce "the
Anglo power structure" and the imperialistic and capitalistic United States,

Gonzales attempted to entice these youths with an alternate vision of their role in the American past and present. This moderate vision had shaped early bilingual policy in California. Rather than rallying educators to embrace bilingual-bicultural education and empower Latino students, Rafferty and Gonzales increasingly wanted to ensure that teachers approached this inevitable pedagogical challenge from the ideological perspective of the bureaucracy they oversaw.

Gonzales's measured approach to bilingual education was predictable since Rafferty had built his public persona around a distinct vision of Americanism as inhospitable to ethnic and cultural particularism. As bilingual education became more closely linked to radical causes such as civil rights or antiwar protests, it collided with Rafferty's strident rejection of identity politics. Rafferty posited Americans as a defined race possessing superior customs and culture, and he believed that the school should cultivate both race pride and an awareness of the myriad and perpetual threats to its existence, especially from abroad. In a widely quoted 1961 speech entitled "Passing of the Patriot," he declared, "I don't know when at long last the American people will rise in all their power and majesty of their great tradition to put an end to this role of international doormat which we assumed of late and which becomes us so poorly."[77] Over the course of the 1960s, the nature of the threat to California schoolchildren and American society shifted from a racialized Soviet menace to political and cultural "others" closer to home, namely, the influx of Latinos after 1965.[78] Their demands on the school system represented a more immediate and unavoidable concern, which Gonzales undertook to address, largely through bilingual-bicultural education policy.

Though Gonzales generally concurred with Rafferty's assimilationism, he put his own imprimatur on the state's policies, publicly describing his own appointment as "a breakthrough by schools [in including] . . . contributions of persons from different walks of life."[79] Still, it is difficult to ascertain exactly how much his ethnicity, or his status as the first Latino appointed to the state educational system, actively shaped his approach to bilingual education. His extensive correspondence suggests that citizens and policymakers across the political spectrum certainly perceived his ethnicity as salient to his professional role. Perhaps most pointedly, Vahac Mardirosian, a pastor at the Mexican Baptist Church in East Los Angeles and the chairman of the radical Educational Issues Coordinating Committee (EICC) instrumental in the blowouts, addressed Gonzales in an angry letter as "*Estimado Señor Eugenio Gonzalez*"—a first name Gonzales never used in official correspondence—and signed "*En espera de tu amable respuesta* [awaiting your esteemed response]," as if to remind Gonzales as well as Rafferty, Reagan, and Nava—who were carbon-copied—that Gonzales belonged to the Spanish-speaking community. Mardirosian explicitly accused Gonzales of "the worst kind of irresponsibility—denying that our Mexican community continues to suffer economic and social inequality." Despite the harshness of his missive, Mardirosian invited Gonzales to speak to the EICC, imploring him "not to ignore our invitation again." Such formulations, including the mock-innocent phrase "Señor Gonzalez, you are . . . presumably interested in the educational problems of the Chicano community," elucidate both that some Californians felt particularly betrayed by Gonzales as a Mexican American and that they perceived publicly highlighting this fact as a viable strategy to turn his attention toward the needs of their—and arguably his—community.[80]

Mexican American ethnic identity, thus, hardly guaranteed a particular perspective on bilingual-bicultural education. Farther right on the political spectrum, Alfred Ramirez, one of the state's most outspoken detractors of bilingual programs, trumpeted in letters to Reagan and Rafferty his own identity as an "American of Mexican descent" and as founder of the American Education Service for Spanish-Surnamed Citizens as investing his opposition to bilingual programs with special credibility. Gonzales, not Rafferty, however, provocatively replied to Ramirez in a terse telegram: "Should you wish to debate the issue you name, I, also an American of Mexican descent, will be available upon agreement of terms."[81] The debate never occurred, for Ramirez would not agree to Gonzales's demand for a venue that would guarantee that "the session be void of hysteric and emotional outbursts already witnessed from uninformed individuals supposedly speaking for a group consensus."[82] Yet it is apparent both from Ramirez's framing of his opposition—he also mentioned a meeting that would include Gonzales, a group of "American businessmen, of Mexican descent," and himself to legitimate his resistance—and from Rafferty's decision to make Gonzales the department's public face of bilingual education that Gonzales's ethnicity was highly germane to his role.[83]

An exchange between Gonzales and a high school teacher from the agricultural city of Indio intimates palpable tension between his ethnic identity and professional responsibilities. The teacher, Alicia Davila Luff, beseeched Gonzales to fulfill his promise "to help . . . any way he could" her students organize a chapter of the UMAS.[84] While Gonzales's scrawl, "I have not been there?" indicated he may have forgotten making the commitment, Luff demanded a "very immediate answer" since "the organization has become very controversial," and "the principal values what you have to say."[85] Gonzales's apparently anodyne reply, disclaiming any authority to address "tensions pertaining solely to local affairs," suggested the libertarianism of Rafferty's administration.[86] Still, his measured tone belied empathy for this fledgling Chicano activism. To Luff's concern that UMAS excluded Anglos, Gonzales rejoined, "The question is not whether UMAS has discriminated against Anglos, or whether the name implies segregation. As a matter of fact . . . the Anglo has, in the past, discriminated against Chicanos and . . . the Chicano has always been segregated, and not only educationally." That UMAS, initially politically moderate, had "lately . . . become more liberal and militant than some would like to see" did not seem to trouble Gonzales.[87] Gonzales ultimately evaded taking a stance and claimed his department "will recognize UMAS, as well as any other student organization, as long as it is not in conflict with our Constitution or our state regulations."[88]

Most telling, however, is a revealing exchange between Gonzales and colleague Dan Reyes, who advised him on how to reply to Luff's "loaded question." "No matter how the letter is answered," Reyes wrote, Gonzales was vulnerable for offering to help UMAS when "some chapters [were] quite militant," associated with radicals such as Phil Montes of the Association of Mexican American Educators and Sal Castro, notorious since the blowouts.[89] Still, Reyes acknowledged that though any response "was sure to find its way to the news media . . . the State Department of Education could use some Chicano support."[90] Luff and Gonzales never mention his ethnicity in their correspondence, but Reyes's closing parenthetical remark— "We Chicanos have to stick together" —illuminates the continued saliency of Gonzales's ethnicity to his position.[91]

Gonzales was at the vanguard of a wave of California Latinos during the late 1960s who were making inroads within the educational establishment as well as developing an increasingly robust collective identity through new civil rights organizations such as MAPA and the Mexican American Legal Defense and Educational Fund (MALDEF). The establishment of the Association of Mexican-American California School Board Members (AMACSB) reveals the nexus between the organizational impulse among Latinos and their specific advances in the realm of education. At its first annual meeting, the AMACSB asked, "What is the proper function of a Mexican-American school board member who identifies ethnically?"[92] By "an overwhelming consensus," the AMACSB declared that school board members "must serve all school children in the district." Still, as Mexican Americans, the school board members "must be positive about the commitment to the special needs of the Mexican-American pupils, but it is not a question of 'rather than' but merely 'in addition to' our overall concern."[93] The AMACSB members knew they operated in a fraught environment.

Having at last secured a place in the educational power structure, Mexican Americans were empowered to advocate for Mexican American youth, but the faintest suggestion that these newcomers privileged "special interests" over the common good—most reflexively associated with bilingual-bicultural education—threatened their still modest gains. A commitment to tread cautiously hardly diminished the collective sense among Mexican Americans that they possessed a newly powerful political voice. Nava emphasized a need to support Mexican Americans across party lines. "Issues or differences of opinion amongst us must be kept within the family in order to present a unified front for maximum effectiveness," he wrote.[94] Presuming that "family" identity superseded partisanship, Nava asserted that "promoting the valid interests of our particular group requires that we have well-placed individuals in both parties at all levels."[95] In fact, it was Gonzales, a Republican who had condemned the blowouts Nava had vocally supported, whom Nava declared deserved the unqualified endorsement of the Mexican American community.

Nava, still widely celebrated as one of the most prescient Latino educational reformers, was not alone in realizing the urgency of collective action and the political danger of splintering the community. Eddie Hanson, a Department of Instruction colleague, wrote in frustration to Gonzales about a speech delivered by Herb Ibarra, an ESL innovator, at the 1968 Teachers of English to Speakers of Other Languages (TESOL) Convention in San Diego. It was "a scathing attack on our schools without offering any solutions for correcting the inequities that still exist," Hanson complained. Interestingly, Hanson criticized Ibarra's commentary for its tenor rather than its content: "The same points (which in general are true as Herb stated them) could have been made without alienating anyone whose support we so desperately need."[96] This exchange suggests that Gonzales and Hanson, like Nava, attempted to "to enlist the full support of people" for Mexican American educational rights. Based on the transcript of Ibarra's speech, their perspectives are hardly at odds. Ibarra defended bilingual-bicultural programs by asserting Mexican Americans' long patriotic past, from "ringing the Mission bell in San Diego" as the first shots of the American Revolution were fired to "the casualty lists of Vietnam [giving] ample testimony to the allegiance of this group of Americans."[97] This moment apparently manifests an exceptional and transient ideological fluidity among politically diverse Latinos committed to improving Mexican American education.

By spring 1969, events that transpired at the third annual Nuevas Vistas conference in Los Angeles evinced the range of increasingly irreconcilable positions among Latino educational activists in the policy universe over which Gonzales presided. Entitled "*Las Vistas Se Aclaran*," the conference was jointly planned by the state Department of Education and MAPA, California's foremost political organization for Mexican Americans, along with the League of United Latin American Citizens (LULAC), an organization known for its assimilationism. Rafferty greeted the conference in a tone of genial inclusiveness, conceding, "As a society we are strapped by the old 'melting pot song,' a part of our historical show which is over," but maintaining that its "melody lingers on."[98] This awkward metaphor conveyed Rafferty's grudging acceptance of his office's responsibility to educate in new ways the "American of Mexican descent who has chosen to keep much of his ethnic identity." Furthermore, the presence of so many approaches to this question prompted Rafferty to comment on the promise of the occasion: "No one knows who may step forward with a crystallizing thought and . . . make those present get the feeling that *sí, las vistas se aclaran.*"

Gonzales also emphasized working together "by concerted fused action and commitment," but directly cautioned the over four hundred educators present to act moderately, formulating "rational, accurate, supported statements" in lieu of "irresponsible charges and countercharges."[99] At the previous year's conference, Gonzales had urged action to "remove the barricades . . . of unyielding years of status quo and 'do nothing'!" rousing the Mexican American from "a long siesta of looking in from the outside."[100] A tumultuous year later, Gonzales declared that having "gained a foothold for recognition and concern . . . it is no longer necessary to hit the schools with a 2x4 for attention . . . to ram the barrel with nuts and bolts to make our point," or to "turn our public school system 'up-side-down' to gain advantages for the American of Mexican descent."[101] The allusion to the blowouts was clear.

By the close of the first day of Nuevas Vistas, however, the centrist climate that Rafferty and Gonzales endeavored to cultivate was already beginning to strain. On Thursday evening, Governor Reagan's speech was interrupted by the explosion of several firecrackers dropped from the overhead balcony. Moments later, wastebaskets around the conference pavilion, linen closets, and empty hotel rooms erupted into seven fires, eventually causing nearly sixty thousand dollars of damage to the Biltmore Hotel.[102] Undeterred, Reagan continued delivering his prepared text, beseeching citizens and educators to tell him "how to equip the child of Mexican descent . . . to compete and succeed in the pluralistic melting pot we call America."[103] Only when twelve audience members began "to clap and shout in Spanish" and moved to the center of floor did Reagan stop speaking. Police summarily removed the demonstrators, and Reagan "concluded his speech without further incident" to a standing ovation.[104]

Reagan's warm welcome back to the podium and Rafferty's meek attempt at Spanish clearly failed to paper over mounting doubts among some about the state's commitment to Mexican American education. Even the governor's and superintendent's inconsistent evocations of "the melting pot"—Rafferty called it obsolete, Reagan an ideal—suggested the tenuousness of the state bureaucracy's philosophical approach to educating Mexican Americans. The violence of the demonstrations, and the ugliness of the aftermath of the conference, lay bare this splintering. Nava, who had so carefully nurtured alliances among Mexican Americans across party lines, quickly stepped forward to defend vociferously the demonstrators' freedom of speech and to distinguish them from the vandals, claiming that "the arsonists got away and the wrong people were arrested."[105] While Nava decried the vandalism, he could not resist reiterating their claim that "Governor Reagan had not done enough for education."[106]

Exacerbating the links between Mexican American educational activism and dangerous radicalism, evidence emerged that the arsonists and demonstrators had been one and the same. Four of them, it was found, had organized the blowouts that Nava had defended so vocally just a year earlier. Though the Biltmore Hotel fires did not injure anyone, the protestors' activism had clearly become more militant since the peaceful protests that primarily involved teenagers. Moreover, the students, two of them Brown Berets, were also implicated in an arson incident at a Los Angeles Safeway store, where a fire had presumably been set in support of the United Farmworkers Organizing Committee's International Boycott Safeway Day.[107] While efforts at cooperation by Gonzales and Nava, whether symbolic or genuine, had managed for most of the late 1960s to coalesce diverse and even contradictory perspectives on how best to educate the Mexican American student, the bolder radicalism and overt criminality of the Nuevas Vistas protestors suggested that these were unraveling.

The letters Gonzales received in the conference's wake reflect the extent of the damage the events at Nuevas Vistas wrought on the bilingual-bicultural education cause. Manuel Banda, of both MAPA and the state's Bureau of Intergroup Relations, wrote to express his deep "regret" about the incident, but also to advocate a larger role for MAPA in future conferences.[108] Banda clearly sensed that the Nuevas Vistas forum was in jeopardy and, with it, arenas in which liberal organizations such as MAPA could advocate for bilingual-bicultural education. Vahac Mardirosian, who identified as more radical, believed the Nuevas Vistas incidents reflected a more dire situation. Referring to the removal of Abe Tapia, president of MAPA, from the stage at Nuevas Vistas, Mardirosian "deplored and protested . . . [Gonzales's] humiliation of a Chicano spokesman" and equated Gonzales's actions with the "safer" option "not to speak out against injustice," thus complicitly shoring up "a powerful and immoral status quo."[109] The *Los Angeles Times* also shifted the tone of its coverage. While the paper exhibited some sympathy for the walk-outs and the demands for educational equity, it was quick to publish an elegiac article about the young undercover police officer who had infiltrated the Brown Berets in the weeks before the fires, "preventing a devastating conflagration and the possible loss of hundreds of lives."[110] The region's newspaper of record now circulated a more threatening portrayal of Chicano educational activism.

The radicalization of opinions on bilingual education was not unique to the Left. To the right of Gonzales and Rafferty emerged a vocal antibilingual education voice.[111] As Latino advocates of bilingual education aligned more energetically with the political Left, some conservatives pigeonholed them with causes the Right had already dismissed as offensively radical. In 1970, John Steinbacher specifically targeted the Nuevas Vistas conference series as misleading "a whole generation of young people who mouth revolutionary slogans and clichés they learned from someone."[112] Refusing to refer to the meeting by its Spanish name, Steinbacher wrote, "New Vistas would run roughshod over the educational system in California." He linked the educators' reformism to the labor activism of César Chávez, claiming that the plight of "the linguistically underprivileged children was as true as the fabricated misery of the downtrodden grape-pickers Chávez was supposed to be busy rescuing."[113] Chávez's politics were a far cry from those of Gonzales or Rafferty, but Steinbacher's reductive analysis resonated with conservatives as bilingual education became more vigorously and exclusively embraced by the political Left.

Southern California entrepreneur and commentator Alfred Ramirez emerged as arguably the most ardent opponent of bilingual programs in this era. He inextricably linked bilingual education with the Left in the public eye, but he did so to the programs' detriment. Already in 1967, Ramirez positioned bilingual education as similarly ludicrous to "teaching Swahili to all blacks in the South" and as a "grotesque tax fraud" verging on socialism, sure to create "a Nation of Mongrels."[114] Such characterizations were fodder for conservatives' growing frustration at the excesses of the Great Society and of ethnic rights movements. Ramirez and Steinbacher also echoed Rafferty in linking bilingual education to an assault on the American family. Ramirez wrote that the "bilingual fraud" threatened to "divide and destroy our country . . . by making political pawns out of children." The two identified as heroines the Mothers Against Chávez, an organization formed by Josephine Gabaldón and other Latina mothers when the Republican Party had failed "to save them and their little children from Chávez."[115]

These rifts within the Mexican American community were laid bare for the larger public in September 1970, when for the first time in thirty-five years, the conservative Los Angeles-based *Cómite Mexicano Cívico Patriótico* decided to cancel its annual Mexican Independence Day parade, intended to attract 200,000 and be "its biggest ever." The decision was quickly echoed by the Latin American Chamber of Commerce in the nearby San Fernando Valley regarding its own festivities. The Mexican American business community was fearful of losing control of these historic celebrations given that the previous Saturday, a Chicano protest of the disproportionate deployment of Latinos to fight in Vietnam had resulted in two deaths, including that of notable Latino journalist Ruben Salazar at the hands of a sheriff's deputy. As an OCR investigation of the LAPD took shape, the Chicano Moratorium Committee ignored pleas to cancel its planned event, announcing that it would recognize Mexican Independence Day "with a legal, peaceful parade and rally which will address itself to the war in Southeast Asia, the police repression and occupation of our community, the murder of Ruben Salazar, and the violation of our constitutional rights of freedom of speech and assembly."[116] Reported on the front page of the *Los Angeles Times*, these divergent opinions over how to commemorate a shared past made it unmistakably clear how contentious the Mexican American community's future would be.

## Defining Latino, Defining America

The tendency to ignore the variegation within the Latino community was a common complaint in the 1960s and 1970s among Mexican Americans of all political stripes, who resented being cast as reified archetypes. Moderate Eugene Gonzales was exasperated by the trope of the "lazy tortilla-eater," while both liberal Peter Chacón and radical Galarza bristled at the notion that bicultural children were inherently educationally deficient. Ramirez expressed similar frustration from the far Right with bilingual education activists—he styled them the "Mexican-American Fraud in America" (MAFIA)—who depicted Mexican American children as illiterate and helpless.[117] Parents were understandably incensed by this tendency. One Mexican American mother from East Los Angeles, E. R. Aguerrebere, wrote angrily to Rafferty to decry the widely quoted statistic that most Mexican Americans in California attained only an eighth-grade education. After graduating from Garfield High, a site of the walkouts, Aguerrebere's son had been accepted by UCLA, USC, and Cal State, "and thus must have been taught something."[118] The "eighth-grade statistic," intended to attract support for Mexican American education, inspired "resentment" in this mother because it portrayed Mexican Americans as victims, thus diminishing her family's accomplishments. She wrote:

> Dr. Rafferty, I was born in Mexico and was brought to the United States when I was two months old. My parents, relatives, and neighbors did not speak English. I learned English in school. I believe I was that child they are speaking of now who can't identify with his blue-eyed teacher, who becomes frustrated because his teacher is insensitive, and finally finds conditions so unbearable he drops out. To me, this is a lot of "bull." I went to school to learn and didn't worry about my teachers' looks or origin . . . I don't hear the kids that just came from Mexico crying for Mexican culture and bi-lingual classes. It's only those who expect to make more money when they get that new position—the Association of Mexican-American Educators.[119]

Indeed, Aguerrebere perceived this ubiquitous "eighth-grade" sound bite as emblematic of what she characterized as "the bi-lingual bunk."[120]

Of course, distancing oneself from radicalism, or even reformism, carried with it social benefits. A cartoon in ¿Qué Tal?—depicting a man in a suit answering a woman's perplexed comment, "But you don't look Mexican?" with the reply, "Well, I'm 1/8 French, 1/8 English, 1/8 Portuguese, and 5/8 VENDIDO!!!! [sellout]"—suggests the prevalence of this self-conscious distancing by some Mexican Americans from Chicano identity and politics.[121] (See figure 2.2.) Just as advocates of bilingualism organized in reaction to damaging stereotypes, to Mexican Americans with conservative tendencies, oversimplifications of their Mexican American identity prompted them to proclaim their Americanism all the more ardently.

Moreover, this historical moment for Latinos was particularly opportune for the cultivation of an ardently American, or even "whitened," identity. By the late 1960s, overtly racist speech had been largely excised from political discourse, a dynamic that operated in two ways: it made it politically and culturally possible, and even advantageous, for some Latinos to identify with

FIGURE 2.2 A cartoon from Chicano newspaper *¿Que Tal?* reveals the intensifying stakes of claiming ethnic identity among Latinos during the 1970s. *Que Tal?* No. 6, April 1, 1971, 5. Ernesto Galarza Collection, Box 55, Folder 6. Reprinted by courtesy of Department of Special Collections and University Archives, Stanford University Libraries.

"Brown Power"; for others, it was an opportunity to dissociate themselves from a racial archetype.[122] In fact, this ambiguity contributed to Latinos' problems with educational achievement, one scholar wrote, as "Mexican-American children are not viewed by the educational system as different, yet are treated differently . . . thereby dooming them to failure."[123] Even as the Chicano movement gained strength by identifying with the more mature African American freedom struggle, moderate and conservative Californians pointed to what they perceived as essential differences between the two groups. Steinbacher continually contrasted Mexican Americans with "the notorious Negro."[124] A degree of Mexican American frustration with the United States was understandable, he explained, in that their "real or imagined feelings of being wronged were based on a wrong of property confiscation"—a violation, after all, of the fundamental American right to private property—as opposed to the "vapid claims of Negro civil rights leaders," which were "based on emotion."[125] Spanish-language bilingual education was to Steinbacher a particularly "insidious plan to destroy American language, culture and property," for it wrongly grouped Latino interests with misguided African American initiatives such as teaching Swahili.[126] Steinbacher and others primarily contrasted Latinos and African-Americans based on the latter's essential racial difference as opposed to what they perceived as the "gimmicky" and completely artificial "creation of a new ethnic identity" among Mexican Americans.[127] State-supported bilingual education was at the core of this "unholy grouping." Steinbacher wrote of Reagan's signing Senate Bill 53 into law that "with one stroke of his pen, the governor had created a whole new ethnic group, the "Mexican-Americans. . . . They were hyphenated Americans for the first time . . . successfully broken away from the American mainspring."[128]

Rafferty, in *Classroom Countdown*, also conveys his implicit sense that Mexican Americans were not to be counted in his consideration of California's "racial mess."[129] Though Rafferty had spent much of his tenure grappling with how to educate the Mexican American student, he focused on African-Americans virtually exclusively when writing about public education's "racial gap."[130] Indeed, the only mention he made of Mexican Americans was an offhanded comment that just as he would not attribute low academic achievement among African-Americans to genetic racial difference, he would not blame similar scores among Mexican Americans on their inability "to read English as well as the rest of us."[131] Latinos clearly embodied a less essentialized minority status than did African-Americans. President Nixon exploited this distinction between Latinos and blacks in his strategic advocacy of bilingual education as well. Historian Gareth Davies points out that to secure Latino support for his re-election, President Nixon favored funding for bilingual programs in order to "show that his initiatives on the behalf [of Latinos] . . . are not 'warmed over black programs,'" and that he understood that 'minority' was not synonymous with 'black.'"[132] Latinos' slippery identity, at times defined as racially other, at times as fluidly assimilable to Anglo culture, made the dynamics surrounding bilingual-bicultural activism especially complex.

The leeway in self-definition that Latinos enjoyed is manifest in the unstudied range of their political affiliations in the late 1960s. Though conventional wisdom suggests that minorities voted overwhelmingly Democratic in this era, the Latino story reveals otherwise. California Latinos supported Reagan's gubernatorial candidacy in 1966, and Nixon described the natural affinities he had observed in Southern California between "family-oriented, law-abiding" Latinos and the Republican Party.[133] Indeed, in this region, GOP support for bilingual education, intended to appeal to Latinos, was sufficiently common to merit Ramirez's observation that well-meaning Latinos had abandoned the Democratic Party in 1966 and "voted by the thousands for the Republicans." At the same time, to ardently conservative Ramirez, even the halting support Republicans such as Reagan, Rafferty, and Gonzales lent to bilingual education made this departure less than "a radical departure from the no-win, appeasement policies of the left wing, Marxist-oriented Democratic Party . . . [These Mexican Americans] were too politically naïve to realize that they had merely voted for Tweedle Dee instead of Tweedle Dum."[134]

Students' calls to reconstruct the social order beginning with bilingual-bicultural education, as well as Title VII of the 1965 Elementary and Secondary Education Act, were clearly inspired by the spirit of the Great Society and civil rights movement. Yet close analysis of Rafferty's and Gonzales's stewardship of bilingual education policy in California reveals the programs to have been a reaction to 1960s liberalism as well as an evocation of it. The California story points to leading Latino historian Guadelupe San Miguel's notion that "those in favor of bilingual education are language specialists, Mexican-American activists, newly enfranchised civil rights advocates, language minorities, intellectuals, teachers and students."[135] Rather, inherent to bilingual-bicultural education's origins and statewide implementation was a conservative sensibility embodied most clearly in the perspectives held by Gonzales and Rafferty. Gonzales, in his pioneering position as the highest-ranking Latino in the state Department of Education, highlights the multiple and specific challenges with which bilingual-bicultural education presented Latinos and political moderates, and the range of sensibilities they manifested in this historical moment.

Counterintuitive to reflexive contemporary associations of bilingual education with the Left, and to the apparent incongruity between Sunbelt Republicans and ethnic rights advocacy, in early 1968, Rafferty, Reagan, and Gonzales could still promote moderate bilingual education programs and remain ideologically consistent with mainstream conservatism. Outright racism and xenophobia had receded from respectable political discourse, while Latinos' historically fluid identity as an "in-between group" engendered as many perspectives on bilingual initiatives as the multiple programs that continued to multiply with the help of federal funding after 1968. Complementing expansive government support was a growing grass-roots advocacy for Latinos in general, and bilingual education in particular, that took its cues from other movements of the 1960s and gained strength in the 1970s. After the March 1968 blowouts, it became clear that moderate legislative reform would not be the only force shaping bilingual programming in California. Mexican Americans had organized to protest unequal treatment in education before 1968, but the sudden and impassioned blowouts resonated with other mass movements of the era, inspiring both support and fear of the protestors and their cause. They ultimately and irreversibly polarized the debate over bilingual and bicultural education in California and nationwide.

# 3

## "BIRDS OF MANY COLORS"

### LANGUAGE, CULTURE, AND COMMUNITY IN 1970s SAN JOSE

More than three decades before Chicano students shook East Los Angeles and legislators of all stripes took interest in the academic experiences of "Spanish-surnamed" students, the idea for what would become one of California's—and the nation's—most important bilingual education programs took shape in an unlikely site. In suburban Long Island, New York, Mexican-born labor organizer and educator Ernesto Galarza and his wife Mae (nee Taylor) directed the private progressive Gardner School from 1932 to 1936 while Galarza completed his doctorate in the history of education at Columbia University's Teachers College.[1] Nearly half a century later, Mae fondly reminisced about the thoroughgoing progressivism at Teachers College and recalled that Gardner students and teachers enjoyed "many, very fine, brand new books . . . beautifully done by very good people."[2] The Galarzas, committed to employing progressive education to further the pursuit of social justice for Latinos, immediately identified two problems. First, the books were "all English, all Anglo," an unsurprising fact given that it would be thirty years until the popular *Dick and Jane* readers would begin to include African American characters.[3] Secondly, Galarza, who had spent his childhood in the Sacramento public schools after his parents emigrated from Mexico, lamented that such pedagogical creativity in children's literature "is not customary in Mexico," where a system built on "memorization . . . traditional stories . . . and a great deal of oral repetition" meant that "there was no inspiration there for these kind of things."[4]

Motivated to create progressive educational materials that would excite young Spanish-speaking children about reading and

learning, Galarza self-published *Más poemas párvulos* in 1943, the first whim-
sical volume of songs and rhymes, originally composed for his young daughter, that would become his celebrated mini-libros. Galarza had already written
seven volumes colorfully describing nature, home, and play by the early 1970s
when the San Jose Unified School District (SJUSD) expressed a need for
Spanish-language materials.[5] The mini-libros, ultimately sold in twenty-seven
states and three countries, earned Galarza the nickname "Father Goose of
Mexican Children." These were only the best-known products of his bilingual
education program, the San Jose-based Studio Lab, which showcases both the
pedagogy's boldest ambitions and the substantial obstacles it faced, even as
it left its indelible imprint on contemporary political culture and educational
practice.[6]

In the 1970s, bilingual education expanded with unforeseen energy and
made major gains in state and federal policy throughout a decade during
which it could seem "like nothing really happened."[7] Exemplifying such
strides was the grass-roots and progressive Studio Lab founded in the early
1970s by Galarza, who had already established a reputation as an activist and
Latin America expert.[8] Though dismantled by the early 1980s, the Studio Lab
made a lasting impression, both in explicitly connecting bilingual education to multicultural pedagogies and, more surprisingly, in articulating and
cementing the crucial role of family involvement in schoolhouse politics.
The undoing of the Studio Lab and its replacement by the federally run
Bilingual Consortium tells another important story about how internal dissension among bilingual educators inhibited the successful implementation
of bilingual education perhaps as formidably as did conservative opposition.

Demographic pressures forced these issues to the fore in the 1970s.
Mirroring national shifts and challenging the region's historical political conservatism, San Jose became home to California's second-largest concentration of Mexican-Americans after Los Angeles. In 1970, the US Census Bureau
reported that Spanish speakers had replaced Italians as the largest linguistic
minority in the United States, and California was at the forefront of this massive demographic transformation. The so-called Hispanic Challenge would
alternately excite and enrage Americans at large in the coming decades.[9]
Latinos, who had for much of American history felt that their language and
culture was excluded from public life, made inroads commensurate with
their growing presence. As late as 1969, the *San Francisco Chronicle* published
a series exploring "the plight of the Spanish-speaking," in which citizens
described feeling that "you're out of luck unless you learn to speak English."
Yet by 1975, bilingual ballots and election officials were introduced throughout

Southern California. It was a significant step from the accounts of unresponsive, monolingual 911 telephone operators whom frustrated citizens had encountered just a few years earlier.[10]

The equity issues Latinos raised—foremost among them bilingual education, but also including police brutality, immigration policy, and workplace discrimination—received unprecedented state and national attention in the 1970s. At the urging of newly organized Latino advocacy groups, the California state legislature approved various expansions of the state's pioneering but relatively moderate bilingual-bicultural education programs. These ventures were diverse, ranging from the ESL model most popular in the 1960s to transitional and maintenance curricula that espoused cultural celebration and even two-way language acquisition, which largely targeted Spanish-speaking students despite the state's linguistic diversity. It was a Chinese-American plaintiff, Kinney Kinmon Lau, who in 1970 brought the suit against the San Francisco public schools that culminated in the US Supreme Court decision *Lau v. Nichols* (1974), mandating that school systems all over the country "take affirmative steps to rectify the language deficiency . . . of national-origin minority group children." Hailed as the court's most important ruling since *Brown v. Board of Education* (1954), *Lau* and ensuing legislation enforcing implementation further codified the national responsibility to address the alarming academic failure of Latinos, who averaged eight and a half years of educational attainment compared to the national mean of twelve years.[11] In bringing the struggles of linguistic minorities into a national conversation that had focused almost exclusively on racial discrimination, *Lau* institutionalized the school's responsibility to assist immigrant children on their own terms, setting the stage for outcome-based educational solutions and marking an important departure from the equal-opportunity, color-blind ethos underlying *Brown*.[12]

Ideological challenges came just as intensely from within the movement as differing philosophies of bilingual pedagogy clashed. Some of the staunchest and earliest advocates of bilingualism and cultural affirmation, such as Ernesto Galarza in San Jose, opposed the bureaucratic and pedagogically limited approach of newer federally funded programs enabled by the 1968 BEA. By 1981, Galarza had abandoned the movement in frustration, subscribing instead to a version of the same pro-family, antigovernment discourse that galvanized the emerging right. Policymakers also suffered as much from philosophical incoherence as outright dissension when they debated the practical and philosophical challenge of the myriad programs being piloted in districts statewide. Such divisiveness only stoked growing conservative opposition to bilingual education, the fiscally inefficient state that supported it, and the general assault on Anglo-American culture it was coming to represent. As every major city in the United States experienced an influx of Latinos in the late twentieth century, by the 1990s educators would claim that, "we are all multiculturalists now."[13] California's challenges of the 1960s and 1970s soon became those of the nation.

## Bilingual Education in the 1970s: Policy Framework

Although the BEA had been a watershed, advocates and policymakers alike knew there was much work left to be done. The western states were the primary beneficiaries of the admittedly meager federal funds allocated for bilingual education; California enjoyed unique support for its existing and emergent approaches and became a national pioneer.[14] As a diverse collection of state and local policymakers and educators in California struggled to construct workable curricula to serve a rapidly growing and dramatically underserved population, federal legislators paid greater attention to the needs of the nearly ten million American Latinos who would populate cities nationwide in the late twentieth century. Bilingual education made tremendous inroads during the 1970s, yet as the movement grew and engaged larger social and cultural concerns, it encountered challenges from without and within.

The funds at stake were modest, but their allocation unmistakably located California at the forefront of a national demographic movement and its attendant educational imperative. If California's pedagogical leadership brought national attention to their bilingual education programs, the concentration of federal allocations to Texas and California generated jealousy from bilingual education advocates in other regions. In New York, where a sizeable and predominantly Puerto Rican population encountered comparable linguistic struggles, Latino advocate and Congressman Herman Badillo, along with twenty other legislators, was "bitterly disappointed" at the "outrage" that California had been allocated over $7 million in bilingual education funding to serve its 500,000 Spanish-surnamed children, while New York had received less than $1.5 million to serve its 300,000. Highlighting the diverse and at times contradictory needs of the nation's Spanish-speaking community, New York leaders also bristled at the designation of many bilingual funds as "migrant education," a category applying to many Mexican American agricultural workers and excluding New York City's largely Caribbean populations.[15] The federal government responded that New York City had been insufficiently "aggressive" in its pursuit of federal funds and that "committees from Texas and California have been far more organized, visible, and voluble," submitting "more organized and better-thought out bids."[16]

For all this external support and the innovation California evinced, the success of the state's bilingual-bicultural programs was less than certain. Bilingual education activists such as Ford Foundation consultant Enrique Hank Lopez were "grateful for the money that has been allocated" but worried the sums were "so small that it makes the program look ineffective."[17] A 1971 report on Mexican American education in the Southwest bestowed upon California the dubious honor of performing "best in a group of losers." The problem was systemic. The state's Bilingual-Bicultural Task Force had been charged in 1971 with developing and implementing policy, and parents on both the political Right and Left quickly became frustrated with what they witnessed in their children's classrooms. Most egregious were the many schools that continued to enforce English-only rules, as well as "the inexcusable Anglo-American bias" exhibited in history courses.[18] In Fresno, parents and members of five Chicano organizations publicly charged their district with continuing to "frustrate the intent and purpose of compensatory education programs, and [its] policy of permitting only token parent participation."[19]

To critics, the role of parents was as crucial as that of the bureaucracy. An Anglo Beverly Hills optometrist and former Los Angeles County school board member wrote to the task force of having observed "at J.C. Penney's a Mexican, or Chicano, or Mexican American family" conversing in Spanish, though the parents communicated with the cashier in English. This observer asked rhetorically, "How can the teacher motivate these children to speak and read English when 'Mommy and Daddy talk to us in Spanish'—we don't need to learn English." He advised the policymakers to think beyond the classroom and "put the blame where it belongs."[20] Curiously, the solution he offered to the state bureaucracy was that they better seek out "parental backing" for their programs; ostensibly he was not alluding to the support of the Mexican American parents who spoke to their children in Spanish.[21] Task-force member William Webster wrote a memo to his staff acknowledging, "We have been taking a beating from all sides," and warning of the damaging impact of such attacks on an already precarious initiative: "We simply cannot handle this kind of negative publicity."[22]

A commitment to serving the language needs of thousands of needy Californian children permeates the task force's memoranda, reports, and correspondence. At the same time, a distinct philosophical incoherence—an apparent lack of understanding of the state's core mission in providing bilingual-bicultural education—is equally manifest. Though many programs employed aspects of all three models of bilingual education, the approaches differed substantially in underlying philosophy and practice. As late as October 1974—three years after the task force had been convened—an internal memo revealed confusion on the most basic question: "What is our operational definition of 'bilingual education?' Does this include ESL?" one member wrote to another.[23]

Throughout the 1970s, California continued to attract harsh criticism for its gross failures in implementation, even as it remained a national leader. A 1976 report drafted by the California Advisory Committee to the federal OCR skewered liberal African American state superintendent Wilson Riles equally if not more vigorously than opponents had attacked his avowedly conservative predecessor Rafferty for failing to provide adequate bilingual-bicultural programming for the state's non-English-speaking students.[24] Such criticism only stoked the tensions brewing between African American and Chicano activists on questions of educational and labor equality. In 1970, Galarza had co-authored a widely cited report on this issue, highlighting that the availability of federal anti-poverty programs had "add[ed] fuel to the intensity of hostility on the part of a few browns and blacks who aspire to control. That makes it difficult for the rest of the people to talk," or build a broad coalition to support its efforts.[25]

Still, in light of the relative "invisibility" invoked repeatedly to describe Latino social standing through the late 1960s, the legislative and judicial advances bolstering earlier efforts to introduce both English as a second language and bilingual-bicultural education during the 1970s throughout California were remarkable.[26] "School Districts With More Than Five Percent National Origin–Minority Group Children," a memorandum drafted by J. Stanley Pottinger and Leon Panetta, both liberal California lawyers working for the federal OCR, declared in 1970 that "programs for non-English speakers cannot be dead-end tracks."[27] Though the OCR lacked the funding to enforce this bold directive, the document called attention to the disproportionate number of Mexican American students in EMR classes, an issue brought before the California Supreme Court the same year in *Diana v. State Board of Education.* Within the next two years, the California legislature banned certain verbal portions of the placement tests, decreed that LES students would have an option to be examined in Spanish, and determined that their placement would be based on a holistic assessment of their record rather than a single test score.

By the middle of the decade, bilingual-bicultural education was making inroads at both the state and federal levels. In May 1974, the California state senate initially rejected by a 24–6 vote legislation that would have broadened bilingual education programming. Within a few months, however, it had allocated greater funding for bilingual programs in response to intense lobbying by newly organized Latino pressure groups.[28] That same year, Congress voted to expand the BEA, while specifying that these funds pay for purely transitional programs rather than the more adventurous two-way ones certain districts had piloted before the restriction.[29] Most significantly, the *Lau* complaint reached the Supreme Court and further codified legal protection for linguistic minorities.

Unquestionably, the *Lau v. Nichols* decision was a landmark in the promotion and institutionalization of bilingual education nationwide. *Lau* mandated public school systems to "take affirmative steps to rectify the language deficiency in order to open its instructional program to . . . national-origin minority group children" prevented from "effective participation in the instructional program" due to "inability to speak the English language."[30] *Lau* specifically addressed linguistic issues, codifying the school's responsibility to assist immigrant children on their own terms. Though some critics pointed out that the logic underlying *Lau*'s mandate was grounded in a problematic commitment to "fixing" language deficiencies, this decision built upon the BEA in its commitment to outcome-based educational solutions, marking an important departure from the equal-opportunity ethos underlying *Brown* and previous legislation.[31]

*Lau* also revealed the complicated relationships and diverse goals evident among California's multiracial populace. Latinos and Asian Americans who spearheaded the fight for bilingual education often found themselves at odds with predominantly African American advocates of racial integration, whose formulae for racial balance would disperse the critical masses of Asians and Latinos necessary to sustain the bilingual programs federally mandated by *Lau*.[32] Asian Americans and Latinos formed an apparently unlikely political alliance, since their academic experiences diverged dramatically in the public imagination; in the mid-1960s journalists and social critics began to cast the former as a "model minority," while low educational attainment was repeatedly cast as a distinctly "Mexican-American problem."[33] *Lau* attorney Edward Steinman purposely selected Chinese-American plaintiff Kinney Kinmon Lau to symbolize the bilingual education struggle, due to the perception of Asians as hard-working and intellectually gifted. MALDEF filed a far less visible amicus brief, though Latinos ostensibly had far more to gain from the decision.[34] Indeed, in his testimony before the Ways and Means Committee of the California State

Assembly, Steinman only mentioned on the fifteenth and final page that "the vast majority (90 percent) of the non-English-speaking children in this country come from Spanish-speaking environments."[35] Commensurately, press coverage of the decision focused on Asian-American gains and repeated a single stock phrase about *Lau*'s implications for Latinos: "The decision would be important to Spanish-speaking children around the country."[36]

Although its legacy was not immediately apparent, *Lau* marked a turning point in education policy. Several journalists commented on the peculiar failure of San Francisco—where the case originated—to establish a standard for Spanish bilingual education, currently a "nationwide jumble of bilingual programs and non-programs, the result being that Hispanic children have severe problems functioning in American schools."[37] While Latinos nationwide negotiated *Lau* differently, it was clear that "ultimately San Francisco's implementation will set some kind of precedent."[38] Notably, by 1979, certain African American advocates also took up the mantle of linguistic equality, calling for the allocation of bilingual education funds to redress the "linguistic barriers" faced by speakers of Black English. Linguist Ernie Smith commented, "It is discriminatory [against blacks] that Asian Americans, Hispanics, and Native Americans are eligible for federal funds when blacks are excluded."[39] Bilingual education activism in general, and the landmark *Lau* decision in particular, distinguished Latinos as leaders in enacting pioneering civil rights and contemporary education policy, even as it highlighted divergent priorities among California's many minorities and among Latinos themselves.

The *Lau* decision provided a framework for bilingual education policy and practice, though advocates still encountered challenges in the coming years. For example, in September 1974, at the beginning of the first school year since *Lau*'s passage, a hiring freeze in San Francisco city schools stymied its potential impact; about seven hundred Spanish-speaking children were sent to schools with unfilled positions on the first day of school.[40] In 1975, however, the federal government issued the "Lau Remedies," forceful and unprecedented compliance directives that proposed full bicultural and multicultural models for elementary schools, to be financed in part by federal coffers.[41] *Lau* clearly shed light on the needs of LES students and on the government's responsibility to address them. Even in a constrained economic environment, Governor Brown in 1976 rejected several education proposals to serve disabled and gifted children, yet he signed the Chacón-Moscone Act

(AB 1329), which appropriated $3.8 million to serve 9,500 children who spoke no or very little English.

This 1976 state measure enacted more stringent guidelines than had the federal act. AB 1329 explicitly defined bilingual education as a right of English-language learners, emphasizing the centrality of learning the "customs and values of the cultures associated with the languages being taught," and thus distinguishing California as a leader in bilingual and multicultural education.[42] In 1978, the federal bilingual act was further expanded and research was authorized at more generous funding levels. Still, critics from within the movement pointed out that the act continued to reinforce the "deficit approach" in suggesting that Anglo students should be included in bilingual-bicultural programs to help language learners rather than to derive any cultural or intellectual payoff themselves.[43] The state and federal support bilingual education attained was substantial—and crucial in both erecting a policy infrastructure and introducing the notion that bilingual and multicultural education were closely connected—but would soon be challenged by prevailing cultural assumptions, fiscal constraints, political imperatives, and even supporters within the movement.

The imprecision of pro-bilingual policymakers in defining their curricula was widespread and detrimental to the programs' viability. A scathing report by the federal OCR on California's bilingual education services specifically highlighted the state Department of Education's failure "to produce a definition of bilingual instruction the school districts can use."[44] While Superintendent Riles rejected the claims of the report as specious, many Californians struggled well into the 1980s to define this new pedagogical approach. Some employed the term *bilingual education* to describe pedagogy uniquely aimed at assimilation and mastery of English.[45] Incumbent San Francisco school board member Eugene Hopp won the backing of Latino voters, though he supported bilingual education to teach kids "to function in a society that is English-speaking."[46] Colleague Rod McLeod followed suit in 1987, subscribing to the rhetoric of bilingualism and multiculturalism, but less clearly to its underlying philosophy: "As a legitimate tool for transition (into regular classes) [bilingual education is] needed . . . but some people use it as a way to maintain their own culture. I don't think that's legitimate."[47] Enabling bilingual education to become even more amorphous in practice, the California Senate Finance Committee voted 7–2 in 1979 to allow each school to design its own programming, a move Latino leader and Assemblyman Peter Chacón called "a slap in the face to the Chicano caucus."[48]

Given the political volatility of the era, it was perhaps inevitable that bilingual education's burgeoning policy framework and emerging profile began to raise public ire, as school board meetings and letters to the editor pages show. Scholars of bilingual education have pointed out that very little opposition came from academics or educational researchers.[49] Indeed, it was a *Washington Post* journalist, Noel Epstein, who emerged as a leading critic of bilingual education programs for their allocation of federal funds to support the particularist notion of "affirmative ethnicity," the idea that ethnic difference should be reinforced.[50] Epstein attributed his surprising stature in this battle to the fact that "there were so few people who wanted to touch this topic that by default I became the national authority."[51] Academics soon stepped into the fold, particularly with the 1978 release of the US Office of Education-funded "AIR Report." Conducted by the American Institute for Research (AIR), the survey studied concrete outcomes: whether bilingual education was effective in teaching children English and in raising their academic achievement overall. It determined these programs' effectiveness was inconclusive at best.[52] The AIR researchers' methodologies were criticized by the growing ranks of bilingual education supporters within academia, but the report gave data to the expanding group of skeptics. By the early 1980s, intellectuals such as Thomas Sowell and Nathan Glazer began to criticize bilingual education for its assault on the assimilationist "melting pot," a concept one scholar claimed bilingual education advocates inherently perceived as "an evil metaphor."[53]

This opposition notwithstanding, Latino children in 1970s California clearly benefited from an energetic and evolving policy framework. Exploring how these measures played out in actual districts and classrooms, however, reveals that bilingual education programs neither emerged monolithically nor were handed down fully formed as federal or state mandates. Just months after the passage of California's 1976 Chacón-Moscone Act, San Francisco educational advocate Carlota del Portillo recalled a presentation by a national bilingualism expert: "I couldn't believe what I saw [during the presentation]. . . . The members of the board were chatting to each other, getting up to get water. They were rude. It shows you how important they thought it all was."[54] Only when local groups marshaled community support as well as district, state, and federal monies could programming gain traction. They often advocated for competing visions of bilingual-bicultural education, however, creating internal discord that could stymie progress as effectively as attacks by an emergent conservative resistance.

## On the Ground: San Jose

By the end of the 1970s, increasing numbers of Mexican-Americans were drawn to San Jose, a center of Silicon's Valley emerging semiconductor industry.[55] Few Mexican-origin San Joseans benefited from the area's economic prosperity, and they called upon Santa Clara County's public services such as the schools to provide crucial bilingual services. Absent a large activist population of African-Americans promoting desegregation, in San Jose the central educational problem of the 1970s was how to best serve the Spanish-speaking community, which would reach one-third of the city's population by the end of the twentieth century.[56] The struggle for bilingual education in San Jose shows how intertwined bilingual and multicultural education were and reveals pronounced practical and philosophical rifts among bilingual education activists. It also highlights the growing power of antistate and pro-family sentiments even among avowed progressives. This confluence of factors, borne out in the conflict between the city's two competing bilingual education programs—the Studio Lab and the Consortium—brought increased attention to the Latino community and its attendant concerns, but thwarted the enactment of useful curricula.

San Jose represented "a very dramatic demonstration of the serious problem of absorbing thousands of new families into society," according to Ernesto Galarza. Galarza lived as a migrant youth in the Sacramento Valley and, after attaining a Ph.D. at Columbia University, returned to California in the 1940s to write and organize agricultural laborers.[57] During the 1960s and 1970s, he remarked that the influx of Mexicans to San Jose "raised problems of ALL kinds—immigration problems, school problems, employment problems." Bilingual-bicultural education, he ascertained, "was simply a part of this complex situation" and might provide solutions.[58] As city teachers picketed to protest the high dropout rate and low reading scores of the district's Mexican American students in the early 1970s, Galarza began to develop new curricula and train teachers in bilingual-bicultural pedagogy.[59] When during the 1971–1972 school year about twenty teachers from districts with high concentrations of Mexican children approached Galarza with "genuine worry" about inadequate curricular materials and chronic truancy, he started the Studio Lab, which focused on elementary education and emphasized creative arts and culture (see figure 3.1).[60] At its peak in 1973, the Studio Lab's seven staff members had trained twenty-five district teachers, developed the proprietary mini-libros, and engaged nearly forty parents—whom Galarza described as "influential, courageous, who took the rap."[61]

Though the Studio Lab was radical from the outset—Galarza recalls that "it quickly became clear to the administrators of the school systems in Santa Clara County that we were going to be very critical of the way education is being managed in our community"—it enjoyed considerable early support.[62] The president of the Whitney Foundation wrote to Galarza to report a meeting with Superintendent Riles, who "had heard of the Studio Lab and wanted to make a point to go down to see it."[63] Even the SJUSD, in its 1973 application for Chacón-Moscone funds, ambitiously described the Lab as "only a beginning."[64] Weary of "education as usual," the Studio Lab first criticized the existing SJUSD curriculum.[65] Asked to prepare a Spanish-language guide on phonics, Galarza "wouldn't *think* of it," refusing to reproduce a "Spanish version of methodology and of concepts that have obviously proved negative for Mexican kids."[66] Instead, Galarza thought it "*absolutely* fundamental" to reshape the curriculum to "to engage the child as fully and as deeply as we could in what we think is basic, to *all* future experiences in learning."[67] Galarza recalls learning from visitors who flocked to San Jose to observe the Studio Lab that "what we were facing was typical of the whole country: no materials—no special instruction—no adaptation of the curriculum—and no in-service training." In San Jose, he realized, "we could see it intensely."[68]

Before long, Galarza's Studio Lab came into acrimonious conflict with the San Jose Bilingual Consortium (SJBC), the primary body through which the SJUSD administered bilingual education. Galarza and the Studio Lab had been providing materials to the SJBC as consultants until 1975, but were summarily dismissed when the SJUSD received a federal Title VII grant amounting to more than a million dollars. In the next two years, the Studio Lab was excluded from the district's future grant proposals, based, according to an administrative complaint filed by Galarza, on libelous comments made by the SJBC about the Studio Lab.[69] Galarza publicly criticized the Consortium's approach as the "stupefying status quo, backed by a million dollars," as opposed to the Studio Lab's efforts "to bring affective experience to elementary kids."[70] As Galarza levied more strident charges against the philosophy and tactics of the SJBC—especially that it defined Mexican American children as "sociologically recidivist" and routinely excluded parents from curriculum and grant development—the fight became increasingly bitter.

Galarza was supported by the parents and San Jose State University students making up the Committee to Organize and Monitor Education (COME), which rallied the community and published a newsletter, *Temas Escolares*. Nonetheless, the Studio Lab suffered. In October 1977, Olivia Martinez of vthe SJBC publicly accused Galarza of mismanaging a fifteen-hundred-dollar

THE STUDIO LABORATORY

NATURE

GATHERED a collection of nature specimens, intriguing sheets of questions and information, pictorial examples relating how to create vibrant classroom situations showing the similarity of Mexican and our Southwest environment.

MUSIC

HELPED children to make simple musical instruments frequently of waste materials, making flutes, drums, violins, and cymbals. Composed lyrics from short Spanish poems, for singing and drama. Taught singing, instrument production, and guitar strumming to teachers and aids.

DANCE

TAUGHT the steps of Mexican Folklorico with the music, history and cultural attributes. Presented for the community these Mexican dances performed by local teachers and children for the stimulation and entertainment of everybody.

CREATIVE ART

CONSIDERED the innate urges of very young children for expression with color and brush. By teaching a few techniques of brush and tempera surprising designs appeared to show and discuss. Related study of pictures and artifacts of Mexican artists and art around them to music, dance and literature. Molding of clay was used for muscular development and artistic dimension.

SPANISH

RECOGNIZED Spanish as the communication tool for many of our pupils as well as an asset for all pupils of the Southwest. Spanish vocabulary was stressed in all classes. This language was heard and dramatized especially by a Mexican trained teacher who used it presenting costumes, songs, literature, anecdotes and history of her youth.

*************

THE ARTS AND LEARNING

LEARNING THROUGH THE ARTS in our philosophy is the primary factor for K through grade 3 with the cognitive studies being an important by-product while from 4th grade on the academic subjects, reading, writing and arithmetic will be practiced more formally though still integrated with other subjects and action.

FIGURE 3.1 The pedagogical tenets of Ernesto Galarza's Studio Lab, founded in 1971. The Studio Lab philosophy conceived of Spanish-language instruction as part of a broader cross-cultural educational project, a perspective that would conflict with that of the federally funded SJBC during the 1970s. N.d., Ernesto Galarza Collection, Box 64, Folder 4. Reprinted by courtesy of Department of Special Collections and University Archives, Stanford University Libraries.

community fund associated with his other organizing activities in order to finance his fight against the SJBC.[71] Galarza maintained that the false accusations over "the dinky little fund" were evidence that "the only defense [the SJBC] could think of was defamation."[72]

The SJBC curriculum survived this standoff, despite what Galarza perceived as its dubious pedagogical credibility. Galarza had pointed out that at the most basic level, "many of the [SJBC teachers] themselves are not bilingual."[73] Like some of their hastily hired counterparts in Los Angeles, "this generation of teachers and aides . . . in all probability represent a generation three times removed from the culture of the original migrants . . . So they have a very faded recollection of what Spanish is."[74] On the question of culture, the contested SJBC grant application had explained that the district lacked the resources to employ Galarza's heavily cultural curricula, but Galarza doubted the ability or desire of the SJBC to infuse the program with any cultural components. "They're interested in bicultural development," he wrote of the SJBC, "but they're not really bicultural . . . this advance guard of persons of Mexican ancestry who are a third or even sometimes fourth generation. . . . They were born here and they were raised here. This is an American environment. They were absorbed. They're acculturated."[75] He surmised that though the SJBC might deploy the rhetoric of cultural pluralism—"they keep talking about bicultural identity"—it was a discursive strategy to give their program "dramatic punch."[76]

Galarza's fight merits particular attention for its resonance with the political rhetoric around education developing across the state and the nation. At the core of his protests were a distrust of the ability of federal policy to provide a meaningful learning experience for students and a conviction that parental involvement was integral to effective education. Challenging the prevailing notion among many liberals that federal policy was an unconditional boon to civil rights and education progress, Galarza baldly stated, "Federal intervention in this matter simply *strengthened* and reinforced what had become a progressively worse deal for the Mexican minority. Our only chance to make a dent on that was local."[77] Sounding remarkably like his contemporaries further right on the political spectrum who decried federal intrusions on local control and the "bilingual fraud," Galarza told a Berkeley Chicano group that "what's happening in this country is that we have a gigantic ripoff called bilingual education . . . a sort of an underground siphon by which public funds are being diverted . . . [from] the education of our schoolchildren."[78] Federal intervention, Galarza came to believe, corrupted inherently:

The climate created by federal grantsmanship has taken hold of BE. . . . The notion that you can run things from HEW, from the Office of Bilingual Education (OBE), that you can select grantees, that you can tell them how to do what and when. You're so distant from these 300-off programs that are scattered over the country . . . that they can no more keep informed on what the OBE does, than the OBE can keep informed on what is happening locally. What is the primary concern that we in San Jose have about bilingual education? They don't know! They don't come and talk to people. This also leads to the temptation to create fiction. Every district in the country that submits a Title VII proposal has *got* to apply to the OBE in Washington. They decide whether this is an important project or whether it isn't. They decide upon the amount. They are consulted with respect to the qualifications of personnel. The decisions are made there, and you can't get at the reasons behind these decisions.[79]

Federal support for bilingual education had come under fire from one of its strongest putative defenders, auguring the challenges it would face and revealing how widespread frustration with costly and at times poorly implemented Great Society reforms had become.

Galarza and the SJBC clashed repeatedly on the role of parents in the development of bilingual-bicultural curricula. Galarza described the SJBC's approach as an assault on parental prerogative. Parental involvement was central to the Studio Lab philosophy. The Studio Lab's supporters, according to Galarza, were "people who started with very small, very narrow motivation. Something happened in their school district that they didn't like—they joined our group."[80] Had the Studio Lab have survived, Galarza envisioned "tapping into family and home life," creating mixed Anglo and Mexican American parental councils for each grade in every school and instituting a system of parent counseling and education.[81] Such active parental involvement was inimical to the hierarchical SJBC model, Galarza believed, "so really it's no wonder they destroyed us."[82] Envisioning an educational program that eschewed assimilation to challenge cultural norms both in the classroom and at home ultimately proved too radical for San Jose's educational establishment, revealing the racial boundaries of the "family values" concept invoked by predominantly white parents when they contested sex education.

A central plank of Galarza's complaint to the Office of Bilingual Education was that the SJBC had not complied with Title VII rules, since "comments of parents were not submitted to the preparers of grant proposals."[83] COME filed a subsequent complaint claiming that parental involvement was rightly the "cornerstone" of Title VII and any effective proposal, and Olivia Martinez's ensuing deposition failed to clarify whether she actually had done more than create "the appearance of parental participation" in crafting the proposal.[84] The importance of parental approval to the public became apparent as these accusations were levied; in January 1978, the SJBC decided to publicly rebut this particular charge of Galarza's many.[85] Similarly, at the 1978 conference of the California Association of Bilingual Educators, an overwhelming number of sessions were dedicated to parental involvement in curriculum development.[86] This burgeoning notion that parents should have a meaningful say in their children's education was sufficiently powerful to engage citizens across the political spectrum, from Orange County conservatives opposing sex education to Mexican American activists such as Galarza.

San Jose's vitriolic classroom wars over bilingual-bicultural education highlight the destructive impact of battles within the advocacy community. Reinaldo Macias, assistant director at the National Institute of Education, described the philosophically diverse actors comprising the bilingual education movement as "a lot of birds of different colors flying under the same banner of bilingual education."[87] Galarza had begun his efforts to redress the fundamental weakness in "America's liberal conscience" in its "inability or disinterest in helping class victims create their own collective means for resisting abuse and for changing the conditions that cause it."[88] By the early 1980s, he commented: "As far as I'm concerned, the system can just rot on its haunches. It's not possible for education to survive and to be useful the way it's going now. And bilingual education is only one part of it."[89] Disillusioned and exhausted by this arduous struggle, Galarza liquidated the Studio Lab curricular library, which the district declined to purchase. In 1981, he walked away from bilingual education activism, announcing, "What little time I have left to live or to think or to act is not going to be spent or wasted in continuing this dialogue."[90] Echoing the challenges facing the state task force, the SJUSD, Galarza believed, lacked "any clear philosophy of where bilingual education should be going."[91] Still, for the ugliness of the struggle and the "deeply systemic" nature of the problems, Galarza acknowledged that at least the moment had come when "the federal government—the state government—the local organizations are talking—at least they're AWARE of the problems [facing Mexican-Americans]. They're talking about it—not that they're doing anything too significant or intelligent about it, but the thing is they're talking."[92]

# 4

## "SOME KIND OF PRECEDENT"

### THE AMBIGUOUS LEGACY OF BILINGUAL EDUCATION

In 1976, Karen Greenwood, a white Angeleno who had spent two years in West Germany while her husband served in the military, returned to her hometown of Whittier "shocked and nauseated at all the bilingual controversy" in which the Los Angeles area had become rapidly embroiled during the couple's absence. In the wake of the *Lau v. Nichols* decision, Los Angeles—home to California's largest concentration of Mexican-Americans—led other cities in introducing accommodations beyond the classroom such as bilingual ballots and phone service. These reforms generated responses such as Greenwood's on the *Los Angeles Times'* editorial page: "So, my Spanish-speaking neighbors, you are now in America where English is the native tongue! Learn it or leave it!" Just as frequent were comments such as that of Angel Galvez, whose op-ed argued, "I certainly don't think it would hurt the phone companies to have at least one operator at all times who can speak Spanish as a service to . . . Mexican-Americans who have come . . . to a country that was once theirs."[1]

The *Los Angeles Times'* polarized editorial page suggests the intensifying opposition the Latinization of classrooms and culture was inspiring. Bilingual-bicultural education was at the center of this complex process, and observers far beyond the San Fernando Valley considered these transformations. In 1976, the Modern Language Association invited bilingual education advocate and Chicano scholar Tomas Rivera to deliver the annual keynote address.[2] In 1979, the very first task the newly established federal Department of Education tackled was the development of bilingual-bicultural education compliance guidelines.[3] As it expanded, bilingual-bicultural education became foundational to modern "multicultural" pedagogy, a movement both champions and detractors agree defines the contemporary educational environment.[4] California's story unmistakably reveals bilingual-bicultural education to be inextricable from the larger movement for cultural recognition, an important reason it has been so ardently defended—and attacked.[5]

Bilingualism and multiculturalism emerged from the 1970s strengthened by a legislative infrastructure and by recognition from the culture and marketplace at large, a development that forcefully challenges the notion that the decade was defined by the rise of the Right. At the same time, the substantial successes of bilingualism and multiculturalism can belie considerable tension both within the ranks of supporters and opponents.

This chapter analyzes how bilingual education was institutionalized and contested in two major but very different Californian metropolises, Los Angeles and San Francisco. Los Angeles, home to California's largest concentration of Latinos and to the biggest public school system west of the Rockies, faced the challenge of complying with *Lau* with special urgency. At the same time, the imperative to comply with another Supreme Court decision, the 1970 *Crawford v. Los Angeles* mandate to desegregate LA schools, quickly showed how diverse and potentially at odds were the demands of a racially variegated population. San Francisco's Latino population was far smaller and unique in California in that Mexican-Americans there comprised a minority compared to Central and South Americans. The city's diverse community cultivated a surprisingly cosmopolitan pan-*Latinismo* around activism for bilingual education, a movement that found an unlikely symbol in a young Chinese-American boy. At the close of the 1970s, the oft-repeated claim about the *Lau* decision—"Ultimately [it] will set some kind of precedent"—indicated the ongoing uncertainty of its impact.[6]

## Los Angeles

If any district was poised to blaze a trail in establishing bilingual education programming, it was Los Angeles. Between 1966 and 1976 the school-age Latino population nearly doubled from less than 20 to over 30 percent, substantially overtaking the city's African Americans, who had previously constituted its most numerous minority. The city's struggle for bilingual-bicultural education played out in especially close relation to the sprawling district's desegregation battles.[7] In 1970, school board member and Latino advocate Raúl Arreola reported on a "truly most fantastic experience" enabled by this unique demographic circumstance: Latino parents, "who had never dared go to their local schools because of their fear and lack of confidence," felt emboldened "to speak freely in the language easiest for them, of their fears, frustrations, problems, suggestions, opinions of their local schools."[8] This situation served to wed bilingual education and Chicano politics to those of the black freedom struggle and the reshaping of educational practice and politics. At the same time, these ethnic activists inspired a reactionary backlash from those wary of what appeared to be the expansion of identity politics. It was a far cry from the compensatory tone of early bilingual education policy that framed the measures narrowly as antipoverty programs.[9]

Even as black and Latino activism was seen as of a piece by some outside observers, the two groups shared little common history beyond their systematic exclusion from many social institutions. While Latinos constituted the primary "racial other" in the Southwest for much of its history, they were often a racial "in-between" group that could at times make claims to whiteness and its attendant privileges.[10] In *Mendez v. Westminster* (1946), often considered the forgotten precedent to *Brown v. Board of Education* (1954), Mexican American parents in Orange County, south of Los Angeles, protested the segregation of their children into a poorly resourced school for Mexicans, on the grounds that children of Mexican descent were actually white.[11] For this reason, not on the basis that separate-but-equal racial segregation was unjust, the Ninth Circuit Court of Appeals in 1947 granted the Mexican children access to white schools. The same year, Ernesto Galarza negotiated these same slippery racial categories while living with his family in Washington, DC. His daughter Karla attempted to enroll in all-black Margaret Murray Vocational School in order to take a course in dress designing and was rejected with the explanation that she was white.[12] The Galarzas ironically found themselves resisting the designation of "white" to allow Karla access to a black school. By 1970, Latinos were hardly considered as white—due in part to the ethnic activism of Galarza and his colleagues—and a series of three reports on Mexican-Americans funded by the Office of Education and Welfare noted various "points of friction" and "a watchful jealousy" exacerbated by the "equally crippling . . . deprivation of economic and educational opportunity" that afflicted both Mexican and African Americans.[13]

In Los Angeles, the obstacles to desegregation of African American students were what allowed Chicano activists to make inroads with bilingual education. As the enforcement of desegregation following the 1963 *Crawford v. Board of Education of the City of Los Angeles* case languished, Latinos seized the opportunity to promote the bilingual-bicultural programs that benefited from the very concentrations of minority students integrationists sought to disperse. The struggles Latino Angelenos faced in advancing bilingual-bicultural pedagogy augured the obstacles that would limit the movement nationally. At one conference sponsored by HEW, a research analyst remarked, "It was common to see therefore there are urgently raised issues in [Western] cities about what the relationship is between desegregation and bilingualism . . . one group or another has come forth and said, 'We don't want to be desegregated. We have a bilingual program, and it is working fine, and we should be exempt.'" Similarly, this research showed that, while 70 percent of Los Angeles Latinos supported desegregation, only 40 percent espoused busing.[14]

While Los Angeles bilingualism advocates enjoyed power in numbers and the support of the legislative framework, moderates within the coalition cautiously began to embrace integration once the city began to desegregate in 1976. Imagining an integrated schoolhouse in which linguistic minorities could thrive alongside African American and Anglo students, they increasingly borrowed from the language of African American educational activists to promote bilingual-bicultural curricula as fostering a healthy "self-concept" and "intercultural understanding" among students.[15] The dual circumstance of Mexican American demographic growth and relative progress of bilingual-bicultural legislation vis-à-vis the lackadaisical pace of desegregation created an environment in which Latino initiatives shaped education and culture. This distinctly Western scenario would be reproduced in major cities throughout the late twentieth century as Latinos came to replace African Americans as the "majority minority" in many urban areas.[16]

Even as African Americans and predominantly Mexican American advocates of bilingual-bicultural education began to make common cause in the mid-1970s—or perhaps in part because of this emerging coalition—they also met harsh resistance from those skeptical of their call for cultural affirmation in the classroom, what appeared to be the misguided errand of public education. As early as 1970, Superintendent Max Rafferty acknowledged that the city was "in a time of crisis" with regard to educational and racial politics.[17] One Angeleno complained, "No sooner we dispose of one crisis, we are confronted with a new one of equal or greater magnitude." He wrote to Rafferty to complain about a "double-header": alleged—rather, imagined—state directives both to force busing and to dispense with grading in fifty-seven Los Angeles schools "so the poor Mexican-American student is spared the terror of getting an 'F' on his report card!"[18]

Los Angeles teachers' unions levied complaints against disruptions they experienced due to bilingual education and desegregation. In 1970, the city's two rival teachers' unions merged into the nationally affiliated United Teachers of Los Angeles (UTLA), only to be attacked by liberals and radicals as too ethnically homogeneous and by conservatives as a "far-out" tool of the National Education Association.[19] Disappointed in UTLA leadership and philosophy, conservative teachers founded an alternative union, the Professional Educators of Los Angeles (PELA). PELA vocally resisted school and faculty integration initiatives, as well as the bilingual education programs that geographically displaced many Anglo teachers and created the expense of hiring of Spanish-speaking teachers, some of whom arguably merited the charge of lacking skills and experience. One researcher accurately noted that even the LAUSD's highest credential for evaluating bilingual teachers "obfuscated the fact that while these teachers exhibit bilingual fluency, they may not have been instructed in bilingual methodologies and instructional approaches."[20] By 1979, "hundreds" of Los Angeles teachers wrote letters of complaint against bilingual education.

In claiming that the disruptions these policies caused were damaging to their own "self-concept," the disgruntled teachers curiously appropriated the jargon of the bilingual programs.[21] Approximately one-fourth of the teachers displaced by efforts to achieve racial balance in 1975 expressed "bitterness and frustration" at the policies of the previous five years, which had negated the privileges of seniority.[22] These two hundred white teachers first approached PELA with complaints about their own discomforts: commutes across LA's sprawling expanse that resulted in ten-hour workdays and disruptions to the coherence of the communities built around their schools. Yet their concerns about the desegregation policies also revealed a new sensitivity to issues of culture and identity: "Many black aides have the affection and trust of the [black] children which the white teachers will never be able to achieve. . . . And just to show the lack of thought of this thing, one predominantly Mexican-American school had its bilingual teachers replaced with Asians. What good does that do? But they got racial balance."[23]

On the one hand, the overwhelming presence of Mexican American language learners in the LAUSD created major obstacles to the development and implementation of effective pedagogy. Yet this same circumstance mobilized Latinos to advocate, with unprecedented if measured success, for bilingual-bicultural programs, a role that placed them at times in collaboration and at times in tension with the city's African American population.[24] Los Angeles, with its empowered racial minorities and elaborate educational infrastructure, came to represent the multiple dimensions of the bilingual education struggle within the pioneering state of California.

## San Francisco

Four hundred miles to the north, the city of San Francisco negotiated similarly challenging questions of diversity and inclusion in the 1970s and 1980s, but in a strikingly different demographic context. Smaller than Los Angeles and even San Jose, San Francisco enjoyed greater economic resources than many of California's other metropolitan areas. The education system in "everybody's favorite city," however, suffered from lower test scores and graduation rates, frustrating the efforts of its school superintendents, three of whom attempted the challenging post between 1970 and 1975 alone.[25] When the third of these superintendents, Robert F. Alioto, took up the position in 1975, he broke with tradition by holding his swearing-in ceremony at Mission High School instead of at City Hall. Mission High was located in the city's most heavily Latino district, signaling Alioto's awareness that the central task of any successful superintendent would be addressing this community's substantial educational challenges.[26]

A decade later, the landscape would look different. In 1986, a bold headline in the *San Francisco Chronicle* proclaimed the advent of "Latino Power!"[27] By 1996, an Anglo columnist defended her right to send her "blond, blue-eyed daughter" to Buena Vista Alternative Elementary School in the largely Latino Mission District, which mixed Anglo and Spanish-speaking students to produce bilingual, bicultural graduates.[28] Like forty such programs in California, the Buena Vista program exposed all students "day-in and day-out to the music, art, language and culture of Latin America."[29] The Spanish-speaking minority's culture and language, which for years had been defined as deficiencies, were thirty years later touted by some as "immeasurably enriching" to Anglos and as providing "a clear economic advantage."[30]

San Francisco's diverse Latino community was instrumental in effecting this change toward a positive multiculturalism. An anomaly in Mexican-dominated California, the city was home to 140,000 Chicanos, Mexican nationals, and Salvadoran, Nicaraguan, Cuban, Bolivian, and Guatemalan immigrants.[31] Though these Latinos in 1970 accounted for only 15 percent of the city's population—in comparison to its 13 percent African Americans and its 15 percent Chinese Americans—the academic struggles of Latino San Franciscans generated as much concern as those of African Americans, earning the city "academic shame" for "registering test scores more befitting an outpost of civilization."[32] Indeed, at a federal conference on bilingual education, California state superintendent Wilson Riles was so embarrassed by the academic performance of the Bay Area city's Latinos that he made the unprecedented decision to "overhaul" the city's beleaguered educational system.[33] This demographically unique population in the process forged a pan-Latino identity, advocated for bilingual-bicultural education, and inspired the multicultural curricula that were both commonplace and controversial by the 1990s.[34]

Latino San Francisco and its campaign for bilingual-bicultural education was crucial to the emergence of comprehensive multicultural curricula that questioned assimilationism and began to address the diverse needs of the city's multiethnic, multilingual population. Well into the decade, many considered San Francisco's peculiar diversity an obstacle to educational attainment. In 1974, the *Chronicle* reported that the San Francisco Unified School District's (SFUSD) academic achievement was "worse not only than the whiter, more affluent suburbs, but also below those of Oakland, Los Angeles, Richmond, and San Diego—cities with many of the same problems San Francisco has."[35] School board president Eugene Hopp explained why the city's performance ranked so poorly statewide: "San Diego, for example, has only two students—English and Spanish. . . . We have some 31 languages because we are a port city with the largest immigrant influx in California."[36] Like early bilingual education policies that identified linguistic minorities as possessing educational deficiencies needing to be "fixed," such acknowledgment of San Francisco's Latinos defined this community by its "problems." The Latino community would not only generate powerful grass-roots activism for bilingual-bicultural programs, but also would endeavor, with some success, to gain recognition of the Spanish language and Latino culture as assets to broader society. Ultimately, this movement generated some of the nation's first K–12 multicultural curricula and a paradigm shift in how ethnic and linguistic diversity was negotiated in the schoolhouse.

Diverse San Franciscans fought for educational reforms based on "linguistic and cultural maintenance" and elected a school board assembled along ethnic allegiances, but there appeared to be no corresponding embrace of disparate cultures within the "Latino" designation. During the 1970s, an organic pan-Latinidad began to emerge in San Francisco, with, as a Latino journalist observed, "educational issues unit[ing] Latinos more than any other." Importantly, the pan-Latinidad fostered there, however, was not solely a reaction to structural adversity.[37] One the one hand, community newspaper *El Tecolote* described its function to counteract "the out-of-focus view . . . presented of our community through Anglo eyes," including media coverage that either sensationalized gang violence or highlighted tokenistic "native costumes and quaint food."[38] On the other hand, Latinos proactively cultivated this pan-ethnicity, with the local Spanish-language media embracing the umbrella term "Latino." In a *Tiempo Latino* article about school disciplinary problems, the writer carefully broke out the various national-origin groups among Asian-Americans, but referred only to "*los latinos*" without differentiation.[39] Editorialist Carlos Barón explained that "the Latinoamerican who lives in San Francisco has greater possibilities to truly understand what it is to be a Latinoamerican." Puerto Ricans, Chileans, and Nicaraguans discover each other, he explained, and the immigrant "who returns will discover that she is no less a Chilean, that she is more Latinoamerican and less nationalistic."[40]

Nearly two decades before the myriad variations of multicultural theory were conceptualized, San Francisco's Latinos embodied its cosmopolitan potential in forging a shared identity and its particularist tendencies in demanding curricula that recognized linguistic and cultural diversity.[41] Some of San Francisco's most passionate bilingual education advocates evidenced this dynamic. Organizer Rosario Anaya, a Bolivian immigrant, shared little with the largely Central American citizenry of her constituency and the Mexican American majority of California's Latino community. Nonetheless, she became one of the most vocal advocates for bilingual education and the director of the private Mission Language and Vocational School, which boasted one of the city's most progressive bilingual education programs. Similarly, belonging to an almost statistically insignificant group hardly precluded Puerto Ricans Raymond and Carlota del Portillo from taking the helm to represent Latinos in the education establishment.[42] As San Francisco's Latinos strove to enact a more pluralistic model in the public culture and educational arena, internally they forged a cosmopolitan pan-Latinidad.[43]

Of course, important distinctions did exist among San Francisco's Latinos. Class, rather than national origin, emerges most strikingly. Many Latinos with sufficient resources left the city, such as the small enclave of wealthy South Americans who relocated to the affluent southern suburb of Hillsborough. Even within San Francisco County, activist Carlota del Portillo reported, "if people have enough money, a lot of them send their kids to Catholic school."[44] Class distinctions were also sometimes manifest within the majority-Latino schools in the SFUSD. Though rarely reported in the Anglo press, this discrepancy was obvious to newly arrived superintendent Thomas Shaheen in 1970 as he visited the city schools. At Mission High he saw "30 kids waiting in line to see a counselor with no chairs, because they have no classes." The school had "boarded-up doors, exposed wiring in the ceiling, and floors that need painting." By contrast, at the more generously resourced Buena Vista High, Shaheen received "no complaints about worn-out facilities and smiling teachers." Buena Vista's bilingual Spanish teachers treated the new superintendent to lunch, "where everyone [sang] Latin American folksongs" in "an atmosphere of warmth and gaiety."[45]

If the civil rights achievements of the 1960s had confirmed doubts about the "Americanization" mission of public schooling, the 1970s witnessed the emergence of a new discourse that recognized linguistic and ethno-racial diversity as a given and even, to some, a desirable feature.[46] The SFUSD had as early as 1965 received national media coverage for attending to "the subcultures of minority groups, the effects of prejudice on majority and minority children," and the role teachers might take to redress these ills.[47] The bilingual-bicultural agenda mandated by *Lau*, as well as activist groups' sustained criticism of San Francisco's school system and teachers' racism and ingrained "knowledge that the child has no future," inspired elaborate multicultural curricula that gave district schools at least a veneer of progressivism.[48]

Just as districts all over California and the Southwest had implemented bilingual education programs before the passage of the federal BEA in 1968, so too did San Francisco experiment with serving its linguistic and cultural minorities before it achieved national recognition through the 1974 *Lau* case. In 1969, San Francisco State University was one of five campuses statewide piloting "Teacher Corps: Rural Migrant People," a teacher certification program that taught a pedagogy that aimed to deliver more than "English wrapped in Anglo culture," the traditional method that left Latino children intellectually alienated.[49] These steps were halting, reflecting the measured commitment of policymakers and educators alike to bilingual education and presaging the ambivalence of future efforts as well. As early as 1971, the district offered an instructional workshop on Latino culture and on ethnic influences in San Francisco, but only four teachers participated.[50] Passionate advocates in San Francisco lobbied policymakers to court state and federal funds, and in 1972 they secured $90,000 in state funds and also the resources to pilot a three-year Chinese-English program.[51] Slowly, programs addressing both linguistic and cultural pedagogical needs were gaining a foothold in the San Francisco city schools.

By 1976, Superintendent Robert Alioto connected the aims of linguistic and cultural pedagogy more energetically. The first "Educational Redesign for the SFUSD" claimed to weave multicultural pedagogy throughout the K–12 curriculum. Elementary classes would benefit from "a comprehensive program of study for each child, including the history of government, citizenship and multicultural-multiethnic heritage of the many groups of people that make up the United States." Students would further ground this knowledge in "the multicultural richness that is San Francisco" in the middle grades and graduate high school having "positively interacted with students of all cultures," harboring "a sense of personal identity and self-worth," and having secured "an understanding of similarities as well as differences among people . . . and an appreciation of the unique characteristics and contributions of diverse ethnic groups including blacks, Chinese, Filipinos, Latinos, Native Americans, and Samoans within a pluralistic society."[52]

This was an ambitious endeavor. However, in both the 1976 and 1978 versions of the Redesign, these lofty goals were only articulated in the opening "preamble" or "philosophy" sections and absent from the hundreds of pages of practical instructions. The preamble to the 1978 "Implementation Manual" made much of the need for "the school system . . . and program of instruction . . . to be dynamic" in response to "the continuously changing needs . . . of the children, community, state and nation," but the only concrete instruction for teachers was to "foster a healthful environment."[53] Expectations for high school graduates were similarly disconnected from the ambitious curricular mission: the sole outcome linked to the Redesign's professed multicultural aims was "evidence of good character and good citizenship."[54]

The practical applications of multiculturalism that do appear in the Redesign hardly suggest the structural overhaul of the introductory sections, but evoke a mentality closer to the "immigrant gifts" view of early twentieth-century reformers, or to the "contributionism" against which feminist scholars were battling contemporaneously.[55] For example, providing "materials representative of the many religious, ethnic, and cultural groups, and their contributions to our American heritage and world civilization" seems less ambitious than "MAKING CROSS-CULTURAL EDUCATION A PART OF ALL EDUCATIONAL EXPERIENCES," as the 1976 policy had recommended, in all caps.[56] Although the exact nature of the gap between prescription and practice can never fully be known, looking closely at the curriculum itself reveals that even the recommended classroom practice falls short of the capacious vision articulated in its opening philosophy.

While the changes carried out in the SFUSD were undoubtedly uneven, Mission High School exemplifies the cultural shift to multiculturalism afoot as well as its attendant challenges. The first comprehensive high school west of the Rockies, Mission High was in the 1970s located at its original 1897 site at Eighteenth and Dolores Streets.[57] Mission High had educated the largely

Italian, German, and Russian newcomers of the early twentieth century. One alumnus commented, "If there ever was a melting pot, we were it."[58] The pride of another alumnus was qualified, "Today when I see old school friends, many tell me how . . . their children attend schools other than Mission High. And isn't this what you would expect from the children of first-generation San Franciscans?"[59] To these former students, the glory of Mission High had been its great success in assimilating its immigrant pupils to Anglo culture.

In the years between these alumni's graduations in the first half of the century and their reflections in the late 1970s, much had changed both inside the walls of the rambling stone building and in the surrounding neighborhood, now the center of the city's Latino community. Between 1970 and 1980, Mission High's graduation rate dropped from a lackluster 20 percent to just 15; in the 1950s, the majority of its student body had attended four-year colleges.[60] These alarming figures and the student body's new composition of Latinos, African Americans, Filipinos, and Chinese renewed Mission High as a vivid symbol of the problems and promises of immigrant education, further underscored by Superintendent Alioto's swearing-in. A decade later, Ramon Cortines made much of having graduated from this institution in his successful 1986 bid to succeed Alioto.[61] In 1996, the principal trumpeted nationally his role at the helm of this predominantly Latino school and flew to Washington, DC, to speak specifically about education in Latino communities.[62]

The melting pot no longer seemed a workable model for Mission High. Instead, this institution exemplified the developing multicultural ethos of this era. By 1970, the social studies curriculum included African Studies, Asian Studies, Black History, History of Minority Groups in the United States, and Latin American Studies, highlighting "the current experience of Latinos in this country . . . with specific reference to the Mission District."[63] A campus education center founded in 1978 aimed to help children respect their own heritage while learning to speak English and advance in Anglo society.[64] Increasingly, Mission High celebrated its cultural roots and location in the heart of San Francisco's Latino neighborhood rather than its ability to help students transcend these origins. In 1974, students received a grant to open a Mission High School art gallery of ethnic art, and the Bank of America commissioned "a monumental Latin mural" from the high school's students that would depict "the heritage, life, and hopes of the people in the Mission district."[65] While the challenge of introducing immigrants to American and San Franciscan culture persisted throughout the twentieth century, the terms of the newcomers' integration, their expectations, and the response of the educational establishment and society at large were being utterly transformed.

Of course, the results of the ambitious initiatives Mission High and the city began to implement in the 1970s were not always as far-reaching as imagined. In a 1987 SFUSD newsletter, the only sign of a continued effort toward the Redesign's original aims was a trip to Mexico by three teachers from the Mission Education Center to better master children's literature.[66] Retrospectively, Latino leaders questioned whether the multicultural education for which they fought might have precluded more substantive reforms. Former SFUSD board president Carlota del Portillo commented, "We might have come far enough to change 'Dick and Jane' to 'Juanita and Carlos' in certain textbooks, but Juanita looks like a geek and is walking with a smiling Latina grandmother who has nothing to do with a real person; this kind of change means nothing. Putting in an Asian or a Latino face without altering the way the characters behave ends up being meaningless."[67] She observed similar tokenism in classrooms, "The SFUSD has never really made a concerted effort to . . . *behave* differently, no matter what the curriculum. We used to spend money allocated for 'so-called multiculturalism' and what I saw when I went to the schools were kids doing the Mexican Hat dance."[68] A nearly forty-year veteran of the San Francisco public education system, del Portillo in 2004 commented on the persistence of stereotypes of minorities: "There are still people who associate . . . Latinos with the inability to handle intellectual rigor. . . . Now they just use politically correct language, but they enact what is in their heart."[69] At the same time, this admittedly ragged transfer of multicultural ideology to the lived experience of students managed to change fundamentally the educational rhetoric of San Francisco's public school establishment. The debates over bilingual and multicultural education were inextricably linked and irreversibly introduced the issues of linguistic, and then cultural, maintenance in education to the city and national spotlight. The bald racism and invisibility apparent in curricula in the late 1960s and early 1970s had evolved into a rhetorically energetic but somewhat hollow version of multiculturalism. (See figure 4.1.)

Throughout the later twentieth century, the public school remained at the center of debates over the obstacles and opportunities of immigrant life. In this bright glare, San Francisco's Latinos exercised a cosmopolitan multiculturalism, forging a pan-ethnic consciousness in the mainstream institution of the public schools, which became at least nominally more receptive to their concerns during the last three decades of the twentieth century. Somewhat paradoxically, as reformers such as the Bolivian Rosario Anaya and the Puerto Rican Carlota del Portillo elided their national and cultural differences, a more particularist multiculturalism became the dominant social paradigm of the

FIGURE 4.1 African American children at a California public school celebrate Christmas with a "Pancho Claus" character in 1969. Such attempts at multicultural inclusion showcase how challenging it was for districts to meet new demands for cultural recognition in the civil rights era, and how superficial were some efforts. Joe Rosenthal, "Kids' Curiosity over Pancho Claus at E.O.C. Party," 1969. African Americans in the Bay Area Collection, Calisphere. Reprinted with permission from the Bancroft Library, University of California, Berkeley.

era and of the curricula for which they advocated. These changes in public education point to an equally important liberal counternarrative to prevalent ideas about a conservative backlash in this era.[70]

Los Angeles and San Francisco provide evocative and distinct examples of how bilingual education activism simultaneously moved public schools and the culture at large toward more explicit engagement with issues of diversity, while at the same time failing to resolve the lack of resources and deep-seated antipathies that often stymied enduring change. While social studies has been seen as the class that embedded a multicultural ethos most deeply in students, the California case suggests bilingual education engendered this shift just as powerfully. In Los Angeles, one Latino journalist remarked in 1975 that attitudes toward Latinos had transformed in the decade since he had suffered an "inferiority complex" about his Spanish tongue and brown skin. By contrast, he wrote of East Los Angeles schoolchildren proudly hosting Anglo visitors from neighboring Woodland Hills for tours of the barrio they called home. At the same time, many of their teachers exhibited "lethargy" and even a hushed racism that kept many Latino children in dead-end curricular tracks.[71] The San Jose Unified Schools embedded a bilingual education program in the district by the mid-1970s, but did so at the expense of a far more progressive program that challenged Anglo cultural norms. In the Southern California district of El Rancho, community leaders collaborated to win a $250,000 federal grant earmarked to enact bilingual/bicultural education for both Anglo and Latino students, a substantial change since the days when such programs were imagined as compensatory for the deficiencies of linguistic minorities. On the other hand, the cultural component the designers imagined offered only the tired contributionist combination of "cultural events, holidays, customs, and food."[72]

A *Washington Post* story reveals the depths of the transformation Latino activism around bilingual education was making in this era and the degree to which these Californian dynamics were sparking national interest. The newspaper reported on the return home after nine years of Vietnam of prisoner of war Everett Alvarez of Salinas, California, the rural region made famous by novelist John Steinbeck. The *Post* emphasized how "the landmarks of Everett Alvarez's existence will be almost unrecognizable," symbolized most vividly by the "Chicano activism" on his college campus, the *"¡Huelga!"* signs brandished by the new presence of United Farm Workers, and the presence of Chicano clubs and a student newspaper at his alma mater Salinas High School, which one teacher described as newly committed to "giving the Mexican-American a better self-concept." While Alvarez's sister excitedly told the reporter that thanks to these social changes, her "All-American" brother would no longer be able to brush off her belief that "Chicanos are the Vietnamese of this country," several members of the community waxed nostalgic about the era left behind, before the embrace of ethnic self-determination, when Alvarez had never felt the need to speak Spanish, and during which, according to this Anglo teacher, "there were never any racial problems."[73]

The relatively sudden presence and rapid progress of recently arrived Latinos in California met with swift and public backlash, as some citizens questioned the right of these new arrivals to participate in civil society at all. If they "are too lazy or disinterested to learn to read, write and speak English, then they don't deserve to vote, have drivers' licenses, collect welfare, or enjoy any of the other benefits that we Americans have earned and are entitled to," a letter to the *Los Angeles Times* complained.[74] More frequently, calls for recognition as a linguistic minority were countered by appeals to preserve a fragile national unity: "Our pluralistic society needs a common language as a binding force." The 1975 decision to offer voting ballots—perhaps the ultimate symbol of civic participation and belonging—in Spanish inspired criticism of school-based bilingual education, as some Californians argued that "the dollars suggested for this program will be far better spent on educational programs to teach all citizens English." This English-only prescription was at odds with the approach of the programs calling for cultural and linguistic recognition—and the creation of jobs and curricula to fulfill these pedagogical goals—multiplying statewide.[75]

The backlash against bilingual education and multiculturalism of the early 1980s has been seen primarily as a conservative onslaught, and a largely successful one at that.[76] Indeed, opponents raised serious doubts about curricula they considered a "jumble of bilingual programs and non-programs" and about the right of Latinos to make demands for such cultural recognition in the public sphere.[77] Fiscal conservatives joined this chorus as they excoriated the cost of big government programs, despite the remarkably small allocations for bilingual education. In addition, the challenges bilingual education advocates met were sometimes internal and almost always regionally specific. Districts were sometimes so desperate to find staff even marginally equipped to engage with these expanding communities that they hastily hired teachers and paraprofessionals lacking skills and credentials, angering established educators and providing fodder for their mounting offense against bilingual programs. Moreover, a host of other educational questions—foremost among them the desegregation of African American students—provided a complicated context for negotiating these concerns. Yet it is important to remember that this conservative resistance to bilingual education gained strength precisely because of the success of its target: Chicanos, bolstered by a strengthened legal framework and a cultural alignment with the black freedom struggles, succeeded in implanting at least the seeds of a lasting progressive multiculturalism in American schools, beginning with California.

# SEX

"Is the schoolhouse the proper place to teach raw sex?" one of the most popular anti-sex education pamphlets of the 1960s asked parents and citizens.[1] In this publication and countless homemade mimeographed pamphlets and impassioned speeches and editorials, opponents to sex education attempted to incite the public to petition schools and lawmakers to eradicate the controversial programs. These 1960s activists positioned the era's initiatives as an unprecedented attempt by immoral hippies to pervert American children and even to turn them into communist sex slaves. Sex education, however, has deep roots in American educational history and has most frequently been used to manage adolescent sexuality rather than to encourage its expression.

In 1913, the American Social Hygiene Association, finding "traditional institutions insufficient to guard youth from urban temptations," convened doctors and social engineers to design energetic school curricula to counteract growing secularism, lax social examples set by immigrant parents, and the general cultural and moral dissolution embodied by the urbanizing, diversifying society.[2] Social hygienists aimed to safeguard adolescent chastity by regulating teenagers' sexual desires during the growing period between puberty and marriage. While these early sex educators condemned Victorian repression for inciting deviant sexuality, they confronted the same paradox that would vex sex education activists and opponents alike in the coming century: in openly discussing sexuality, weren't sex educators encouraging sexual exploration rather than limiting it? Conservative sex educators thus exalted reproductive sexuality, safe within the nuptial home, and attempted to de-eroticize their subject matter by forsaking any discussion of sexual pleasure in favor of rational, scientific explanation.

These fundamentally conservative strategies hardly served to stem controversy, which has attended sex education throughout its history. The thrust of the opposition which immediately emerged—most notably a crusade to purge "sex hygiene and personal purity education" from the Chicago public schools in 1913—remained largely consistent throughout the century. Opponents complained that educators trespassed upon the domain of the family and church, and accused sex educators of "sneaking" sex education into science and health classes, undermining parental prerogative and corrupting innocent youth. Even in these early battles over sex education, the central question was who other than parents was qualified to teach children about sexuality. As with any innovative pedagogy, early sex educators—who were smeared as perverts—were inexperienced with new material, yet found themselves negotiating highly sensitive moral questions. In an era defined by social dislocation and the expansion of the school's role in children's lives, sex education seemed to threaten parents' control over their children's moral development.

During wartime, when young Americans faced military service, sex educators emphasized disease prevention, highlighting the public health perils embodied by foreign women. One government-issued poster series for boys popular in the 1920s advised that " 'the sex instinct' be controlled and directed," but also cast this impulse as the source of "ENERGY, ENDURANCE, FITNESS."[3] In the 1930s, however, the exigencies of the Depression forced many programs to be cut back or stripped down to emergency disease prevention.[4]

The "family life era" in the history of sex education dawned in the postwar period. From the 1950s and the sexual revolution until the advent of the AIDS crisis in the early 1980s, sex educators expanded their curricular reach beyond disease prevention and mechanical explanations of reproduction. Capacious sex education pedagogies dealt with issues of family life, gender, dating, and marriage. Widely screened instructional filmstrips took up topics such as how to be popular and how to find emotional balance, and for boys, how to identify and avoid the advances of homosexuals.[5] Many sex educators perpetuated the work of their conservative antecedents in social hygiene, shoring up normative values prizing chastity and the nuptial home and encouraging shame for transgression of these mores. Sex educators in the San Diego schools in the 1950s, for example, prominently advertised their happy and prolific marriages as credentials for the job and described their responsibility as imparting "the truth" about matters of gender and morality.[6] Such curricula tended to enshrine the white, middle-class family and to pathologize or omit all non-reproductive sexuality, particularly masturbation and homosexuality.

The seismic cultural changes of the 1960s gave the programs of the era a decidedly liberal tone and provided new grist for traditionalist opponents. The Supreme Court both narrowed the definition of obscenity and proscribed prayer in schools over the course of the 1960s. Immediately, provocative images on book covers, billboards, and movie posters abounded. Still worse for conservatives, the Court then outlawed prayer in school, constraining schools from acting as a moral counterweight to these newly unregulated images and ideas permeating public life.[7] Whether these legislative changes galvanized or constituted the sexual revolution, American youth experienced a revolution in morality and comportment over the course of the 1960s. Unrest over civil rights and the emergence of an ethos privileging self-fulfillment over traditional obligations to family contributed to the sense that the very tenets of society were in flux. The era's family life and sex education programs became mechanisms to deal with these dislocations, as sex educators of all stripes conceived of school as a site for managing adolescents' desires in the face of temptation.

Increasingly vocal opponents, however, derided the programs as troubling outgrowths of the very trends such curricula were devised to quell. At the core of the heated debates over sex education that flared in the late 1960s and early 1970s were two familiar concerns: the school was intruding upon parental rights to teach about sex, and any discussion of sexuality amounted to encouraging sexual experimentation. Even moderate speech would diminish the silence and shame that had supposedly kept previous generations safe from moral ruin. Sex education programs in this era, as moderate as they may seem in retrospect, were revolutionary in bringing the wider society's new openness about sexuality into one of the last bastions where sexual speech was silenced: the classroom.[8] To conservative citizens' groups and national religious organizations, all that was wrong with the corrupt society was emblematized by sex education.[9] The visions that reformers—both those in favor of and against sex education—entertained throughout the twentieth century came into especially sharp focus in the crucible of 1960s California.

# 5

## "THE POT WAS ALREADY BOILING"

### PARENTS, TEACHERS, TAXES, AND SEX EDUCATION IN SAN MATEO

"Battle lines [are] being drawn all over the state . . . over what might be the most controversial offering in the public school curriculum," read the front page of the *Los Angeles Times* on December 23, 1968.[1] The article did not refer to ethnic studies, science instruction, or the teaching of religion: it was sex education that bitterly divided California cities as regionally and socioeconomically diverse as Oakland, Merced, and Ventura.[2] The Sexuality Information and Education Council of the United States (SIECUS), vilified as "leading this shocking and amoral sex education drive across America," amassed a growing list of groups founded expressly to oppose sex education in the schools. By the end of 1969, it counted 316 such organizations nationwide, 203 of them headquartered in the Golden State.[3] This fervor from Sacramento to San Diego challenges the narrative locating the crucible of modern conservatism primarily in southern California's Orange County and suggests that the power of the New Right derived significant strength from the support of a wide swath of Americans outside of conservative strongholds, many of whom found their voice around educational questions.

The most incendiary and acrimonious fight transpired in the San Francisco Bay Area community of San Mateo. Ultimately, the Educational Programs Committee of the State Board of Education threw up their hands in frustration and abandoned the pursuit of a universally workable series of health education guidelines.[4] To the state committee, the intensity of the battle parents and educators in San Mateo waged over sex education in the late 1960s pointed up not only their project's futility but also California's troubled educational system and political future. The San Mateo controversy shared with many other districts the questions of teacher quality, taxpayer rights, and the besieged nuclear family—issues that overshadowed the anti-communist rhetoric that figured so prominently in Orange County.

Across California, it was this triad of fundamental concerns that inspired parents and citizens, some of them previously apolitical, to organize. The tenor of San Mateo's fight over sex education evokes these shared concerns and explains how and why resistance to costly progressive education programs began to gain such momentum among Californians in this era.[5] While the programs at stake were largely born of liberal efforts to remedy the effects of an increasingly sexually explicit culture, they were targeted by the early 1970s as an insidious and expensive affront to the American family, the very institution they were conceived to safeguard.[6]

San Mateo's struggle merits particular attention for its uniquely powerful impact. Citizens for Parental Rights (CPR), San Mateo's largest opposition group to family life education, sued the county schools in 1968 for "the unconstitutional invasion of privacy and destruction of morality" represented by the offensive curriculum. CPR pursued the case as far as the US Supreme Court.[7] The San Mateo conflict galvanized Governor Ronald Reagan and Superintendent Max Rafferty to convene the Moral Guidelines Committee (MGC), an appointed body charged with the unprecedented duty of designing an explicit code to teach morality across the curriculum. California's debates over sex education thus inspired a broader discourse within the state and federal legal and educational bureaucracies about parental rights and the definition of morality in a changing society. These vivid controversies reveal how sex education invoked a broad range of associations and fired the passions of Californians beyond the "vocal minority" populating the colorfully named conservative parental associations: the Movement to Restore Decency (MOTOREDE), Parents Organized to Stop Sex Education (POSSE), and Mothers Organized for Moral Stability (MOMS), among others.

San Mateo's classroom wars helped to consolidate a grass-roots ideology of "family values" as besieged by a profligate, fiscally irresponsible cultural and political left. The ultraconservative John Birch Society supported these local campaigns against sex education, but in San Mateo stepped in well after the proverbial "pot was already boiling."[8] Perhaps most importantly, these battles show that the citizens who saw their opposition to sex education as part of a conservative turn in their politics in the early 1970s were acting out of both economic and cultural self-interest, a convergence to which the New Right owes much of its power.[9] At the same time, if San Mateo's controversy was the seedbed for sex education classroom wars as far away as suburban New Jersey and upstate New York—as the *Wall Street Journal* reported with urgency—this fracas, which dragged on for six years, also reveals an enduring progressivism in American schools and culture at large. San Mateo's CPR pursued their mission to remove the curriculum all the way to the U.S. Supreme Court, where it was summarily dismissed for "want of a substantial federal question." San Mateo students remained able to study (or opt out of) *Time of Your Life* (TOYL), and the programs that emerged in the 1970s only expanded sexual discourse in schools, challenging the idea of an ascendant traditionalism.[10]

## The San Mateo Story

The best-known battle over sex education rocked the community of San Mateo, made up largely of white middle-class families and located about twenty miles south of San Francisco.[11] The *Wall Street Journal* attributed the debates foremost to the community's initial reaction to the 1968 broadcast of TOYL, a sex education film used in county schools that candidly recognized sexuality and celebrated critical thinking around moral topics, perspectives all but absent from popular 1950s instructional texts such as Evelyn Duvall's tellingly titled *When You Marry*.[12]

In contrast to the fervor San Mateo's curriculum would inspire, the program was one of many statewide that began most auspiciously. Part of a two-year "trial and evaluation" program initiated by Bay Region Instructional Television for Education (BRITE) and KQED, the local public television station that developed the TOYL filmstrip based on the San Mateo County curriculum guide, the program was born of "widespread community demand . . . [that] for the most part was external to our schools," according to Superintendent J. Russell Kent. The curriculum was conceived and approved by "a broadly based committee . . . representing every school district, the religious community, the legal community, parent groups from both public and parochial schools, and a variety of civic bodies."[13] Written by esteemed local child psychiatrist William Ayres, the program's centerpiece was the TOYL filmstrips, each under thirty minutes long and screened weekly in 120 districts across fifteen counties.[14] Reflecting on their experience with the program over the previous two years, 81 percent of parents polled in San Mateo County thought their children had benefited from TOYL, and 84 percent believed it harmless. Among the three districts randomly selected for polling, even greater percentages of parents expressed comparable sympathy or at least equanimity toward the film series.[15] TOYL gained such widespread acclaim that a nonprofit educational television station purchased its national distribution rights even before the two-year trial period elapsed.[16]

Sex education may have been almost universally contested, but the spark that ignited controversy differed across communities. Anaheim school nurse Sally Williams recalled that in her community, problems arose due to the shared conviction among her colleagues that "basic biology was not enough." In 2 of the 120 San Mateo districts piloting the curriculum, however, it was the treatment of male biology in the TOYL episodes screened in grades four through six that touched off the firestorm.[17] Many complained that the explicit anatomical descriptions at too early an age would "stimulate experimentation and inappropriate talk among children."[18] Lawrence Smith of KQED relayed to the State Board of Education that Lessons 1–9 of TOYL, dealing with interpersonal relationships, were shown in San Mateo schools without incident, but that Lesson 10, "The Male," garnered hundreds of phone calls and protests.[19] This insistence that family life and sex education programs were merely too graphic persisted among some Californians, even as the issues at stake mushroomed to engage far more abstract questions. Nearly a year after the TOYL controversy erupted, Dr. Thomas Harward of the state board, a consistent opponent of sex education, clung to the belief that the problem with existing curricula was "too much emphasis . . . on sex and anatomy . . . and not enough on emotions."[20] Soon, the threat that TOYL represented to these parents would grow from the most finite and predictable worry that it exposed their children too early to information about sexual intercourse to an almost abstract paranoia that it was an assault on the family unit, American society, and morality.

In San Mateo, all the decorous and technical description of TOYL's "biological explicitness" transpiring in official testimony obscured an issue core to mobilizing opponents, as district Assistant County Superintendent of Schools Armin Weems clearly articulated in August 1968: "[The district's] only disagreement is on the depth [Ayres] went into on masturbation."[21] The TOYL teacher's guide to the controversial lessons spared no detail on topics like masturbation, and many parent letters reflected as much. The guide was designed as a conversation between an inquisitive "Child" and Dr. Ayres. The explanation of masturbation, sandwiched between the queries "How often does sperm come out?" and "Can a boy's testicles get wrecked if he gets kicked?" explained "wet dreams" and the natural impulse for a boy "to handle his penis so as to cause the sperm to come out . . . in private."[22] As in his testimony before the state board, Ayres assured the child that "we know as doctors that physically it does not hurt boys, and as psychiatrists that it does not hurt people emotionally to masturbate" but acknowledged that "certainly people who think it is wrong might talk to their minister, priest, or rabbi."[23] This contention linked a concretely physical behavior to larger moral and religious beliefs, signaling why masturbation inflamed such controversy. Similarly, the teacher's guide's culminating lesson included concepts as broad as "We are evolving from a rural, non-technological to an urban, technological society," and as potentially revolutionary as "Social institutions, such as marriage, church, family, etc., tend to be stabilizing factors, but are also mutable."[24] On a practical level, the guide insists on coeducational viewing and discussions of "The Female" and "The Male," enabling boys and girls to "more easily be able to ask their own question in front of members of the opposite sex."[25]

Talking about masturbation is of course a uniquely enduring taboo.[26] Open engagement with sexual acts that privileged pleasure over procreation and transpired outside of the heterosexual nuclear family rankled some citizens. Unabashed discussion of masturbation and homosexuality in tax-supported classrooms seemed to many the coup de grâce of the sexual revolution, which had all but shattered the silence and shame around sexuality that upheld, for many, the moral order. Reflecting on his tenure as governor six years later, Ronald Reagan would with "sincere outrage" single out a play "put on under university auspices" during which "a young man simulated masturbation" as indicative of "permissiveness and laziness at every level of the university system."[27] Encouraging such openness in tax-supported schools was a burden too great for many parents to bear, especially as it emboldened sexual liberals. On the other hand, Anaheim school nurse Sally Williams forthrightly considered candor "of vital importance" since "some of these questions students feel they cannot ask their parents concern homosexuality and masturbation."[28] In her film appearance with SIECUS president Mary Calderone, the two went so far as to encourage discussion of female masturbation, an issue considered so ineffable by many that it rarely even entered debate.[29] Along with the frequent and ill-considered use of the word *stimulate* (apropos discussion), TOYL's treatment of masturbation assumed an environment in which sexual speech was encouraged and in which the very foundations of society—the family and its attendant moral code—were taught to be in flux.

Even Ayres, who so matter-of-factly defended his project, vacillated and backpedaled in describing TOYL's treatment of the "solitary vice":

> The series does not follow the accepted medical position of saying it is harmful for parents to prohibit masturbation. . . . In recognition of the

importance of the religious issue, the series states that it is not harmful not to masturbate. In the same way, it is not mentally . . . or physically harmful for an orthodox Jew to eat pork or for a Catholic not to attend Mass. Such a statement, however, in no way diminishes the fact that these are very important issues within their religions. Religious beliefs are important and children are encouraged to adhere to them . . . in the series there is mention that masturbation can be excessive and may be a problem if it is misused . . . Unless excessive, masturbation now is primarily a religious issue and it seems appropriate to tell children that this behavior falls within the consideration of their religion, not within medical concerns of physical damage, mental aberrations or sexual perversion.[30]

Ayres's uncharacteristic stammering, layers of qualification, and garbled invocation of religion illustrate the persistent notion that masturbation threatens the nuclear family and thus the social fabric.[31] That much of the San Mateo furor arose over masturbation suggests the broader and potentially more volatile purpose of the curriculum and a host of similar programs statewide. The lofty aim of TOYL—to foster children's social, emotional, and civic growth—was certainly more ambitious than merely providing technical descriptions of the reproductive organs and process.[32] Moreover, the program's teachings consistently encouraged self-expression over self-regulation, a shift in focus with potentially socially disruptive implications.

Educational administrators in San Mateo County attempted to distance the district from TOYL, to little avail.[33] Following the initial complaints, the county board of education released an official statement declaring that "approval or disapproval [would] be made" on TOYL only when "a full evaluation of subject matter, script, and grade level placement has been determined following a thorough analysis."[34] The San Mateo Medical Society quickly added that it was "not in any way involved with TOYL."[35] The Office of the Superintendent had initially commissioned TOYL "in response to a definite need recognized by the whole community" and had thought the film sufficiently uncontroversial to have made "little provision here for review by BRITE and none by school officials nor for any final approval of either the script or the final televised program prior to, nor following, for that matter, its being broadcast to the schools." When controversy flared, however, this office noncommittally diminished TOYL as "an optional supplement that has yet to be approved or disapproved."[36] District educators and bureaucrats also insisted that they relied primarily on the county-developed teachers' guide—on which TOYL was actually based—for fear that materials created by outsiders would inspire greater controversy. Yet school officials could not simply cordon off TOYL from the rest of their curriculum. Although they insisted that the reviled SIECUS exercised "no influence whatsoever on the development of the . . . course guide" and that the county's curriculum was distinct from TOYL and "not patterned after any program in Europe or any other part of this country," the San Mateo educational bureaucracy could not silence a burgeoning discourse engaging—and indicting—broader offerings in family life and sex education.[37] Nor could it stem the increasingly national interest in this program, which manifested daily in letters from as far away as El Paso, New York, and Nashville.[38]

The opposition that originated in San Mateo gathered quickly and built on the support of other Bay Area activists, becoming core to the opposition to sex education burgeoning statewide. Margaret Scott, publicity chairwoman of CPR and lead plaintiff in the case against San Mateo that the group took to the US Supreme Court, personally credited her organization's campaign with "reaching the crusade into every state of the union, including Alaska and Mexico [sic]."[39] Only months later did the now better-known "sudden and savage turnabout" on programs such as that in Orange County's Anaheim occur.[40] In fact, Scott and other CPR members traveled to Anaheim and other Southern Californian communities to mobilize parents and share tales from the struggles of their communities to the north, located dangerously close to "Berkeley and Stanford and San Francisco, those hippielands [that] have . . . anesthetized people into expecting almost anything."[41]

Scott and other Bay Area conservatives took it upon themselves to inform people all over California that sex education represented "more danger than even the bomb or Vietnam or poverty." Invoking religious values, Scott warned people that the sex educators would "rob them of their goodness and of their faith in God and their country." The "long-suffering decent people of America," she maintained apocalyptically, "must . . . fight to the death to defeat this program in any way God gives us the strength and wisdom to prevail. . . . If we do not, we cannot survive."[42] Addressing "a capacity crowd at a Pro America luncheon" in the Central Valley city of Bakersfield, Margaret Scott urged concerned parents to contact her associates in Redwood City, another Bay Area community, who had developed materials expounding on the perils of family life education and organizing effective opposition.[43] Scott was hardly alone among her fellow Northern Californians. Gertrude McLellan, a Sacramento mother, co-founded with Eleanor Howe California Families United, which went on to become the state's largest anti-sex education organization.[44] In San

Francisco, caricatured by many conservatives as a hotbed of immorality and sexual debauchery, opponents to sex education were equally strident. Marjorie Lemlow, of the citizens' group Mothers Support Neighborhood Schools, decried the "SIECUS sexology" imparted in city classrooms and the secrecy so intense shrouding the curriculum that she had "to wrest it from the city attorney with threats."[45]

Exacerbating the conflict, the vigorous public statements of program designer and filmmaker Ayres and teacher Marilyn McCurdy, who substantively created and narrated the program, could seem deliberately oblivious to parental concerns. Apparently unaware that speaking with children about sexuality in any capacity, much less at school without parental supervision, was highly incendiary in the late 1960s, they emphasized precisely this aspect of the program.[46] Rather than downplaying TOYL's content, Ayres, an honoree of the American Pediatric Psychiatric Association, responded to concerns about the films' explicitness that "nine to twelve-year-olds' cognitive abilities demand that they be shown concrete images," a perspective clearly antithetical to that of citizens concerned about "titillating" impressionable children.[47] Similarly, Ayres touted "the quiet attentiveness in the classroom and the many, many serious respectful questions which the children ask during such classroom teaching [as] testimony to their natural—not artificially stimulated—interest," as if ignorant of the degree to which the image of small children rapt by celluloid images of genitalia, and then encouraged to inquire further on these topics, would horrify parents who balked at any type of sexual speech, particularly outside the home.[48]

Ayres went on to say that "one of the most gratifying aspects" of the program was "increasing the amount of sex education in the home rather than reducing it."[49] Eighty-two percent of the polled families in the Santa Cruz City Schools may have indicated that TOYL "made it easier to discuss sex education at home," but in citing this statistic to bolster his position, Ayres overlooked the fact that many parents looked askance at any such discussion.[50] His insistence that family life education in general, and TOYL in particular, helped redress "most adults' inadequate knowledge of many areas of sexual development or . . . folklore beliefs that are inaccurate" hardly mollified concerns that sex education could disrupt the social hierarchy.[51] Indeed, these bold assertions of pedagogical or "expert" authority actually served to galvanize a defensive activism around the home as a place to be energetically protected *from*, rather than *by*, such pedagogical efforts. MORE, one parent group from Bakersfield, described itself as "mothers who believe in the concept that some things about life are kept personal and private . . . a positive action group founded on the principles that responsible education does not eliminate the parents but safeguards and protects parents' rights so that education takes place in the home, as well as in the classrooms. . . . we are rising to the challenge of those who say we cannot or will not keep this responsibility . . . and we insist on maintaining this privilege at any cost."[52]

These defenders of the home were of course facing a society in which sexual discourse was reverberating in multiplying venues and at amplified volumes, reinforced by a series of US Supreme Court decisions narrowing the definition of obscenity and thus permitting billboards, novels, and television programs greater leeway to keep "Americans in a constant state of sexual excitement."[53] The birth of the Free Speech Movement on the campus of the nearby University of California, Berkeley, in 1964 only cemented the link between discursive freedom and broader critiques of authority. The enthusiastic accounts sex educators shared of fostering discussions of sexuality in their classrooms further eroded the status of the schoolhouse as a bastion of moral authority. Ayres joined a growing chorus of sex education advocates who similarly celebrated such openness and were apparently tone-deaf to its controversy.

Liberal State Board of Education member Dorman Commons told his colleagues he was impressed with the films' ability "to open up lines of communication between parents and children."[54] In a different film co-produced with SIECUS founder Mary Calderone, Sally Williams effused: "[The students] come in, on their lunch hour. They come in before school, they come in after school, and they say, 'I've got a question for you, I've got a problem, ah, what do you think about this and such?' and it's beautiful."[55] Williams proudly described how "all kinds of questions are explored in Hal Rice's 12th grade class including whether teenagers are accepting the values of adult society or developing their own."[56] Such bold encouragements to critique authority provided fodder for an increasingly fierce opposition, which germinated early on in San Mateo and quickly gained traction regionally and statewide.

How radical was San Mateo's polemical program? Superintendent Kent insisted, "If the SMC Teachers Guide has any special claim for distinction, it is to be found in its heavy emphasis upon moral and upon spiritual values."[57] Ayres's vocal and tenacious commitment to increasing knowledge about sexuality among children at times ironically underscored the moderate impetus behind TOYL. He maintained that "accurate information decreases false ideas and needless anxieties," but he suggested that the program was primarily an effort to mitigate the effects of children's exposure "to material in newspapers or magazines and the overhearing of conversations about sexual issues."[58] An interview between teacher Marilyn McCurdy and state board member Eugene N. Ragle reveals as much. While Ragle's questioning nearly succeeded in painting McCurdy as profligate, McCurdy ultimately salvaged her respectability.[59] Ragle attempted to corner her with a damning line of questioning:

RAGLE: Then, as far as you're concerned, perhaps as a teacher and as a producer of the film, in the field of right and wrong in the matter of morals or ethics, there are no absolutes—is that what you're saying?
MCCURDY: No, I think that we very firmly reinforce the values of honesty—of the basic values that we do stand for . . . The fact is that we try to help the children think through the situations for themselves and they do come up with the moral answer themselves. This is what I have observed in classroom after classroom.
RAGLE: What would you do if they did not?
MCCURDY: I would, as a classroom teacher, guide them to see this and if they were not seeing it I would bring up a question which would allow them to look at it in this way.[60]

Extensive inquiry into the "apparent lack of the moral aspect of the subject in the program" thus revealed that despite the frankness of its creators, TOYL was actually designed to curb the licentious behavior opponents were convinced it encouraged. McCurdy argued that lack of sex education encouraged libertinism, rather than vice versa: "Actually the fear of increased experimentation is not borne out . . . In fact, the combination producing experimentation seems to be ignorance, unsatisfied curiosity, inadequate self-control, lack of moral training, and the presence of the physical drives rather than intellectual knowledge."[61] Even students expressed some fairly conservative arguments in favor of the purportedly radical programs. One student who beseeched the state board for more programs at the February meeting commented, "Intercourse should be saved for marriage. You do this because if you do it you have a better understanding of your wife or your husband, and you feel that you're both clean, spiritually and physically. . . . Marriage doesn't start until you understand each other."[62] On the one hand, this student clearly advocated an open dialogue about sexuality and envisioned a companionate marriage. On the other hand, he subscribed to the notion that extramarital sex taints youth who should preserve themselves for the apogee of sexual expression: heterosexual marriage.

Advocating for, or even implementing, sex education thus hardly indicated an embrace of radical sexual politics. The *Los Angeles Times* reported in December 1968 that a teenage girl who had inquired in a sex education class about oral contraception had been punished for her indiscretion with a trip to the principal's office.[63] Of course, discussing the recently legalized Pill highlighted the waning power of the longest-standing reason to forswear premarital sex: fear of pregnancy.[64] Certain aspects of TOYL resonate with this sensibility and echo the conservative marriage guides of the 1940s and 1950s with which their authors were surely familiar. Lesson 14 spells out, in block letters, the key concepts for teaching a lesson on "Growing Up": "SEX CAN AND SHOULD BE CONTROLLED. SEX SHOULD ALWAYS BE SECONDARY TO THE RELATIONSHIP. SEXUAL INTERCOURSE WHICH OCCURS IN EARLY ADOLESCENCE IS HARMFUL IN TERMS OF THE CHILD'S DEVELOPMENT."[65] Unabashedly pronouncing that "any form of sexual affection should be regulated," the TOYL program as a whole is an amalgam of sexual conservatism and liberalism. Lesson 12, titled "A New Life," begins with the pedagogical imperative that "Sex is biologically, psychologically, and spiritually related in its most basic sense to marriage."[66]

Simultaneously, however, the guide writes that sexuality "should exist in an atmosphere of love and confidence, free from anxiety and guilt."[67] Still more adventurously, buried within the third paragraph of Lesson 12, is the precept that sexual intercourse "is not performed merely for procreation."[68] According to Ayres, the program as a whole shored up a fairly temperate conception of family and sexual mores: "The series does not change human nature and mothers still need to counsel their daughters as they have for generations on how to deal with the inappropriate remarks of boys."[69] Still, sex educators generated an anti-sex education backlash among people who already began to claim "the American family" as its exclusive domain to defend against the incursions of the 1960s. The San Mateo curricular materials were thus comparable to those in other districts in exhibiting a new willingness to speak openly about sexuality in order to advocate moderate conclusions, yet in the process inspired conservative backlash.

Relative to older programs in San Diego, San Francisco, and Long Beach that had been uncontroversial, the new curricula represented a marked shift.[70] In state-level discussions of the solutions to the increasingly intractable sex education fracas, the nearly thirty-year-old San Diego program was repeatedly raised as a model to emulate. In 1965, the San Diego County grand jury had thoroughly investigated the program and "concluded that it was not only a good program, but one that could be used as a prime example across the state."[71] Developed during the Second World War, the San Diego program raised few objections for it spent "most of [the students'] time . . . with the psychological, and emotional and moral attitudes involved—very little . . . on the anatomical and actual reproduction per se."[72] Perhaps most importantly, champions of the San Diego model repeatedly celebrated the teachers as being of "high moral standards."[73] Persida Drakulich, a sex education teacher in the district, rattled off her extensive "professional and personal qualifications," including multiple health education credentials and having "been married 22 years [with] two sons—a boy in college and a boy in high school."[74] Her seamless integration of her marital status into her professional resume highlights the threat sex education represented to the nuclear family. Indeed, Drakulich attributed "the success of this 30 year old program" to a perspective that she maintained far more tenaciously than Ayres and Williams: "The home and the church are the primary sources of family life and sex education. . . .we continually strive to supplement their efforts . . . to stem the tide of unhappy social involvements."[75]

Finally, the role of the sex education teacher in San Diego was very different than that described in San Mateo. Eschewing any accusations of moral relativism or of harboring "situational ethics," Drakulich explained that "our students appeal to us for the truth." Purveying this infallible "truth" and "sound knowledge," Drakulich elaborated, allowed the school to intercede "before they [the students] get into trouble through ignorance."[76] "Getting into trouble," which to earlier sex educators had referred to venereal disease and premarital pregnancy, evoked a far broader and scarier range of associations in the age of the sexual revolution. Drakulich and her colleagues in San Diego shared with their more controversial peers in other communities a perception that ignorance represented a danger to students, but they differed on how sex education should remedy this situation. Teachers who privileged students' independent decision-making capabilities were easily tarred as debased libertines. The San Diego teachers' approach offered "the truth." By contrast, the breadth, depth, and pedagogical freedom that characterized other such curricula developed during this era contributed to their volatility, even though the critical inquiry they espoused often led to the same conservative conclusions.

The vast majority of the programs in California at this time evoked what might be called the "family life era" in the history of sex education, a period stretching from the close of World War II to the outbreak of the AIDS crisis in the early 1980s.[77] During this nearly three decades, sex educators were temporarily relieved of the urgent threat of preventing venereal disease and dramatically expanded their purview to address social, emotional, and gender relations. The TOYL teacher's guide, for example, articulates its aim so grandly it might have been a course in psychology or social studies. "Hopefully," the guide states, "this series will help the children understand the meaning of their own and other people's behavior, and will further help them in their interpretation of their world."[78] This broad reach was arguably what made the program so inflammatory. Certainly, Orange County Congressman and ardent sex education opponent John Schmitz reminded the state board and the listening audience that "most people have the idea of sex education of what they remember when they were in school . . . you know—that this is an ovary and this is a testicle—a kind of geography course on anatomy—and not what we're talking about now."[79] This novel expansiveness, Schmitz pointed out, had quickly permitted family life education to become "obnoxious and pornographic."[80]

San Diego's case is again instructive. While the county's sex education program never stirred controversy, Max Rafferty received various letters from local parents employing rhetoric nearly identical to those blasting sex education, but complaining about the proposed social studies curriculum. One irate mother claimed that the as-yet-unapproved framework was already in use in San Diego schools and decried its guiding questions: "Why do these phenomena behave as they do? Who am I or who are we, or who are they? And what should I, or we, or they do next?" This mother issued precisely the criticisms her peers in other towns and cities levied against sex education: "In most families, these questions are discussed and answered within the framework of our religious beliefs. . . . [The schools] should not be allowed to undermine our children's religious teachings . . . as [the social studies framework] will inevitably do."[81] Therefore, in San Diego, where the sex education curriculum was entrenched and taught by longtime teachers perceived as upstanding, it was an emergent social studies curriculum that inflamed parental anxiety about the declining power of the family.

That these concerns were so similar reveals that the underlying doubts were both broader and more deeply rooted than the minutiae of the sex education or social studies curriculum initially suggest. Thus, systematically comparing sex education curricula statewide, as the state Educational Programs Committee attempted to do in late 1968 in an effort to understand which aspects of the programs were most incendiary, was not only difficult but perhaps ill-considered, since the discourse and substantive debates so quickly departed from the texts or curricula at hand.[82] Although especially ardent in San Mateo, opposition statewide converged around three fundamental accusations: one, the curriculum threatened parental authority; two, it was taught by unqualified and morally profligate teachers; and three, it represented an obscene burden upon increasingly strapped taxpayers. These concerns intertwined strands of classic and contemporary conservatism and quickly reverberated in communities all across California.

## Parents, Teachers, and Taxes

All over the state, incensed parents blamed teachers for alienating them from their children by engaging in conversations and promoting attitudes that challenged parental authority and the sanctity of the nuptial home. In Ventura, a northern suburb of Los Angeles, where one newspaper headline announced parents to be "thrashing out [the] sex education dilemma," the organization Ventura Concerned Parents (VCP) ascribed to "this new SEX EDUCATION . . . the intent . . . to preempt parental prerogative and to impose sex information upon our children . . . WHETHER WE LIKE IT OR NOT! This is being accomplished with a total disregard for the moral frame of reference."[83] VCP defined its "fundamental objective to unite parents and other concerned persons . . . for the purpose of tempering and resisting local and state sex education as a compulsory course of study."[84]

Sex education was just one menace to family unity. Countless letters from parents statewide decried "the dope, crime and sex" proffered in and by the public schools and generally echoed one mother's excoriation that "the American school system is no longer an institution to me . . . my four daughters would be safer at home."[85] Ayres and McCurdy presaged this opposition, posing the question, "ARE THE SCHOOLS TAKING RESPONSIBILITY FOR THE CHILD'S SEX EDUCATION AWAY FROM THE HOME?" in block letters in the introduction to their teacher's guide.[86] Their explanation, though meant to reassure, was characteristically oblivious to the issue at hand: many parents were not eager for their "children to go home and be as able to discuss [with them] their newly gained knowledge in the field of sexual development as they are about social studies and science."[87] Teachers who encountered "parents made anxious by such discussion" should, according to TOYL, provide them "with support to view this as a wonderful opportunity to carry out their responsibility and not as the school taking it away from them."[88] Ayres's lack of classroom experience showed. Despite his reassurances, parents felt slighted by a program that appeared to be moving forward without their, or possibly any, qualified leadership.

Even cursory scrutiny of the program's implementation confirmed many parents' concerns. Nearly a year after the earliest protests in San Mateo, county board member Florence Cadigan testified before the state Educational Programs Committee that "schools that used the TOYL film were selected by each district" and could not identify the individual schools that screened TOYL. While the county office "encourage[d] boards to use its guide," she admitted that educators tended to confuse the recommended text with TOYL. Cadigan's remarks exposed the lack of uniformity and curricular control that so angered anxious parents, especially in her candid claim that "advance notice is *usually* sent to parents when the materials are to be used."[89] Similarly, when board member Mrs. Edwin Klotz asked McCurdy whether parents were permitted to preview films, McCurdy rejoined inconclusively, "This is handled differently in the different districts. There is no general rule. . . . [Parents] do not see it with the children, but usually on the TV at home—while the children are watching it at school. . . . This will increase the communication between parents and students."[90] This nonchalant admission that parents and children usually viewed the film simultaneously, and her clear goal that the program should increase communication between parents and children rather than defer to parental authority, only inflamed existing resistance. Nor did McCurdy's weak assurance that "teachers try to . . . reserve those subjects which fringe on moralistic values for family discussions" counteract this concrete evidence of a systematic or at least de facto disregard for parental prerogative.

By the time the controversy broke, Ayres began to temper his tone, claiming the programs "strongly increas[e] the parents' opportunity . . . to discuss and reinforce the particular home and religious training the parents wish to impart to their child."[91] This deliberate concession to parents did little to abate a growing sense that most sex education was "nothing but pornography and . . . what parents want to avoid," according to State Board of Education member John R. Ford.[92] Two days later, on Valentine's Day 1969, desirous of "seeing our society on a much higher plane than what we see in the world today," the board requested that the state department of education draft guidelines for teaching of sex education; ultimately five of the six guidelines explicitly highlighted the preeminence of the family unit.[93] One study of a failed attempt to implement sex education in nearby Sacramento strongly suggests that parental fear of losing control over their children's education was at the core of the opposition. Adults in Sacramento indicated the following elements held "great importance" in determining their decision to reject sex education: parent opposition (42 percent), organized group opposition (50 percent), poor communication (27 percent), and perceived lack of parental involvement in the program (22 percent).[94] These categories are permeable and imprecise, but parents were clearly opposed to these programs primarily because of a sense of their faltering authority at the hands of less qualified educators.

To many parents, unqualified and profligate teachers were the villains erod-ing their authority—and on taxpayer dollars, no less. This contention loomed large at a March 1969 meeting of the Educational Programs Committee of the State Board. The committee paid special attention to the San Mateo case.[95] Committee members briefly acknowledged the exceptional classroom cir-cumstance sex educators faced in that parents could exercise their recently won legal right to remove their children from such classes.[96] The committee then relentlessly criticized teachers. Most diplomatically, state board member Mrs. Seymour Mathiesen opened the meeting by addressing teacher train-ing, which she described as a core "concern shared by many people."[97] Even the moderates, who generally supported the program, expressed serious and pointed doubts about the fitness of sex educators to instruct children. Board member Dr. John R. Ford, a frequent defender of family life education, con-tended that in a properly executed program teachers should "guide the chil-dren into the right conclusions after certain situations are discussed" and that "there are many teachers who are teaching the subject who do not have the same moral standards that we would like and hope that all teachers would have."[98] The parents who raised the "great deal of objections" in the "volume of mail" the board received were less diplomatic. They saw in such pedagogy both nefarious motives and apocalyptic consequences.[99]

Sex education clearly represented to many parents only the most flagrant example of a school system in which teachers had forsaken their moral com-passes at a historical moment when such guidance was paramount. A letter from one San Mateo mother recounted her anger at a worksheet assigned in her seventh-grade child's world history class, which asked students to con-sider the idea of "just asking for volunteer soldiers in the event of an all-out war . . . instead of our present draft system."[100] Angry that the students should be addressing "such a controversial subject," she asked, "Does a teacher have the right to teach her views on peace and war? How can parents and taxpayers prevent the brainwashing of children?" Though it was world history that had angered this mother, she used this anecdote about teachers' moral unfitness, specifically related to the selective service draft during the Vietnam War, to build to a conclusion about sex education: "Are teachers allowed the freedom to teach as they please. . . . IF SO, are the majority of teachers capable of teach-ing a subject like FAMILY LIFE EDUCATION? I think not!"[101] Allowing teach-ers of suspicious reputation not only to teach about that bedrock of society, the nuclear family, but also potentially to denigrate it, was a risk too great to bear for many parents, especially at such a precarious moment.

In San Mateo and statewide, parents repeatedly excoriated public school educators as unfit to teach any subject engaging morality, though significantly never mentioned the specifically communist threat fueling opposition in Orange County. Mrs. Johnson, an anti-sex education activist mother from Anaheim, waxed passionately at Sacramento's state board meeting in April 1969, but without mentioning the specifically communist threat that resonated in her home region influenced by defense-industry culture. Mrs. Johnson referred to her daughter's "sex teacher" alternately as "he" and "she," suggesting little was sure about the teacher beyond his or her certain perversity. The English teacher had "spent the entire class period discussing the play 'Hair'" despite telling students outright "that it wasn't recommended for junior high or senior high students," not to mention assigning a play that "contained at least 27 obscenities from foul language to prostitution."[102] Mrs. Johnson underscored the damage this pedagogy wreaked on their family. The social studies teacher, after pontificating to the impressionable children on her unpatriotic politics, "went on . . . [to say] that she knew how the students felt—that they can hardly wait until they are big enough to kick the father between his two running legs."[103] These attitudes seemed pervasive among the faculty, as teachers beyond "sex class" all promoted "immoral attitudes against [parental] beliefs and wishes."[104] Johnson lambasted the questionable judgment and moral fiber of all of her daughter's teachers, but stopped short of impugning their opposition to communism.

Hostility toward teachers came from all quarters. As frequently as parents slammed them as permissive, others denigrated them as "totalitarian."[105] Another Orange County mother poured out her wrath on the "dictator teachers" commandeering her child's educational and moral development.[106] From Santa Clara County, neighboring San Mateo, one mother wrote Rafferty, "Children were treated like sheep . . . herded together, each must fit the mold."[107] Her daughter and classmates were "labeled as troublemakers as early as kindergarten" if they displayed "some imagination or dared to question the system."[108] It was thus excessive discipline, exacerbated by the "evasiveness and lying" of teachers, rather than the academic and moral laxity many others blamed, that this mother posited as fomenting "the desire to burn down our colleges to get back at an unjust system."[109] What remained constant among the stacks of letters sent to Rafferty and the board was the shared conviction that teachers were unfit to provide moral guidance for their children.

Overwrought as many gripes were—one Santa Ana mother likened modern pedagogy to "putting strychnine in the drinking water" —expansive and modern family life programs were fairly new, and no universally acknowledged professional credentials for teachers yet existed.[110] Superintendent Kent boasted that four hundred of the county's teachers had completed in-service training with the support of Notre Dame College, but even the most established teacher training programs had emerged "at some local colleges over the last two or three years," as McCurdy told the Educational Programs Committee.[111] Just months earlier, San Francisco State College had begun offering a master's degree in family life education.[112] McCurdy's claim that "many local school districts are conducting workshops and in-service training for their teachers" did little to assuage doubts that teachers were being trained as sporadically as parents were consulted about programming.[113] Jack Mitchell, an instructor featured in a pro-sex education film, described the career path that led him to teach adolescents about family life and sexuality, reinforcing such suspicions: "The fact that I taught social studies didn't seem to make a great deal of difference. They simply wanted people that they thought would be, ah, warm with kids, people that liked kids and wanted to see this kind of program develop . . . and I thought about it for about five minutes, and I said "where do I volunteer?"[114] Upon completing a summer workshop, Mitchell was teaching sex education in California classrooms in September. Passionate reactions among conservatives to innovative curricula might suggest misplaced fears, but such programs were frequently taught by novice teachers ill-trained to impart especially sensitive material during increasingly contentious times.

Nightmarish tales of dubious veracity reiterated the sense that sex education was a tool of immoral teachers to arouse sexual curiosity in innocent children.[115] One parent group from Santa Cruz County, where TOYL had also been piloted, wrote a detailed three-page letter to Rafferty describing the case of an eighth-grade English teacher named Candy Love who told students to "get off their dead asses," wallpapered the classroom with posters declaring "Peace and Love" and showing Peter Fonda on a motorcycle, and placed an image of "known drug user Jimmie [sic] Hendrix directly behind the American flag, so that this was seen every time one looked at the flag, or saluted it."[116] Contributing most to the "outrage," according to the father, were the overtly sexual comments such as "blow me" and "suck me" that students had scrawled on a "graffiti sheet" Mrs. Love had affixed to a wall in the interest of letting "students write what they thought of anything."[117] The father pointed out that "the administration had seen this room, and thereby approved it" and that "Mrs. Love was selected from 200 applicants," suggesting "a hopeless situation . . . [to which] we are forced to expose our kids"; he believed educators were working proactively to "fill schools with dope and filth and sex" and to "teach [students] to make babies so they can kill them."[118] This type of narrative of a debauched teacher supported by a morally dubious infrastructure inspired an emerging consensus among Californians. (See figure 5.1.)

The fruitless efforts of one educator to check the growing distrust of teachers statewide reveals how embedded this bias had become. Dr. Howard Busching of the Northern California Council for Family Relations, an ordained clergyman and full-time professor of marriage and family life education at San Jose State College, pointed out that he taught every semester "because of the demand of the people out there in the community . . . who want training in family life education."[119] He touted the statistic that the American Council of Churches, representative of 80 to 85 percent of Protestant churches, had "gone on record in favor of family life education in the public schools."[120] Busching pled with Californians at the hearing to "look at what is actually being done" by speaking with practitioners and students, rather than listening to "rumors or allegations or name-calling or

FIGURE 5.1 Southern California women dressed as cheerleaders to support Max Rafferty's campaign for US Senate in 1968. The campaign failed, but Rafferty was instrumental in mobilizing political action among conservative women and men. Max Rafferty Collection, Box 1, Folder: Photos. Reprinted with the permission and by courtesy of the Special Collections Department, University of Iowa Libraries.

emotionality or sentimentality."[121] When he ventured to claim that "there is definitely moral and spiritual content in family life education," the audience booed loudly.[122] After several minutes of advocating for the "love education" aspect of existing programs rather than the focus on sex per se, Busching changed strategy.[123] Abandoning his original contention that a quiet majority supported sex education, Busching acknowledged his views to be at odds with popular opinion and entreated the board to buck "making decisions on the basis of a vote of the people," but to heed the "testimony of people who are competent through training and experience." Busching concluded, "In short, I call upon you to believe in your educators."[124] Among a populace rapidly losing faith in its teachers, this plea rang hollow.

The continued expenditure of hard-earned tax dollars to pay for these questionable teachers and their curricula stirred emotions among Californians who simultaneously faced rising tax bills and a proliferation of less orthodox curricula. Even parents who discerned a distinctly Soviet plot behind such programs felt that unaccountable teachers salaried by an unreasonable tax burden were at the crux of the problem with California schools. Two parents in La Cañada, near Los Angeles, wrote Rafferty a multipage, single-spaced letter echoing their southland neighbors in railing against "the Karl Marx lie and subversives in the schools," as manifest in sex education and other questionable curricula.[125] Yet the co-signers underlined only one sentence in their lengthy screed: "We certainly do feel that our tax money should be spent on equal education for all taught by qualified teachers on proper subjects."[126] Singer Bing Crosby stepped up to support the collective and rising "opposition of the public for more taxation for state schools" among "small home owners," who in recent years found shouldering the costs of "the four thousand subjects taught in state schools" unbearable since many such subjects "are not the taxpayers' responsibility and should be paid for by recipients."[127] Rafferty responded to Crosby's suggestion that "the schools should get back to essential fundamentals" by assuring him that though some "so-called frills are still being offered in elementary and secondary schools," his eight-year tenure had dispensed with many of them.[128] Sex education seemed one particularly offensive area on which to squander public funds.

A sense of victimization at the hands of an egregiously inefficient system spawned a new activism among many parents and gave politicians a powerful new rhetoric. Congressman Schmitz articulated his passionate resistance to sex education in the broader context of California's wastefulness on educational "frills."[129] He expounded at length to the Sacramento audience as to why sex education was both practically impossible and undesirable:

We are continually having a problem finding money to support the schools. And this is a very serious problem. . . . If you have an automobile where you can't make the payments, there's no sense putting a TV set up in front of your car. It's debatable whether you should watch TV while you are driving a car or whether you should watch TV at all. But it is certainly not debatable that if you don't have enough money to make the payments for the car in the first place, you shouldn't go into fringe or frills that are debatable as to whether you should have them at all. I hope the analogy is not missed here. We are having trouble paying for reading, writing and arithmetic. . . . We have trouble meeting the costs of the basics. . . . I do not think you should go out, even on a limited program, into such controversial field as this, when you face this danger of being unable to pay for it and also of setting the foot in the door and then allowing it to be expanded.[130]

Parents whose children attended private school also resisted funding the public schools' "special training for young revolutionaries" and found Superintendent Rafferty supportive of giving them tax rebates.[131] This climate led William J. Cardinal, a father from San Ramon, to write to Rafferty that "you better believe the pressure is on" parents to finance a misguided school system. Kindergarten teachers were apparently explaining to young children why there were no funds available for their education and asking for parent volunteers to do their "chores" such as yard work, a strategy Cardinal considered "in very poor taste."[132]

Some unlikely voices joined the chorus calling for tax relief. One teacher, hardly alone among her peers, wrote Rafferty as a "teacher, concerned parent, and overburdened taxpayer," challenging him to devise "a plan for action" to stamp out sex education.[133] A fellow teacher and self-described "minority among educators" for her Republican politics explained that "this wasting of our tax money offends me . . . and I wonder at the naivetee [sic] of most Democrats who can't seem to understand that this is TAX MONEY which THEY PAY TOO. . . . isn't there some way we can control its wise use to some extent? And is it any wonder our schools are in such trouble? No amount of additional funds can fix that kind of rathole. In fact, I am beginning to wonder if more funds don't simply encourage it."[134] One professedly liberal couple from Torrance wrote to Rafferty to express support of the "courageous teachers of our great state" striking in nearby Los Angeles, a cause for which Rafferty had little sympathy, but mostly to point out that "the big financial trouble" of "every school district in our state" could not be met with more taxation. They wrote, "More taxes is not the answer. The people of California have already had the last tax hike they intend to tolerate for a long, long time."[135] Board member Dr. Ford acknowledged the worsening fiscal climate, but employed the idiom of his attackers to challenge the notion that sex education was superfluous: "Some have mentioned about the frills of sex education—sex education as being a frill. Am I to understand then that personal hygiene is a frill? The doctrine of the necessity of cleanliness, including the sexual organs, is a frill? Am I to understand that the physiological functions of a body that are so necessary in maintaining a healthy existence morally, ethically, spiritually, physically, is a frill?"[136] Yet this plea to value sex education even in its most conservative form—Ford specifically advocated "a moral code of ethics" like that in the San Diego curriculum—gained little traction.[137]

Students, perhaps surprisingly, participated energetically in these conversations—the State Board of Education even appointed a student advisory board on sex education—and invoked a range of viewpoints on the questions of parental authority, teachers, and taxes. Teenager Mark Borba of Riverside reported that the students had unanimously decided that the state should require a comprehensive program of sex education to deal with "all of it . . . relationship of the sexes in general—family life, to get along, marriage life, morals, and what not . . . due to today's rising rate of illegitimate births, early teenage marriages and divorces." The "generation gap" widely accepted as defining this era notwithstanding, some students echoed their parents' concerns. The student advisory board, albeit selected by administrators, went further than many adults, recommending that "the sensitivity required in dealing with a subject of this type" demanded "that qualified teachers have at least a college minor in psychology." Freer of fiscal concerns than their taxpaying parents, the students further suggested "a possible expenditure in state aid to help present teachers receive this education or to assist schools in bearing the burden of higher salaries that will be required in the hiring of competent instructors."[138] Even as some students bashed sex education and "the leftist-liberal bias" they perceived among their teachers—one Bay Area high school sophomore worried about "creeping socialism" in his history class—the very public debate over sex education was quickly drawing children and adolescents to take a vocal stand on precisely the issues many of their parents wanted to shroud in secrecy.[139]

Reflecting the perspectives of adolescents and adults, the thousands of letters Rafferty received and the pages of public testimony regarding the San Mateo case and others confirm that while anti-communist rhetoric polarized opinions very quickly in Orange County's classroom wars over sex education, the relative absence of this element in other regions sapped some hysteria from at least the early debate.[140] Instead, a more broadly based conservatism, anchored in a longstanding antipathy to government spending, moral relativism, and robust patriotism, resonated among wider swaths of Californians and coalesced around sex education. In an observation that would within a few months seem naïve, Ayres in July 1968 described his sense of the controversy in San Mateo: "Neither side imputes any desire to harm. . . . Some people who disagree with this series are alarmed. I believe them to be sincere parents whose concern is for the best interests of their children in the community. Obviously there is a clear disagreement as to what is helpful to children and appropriate for school instruction, but I believe we have in common a wish to help children to be moral, strong and intelligent."[141] Disagreement over sex education persisted and became more embittered in the coming months. The appeal of the anti-sex education cause to Californians reflects the fact that at least at its inception, the terms of the debate were reasonable enough to engage even moderates concerned about the growing impact of a sexualized society—and pedagogically adventurous school system—on their children, as well as on their shrinking wallets.

Deep concerns about teachers, family, and taxes fueled fights over sex education in a state undergoing tremendous demographic and cultural change. At the April 1969 state board meeting, Dean Hanson, a father from Redwood City and a plaintiff in the CPR case against San Mateo County, explained at length that the foolhardy notion of public schools offering family life education to an increasingly, and to him troublingly, diverse citizenry: "The trouble is that there are so many different kinds of people in the world with different educational backgrounds, varying degrees of insight into human nature, with all kinds of sex complexes, that it would take the wisdom of a Solomon and the diplomatic skill of a Talleyrand to unite them and devise a program that would win their united support."[142] Of the course title, he rhetorically asked Ayres, "Whose family are YOU talking about?"[143]

To this father, and to the many other parents who inveighed against sex education as abetting the dissolution of the family, any curriculum short of indoctrination with traditional moral standards could only hasten such moral decay. The key players in the fights over sex education were predominantly white and middle class, but the backdrop of pluralistic California infused the debates, albeit often implicitly. While Frances Todd of San Francisco articulated the universal need for education about "human maturation and reproduction, a natural, not unusual, aspect of the family life of all people regardless of their ethnic, political, or religious backgrounds," an ardent opponent and representative of MORE felt the need to reiterate how universally offensive the programs were. She relayed that "even a Mexican-American father said to me" that parents wished to reserve "the right to talk about such matters with their children," and she boasted of "signed statements from Modesto to Tulare County" that expressed as much.[144] Deputy State Superintendent Eugene Gonzales, better known for his prominent role in establishing the state's bilingual-bicultural education programs, was charged with simultaneously negotiating the classroom wars both these and sexuality education inspired.

To members of CPR, and the many hundreds who wrote letters to support them, parents hoping to impart to their children traditional ideas about family and privacy felt far better addressing such questions themselves rather than entrusting them to anonymous and novice teachers. Although the largely Anglo participants in these heated debates rarely referred explicitly to ethnicity, their comments reflect a decided xenophobia. The previous fall, Hanson had joined 1,200 other Redwood City parents to protest the introduction of TOYL and had echoed a discourse gathering steam in Orange County allies that defined the locally developed program as vaguely foreign. Hanson invoked examples of how the series, part of a "headlong rush into immorality," mimicked Swedish schools, in which "students feel they should have special rooms set aside in schools so that they can have sexual intercourse during class breaks. In that way, the couples could be sure parents wouldn't surprise them." Hanson also noted the kindergartens of West Berlin, which purportedly boasted "a loving room, where children can, if they wish, experiment in the first stages of sex. If he wants, little Fritz can escort little Heidi to her home and sleep with her overnight."[145]

Significantly, even when these activists connected sex education to a foreign menace, none of the dystopic societies they describe are communist. In an exceptional example of an anti-sex education activist beyond Orange County drawing explicit geopolitical outcomes from the implementation of sex education, Hanson specifically evokes West Berlin and "fascist Germany of 35 years ago" as the nightmarish outcome of sex education, rather than the Soviet Union. The scenarios they imagined were interchangeable: Hanson could have been a southland activist when he asked, "Who really owns my children? It is as though our children no longer belong to us, but to the State." But the fact that he drew only an implicit link to communism reveals both that this did not dominate his worldview and, perhaps most important, that he did not think it would resonate with the larger public of parents and policymakers in Sacramento.[146]

Hanson concluded by returning to questions that he knew from experience would inspire sympathy among audience members: teacher quality and tax expense. He closed by pointing out the foolhardiness of funding sex education when basic programs were lacking, as expressed by a Redwood City school board member: "Family life education isn't going to do them any good if they can't count to 28 days. And they have to learn to read labels or they will take the wrong pill bottle."[147]

It is clear by 1970 that sex education programs were contested statewide and that these curricula, while radical in breaking the nervously guarded silence over sexuality, also delivered a fairly tame message. While sexual liberals and moderates were trying to redress what they saw as a crisis in American family and sexual mores during the 1960s, sex educators and their advocates misinterpreted the volatility of this approach.[148] Opponents of these programs perceived sex education itself as a troubling symptom of the very trends it had been created to mitigate. They succeeded in dismantling and diluting numerous programs, though in mounting their campaigns they sacrificed the silence around sexuality they purported to guard. Most notably, organization against sex education served primarily to enable conservatives to identify as the exclusive defenders of parental authority and family unity against a morally suspect, liberal-dominated society and school system. Sexual liberals unwittingly germinated the notion of "family values" in their introduction of sex education programs, which enabled grass-roots conservatives to cement the family as the domain of the Right and as besieged by immoral progressives.[149] The story of sex education reveals how the popular sensibility into which these national organizations tapped came to flourish during the late 1960s and on through the 1970s.

Despite the violent undoing of the progressive Anaheim program and the ignominy heaped upon sex education advocates in San Mateo County and beyond, a conservative cultural victory was hardly assured. The CPR began to rally for a protracted journey to the Supreme Court that would last seven years and end in defeat in 1976.[150] The April 1969 state board meeting had closed with the unanimous, albeit nonbinding, recommendation that "sex education be included as a necessary part of local educational programs," which the New York Times declared a "lost battle for California conservatives."[151] In 1970, Superintendent Rafferty was defeated by liberal African-American Wilson Riles, and the conservative "Paradise Regained" he had optimistically predicted as the inevitable successor to the "Sick Sixties" hardly seemed imminent.[152] An empathetic note to Rafferty, who had opposed many sex education curricula, upon his defeat reveals that certain conservatives certainly did not see the tides turning in their favor: "I am still 'in shock' and grieving for California's school children. I knew we were moving to the left but I had no idea how fast or how far until your defeat."[153] As a new decade dawned in California, the fate of sex education was hardly certain.

# 6

## SEX EDUCATION AND THE UNMAKING OF ANAHEIM'S "GOLDEN AGE"

On April 10, 1969, the eight men and two women of California's State Board of Education listened to parents, students, and teachers who packed a Sacramento auditorium for several hours to share their polarized views about the place of sex education in public schools. The board members were split on how to consider the unprecedented fervor over what had until recently been an uncontroversial area of curriculum; in the Orange County city of Anaheim, 99 percent of parents had approved sex education as recently as 1967.[1] Dorman Commons, a liberal businessman who had served on the board since 1961, cautioned his colleagues against "being led astray by the amount of mail" opposing sex education, considering the "stock phrases" and generally weak "quality of the criticism and the source of the material."[2] His colleague, physician Thomas G. Harward, was aghast, however, at the intimation that anyone but genuinely and rightfully concerned parents had inspired this groundswell.[3] From as far away as New York City and Kansas, students, parents, educators, and journalists wrote to Californians asking both how to found sex education programs and how to combat existing ones.

After several hours, board president Howard Day had just adjourned the hearing when "two mothers who . . . have traveled over 400 miles . . . all the way from Anaheim," pushed their way to the microphone.[4] Though two other representatives from the growing southland city had already spoken, the women insisted, "We do have information that you haven't heard before."[5] Introduced by Mrs. Raymond L. Burns, a leader of Anaheim's anti-sex education movement, Mrs. Dwight L. Johnson took the stage and regaled the crowd with horror stories about the Family Life and Sex Education (FLSE) course to which her daughters had been briefly exposed at

Oxford Junior High School before she exercised what she felt was her waning parental power to remove them. On "the very first day" of "sex class," Johnson explained, the teacher "talked about homosexuals" and shared "a newspaper clipping of a white man who had been changed into a woman and married his colored chauffeur."[6] After reportedly detailing the procedure for a sex change operation, "the teacher concluded the class by saying that there wasn't anything abnormal or wrong with homosexuals." Johnson appealed to her audience's common sense: "Now I think we all know a little different than that."[7] Even the one class hour the young girl had endured "left her afraid to sleep alone for over a week, and having terrible nightmares when she knocked her lamp to the floor because she dreamed the white lamp was the bride trying to do the sex change on her."[8]

Johnson's sense of what was at stake in the sex education controversy that had convulsed her community ran far deeper than her daughter's sleepless nights, or even her one-time exposure to a litany of perceived sexual perversions. Johnson had immediately withdrawn her daughter from FLSE, but was shocked to find her child "getting sex in almost every class."[9] Offerings from social studies to literature to science were challenging her parental authority and threatening her daughter's modesty and patriotism. The auditorium first erupted in laughter when Johnson recounted how her daughter viewed the film *Rosemary's Baby* in school and then likened its Satanic infant protagonist to President Nixon, but Johnson summarily admonished the crowd: "You might sit here and laugh and think it's quite funny—but I think degrading our president is another thing, especially to the youth of our country."

This new pedagogy also jeopardized students' relationships with their families, Johnson continued, as teachers often told their students outright "that if they had a problem to go to the teacher, not to go home to their parents, because students these days cannot communicate with their parents."[10] To the speakers and many of those who crowded the meeting on that Thursday, sex education had assumed far greater significance than merely a curricular offering in grades seven through twelve. The programs they attacked were indeed more capacious than the curricula many California schools had offered since at least the 1940s, when basic reproductive or venereal disease prevention information was often enfolded into biology or health class. Though they still stressed heterosexual marriage and traditional gender roles, newer family life courses engaged more expansively with "students' values and attitudes about sexuality, family life, and relationships."[11] Clearly, sex education in Anaheim and California at large was becoming emblematic of the sea changes in authority and morality that characterized the 1960s.

Unpacking the Anaheim case helps explain what made sex education such a political lightning rod in communities across the state during the late 1960s and reveals how this particular city came to be understood a bastion of Orange County conservatism.[12] Considering this battle in state context, particularly in juxtaposition to the equally heated controversy in San Mateo, uncovers specific and mounting doubts about the appropriate role of public education and teachers' authority, particularly vis-à-vis the family.[13] In tracing the origins of Anaheim's bitter debate and the distinctly anti-communist idiom in which it was waged, this chapter shows how closely intertwined were questions of sexuality, morality, education, and nation, as well as the limitations of the rightward turn in American political culture. In Anaheim, the "Antis" constituted a highly "vocal and vigorous" minority, but they were a minority nonetheless.[14] By 1970, FLSE was dismantled, but students were beginning to voice loud skepticism of the Antis and their characterization of sex education as the "devil's work." Even the controversial FLSE program, with its focus on heterosexual marriage and silence on sexual pleasure, began to seem tame to youth coming of age in the era of the Free Speech Movement and the sexual revolution. All over the state, and increasingly the nation, sex education was becoming convenient shorthand for the troubling redefinitions of social relationships.

## The Anaheim Controversy

Amid the citrus groves, tangle of freeways, and commercial development that characterized Anaheim and California's southland, the battle over FLSE was already in full swing by the time the state board convened in April 1969. Educators in Anaheim had become so inured to the fierce rhetoric of their local debate that when Superintendent Paul Cook's secretary received a vicious phone call alleging her promiscuity and threatening her life, she calmly typed up a memo for her boss: "Abusive telephone call at 1:00 p.m., 12/9/1968; I didn't lose my cool."[15]

This phone message was saved in a stack of correspondence addressing the FLSE program being taught across the district in grades seven through twelve. Few letters supported FLSE, and most adopted the caller's menacing tone. One, neatly typed, revealed the depths of Anaheim's political conflict over the program:

The Russians said they would "bury us" . . . They are succeeding wildly . . . They manage to get people like you in as head of the schools.

Then they advocate all types of new programs in the schools that will brainwash the children's minds and eventually render them mad and insane.[16]

Sex education, the writer charged, was the vehicle for this Russian subterfuge, and citizens were preparing to use force "to eliminate all these rotten . . . slimes and try to get the country back to sanity. . . . The persons responsible for introducing this sex program into the schools are sadists and sex perverts, and should be lined up against a stone wall and shot. . . . Abolish the sex programs from the schools. Otherwise—you are going to face eternity at any time." The letter was signed "Association for Decency in California."[17] These threats had become commonplace by December 1968, when the Anaheim FLSE program, celebrated since its formal introduction in 1965 as one of the most progressive in the nation, was regularly smeared as a distinctly communist menace to children's moral and civic health. Since the summer, local activists in this Orange County city, home to Disneyland, had been congregating in homes and hotel rooms, screening cautionary films for the public and barraging the local press and school board with letters establishing a link between FLSE and a communist plot to brainwash Anaheim's schoolchildren.[18] Within a year and a half, this vocal opposition would "water down" FLSE until it was unrecognizable, take over the school board, and force the superintendent to resign.[19]

The opposition's success, and the vitriol of its attack, is particularly surprising because sex education had been taught in Anaheim since the 1940s, when preventing venereal disease was its primary aim. While a smaller controversy flared in 1963 over a class watching a movie addressing masturbation, none of the opponents in this earlier battle portrayed the threat of sex education as anything more than impropriety. It certainly was not the harbinger of communist revolution that protestors in 1968 discerned. In fact, 92 percent of parents polled after this 1963 protest supported expanding sex education district wide. Encouraged by this overwhelming backing, Superintendent Cook convened a citizens' advisory committee to develop a more robust program, which was implemented in classrooms that reached 32,000 students in 1965.[20] By 1968, the curriculum had been published nationally and commended by the president of SIECUS.[21] Why, then, in this Southern California city, where sex education had long been a part of the curriculum, did the district secretary receive threatening phone calls? What unleashed the onslaught of correspondence and activism?

## Family, Industry, and the School: The Anaheim Ideal

Anaheim's sex education story begins in the 1950s. Located in the heart of Orange County, the city benefited handsomely from the postwar economic relocation from Northeastern and Midwestern cities to western suburbs, growing from 15,000 residents in 1950 to nearly 170,000 in 1970.[22] As Midwesterners followed jobs and ex-servicemen returned to take advantage of cheap land, low housing costs, and low interest rates, Anaheim became the fastest growing city in the fastest growing county in the nation in the 1950s, earning longtime local teacher Louise Booth's estimation as "our golden age."[23] The arrival of Disneyland in 1955 cast its own aura over the community, bolstering local businesses as legions of fun-seekers flocked to Anaheim.[24]

Disney selected Anaheim because its culture seemed particularly suited to the Disneyland idyll, already removed from the America park-goers were purportedly escaping, as well as from sleazier East-coast amusement venues. Mass entertainment was familiar to the area, as was a certain political cast. Nearby Knott's Berry Farm proprietor Walter Knott was a staunch conservative, and the farm not only boasted a large collection of antipornography and anti-communist literature but also hosted Republican Party events.[25] Commercialized fun parks with a patriotic sheen thus shaped 1950s Anaheim culture, dominated by larger-than-life Disneyland.

Local cultural events reinforced conventional morality. Anaheim's Halloween parade celebrated a mix of traditional gender roles, industry, and patriotism, featuring a beauty pageant funded entirely by local businesses.[26] The parade's founding purpose was "partly to show civic pride, but mostly to redirect the energies of local youngsters" who might otherwise get into mischief.[27] In 1961, for example, parade organizers co-opted a common prank of vandalizing windows, as local businessmen provided materials to decorate their storefronts.[28] Ironically, a *Gazette* columnist bemoaned the passivity this fostered: "[Everything] must be supervised and the kids must be coached by some appointed official. . . . They don't even know how to . . . get into some real old-fashioned harmless mischief."[29]

This ethos of business, anti-communism, and social conservatism also permeated the rapidly growing school system and commercial community. Kwikset Locks cultivated an especially close connection with the Anaheim Union High School District (AUHSD), co-sponsoring "Public School Week" to celebrate the link between schools and business, and "Industrial Progress Week" to recognize Anaheim enterprise "funneling money from all over the free world."[30] While the unity of civics, industry, and education is clear, the Kwikset fashion show and "Queen of Anaheim Industry" beauty pageant reflected the increasing numbers of women leaving homemaking for industry.[31] At the Kwikset fashion show, female workers modeled "styles for women in industry and business," though pageant organizers were quick to remind their potential audience that bridal and children's clothing would figure prominently in the event, reinforcing traditional family values.[32]

Anaheim schools in the 1950s and early 1960s fostered conformity and discouraged and defused rebellion. The city's cold warrior culture was never far from the classroom; both within and beyond Anaheim's multiplying schools, students too embraced the values of enterprise and anti-communism. It was an era in which the professed attitudes of teenagers appear to have been roughly the same as those of adults, and in which rapid growth and social change had yet to disrupt the consensus and stability within the schools. In many California schools in the early 1960s, administrators and pupils actively worked to promote traditional gender roles. Girls' dress codes elicited considerable coverage in the student press, and boys quoted concurred with the strictures, remarking that "girls should be able to wear anything they want, but not to school."[33] Boys' dress codes, by contrast, went unmentioned.[34] Most clubs and physical education classes were sex segregated. Dances and pageants naming a king and queen were commonplace, and exclusively mother-daughter teas and dessert parties were often held at AUHSD facilities.[35] Gender reversal was also part of school festivities; frequent Sadie Hawkins Day celebrations assured that any sexual aggressiveness of female students would be channeled into their "act[ing] like perfect gentlemen" under supervision, and boys competed to be "Mr. Irresistible" in a mock pageant.[36] Delineating the differences between the sexes effectively sanctified existing gender relations; at the same time, these reversals subtly portended the revolutionary shifts of the late 1960s.

Students actively participated in this process. The school-approved, student-run "Beatnik Ball" vividly evidences this mode of taming rebellion through co-optation, whether or not the students were aware of it.[37] In billing this school-sanctioned costume party as "the coolest, weirdest, and swingingest dance of the year," students and faculty constructed beatnik counterculture as a temporary masquerade, merely a foreign identity with which Anaheim students experimented under adult regulation. Anaheim students in the early 1960s seemed not to resist too strenuously. The student newspaper sternly admonished even mildly unseemly behavior by among students: holding hands in the halls, "munching" in class, and dancing too close at school functions.[38] Some shared their parents' anti-communism outright, as revealed in an editorial correction to a quote in the newspaper. A junior had described her reasons for learning Russian as "to get along with [Russia and] . . . understand its language, its people, and its customs." The student editors, however, restated her motive as "to combat Communism,"[39] which suggests that the Cold War may have concerned some Anaheim students as much as their parents. This is hardly surprising, considering that by 1961 an expressly anti-communist curriculum was proposed for adoption district-wide.[40] The same year, the AUHSD excused students to attend international right-wing figure Fred Schwarz's weeklong School of Anti-Communism; over seven thousand Anaheim children participated in his Youth Day.[41] Planned locally at Knott's Berry Farm and hosted at the Disneyland Hotel and Anaheim High auditorium once the hotel reached capacity, the School vividly embodied the aligned anti-communist aims of education and business, Disney-style, in Anaheim.[42]

The sheen of industrial prosperity, profitable fantasy diversions, and ideological unity did not encompass everyone in the region, even in these early years. Partly due to its racial and socioeconomic homogeneity, Orange County in the 1950s and early 1960s is often viewed as monolithically conservative.[43] Yet by the 1960s, after national media attention to the black freedom struggles, at least some locals held racially progressive opinions. A *Gazette* columnist, for instance, condemned the acquittal of black youth Emmett Till's white murderers as typical of the "southern way of *death!*" One former student recalled that when one of the high school's two black students ran onto the football field, "everyone clapped really hard . . . [it was as if] everyone was prejudiced and trying not to be."[44] Susan Penton, a former student of Smedley High, in relatively diverse Santa Ana, similarly recalled that white, Mexican, and black students "almost killed each other" when the school was integrated in 1956, but that "by ninth grade, we had learned to appreciate each other's differences." During a football game, one of Smedley's "absolutely gorgeous" male cheerleaders, "who was one of the most popular boys in school" and also "half black and half white," found the opposing team unwilling to shake his hand. Penton recalls that the Smedley cheerleaders responded "in a true united front, by turning backs to their side of the field." "You could hear the cheers from our bleachers for miles," Penton wrote in 2007, alluding again to a certain racial tolerance infrequently ascribed to Orange County.[45]

Whether or not their cheers and applause were genuine, the fact that at least some students perceived that projecting an image of racial tolerance was socially necessary suggests a nascent social conscience that would flower in the late 1960s. At a moment when racist backlash against *Brown v. Board of Education* ran high, such solidarity across color lines reveals some political diversity within Anaheim's conservative polity. In a sense, these racially tolerant attitudes of the 1950s and early 1960s might be considered to be commensurate with their anti-communism; a popular tactic of Soviet propaganda was to decry American racism, to which the United States responded by trumpeting its (often exaggerated) progress in racial equality.[46] Yet by the late 1960s, anti-communist rhetoric around sex education intensified, and so did racist discourse. Racial progressivism might have bolstered anti-communism diplomatically, but on the ground in Anaheim, the two were not inextricably intertwined.

Despite the droves of students who appeared at the School of Anti-Communism, adults also hosted a surprising number of church and secular events celebrating "international understanding" and "world community" and sent many children to study abroad.[47] The independence of the AUHSD, fabled or actual, was also defended by community members wary of encroaching libertarian newspapers "dedicated to . . . sack[ing] the public schools . . . [through] doctrine and dogma."[48] Similarly, the *Gazette* bemoaned the promiscuous use of "communist" to mean "anyone who doesn't agree with a particular line of thinking."[49] Perhaps most salient to attitudes about sexuality, a seven-month pregnant salutatorian addressed the crowd at Anaheim High's 1961 commencement. The expectant father, also graduating, years later described his parents' bitter reproach. Yet bestowing this very public honor on an obviously pregnant and unmarried teenager suggests that in the early 1960s a significant segment of the community accepted that premarital sex might not be categorically ruinous.[50] Such examples represent unquestionable fissures in a generally conservative cultural foundation and help explain why a progressive sex education curriculum could have been initially welcomed. By the late 1960s, however, the program's vociferous opponents would make it difficult for some to see sex education as anything but the vanguard of a communist takeover jeopardizing the community's essence. Still, the Anaheim example is not merely an instance of an ascendant Right; rather, the voices of the students and the status of the opponents as only a(n albeit vocal and well-organized) minority suggests that the Anaheim case is just as revelatory of a consolidating sexual, and educational, progressivism.

In light of the 1968 battle, Anaheim has become so intertwined with the reaction to sex education that the fracas over FLSE's implementation almost seems inevitable. But in 1963, the district had a popular mandate to expand its sex education program, which raises questions about the depths of the community's conservative politics.[51] In 1962, when a parent group angered by a film addressing masturbation and discussions of premarital sex demanded abolishing the whole curriculum, the AUHSD re-examined its sporadic offerings.[52] Though sex education was temporarily suspended, the citizens' committee appointed by Superintendent Cook determined by survey that over 90 percent of parents favored expanding the courses, and supportive letters poured into the district and press.[53] In this earlier battle, opponents merely considered the program inappropriate for discussing sex. There was no mention of communist subversion lurking within lessons on dating etiquette and the dangers of petting when the newly designed FLSE courses were introduced in several schools in 1965. The courses met little resistance until 1968, when FLSE catalyzed the virulent reaction that gained Anaheim national and scholarly attention.

The reaction was fierce and gained surprisingly widespread traction, although it was fulminated primarily by a highly vocal minority encouraged by national groups such as the Christian Crusade. In Anaheim, the Citizens Committee of California (CCC), originally convened to support Barry Goldwater's 1964 candidacy, formed the backbone of the local movement. Proponents of sex education attributed the success of the opposition to "really big people" in outside groups such as the John Birch Society and pointed to "irrational voices" who generated "a tremendous amount of mail" that served to drown out "the quality of support that family life education is receiving from most people."[54] The John Birch Society convened a special group –the Movement to Restore Decency (MOTOREDE)—to battle sex education, and generated enough local support to pack local, county, and state school board meetings with "cheering ultra-conservatives" and to inspire "tides of conservative votes" for school board members who not only attacked sex education but also progressive curricula such as the history textbook Land of the Free, which espoused racial tolerance.[55] Conservatives insisted opposition was homegrown despite polls that showed Anaheim's overwhelming support for the programs. Still, multiple state school board members were skeptical of supporting improving sex education rather than prohibiting instruction.[56] Historians have often explained the Anaheim controversy as having occurred only because such national groups manipulated local personages and circumstances to advance their agenda, an analysis that overlooks the interplay of distinctly local and national factors.[57]

A surviving set of 1965 FLSE course evaluations enthusiastically celebrated breaking the silence around sexuality, suggesting the tensions that would climax in 1968 and providing a rare window into how the sexual revolution resonated in Orange County. The evaluations celebrated the instructor's "frankness," his "talking to them like adults," and his warnings against premarital sexuality. "If we wouldn't of [sic] had this, I think I might have been sorry later. And I mean this." Several echoed one girl who "wish[ed] with all [her] heart that they could have had this course, say, three years ago, because I . . . would be a much happier girl today."[58] Yet a few responses portended the new sexual mores of the late 1960s. One male student, for example, commented that focusing on "getting a nice girl" was pointless when "there are so many around that are ready, willing, and able, and already have."[59] Reflecting back decades later, another former FLSE pupil recalled that she and her friends had disdained masturbation, though not for its sinfulness: "It seemed so ho-hum in the feast of sexual activities there was to choose from."[60]

These student reactions imply that FLSE was not as progressive, the community not as parochial, and the response not as monolithic as the later 1968–1969 furor implied. Most notable is the overwhelming parental endorsement of discussing sexuality at school. By 1969, journalist Mary Breasted commented that "conservative sexual attitudes seem, in fact, so common in Anaheim . . . that it is difficult to understand how any . . . superintendent could have for a moment entertained the thought of putting sex education into his public schools."[61] At the same time, the *Los Angeles Times* ran an editorial acknowledging the attacks on sex education were "widespread both at the local and state government level," but deriding these efforts as "silly" and wondering if groups such as the Antis would next suggest "burning the Encyclopedia Britannica."[62] In this first battle, however, the broad support for FLSE and the student reactions suggest that at least until the mid-1960s, the ideals of the sex educators and of Anaheim's citizens were largely consonant. By 1968, the curriculum was effectively unchanged, but the debate it sparked portrayed an Anaheim split along newly jagged fault lines barely discernible just five years before.

The controversy in Anaheim can be properly understood only in the context of this changed world of 1968, when a prosperous sun-drenched city built on family entertainment, staunch anti-communism, and racial homogeneity began to see the effects of a liberalized and sexualized culture on its newsstands, its thoroughfares, and—worst of all—in its classrooms. (See figure 6.1.)

FIGURE 6.1 The palm-tree-lined streets of suburban Anaheim in 1970. "Residential street, Anaheim," August 28, 1970. Reprinted with permission of the Anaheim Heritage Center at the Anaheim Public Library.

## The Emerging Conflict Over Sex Education: National and Local Contexts

Despite an earlier consensus on sex education, local activist Eleanor Howe was able to attract enough opponents in 1968—known as the "Antis"— to hijack several meetings of the district's board of trustees and demand special sessions to address FLSE, which they decried as a mechanism of communist takeover. The Antis' success in stoking the anti-communist flames five years after the first battle revealed how much more was at stake than sex education. Local developments alerted Anaheim conservatives to the darker consequences of the era's rapid expansion, and this heightened alarm made any trespass upon conventional morality, such as discussing sexuality with children, appear doubly threatening. The opponents' complaints became shriller and more urgent, and the ears they fell upon far more receptive.

Rapid growth contributed to a breakdown in civic unity and to the sense of urgency among certain citizens. By 1962, Anaheim stretched to accommodate nearly 130,000 residents, and large public entertainment venues continued to fuel expansion.[63] Local civic and business leaders leveraged Disneyland's success in developing the Anaheim Stadium (1966) and Convention Center (1967), which along with La Palma Park hosted AUHSD functions.[64] Yet the strong bonds between school, business, and the Anaheim community were fraying. Anaheim's squeaky-clean culture no longer represented such a pleasant continuum, as the city was surrounded by a "glitter gulch" of prostitution and petty crime by the mid-1960s. In 1967, Disney executives secured the "magic kingdom" with a zoning ordinance prohibiting buildings high enough to see into the park.[65] Other public arenas did not erect such ramparts, and ominous signs appeared: the stadium banned rock concerts when marijuana sprouted in the outfield, and sex education opponent John Steinbacher claimed students often "ran around in the Stadium having sex."[66] Perhaps the most symbolic intrusion was in 1970, when Disneyland was barricaded with a riot-trained, armed police force intended to check the "unauthorized invasion" of the Yippie Pow-Wow, advertised across the nation with 100,000 leaflets. While only three hundred yippies appeared "to liberate Minnie Mouse, have free rein of the park, and infiltrate Tom Sawyer Island," such an appeal speaks to Disney's symbolism of older social mores increasingly out of sync with changes afoot in Anaheim and nationwide.[67]

Local schools also reflected tensions of growth. Anaheim teacher and local historian Louise Booth cites "the estrangement of educators from the business and social world of Anaheim" in the late 1960s as evidence of the AUHSD's downfall.[68] Defensively, the district changed Berkeley Junior High's name to Apollo Junior High when the University of California campus four hundred miles to the north became associated with student rebellion, but neither students nor teachers embraced conservatism wholeheartedly.[69] Fifteen high schools had opened in the 1960s, attracting an influx of younger teachers, some themselves "products of the rebellious 1960s."[70] Disrespectful of the "accepted order" and brainwashed from "long emphasis on the 'self,'" these teachers, Booth argued, held beliefs at odds with the older generation and upset traditional schoolhouse hierarchies.[71] When newer teachers unionized, older teachers spurned them for abdicating individual responsibility in favor of "groupthink."[72] Curricular changes such as the introduction of creative writing and foreign language classes, however, were most pronounced, due to Superintendent Cook's progressive leadership.[73] Flexible scheduling allowed students to design their studies based on individual interest, and angered critics charged that teenagers would "schedule themselves out of an education." Already radical for emphasizing students' freedom of choice, flexible scheduling sparked even more criticism when it foundered, permitting unmotivated teachers and students alike to shirk their workloads; one former student loved that he could now "surf every single day."[74] The social order of the school as it had been known in the 1950s and early 1960s was disintegrating from within, and progressive curricula seemed to accelerate this undoing.

This instability also disrupted the gender binary that had been so carefully nurtured in Anaheim's schools. Participation in sex-segregated clubs waned, the first female principal took office, and—as Booth lamented—boys' and girls' fashions were increasingly indistinguishable.[75] Students recognized how the fledgling FLSE program, with its mixed classes and frank discussions, vividly embodied this trend. One high school journalist justified FLSE: "Divorce rates and statistics on illegitimate children . . . prove that the courses were needed. . . . Discussions of everything, from premarital sex to homosexuality to venereal disease to the role of the father in marriage were needed . . . [to drop] the inhibitions of a puritanical society."[76] Teenage mother Priscilla Feld welcomed the dramatic discursive shift during her high school years in the 1960s: "I had teachers and counselors ridicule me. . . . Then the free love movement came along and everybody was talking about sex."[77] These transformations were particularly troubling to many adults when manifest in their children. While Booth derisively called her students "the most pathetic, uninterested teenagers to ever warm a chair," local newspapers exposed deeper anxiety.[78] Through the 1960s, articles about youth delinquency filled the Anaheim press.[79] While journalists tended to paint the national picture as disastrous, they attributed Anaheim's youth rebellion to a handful of perpetrators among an otherwise wholesome population. For example, a national newswire story on juvenile lawlessness stressed the ubiquity of degeneracy in "the school room, the living room, the court room and . . . streets." An Anaheim editorial on the same topic emphasized that "the majority of our youth are proving themselves eminently qualified to assume future world leadership."[80] Thus, despite ominous signals of youth rebellion at home, local leaders reassured themselves that the "fine young teen-agers" of their suburban enclave were distinct from a small "undesirable minority."[81]

With the schools apparently falling victim to questionable values, the family assumed far greater importance as a bulwark against immorality. The press primarily recommended stronger parental discipline. "If they ran this country the way I run my home, there'd be a lot less trouble," read one father's declaration to his cowering wife and child in a newspaper cartoon; the serious implication was that strengthening family hierarchy would counterbalance the dissipation of the larger society.[82] "Points for Parents" cartoons modeling effective methods of enforcing rules for teenagers dotted the *Bulletin*, emphasizing how to appear less authoritarian while exacting greater obedience.[83]

Anaheim teenagers recall a growing chasm between teenage behavior and parental morality. Priscilla Feld, who married her boyfriend under duress after becoming pregnant at fifteen, explained that while "everyone had sex . . . adults had their heads in the sand." Sexual mores were changing among youth, but many parents clung to an increasingly obsolete model of normalcy: "They owned a home, their kids were in sports or cheerleaders, so all must be well," Feld commented.[84] Another teenage mother, Melissa Finch, sensed her generation was "breaking the mold" that prescribed their parents' behavior.[85]

The Orange County enclave was hardly immune to national trends: between 1966 and 1968, the number of young unwed mothers reporting to the Orange County welfare adoption department climbed even faster than the national average, and by 1969, plans for the county's first home for unmarried mothers were underway.[86] Teenage out-of-wedlock births symbolized a threat to the idea that sexuality and reproduction—and discussions thereof—were to remain within the family. While some parents attempted to maintain a disintegrating code of silence, ignorance about sex and contraception in an increasingly sexualized milieu arguably contributed to this rise in unwed teenage pregnancy. FLSE's candor in the classroom, while introduced in large part to remedy such issues, seemed to a vocal minority simply another attack on the dissolving family. Its frank engagement with nonreproductive sexuality—premarital sex, masturbation, homosexuality—seemed not only to co-opt the family's domain over these matters, but also to condone nonreproductive, out-of-wedlock merely by mentioning it.[87]

In the midst of these tensions, an attempt to smear Republican US senator Thomas Kuchel as homosexual underscored the increasing reaction among certain citizens to the sexualizing society. In office from 1953 until 1968, Anaheim native Kuchel was a pillar of the community. Founders and owners of Orange County's oldest newspaper, *The Anaheim Gazette*, he and his family were often honored locally.[88] By 1965, however, Kuchel, a champion of civil rights, was losing favor among increasingly conservative Southern Californians. When Kuchel failed to support Barry Goldwater in 1964 and denounced right-wing extremism, the Los Angeles County Young Republicans condemned his "socialistic voting record and left-wing philosophy."[89] On the heels of this ostracism came a press release implicating Kuchel in a "sordid government homosexual sodomy incident in 1950" and a subsequent fifteen-year cover-up to hide the news from constituents.[90] Because of Kuchel's social standing, the architects of this press release knew that the blow would reverberate within Anaheim's already volatile climate. If the upstanding Kuchel exhibited such profligacy, it seemed Anaheim's way of life was threatened right to its core.

The press release claiming to expose Kuchel and the ensuing cover-up speak passionately to the Cold War-era association between homosexuality (and sexual deviance in general) and communist subversion. Fingering Kuchel as covertly homosexual fit seamlessly into the image conservatives painted of him as unpatriotic and dishonest. It also evinces a growing distrust of the federal government for withholding such information from the populace.[91] The press release linked the Kuchel cover-up to another complaint against the legal system: laxity in sentencing child molesters. The most recent national "sex crime panic" had receded by 1955, but the persistence of homophobic politics explains how this group of conservative Republicans dissatisfied with the country's overall moral degeneration effectively exploited Kuchel's purported debasement.[92] This constellation of associations crystallized in the case of Senator Kuchel. Both his dismissal from the party and the sense among the writers of the press release of the resonance these allegations would have in Anaheim suggest that the populace was becoming more politically conservative in response to sexualized threats to the moorings of their social order. It was in this climate, and in the very same month, that the revised FLSE program was introduced in Anaheim classrooms.

Life in burgeoning Anaheim was becoming more closely linked to national issues, which was encouraged in many ways by citizens. Notably, the success of the economic drivers of Disneyland, the Stadium, and the Convention Center depended on a consistent flow of outsiders.[93] Local newspapers in the 1960s drastically expanded their purview from regional to national coverage. The nation was changing, however, and as the stable and prosperous "good sixties" early in the decade intensified into the hedonistic and radical "bad sixties," Anaheim's adults, particularly the small and vocal cadre that would oppose FLSE so vehemently, construed their conception of the good life as increasingly at odds with social, political, and cultural national currents.[94]

The turning point in conservative Orange County, and Anaheim in particular, was arguably in 1964, when Republican Barry Goldwater's loss to Lyndon B. Johnson crushed his far-right supporters and signified fissures in the GOP. Goldwater's loss was acutely felt in Anaheim, where citizens had organized in living rooms and schools to support his campaign. The CCC was one such group. After the defeat, the CCC turned inward to fight defensive local battles, most famously in 1968–1969, when it led the fight against FLSE. Thus, Goldwater's defeat helps explain why opposition to sex education crystallized in the late 1960s, rather than in the earlier battle, and why it garnered such intensity in Anaheim. Johnson's election was painful evidence to Anaheim conservatives that its vision was at odds with that of the nation. Alarmed citizens forsook national political activism in favor of defending Anaheim from what they construed as encroaching moral erosion.

Out of the Goldwater campaign emerged a decidedly regional and newly bitter antipathy in Anaheim toward the East Coast. Since the flush 1950s, western enthusiasts who came to Anaheim (including Walt Disney) for its regenerative opportunities and "gold rush atmosphere" had championed their distinctively western lifestyle.[95] An advertisement for the California-based Union Oil Company conveys this early western boosterism. An urbane "lady from Boston" beams at a tank of gasoline, having learned "what so many other former Easterners have discovered—that Royal 76 is the West's most powerful premium." The copy concludes, "The lady from Boston just learned it. The West knew it all along."[96] That this message of western savvy and East-coast oblivion was considered resonant with Anaheim readers suggests that at least a subtle contest between East and West characterized the populace's emergent worldview, especially after Goldwater's defeat. He had relentlessly stoked the image of his opponent, New Yorker Nelson Rockefeller, as a distant elitist soft on communism and clueless about California concerns, famously commenting that the country might be best served "if we could just saw off the Eastern Seaboard and let it float off to sea."[97] Johnson's victory was thus a symbolic blow to the ideals Goldwater personified and reverberated loudly in Anaheim.

The national signals on both coasts were alarming, by any standards. Upstate at Berkeley, free speech activism had evolved into the "filthy speech" movement, forcing "nearly everyone in California," according to one historian, "to re-examine their views about morality and censorship."[98] More broadly, between 1957 and 1967, the US Supreme Court overturned several obscenity regulations, effectively sanctioning unabashed portrayal of sexuality in literature and the media.[99] A growing singles culture, championing sexual autonomy outside of marriage, further challenged family stability. Helen Gurley Brown's *Sex and the Single Girl* (1962), a guidebook for the sexually and economically independent woman, became a bestseller. Bars, apartment complexes, and dating services geared to the unattached, sexually free life of modern singles sprung up.[100] Not only had the carefully guarded silence around sexuality been shattered, but so had the exclusive connection between sexuality and the nuptial home.

The national landscape threatened more than family cohesion and sexual modesty. The civil rights movement, to which progressive racial attitudes in Anaheim had been somewhat sympathetic earlier on, had turned militant toward the end of the 1960s. While many historians concur that the ethnic free-dom struggles "spurred the idealism, egalitarianism, and rights-consciousness that . . . challenged social relations," the residents of Anaheim did not fully share in this experience. For one, the population included virtually no African Americans.[101] Moreover, the proximity of the 1965 Watts riots frightened many Anaheim residents to the south. Jessica Wendell, home for the summer from college, recalled her parents forbidding her to go out lest the rioting reach Orange County.[102] Priscilla Feld's parents "had moved from Compton to Anaheim for exactly that reason—my parents were terrified of blacks."[103] Race deepened and exposed generational rifts: David Wells knew his mother was "bigoted against blacks . . . and we fought about it."[104] More commonly, the dramatic scenes of racial violence punctured the bubble around their homo-geneous southland city.[105]

## Imagining Sex Education

Anaheim residents who viewed the national culture as anathema to their hopes and dreams felt besieged. As the US Supreme Court's definition of obscenity narrowed, conservative impresario Walter Knott cultivated one of Southern California's largest collections of antipornography literature.[106] As strip clubs abounded in northern California, Anaheim's only topless venue was slated to become an evangelical church.[107] Similarly, opponents of FLSE in 1968 construed the curriculum as a vehicle for powerful outsiders to turn their children's loyalties away from family and country to godless communism and sexual license.

Notions about race shaped ideas about sex education. Certain residents of homogeneous Anaheim perceived African Americans as yet another external peril linked to communism and moral erosion, an idea propagated by many national right-wing pamphlets that fanned fears about a commu-nist revolution "in which Negroes are to play a major role."[108] One Anaheim parent wrote to Superintendent Rafferty to complain about the explicit sex education curriculum, but spent most of her letter decrying a visit to local Loara High School from a Black Student Union member. "My children will NOT be mere pieces of meat in a racial stew," she declared.[109] Echoing Mrs. Johnson's race and class concerns about her daughter learning of a white woman marrying her African American chauffeur, fellow Anaheim mother Jan Pippenger substantiated her opposition with several unverifi-able anecdotes linking racial mixing. According to Pippenger, the lights in an Anaheim FLSE class were darkened, "wild African music" played, and students experienced "strange sexual feelings."[110] In Ohio, she relayed, black and white children were forced to dance together in sex education class.[111] This was especially alarming, she explained, because communists planned to "use the colored people to get things all stirred up" before the revolution.[112] Such apocryphal "depravity narratives" were ubiquitous in the opponents' rhetoric and always located the fabled transgression in the east; these dubious anecdotes suggest the affinity of racial, sexual, economic, and geographical "others" to communism in the conservative imagination.[113] Their falsity hardly mitigated their damage. Opposition leader Townsend acknowledged that even if "it didn't happen, it certainly was out as happening, and was being run around the country and talked about on radio and TV. In the minds of the people, it happened."[114]

These constructions of an outside threat were propagated by a passionate minority in Anaheim. To only a committed few were such menaces a rallying cry. Without a medium to convey this alarm, the fervor of CCC activists such as Townsend, Pippenger, and Howe might have foundered at a Goldwater coffee klatch. The ultraconservative *Anaheim Bulletin* provided precisely that bullhorn. Purchased in 1962 by libertarian R. C. Hoiles, in 1968 the *Bulletin* began its attack on FLSE with coverage of a local sex education conference, described as "a clandestine meeting of sexologists."[115] For two years, newspapermen Sam Campbell and John Steinbacher barraged Anaheim, six issues a week, with damning coverage of the FLSE debates. Defenders of FLSE claimed that the *Bulletin* was as responsible for destroying the program as the opponents themselves; ousted Superintendent Cook called its coverage "as venomous and distorted a series of attacks in a local newspaper as you could *ever* wish for."[116]

In her tireless fact-checking, Mary Breasted found in the *Bulletin* many misrepresentations and exaggerations of the district's actions and of the FLSE curriculum. For instance, Cook's decree to allow only parents of FLSE students to audit lessons garnered the headline "COOK BARS PARENTS FROM SEX CLASSES."[117] In the *Bulletin* and elsewhere, opponents only referred to FLSE as "sex instruction," insisting it was a class in sexual technique. School nurse and FLSE architect Sally Williams explained her helplessness: "Newspapers have you over a barrel. They ask you something that is totally outrageous, something that never did happen, never would happen, never could happen, and then they say, 'she denied it.'"[118] The well-organized Antis cleverly used the *Bulletin's* resources and reach to put FLSE advocates on the rhetorical defensive. Townsend, for example, also covered the Anaheim battle for the regional newspapers, drumming up wider support.[119] The authenticity of these accusations was meaningless, and the stories took on a life of their own. Still, while FLSE proponents portrayed the *Bulletin* as amplifying the protests of very few, the paper's financial health and wide circulation speaks to a spreading conservative sensibility.

By the opening of the second FLSE battle in 1968, the *Bulletin* had seized upon "organizations" as threatening individual freedom and misdirecting loyalties. The 1964 establishment of SIECUS, expressly to disseminate scientific information about sexuality, fit seamlessly into the familiar configuration of a large institution with a nefarious agenda, embodied most vividly in the Anaheim press by the United Nations and its supposed designs for a "one-world child" devoid of family, spiritual, or patriotic allegiance. Nationally distributed films such as *Pavlov's Children* and pamphlets such as "Is the Schoolhouse the Proper Place to Teach Raw Sex?" relentlessly hammered at connections between sex education and internationalism and their nightmarish consequences (see figure 6.2).[120] The link between the United Nations and the FLSE was tenuous. SIECUS, however, provided a perfect target for opponents convinced of sex education's role in a larger conspiracy.[121]

Founded by Mary Calderone, previously of Planned Parenthood, SIECUS endeavored with frank discussion to clear the fog of guilt and ignorance surrounding sexuality. In the process, conservative circles labeled Calderone a "dirty old lady" leading the charge to pervert American children. To opponents, encouraging children to make "rational and responsible choices about their personal lives" removed sex education from the responsibility of parents. Furthermore, "integrating sexuality into our view of what constitutes whole and complete personhood" challenged the notion that sexual identity was only properly awakened upon marriage.[122] Breasted, however, pointed to certain unmistakably conservative strands in SIECUS's ideology, stating that "[they] were also interested in controlling the sexual behavior of the young . . . and every bit as interested in preserving the conventional morality as were the Antis."[123] SIECUS was radical only in marshaling science, rather than silence, to the conventional end of discouraging extramarital sexuality.

Nevertheless, SIECUS proved "a brilliant choice for a new target of the Right."[124] Led by an aristocratic "East Coaster" educated at elite schools and trained at Planned Parenthood, SIECUS was a top-down, New York-based group. If these traits were insufficient to raise the hackles of those who believed sexual issues were best silenced, large organizations were inherently suspect, and anything eastern was vaguely corrupt, SIECUS co-founder Isadore Rubin was also an alleged communist. When Anaheim school nurse Sally Williams joined as a consultant in 1968 and co-published a version of

FIGURE 6.2 The cover of the bestselling anti-sex education pamphlet "Is the Schoolhouse the Proper Place to Teach Raw Sex?" by Gordon V. Drake of the Christian Crusade, 1968. Reprinted with permission of the James D. Bales Library, Special Collections, University of Arkansas, Fayetteville.

FLSE with a SIECUS associate director, opponents who had been drawing far-fetched links to the United Nations suddenly had tangible evidence of sex education's bond to large, unfamiliar organizations. That Williams and her local staff had designed FLSE well before SIECUS's establishment—explicitly explained in the preface to the 1968 volume—meant little to opponents, who fabricated relationships between Williams, SIECUS, and FLSE.[125] Conspiracy theorists were not the only ones to voice such qualms. Rafferty staunchly opposed SIECUS's open discussion model, describing "sex delinquency" among youth "as an offense against both God and man."[126]

Statewide, this vilification of SIECUS reverberated with sufficient power that in response to public pressure, the legislature prohibited (Senate Bill 413) "SIECUS materials" in sex education classrooms in April 1969. Considering how fervently sex education opponents argued that the state inserted itself too vigorously into the schoolhouse, the fact that they invoked greater state power to limit sex education speaks to the profound threat they felt these programs represented. Particularly since SIECUS produced no classroom materials independently, the ruling, and to some extent the demand for it, was symbolic.[127] The fury channeled at SIECUS had little to do with its actual links to Anaheim's FLSE or that in place elsewhere; the organization had merely become a repository for venom directed at sex education and its associated evils.[128] Calderone, aware of the particular vitriol channeled toward her and SIECUS in this region, wrote to a correspondent with a perceptible shudder, "I shall never, ever, move to Southern California."[129]

## The Second Battle, 1968–1969

The stars began to align for the Antis in late summer 1968. Since the curriculum's 1965 introduction, 99 percent of seventh to twelfth graders had enrolled in the four-and-a-half-week program without incident. After attending every board of trustees meeting flanked by several parents, Eleanor Howe was granted permission to hold an October "workshop" to present the opposition's perspective. Over the three hours in a packed auditorium, the shape of the debate over the following year and a half became clear. The Antis had assembled a full program: fulminations against SIECUS, outside "experts" attesting FLSE was brainwashing by a sexualized society, and apocalyptic promises of children surreptitiously receiving gonorrhea treatments and abortions while contraceptives were dispensed in the school cafeteria.[130] The alternatives they proposed ranged from total silence to supplementing minimal scientific information with a heavy dose of Christian moralism—preferably at home or in church.

The CCC, perhaps through contacts from its Goldwater days, recruited supportive speakers from all over California. Senator John Schmitz affirmed that destroying FLSE was of statewide importance; otherwise it might be foisted on all of California, and then the nation. Dr. Melvin Anchell of Long Beach, a nationally recognized opponent of sex education, claimed, "We have become so brainwashed that we think we've got to teach children how to engage in the sex act."[131] The proceedings on this October evening revealed the delicate balance the Antis struck in portraying their struggle. On the one hand, they saw themselves as the decent few seeing clearly through the perverse haze of a sexualized society to recognize sex education's nefarious agenda and had to fight relentlessly against these formidable forces. On the other hand, the support of influential outsiders served as a reminder that powerful advocates in halls of government and with university degrees sympathized with their fight and perceived its wide-ranging importance.

The three-hour session did not exhaust the Antis, who persevered through a year of board meetings with similar energy. They looked beyond Anaheim to accuse instigators such as SIECUS and Berkeley hippies and also benefited from a growing focus on sex education among national right-wing groups. Gordon Drake, author of "Is the Schoolhouse the Proper Place to Teach Raw Sex?," was hosted by Walter Knott in Anaheim. Steinbacher's three-part exposé in the December 1968 *Bulletin* on the purportedly covert sex education conference in Anaheim was distributed nationwide. The pillorying of Williams for her SIECUS affiliation continued through the winter, and by January the John Birch Society had founded MOTOREDE, which formed a political bloc with the multiplying grass-roots organizations dedicated to eradicating sex education. It secured the California ban on SIECUS materials, as well as the summer 1969 statewide decision mandating that students receive written permission to attend sex education class, rather than to be excused. Rafferty's extensive correspondence with citizens begging for state action to limit sex education, impulses with which he agreed, reveals he largely stayed true to his libertarian principles. He perpetually responded to such citizens with statements such as "There is no question but what some teachers abuse the privilege of instructing young people . . . the solution is most quickly to be found on a local level, especially since California law mandates local control of local school problems by locally-elected boards of education."[132] That Rafferty supported any state action to circumscribe local sex education prerogatives speaks to the depths of the concern over this program he shared with other archconservative legislators and citizens. The Anaheim case reveals a larger shift afoot, that from a libertarian to a more forthrightly interventionist conservatism.[133]

By the fall of 1969, no students received sex education, for once the Antis had won a board majority they reduced FLSE to a "birds-and-bees" course covering only the basic mechanics of intercourse and reproduction.[134] Implementing the revised program was then postponed until February 1970, contingent upon "each school's ability to absorb the program."[135] Cook commented that the "watered-down" program was "practically worthless."[136] As much a casualty of the debate as the curriculum, Cook kept his title of superintendent but only consultative power; after a heart attack he retired in 1969, even before his contract expired.[137] With FLSE dismantled and Cook in retirement in San Clemente, the Antis redirected their energies locally and nationally. Howe marched on to Washington, DC, to fight federal financing of sex education, and the CCC turned to stamping socialism out of the social studies curriculum.[138] The emergent Right began to vilify a public school system that seemed to be demanding increasingly more money to fund ever more unorthodox, even immoral, curricula.

The fight that racked Anaheim was unquestionably bitter. But amid the venomous and hyperbolic accusations of communism and perversion, it is difficult to ascertain the substance of the curriculum purportedly at stake. One fairly stark conflict seems to have been FLSE's goal to promote a degree of moral autonomy versus the indoctrination the Antis espoused. Accordingly, Howe excoriated Sally Williams for dismissing FLSE teacher who responded to the question "What do you think of necking on dates?" with the absolute "Don't do it" and disapproved of the advice of her son's teacher not to blindly obey their parents, but to "decide for yourself what is right and what is wrong for you."[139] A MOTOREDE member claimed unequivocally that regarding sexuality, "the fact is that children want and need indoctrination."[140] Yet a linchpin of the individualist, libertarian Antis' argument was that the sex educators represented an encroaching totalitarianism that eradicated free thought. In a public debate between Steinbacher and Cook, which took place after the dismantling of the program, the vocal journalist revealed this contradiction. "Most people . . . will reject any attempts to indoctrinate their children . . . such coercive force is known as Fascism."[141] Ultimately, Steinbacher called on the audience to "reject outmoded and irrational totalitarian concepts and to begin to think as free moral agents," invoking a goal sounding quite similar to FLSE's aim: "to develop a set of personal standards and ethical beliefs."[142] In this formulation, the substance of the conflict is protean; the only given is that the Antis and Cook will lock horns.

Examining the curriculum more deeply reveals a similar disjuncture between the bitterness of the debate and the actual divergence between the visions of the Antis and of FLSE. For all the anxiety about perversion and the dissolution of the family, Williams explained that FLSE intended "that the boys and girls who complete this program will create more stable marriages." The evenhanded "pro-and-con" tone of the course notwithstanding, it steered students to conclusions commensurate with the Antis' aversion to extramarital sexuality. "We discuss the values and consequences of promiscuity and [the children] find no values. They look down on those people who 'sleep around.'"[143] The culminating lesson in the five-year program centered exclusively on marriage, and the appendix dedicated to premarital petting portrays an ominous and unstoppable chain of events from "the simple 'I like you, I hope you like me' kiss" to the "permanent mistake" of premarital sex and possibly pregnancy.[144] Moreover, despite acknowledging sexual pleasure, the curriculum equates intercourse and marriage: "Bodies are ready for marriage while they are still in high school."[145] The curriculum guide forthrightly spelled out a key concept in its final lesson: "The family unit is the only socially approved agency of reproduction."[146] Still, Anti parents repeatedly interpreted efforts by public schools to teach about family, gender, or morality as an attempt to undermine parental authority and intrude on the private home. However, the bitter fight over sex education actually reveals a deep consensus among its combatants over the primacy of heterosexual marriage and reproduction.

Prescriptive curricular materials are insufficient, however, to convey how Anaheim's adolescents experienced the program. Yet, as the student responses to the 1965 pilot course suggest, both FLSE's mission and the message it conveyed confirm the course's generally conservative thrust. Notably, however, many students gratefully acknowledged the instructor's "radical" candor, even as it reinforced the "idea that sex before marriage is immoral."[147] One student even commented, "I think it's important we learn about homosexuals. If not, how will we know how to cure them?"[148] If the course upheld the conventional morality, why were students so enthused? Irvine has suggested that entities such as FLSE and SIECUS, products of the sexualized 1960s, were revolutionary in bringing the new openness about sexuality into one of the last bastions of sexual silence—the classroom. The recollections of FLSE alumna Priscilla Feld corroborate this sense: "It was a very confusing time to grow up. . . . No one ever talked about anything [because] they were afraid to talk about anything."[149] While the curricula at stake hardly espoused a radical sexual and family politics, these reformers' willingness to discuss sex even to guide children to moderation, however, was revolutionary and thus bitterly fraught.

In this sense, if the debate was about sexual speech and not the content of the curriculum, the Antis lost. The opposition, so morally repulsed by sex educators uttering "penis" and "vagina," stayed up late mimeographing their *Adult Bulletin*, a pamphlet intended to lay bare the seediness of FLSE. They packed auditoriums to listen to their apocalyptic prophesies of the sex perverts FLSE would produce and to the war stories of the filth other opponents confronted in their towns. At board meetings, the CCC defied the time limit, reading aloud continuously from the purportedly objectionable FLSE texts. Surveying the crowd at the October 1968 FLSE workshop, an AUHSD trustee remarked, "If we were sure we would have this much interest in the things that the Board does, we would always meet in an auditorium."[150] Once famed for Disneyland and defense, Anaheim drew national attention for its discussion of sexuality at new volumes and venues, all in denunciation of talking about sex.[151]

While the Antis opposed explicit sexuality on newsstands and on television, their specific goal was to protect innocent children and family unity from FLSE's divisive perversity. Howe, who first came before the board, claimed her attention had been piqued when her son had asked to be excused from a disturbing "sex class."[152] The *Bulletin* repeatedly ran stories of parents tending to their traumatized children after attending FLSE. Occasionally there were first-person accounts by outraged students.[153] FLSE, according to the Antis, was dividing Anaheim's otherwise tightly knit families. However, the debate itself sparked, or at least revealed, serious discord between teenagers and parents. At the first workshop, the image of children and parents united against the evils of FLSE dissolved when a student got into a shouting match with a prominent anti-sex education activist. The student defended FLSE, and a mother in the audience screamed, "Yeah, but are you a virgin?" Howe hastily interjected that "this program was not intended to be a debate with the students."[154] In this brief interaction, early in the controversy, the premises of the Antis already began to collapse. The silence around sexuality was irreversibly shattered, as was the image of protective parent and vulnerable, sexually naive child. Along with the vocal boy were two full rows of classmates, who "waved their hands in the air and shouted out inquiries."[155] Intended to prove the impropriety of discussing sexuality with children, the Anti workshop only drew more students into the widening conversation about sexuality and showcased their interest in the matter.

It was the students' voices, which grew louder throughout Anaheim's controversy, that revealed the shifting terrain in the theater of this war over sex education. The debate generated heavy coverage in the Los Alamitos High School student newspaper *The Crusader* well into 1970. Editorials beseeching the "silent majority" supporting FLSE to speak up, student opinion polls on premarital sex, and mockery of the Antis' theory that "the dynamic duo of Satan and the Communists" was behind sex education trumpeted a very different image of teenagers than the innocent victims the Antis portrayed.[156] The debate prompted students to articulate their views on larger issues of censorship and free speech, and their conclusions were unmistakably at odds with the views of the Antis. One senior was incredulous at the FLSE controversy. "How can anything that's the truth be offensive?" he asked. Most notably, the students chafed at being portrayed as impressionable or immature. To prove their savvy, they wrote at length about their opinions and experiences of dating, premarital sex, and abortion.

If the Antis needed further proof that their crusade had fostered this irreverence among Anaheim's teenagers, one student spelled out the moral she took from the debates: "I think the biggest lesson we can learn from Mrs. Pippenger is that every person must be responsible in a true democracy, otherwise a minority of people, such as Mrs. Pippenger and company, can take over."[157] Much as Cook had personified the FLSE program during the debate, in its wake the Antis came to represent an old guard at odds with the students' worldview. In 1970, Townsend and Howe explained to an auditorium of students the communist designs behind both FLSE and social studies curricula, and several students reacted rudely. One teacher responded matter-of-factly. "We anticipated some hostility. The sex education program was very dear to the students. He's conservative—they're liberal."[158]

By 1970, then, FLSE had been dismantled, but so had the image of the cohesive Anaheim family allied against the outside influences of immorality and communist perversion. Moreover, the students' inhibitions about discussing sexuality had apparently dissipated in the course of the highly public debate and the mounting national sexual revolution. Since the relative acceptance of sex education in the early 1960s, it seemed, threatening national and local events prompted a general retrenchment to more conservative mores, one of them an aversion to discussing sexuality with children, especially outside of the family. In the dizzying midst of grand sociopolitical shifts and local upheaval, Anaheim conservatives invested FLSE with their particularly acute anxieties about changes over which they had little control. Launched locally, but with sufficient national reach to resonate symbolically as an outside threat, the program was small enough to be defeated but sufficiently large to incite alarm. Most importantly, this local controversy sheds light on the lived experience and polarizing trajectory of the 1960s, the centrality of the classroom to how these changes were both wrought and challenged, and a vocal minority's ability to profit from such volatility. Anaheim's location in exceptionally white Orange County, with its defense-industry-driven economy, breakneck population growth, and spurned Goldwater constituency projected through an archconservative press, escalated the terms of the debate and rendered sex education a particularly insidious threat to a polity simultaneously sheltered from, but nervously aware of, the transformations reshaping their nation, state, and community.

The battle over sex education waged in Anaheim reveals the politics of family and sexuality to be at the core of a developing conservatism. Furthermore, it suggests that at least in certain communities, anti-communist rhetoric retained its power long after McCarthyism waned and that it derived particular energy in the realm of family and youth sexuality, as would become clear in the 1970s and 1980s with the development of the "family values" wing of the New Right. Still, the Anaheim battle, shaped by its specific local and cultural context, was not as paradigmatic of the struggles over sex education occurring statewide or nationally as the scholarly literature suggests. The anti-communist rhetoric that garnered it such media and scholarly attention also rendered it singular. In other parts of California, where parents' and citizens' groups just as adamantly resisted sex education, anti-communism played a far less important role.

In fact, the focus on Anaheim not only overemphasizes Orange County as the exclusive seedbed of modern conservatism, but can obscure the educational questions, such as a growing mistrust of teachers and of programs construed as "frills" in financially strapped districts, that assumed a more prominent place in many Californian communities and gained traction with citizens not especially moved by the threat of creeping communism. Thus, further exploring the heated controversies in California also uncovers the profound concerns—funding issues, curricular quality, and educational authority—that explain why everyday Californians joined ardent social conservatives to oppose sex education. Anti-communist activists were able to rally an enthusiastic following in Anaheim in the late 1960s because parents and citizens in the district were also anxious about these larger questions. By the close of 1970, with many sex educators dispirited and curricula dismantled, these battles inspired a far broader statewide discussion about morality, diversity, and education—weighty issues with which the state educational bureaucracy and the polity would wrestle well into the 1970s.

# 7

## "WHICH WAY AMERICA?"

### CALIFORNIA'S MORAL GUIDELINES COMMITTEE AND THE FORGING OF A PATRIOTIC MORALITY

Reeling from both campus activism and the shocking assassinations of civil rights leaders Martin Luther King Jr. and Robert F. Kennedy in the summer of 1968, Californians shaken by this political turbulence invested tremendous energy in considering the role of the school in contributing to—or ideally, containing—such unrest. Sex education was at the center of these discussions, as letters piling upon the desks of the State Board of Education members grew angrier and more strident in linking the programs to a fraying of the social fabric keenly felt across the political spectrum. Pressure built upon Superintendent Rafferty, a staunch advocate of local control and sworn opponent of sex education, to levy a state-level response to the building crisis.

Just after the Fourth of July, the board implored Rafferty to create a committee that would devise for teachers and administrators a "set of 'guidelines' designed to identify those principles of morality established by tradition and heritage, as well as enforced by the laws of this state and of the US."[1] From its inception, the proposed bent of the framework, born of trepidation about the specific perils of sex education, clearly also sprang from angst about the turmoil in the larger social and political climate. "We specifically want to identify that kind of behavior and activity alien to our heritage, and/or unlawful or contrary to public policy," the board told the nascent committee.[2] Board president Howard Day later recalled how fears of spreading civil rights activism and campus unrest inspired the board to act: "It was mostly at the college level then . . . we could see it coming and were trying to head it off by setting up guidelines . . . that would give students an alternative to militancy."[3] Keenly aware sex education was a proxy for such broader concerns, Rafferty obliged, and with the guidance of Governor Ronald Reagan and the board on July 11, 1968, he charged the Moral Guidelines Committee (MGC) with the ambitious task of "lead[ing] California out of the moral decay into which it is presently descending."[4]

Governor Reagan declared this errand to be "the single-most important task facing the state of California," reflecting widespread concern about the state's moral climate.[5] Conservatives were the most vocal in articulating a palpable and widely shared sense that an unpatriotic "new morality" being forged in California schools required official countervailing efforts, but liberals also expressed worry about the moral fiber of American youth.[6] When Dr. Frances Todd of San Francisco testified at a 1969 hearing on sex education, she asked rhetorically, "Does a parent or teacher have a choice of whether or not morals and morality are taught in the schools?" and answered roundly, "No."[7] Todd garnered boos and hisses when she asserted this privilege of the schoolhouse, but in this newly fraught climate, such entreaties to leave the instruction of values uniquely to the home felt increasingly obsolete. Even MGC member Reverend Robert Williams wrote that though "as a layman," he had known "we need to get back to the basics of reading, writing, and arithmetic," the current social climate had made clear that "without moral instruction, the other will be lost in a war for the minds of men."[8] When liberal Latino advocate Julian Nava challenged Rafferty for the state superintendency in 1970, he lamented "weakened family ties and the decline of strong neighborhood feeling" as "burdens that have now fallen on public education . . . and have been added to the 3Rs."[9] At the dawn of the MGC, the public schools seemed the proper place to impart these lessons.

Many citizens well beyond California's classrooms felt that the social climate to which the MGC responded was extraordinary, and that its response must set an unambiguous precedent. From distant Fall River, Massachusetts, a clergyman wrote to the committee of his "deep distress" about the "breakdown of morality . . . at all levels," manifest in America "being a pluralistic nation." He feared that "any attempts to hold traditional standards of morality and even discipline in our public institutions faces the risk of being challenged . . . and the challenge upheld." Obliquely referring to the recent US Supreme Court *Schempp* and *Vitale* decisions that relaxed obscenity laws and constrained prayer in school, this cleric specifically congratulated the committee for its "intelligent effort" to "conceive an approach based on national heritage."[10] Citizens and committee members perceived California's curricular struggles to engage the nation's history and hold sway over its destiny. Committee chairman Edwin F. Klotz mused that the question the MGC actually undertook to answer was "Which way America?"[11]

Over the next several years the MGC endeavored to fashion a moral code California teachers would impart to their pupils.[12] Already in 1968, opponents of sex education anchored their critiques in more extensive social problems, auguring the vastness of the terrain the MGC would attempt to navigate. For example, Gordon Drake expanded his anti-sex education arguments to a full-length book entitled *Blackboard Power : NEA Threat to America*, which Klotz lauded as a "reliable and scholarly" account of contemporary education debates.[13] Similarly, committee liberals saw attacks on sex education as a sign of a dangerous assault on freedom of expression in the schools. Emerging from a contested climate that permeated even the leadership of a committee intended to stand above the fray, these statewide "moral guidelines" were intended to apply, and be at least nominally acceptable, to the most dynamic and diverse state of the union. By 1974, when the MGC disbanded, the clergymen, teachers, parents, and administrators comprising it had taken up questions of curriculum engaging religion, science, morality, history, and social studies.

While the sex education battles of this era are seen as emblematic of the ascendant political Right, the MGC suggests a more complex story. First, the committee's liberal faction ultimately triumphed in passing its version of the moral guidelines, which both questioned indoctrination and celebrated cultural pluralism. Both committee liberals and conservatives and the hundreds of citizens who commented on the MGC's proceedings on editorial pages and state hearings increasingly concurred that "a new morality" was overtaking American youth and that the public schools had a responsibility to respond. At the close of its proceedings in 1974, the MGC's impact was uncertain, but its tenure both revealed how central educational issues were to citizens' sense of their future and how closely morality and nationhood were linked in the public imagination. This unlikely and uneasy consensus around the social necessity for a "patriotic morality"—and a waning trust in the school system to propound it—also implies that the "rightward turn" of the 1970s was hardly assured.

## Conceiving the Committee

The MGC was unprecedented in embodying an energetic state response by self-proclaimed champions of limited state involvement in education, Governor Reagan and Superintendent Rafferty. To some extent, their exceptional response reflects the intensity of the frustration some citizens felt with the cultural climate apparently investing immoral sex education programs with new and dangerous energy. One father angrily commented, "They've taken God out of the schools and put sex in."[14] A prescient Long Beach mother cautioned that ill-conceived sex education programs threatened to bring about a massive tax revolt.[15] MGC member Reverend Robert F. Williams raised the stakes of the controversy, warning that in growing numbers of community meetings, frustration with "sex education and civil disobedience" inspired discussion of bond issues and tax override initiatives, indicating "growing displeasure, and perhaps even distrust on the part of our people regarding our school administration."[16] The shared sense of panic, expressed loudest by social conservatives, merited a call for state intervention by opponents to this burgeoning progressivism, a powerful impulse that galvanized the convention of the MGC and invested it with tremendous purpose.

The MGC was not without precedent, nor was it California's only state-level response to a perceived moral crisis. The original 1866 California School Code required that instruction in morals take place at every grade level and "impress upon the minds of the pupils the principles of morality, truth, justice, patriotism . . . and instruct them in manners and morals and the principles of a free government," but such pedagogy had for the past century been left to the individual teacher's discretion.[17] Consultants to the MGC recalled a comparable 1950s effort "to infuse 'moral and spiritual' values into the curriculum" to counter the "loss of identity, community and gradual erosion of their own cultural values" effected by postwar displacements that "revised permanently the life patterns of American citizens" and were arguably of similar gravity to the sexual and civil rights revolutions creating the knotty problems animating the MGC's work a decade later.[18] In 1969, California Senate Resolution 99 had proposed that the Committee on Rules convene a committee to study sex education and the heated objections it inspired. That same year, ultraconservative state senator John Schmitz introduced Senate Resolution 60, which stated that "no new sex programs" should be initiated until the Committee on Rules could review them in full.[19] The legislature passed Senate Bill 413 (of which the Department of Education disapproved), stating that no child should be forced or expected to attend any class in which human reproductive organs were mentioned. To attend such a class (rather than to be excused, as held by the previous education code), students would need to furnish a note from their parents.[20] Less concerned with the threat of communistic state control than some strident voices suggested, most Californians wary of sex education took only a slight pause before invoking the state to protect their rights as parents and taxpayers.[21]

That the power in question resided at the state rather than federal level certainly helped allay fears of an intrusive government presence. So too did the fact that Rafferty, who had built a Senate campaign and an illustrious national media persona around a "return to the little red schoolhouse," led the bureaucracy. Rafferty often responded to requests to intervene in local affairs, "I have about as much right to enter your district as I do to enter your bedroom." Interestingly, the American Legion vociferously backed mandatory state enforcement of the guidelines and just as forcefully attempted to silence appeals by moderates for voluntary adoption.[22] This selective support of state power indicates a transition from an older libertarianism to a newer outlook condoning state intervention on specific, especially threatening questions. In this case, a robust state was desirable even to ardently conservative Californians, as long as these resources were marshaled against the troubling tides of tax-supported immorality and erosion of the family. Of this willingness, the MGC was born.

Rafferty faced uncertain tides when he returned to his superintendent post in 1968 upon his failed bid for the US Senate, and the MGC, assembled to stem "the moral crisis sweeping the land and all aspects of American behavior," presented an opportunity to cement his legacy.[23] His appointments to the nine-person committee reflected this intention. Klotz, a politically conservative special assistant to the State Board of Education who described himself as a scholar of Hispanic Studies, was the MGC's shrillest voice. He was eventually removed from his position for giving lectures so reactionary that they conflicted with board policy.[24] Before a Stockton audience of two hundred, for example, Klotz warned of curricula designed by "well-organized and well-financed sensualists who think sex is fun."[25] Appointee Hardin Jones, a medical physicist at the University of California's Berkeley campus, led the conservative wing of the famously liberal faculty and sought "moral revitalization" to counter the "blatant advertisements" for homosexuality and drug use ruining the country.[26] Other Rafferty appointees included Republican legislators: assemblymen E. Richard Barnes of San Diego and Floyd Wakefield of Downey, and Mormon state senator John Harmer of Glendale, whom colleague John T. Kehoe remembered inviting "ridicule" as the tee-totaling "freshman senator always drinking orange juice."[27] Reverend Robert Williams, whose Church of Reflection congregated on Knott's Berry Farm and was financed by its munificent and reactionary proprietor, Walter Knott, was also an appointee. [28] Everyday Californians also openly called for representation they believed would reflect their inclinations. Mrs. Doris Caldwell of Clovis, a small city near Fresno, requested that a local minister who had given her "and many others guidance and inspiration during [their] fight against sex education" be appointed. Such "honest, sincere, and capable men" were "tops in [her] books" and deserved the stewardship of Californian education.[29] Similar requests flooded Rafferty's office.

Spearheaded by Klotz, the committee members proposed one version of the moral guidelines: a lengthy screed against secular humanism and debased sex educators, which was unanimously received by the board in May 1969.[30] Ultimately, however, the moderates on the committee, who gained an even greater voice when the MGC was reconfigured in 1970, ruled the day, and the board adopted a pared-down set of guidelines devoid of such high-flown vilification. The initial "Klotz version," as it came to be called, was footnoted only as an optional reference work. Both documents emerged from grand discussions about school and society as the MGC eventually ranged far from its initial focus on sex education to engage curricular quandaries in science, history, religion, and civics. The MGC emerged with a notion of "patriotic morality" acknowledging the inseparability of ethical and national identity, contributing to an atmosphere in which increasingly present bilingual-bicultural education programs appeared especially inimical to the coalescing political Right. Still, the ultimate adoption of the more moderate guidelines reveals the continued contestation of California politics, even as the oft-proclaimed "rightward turn" took hold. As divided as their perspectives were, committee members emerged from these deliberations enshrining patriotism and parental prerogative, even as MGC liberals emphasized America's unfulfilled promise and "personal value systems."

Nationally, California was poised to take the lead in defining and teaching moral education. Almost as soon as the committee convened, Klotz wrote to state superintendents seeking existing examples of moral guidelines and discovered that most states had no explicit standards in place.[31] Of the three that did—Michigan, Florida, and Iowa—Iowa's 1955 version was no longer even in print. North Carolina had also appointed a commission, but as of 1968 it had yet to issue any reports or guidelines.[32] Upon completing this survey, Klotz commented, "Many indicate an interest in what California is proposing—and want to be kept informed."[33]

California districts had already been employing diverse local strategies to impart ethical standards to their schoolchildren. This was in many instances in direct response to the shock waves of the era's social revolutions, but not all efforts arose from a perspective of moral absolutism. On the contrary, local curricula showcased the range of moral perspectives manifest in the Golden State. In Modesto, teachers argued that American heterogeneity demanded that all teachers accept that "that which constitutes the moral life will change from situation to situation," since "it is not possible to defend the position that certain specific values are held in common by all Americans and therefore should be taught in our public schools."[34] To these educators, the dynamic nation necessitated a similarly flexible moral code "not necessarily religious, traditional, or customary in nature . . . but intended not merely to reflect the existing culture and/or perpetuate the heritage of the past."[35] By contrast, other districts endeavored to act as a bulwark against these cultural shifts. In Sierra-Plumas, near the Nevada border, the schools emphasized "sound principles" and "personal integrity" in order to provide students with "protection from all disturbing elements."[36] Curiously, the Anaheim morality curriculum, hailing from a district whose leadership on such questions was highly controversial, was marshaled in cities as far away as the northern community of Santa Rosa.[37] Like those who wanted to integrate sex education into every subject rather than teach it in isolation, many districts reported weaving morality instruction throughout the curriculum.

Significantly, when asked to submit their "morality curricula," an overwhelming number of districts compiled instructional materials teaching civics and citizenship. In communities as varied as working-class Fresno and the affluent bedroom community of Orinda in Marin County, educators were already imparting a version of morality that equated patriotism with ethics and united the "solemn promise to be faithful in thought, word, and deed" to country and family with moral and civic order.[38] Some such programs were suffused with explicit spirituality. A program pioneered by MGC member and retired minister Joseph Forcinelli evinces how ethics, patriotism, and religion intermingled, and not only in traditionalist pedagogies. In his Southern Californian district of Claremont, Forcinelli voiced a need to "introduce religious studies into the schools." He did not advocate teaching any doctrine but forthrightly asserted his commitment to "one major goal . . . to allow the student to arrive at his value system, based on his own choices." Forcinelli was the director of a one-man humanities department in which courses in philosophy and African studies complemented those in religion. He believed that, in a climate characterized by "ethnic strife, intolerance and violence," teaching respect for "the values of all mankind" was imperative and amounted to "education for better citizenship [including] the teaching of morality, truth, justice and religion."[39] Even from this admittedly liberal political perspective, morality was bound up with questions of spirituality as well as diversity.

California's changing ethno-racial landscape clearly informed the MGC's proceedings. Invoking much of the same inflated rhetoric about race, conspiracy, and godlessness that shaped the discourse on sex education, Californians vigorously chimed in on the MGC's deliberations. Like the interlocutors in those debates, the members of the MGC and the policymakers who hand-picked them were overwhelmingly Anglo, but raised racial issues insistently and anxiously. For example, while testifying before the board in favor of the Klotz guidelines, Mrs. R. M. Evans of the La Mesa Republican Women's Club excoriated humanism and its "soul brother" behavioral science for infiltrating the schools and "our children's minds" with the goal of "destroying American culture and heritage . . . so that they can become citizens in a one-world government."[40] A clergyman representing the Christian Service Ministries at a November public hearing in Sacramento was more explicit, gravely warning the MGC against caving in too much to "the backlash of the minorities."[41] Clearly, the fight over morality assumed ethno-cultural valance.

At an April 1969 hearing, one of the few suggestions citizens enthusiastically embraced was to make the guidelines more "historical and specific to American culture."[42] This request was significant for two reasons. First, the committee's mandate, born of the sex education furor, had never been to engage so broadly with the sweep of American history or culture, or even with social studies or civics curricula.[43] Second, this entreaty clearly spoke to a concern among Californians at a moment when the course of American history and culture was so clearly in flux that crafting and adhering to an explicit set of rules hearkening back to some simpler and perhaps imagined national ethos was appealing. The MGC was reshaping essentially the whole public school curriculum, not just sex education, and linked its mission to national purpose, emphasizing that California children should understand three points, imparted across the curriculum: first, "America's religious heritage"; second, "the religious views of our Founding Fathers"; and third, "the bases of morality understood by our Founding Fathers."[44]

Sex education had inspired these discussions but quickly became subsumed by a host of wider concerns. An exchange between Patricia Hill, a health consultant hired by the state, and two policymakers, lays bare its capacious task. Hill wrote that the committee "may have come out of sex education, but the MGC took on a life of its own."[45] The state bureaucracy had retooled its "Framework for Health Education" several times, reworking the 1952 version that remained in practice for the following sixteen years until 1968, when it piloted a new version in representative districts statewide.[46] The 1968 document provided broadly that California children in grades one through six must receive instruction about "health, including instruction in the principles and practices of individual, family, and community health."[47] Certainly, the initial and unsuccessful efforts of the State Board of Education to subsume regulation of sex education under these general rubrics for "health guidelines"—alongside concrete and technical information such as recommended nutritional allowances and instructions on proper hand-washing—very quickly appeared naïve as these debates gave way to arguments about morality, patriotism, and religion, not to mention science and history.[48]

## Polarization

The MGC's strident conservative voices and the far less clamorous but ultimately triumphant ones in the political center all strove to resolve the "moral crisis" in California schools that the sex education battles had revealed and helped foment. They were passionately divided on how to do so, however, and the MGC soon split into what a member described as "the progressives and the old guard." In May 1969, the conservatives produced a set of guidelines primarily authored by Klotz.[49] This lengthy document received wide press coverage for its reactionary tone: it defined morality in absolute terms, condemned "humanism as Communism," and relied both on moral leadership training given to the Navy and Marines and on an antiquated textbook "from more than 100 years ago," *Cowdery's Moral Lessons*.[50] The *Los Angeles Times* described this version as sweeping and uncompromising, condemning "all forms of nonreligious secularism as a basis of morality" and crediting such perspectives with causing "the moral decay observable all around us." Echoing the most vitriolic condemnations of sex education, this version saw moral corruption lurking everywhere, including "the United Nations, the U.S. Supreme Court, the motion picture industry, group therapy, sensitivity training, current teaching practices, anthropologist Margaret Mead, sex education, philosopher John Dewey—and Communism."[51] A more moderate version, the one ultimately adopted, was barely noted in the press. This second document acknowledged the need for moral pedagogy to resonate with the nation's changing demographics and advocated moving the nation "closer to the fulfillment of its ideals" rather than adhering to a singular code of values.[52]

While Reagan and Rafferty agreed on the need to adopt stringent guidelines to redress the "general breakdown" in morality, it was one Reagan appointee who led the committee's major schism and who chiefly authored the second set of moral guidelines. Reverend Donn Moomaw (see figure 7.1) was the Reagans' affable minister of Bel Air Presbyterian, and known as much

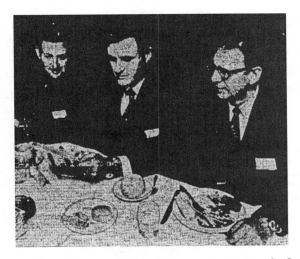

FIGURE 7.1 Reverend Donn Moomaw, State Board of Education member who was both Governor Reagan's pastor and an appointee to the MGC, meets with other educators in 1970. Moomaw surprised members of the MGC by ultimately supporting the guidelines designed by the progressive faction in the group. Reprinted with permission of *The Modesto Bee and News-Herald* and by courtesy of Newspapers.com.

for his reputation as a former UCLA all-American football player as for the fact that he was considered a conservative appointee to the State Board of Education, but occasionally "championed some liberal causes."[53] Suggesting some cracks in the state's conservative apparatus, fellow committee member John T. Kehoe remembered that, "for some reason not all that clear to [him]," despite Reagan and Moomaw's warm rapport, "Rafferty never related well" to Moomaw. Rafferty had derided Moomaw as "an ultra-liberal and a comsymp," Kehoe recalled.[54] Although Rafferty and Reagan maintained a united front in public, Reagan had at first resisted Rafferty's Senate nomination in favor of the moderate Kuchel. While the Presbyterian Reagan's presidency energized the Christian Right, Reagan himself harbored a "carefree attitude on religion" and endeavored to rid "America of a God of judgment and punishment."[55] Reagan described himself as devout, but this rift in the MGC suggests the range of perspectives at play, even within the coalescing conservative movement.

Kehoe described the divisions within the MGC. Within months, as "grass roots were rising to such fire," Klotz had become "the right arm to

Dr. Rafferty." Moomaw "was given heavy criticism among the Rafferty conservative Republicans, among the Republican women, and the fundamental church groups."[56] Moomaw had spoken out in favor of progressive family life education programs on several occasions, and liberal assemblyman Alan Sieroty, known and in some circles reviled for his support of a liberal "abortion bill," lauded Moomaw's expansive vision of sex education at a heated State Board hearing. "My hope is that the Board will adopt a policy of adopting the total personality, as Donn Moomaw suggested in his invocation. This should include a program of FLSE which is integrated into the curriculum from the kindergarten through the 12th grade, which stresses responsibility to oneself and to one's fellow human being, as well as scientific information—biology, reproduction and so forth."[57] Just as resolutely, Klotz "zealously recommended the Navy and Marine Corps' character training pamphlets for use in the schools," and his version of the guidelines won praise as "a masterful work" by his colleague state senator Harmer.[58] In 1969, Kehoe remembered, "all of the fundamental church groups . . . were very comfortable with the make-up of the group."[59] MGC conservatives pointed out the fallacy of the San Mateo Teacher Guide's "secular humanist" discussion of " 'good' without defining 'good' " and repeatedly advocated the San Diego curriculum's embrace of absolute truths as imparted by an infallible teacher. Yet these ardent entreaties found formidable opposition among MGC members aligned with Moomaw.[60] In the eyes of conservative observers, some from as far away as North Carolina, it was the liberal "Moomaw crowd" who "were so powerful" that they could exclude Klotz completely.[61]

On May 8, 1969, the State Board of Education, newly dominated by a Reagan-appointed conservative majority, unanimously received the Klotz document and even added a stipulation that instruction in creationism accompany existing lessons in Darwinian evolution. Under the heading "SILENCE," the left-leaning *San Francisco Chronicle* recounted in an ominous tone the circumstances under which the approval occurred: "No one, either on or off the board, spoke a single word of criticism against the report before the board acted. Perhaps this is because the document was carefully kept under wraps by [Board President] Day and Rafferty."[62] The eulogizing of days past when "the State Board of Education would have simply choked on and thrown away" the adopted guidelines continued in the *Chronicle* over the following days.[63] Editorialist Ron Moskowitz wrote that approval of the report, though protested by a "flood of telephone calls and letters demanding to know why a fundamentalist Protestant, Bible-slapping approach to morality is being seriously considered," seemed the inexorable outcome of a Reagan- and Rafferty-appointed group.[64] Apparently triumphant over family life and sex education programs and the liberals who supported them, the Klotz guidelines were to be distilled into a more manageable form by the MGC for ease of use by teachers. Perhaps in an effort to quell dissension, Howard Day appointed Moomaw to oversee this task, and in this next phase of the MGC, it became clear that the passage of the conservative guidelines—what Moskowitz had called a "covered-wagon approach to jet-age problems"—was anything but a fait accompli.[65]

Indeed, the fatalism of the liberal San Francisco press was somewhat overstated. Day immediately indicated at the May 8 meeting that despite the energetic approval of some of his colleagues, board acceptance of the guidelines did not constitute endorsement. Within a month, the board released an official statement reiterating that "received" did not signify "adopted." Moreover, the board had just weeks earlier dismissed Klotz as special assistant for "often making right-wing speeches that did not represent the board's position on public matters."[66] The MGC thus returned to the drawing board, but under changed leadership.[67] Far from reining in the discourse to engage sex education narrowly, Moomaw's committee also took up the themes of patriotism and national identity, quoting the Declaration of Independence and the Constitution heavily throughout the eight-page document it crafted. Perhaps emboldened by the surprising resistance to the conservative guidelines, or as convinced as his opponents of the nation's dire need of moral direction, the moderate cleric Moomaw and his supporters devised and ultimately pushed through a very different, but similarly sweeping, version of the guidelines.

Though far more succinct than Klotz's eighty-one-page document, the Moomaw guidelines were equally oriented around notions of "morality," "truth," "justice," and "patriotism," even while explicitly articulating that "the public schools of this state are not to assume the roles of the home and of the religious institutions in teaching the moral and spiritual values necessary to self-fulfillment and responsible participation in our society."[68] Moomaw defined the "love of country" that should be cultivated in the schoolhouse, apparently echoing his more conservative colleagues' fusion of godliness and patriotism in the claim that "love of country . . . takes place within a context of higher ethical, and indeed, religious, commitments. . . . The nation has recognized this transcendent element in many ways . . . for example, the motto 'In God We Trust.' "[69] However, Moomaw's version emphasized how California, "in all the rich diversity of its people," was representative of America, and under the rubric of "truth," rejected "dictatorial indoctrination" for the "critical inquiry and sound judgment" integral to rejecting "propaganda," "legend," and "trivia" regarding the "contributions of various religious and ethnic groups."[70] Patriotism, moreover, did not amount merely to "esteem for one's country," but to a commitment to "move it closer to the fulfillment of its ideals."[71]

To both Klotz and Moomaw and the publics they served, questions of citizenship, spirituality, and diversity evolved naturally from debates over sex education. They agreed that a society thrown into such intense conflict over a relatively minor curricular offering such as sex education was clearly a highly volatile social context, and that the public schools should be responsible for establishing equilibrium. The difference between these groups was their vision of how this would transpire. The documents represented diverging worldviews and mirrored an evolving polarization within the MGC and among the broader populace. Moomaw acknowledged to the *Los Angeles Times* that while his committee had been accused of "advocating 'one-worldism' and sensitivity training," the document's "sensitivity about race and disadvantaged peoples" represented a new and necessary perspective. He commented, "Maybe we are coming into a whole new decade of morality in the 1970s and ought to give real thought to these areas."[72]

The debates surrounding the MGC raise questions as to how strong right-wing reaction was in the early 1970s. Some internal observers remembered that conservatives were increasingly marginalized in the state bureaucracy, particularly after Rafferty's stewardship came to a close in 1970. Kenneth F. Cory, a state assemblyman and consultant to the state board during Reagan's gubernatorial term, dismissed both the governor's leadership in education and the impact of the far-right conservatives who emerged so vividly on the MGC. Cory recounted, "Basically, my view of the governor's office [on matters of education] was that it was irrelevant." Of Alex Sherriffs, a Reagan advisor who had initially counseled Reagan and Rafferty to convene the MGC, Cory commented that he "had all sorts of weird, right-wing things he wanted to do in education, but I don't think anyone, even the right-wing nuts took him seriously."[73] Ultimately, by a 9–1 vote, the board adopted the version put forth by the more liberal Moomaw faction on January 8, 1970. By a 6–4 vote, the document the conservatives produced—which excoriated secular humanists and communism—was footnoted merely as an optional reference work.[74] The MGC and its outcome thus suggest a persistent moderation amid a period remembered for grass-roots conservatism in education.

As Klotz and Moomaw faced off within the committee and then before the board, the grander implications of the struggle were cast into sharp relief.

Over forty Californians spoke—mostly in support of Klotz's "Guidelines for Moral Instruction in California Schools"—at the hearing during which Moomaw presented his "treacherous" version.[75] Harry Fosdick of the California Teachers Association warned against bowing to the disproportionately vociferous Klotz supporters: the "one kind of religious and political philosophy—essentially that of fundamental Protestantism"—represented in the conservative version made it "impossible to expect a board representing our total pluralistic society to give this serious consideration in its present form."[76] Though the Moomaw document prevailed, two telling modifications were included. First, a paragraph was added explicitly articulating that "schools should supplement the roles of the home and religious institutions" and that schools bore "an awesome duty to instill in each child . . . high regard for his own heritage, and to encourage in each devotion to the American ideal of a free, yet ordered republic."[77] Second, the revisions included specifying that "until now, the dominant religious and moral influence has been . . . [the] Judeo-Christian heritage and its Biblically derived teachings."[78] While Moomaw was able to preserve the pluralistic spirit of the critical inquiry his version espoused in encouraging "fair evaluation [of] the various approaches to the moral life held by different segments of society," inclusion of a very specific and traditional definition of moral authority was unmistakable.

## Consensus and Patriotic Morality

The Board and MGC were well aware that "the utility of these guidelines necessarily depend[ed] on their implementation." For all the committee's painstaking work, there was still no "material for teachers to teach."[79] Similarly, Moomaw knew that the entrenched tradition of local control over education meant that, ultimately, "all we can do is lay [the guidelines] before teachers and hope for the best."[80] As late as 1972, the *Los Angeles Times* reported that it might still be another six years until teachers were sufficiently trained in the moral guidelines pedagogies.[81] On July 27, 1970, the board appointed a third group, the Moral Guidelines Implementation Committee (MGIC), to devise curricula based on the adopted Moomaw guidelines. While the press had closely covered the proceedings of the MGC for nearly two years, this next phase engaged the public still more intensely, as citizens imagined what the teaching of morality would actually look like in their children's classrooms. Conservatives continued to speak out as education provided a new unifying issue, but their heightened sense of being under siege, as well as the persistence of liberal voices, suggests political variegation. What emerged unquestionably was that, regardless of political sensibility, citizens perceived morality as bound up with national purpose and the school as a key site for crafting an ethical citizenry. The MGC's tenure helped reveal how difficult—perhaps impossible—this errand was.

At a January 1970 hearing to discuss the recently adopted Moomaw document, nearly fifty citizens took to the stage to propound their views, conflating concerns about morality, patriotism, and school finance. A Santa Monica mother, Mrs. Marilyn Angle, levied the familiar charges of secrecy, moral relativism, and secular humanism, which amounted to "advocating anarchy" in the schoolhouse and diminishing her authority as a mother.[82] To Angle, the adopted version offended the public interest and the Ten Commandments, and she confidently surmised, "The taxpayers will not stand for anymore subversion of their children in the name of State."[83] Similarly, the conservative League of Men Voters requested a delay in adoption because the MGC had not taken into account "the feelings of the men and women who make public education possible, in this great state, the taxpayers."[84] Margaret Scott, already widely known for her anti-sex education activism with the San Mateo's Citizens for Parental Rights, flatly denounced the document's "humanistic revisions."[85] It only deepened the rift between the Moomaw and Klotz constituencies that the next person to speak was Lloyd Morain of the American Humanist Association, who not only supported Moomaw but advocated still more progressive revisions: "[The Moomaw Report] is a fine and thoughtful statement. If this were 1960, I might even express enthusiasm for this version. . . . But this is 1970 . . . and [it] might be revised to reflect even more humanness, give increased recognition to the fact that new information often calls for new evaluations . . . hopefully . . . attackers in the long run might find that they will need the humanists to save their own humanity."[86]

Unlike MGIC members engaging in official deliberation, the many citizens who lined up to speak at the Los Angeles public hearing were unconstrained by the recent legal restrictions on invoking God in public schools. Although churches themselves hadn't figured as primary sites for organizing for these parents, they waxed freely about both the tragic absence of religious morality in schools and the Moomaw document's role in codifying this troubling turn. Henrietta Pankhauser, a mother from Livermore, a town near Oakland, explicitly addressed what she perceived as a widespread misinterpretation of the *Schempp* and *Vitale* decisions: "There seems to be a good deal of confusion following the 1963 . . . decision. . . . What is forbidden is the *advocating* of a particular religion . . . and the principles of secular humanism appear in every paragraph, to the near-total exclusion of genuine moral principles as we understand them."[87] To Pankhauser and the majority of those who joined her to address the board in protest of the Moomaw guidelines, this new religion had all but supplanted "the Judeo-Christian heritage on which our basic moral standards and heritage are based."[88] The committee struggled profoundly with how to "acknowledge the significance of religion in shaping our moral and ethical precepts" without breaching the law or the expanding range of sensibilities characterizing the populace.[89]

While the public marshaled religious devotion in support of the Klotz guidelines, some clerics such as Sister Louise Cramer of the Western Catholic Educational Association energetically applauded the work of the Moomaw Committtee. By contrast, Holocaust survivor Rabbi Juda Glasner of Tujunga's Congregation Mischkan Yicheskel—neither an American-born citizen nor a Christian—spoke at the hearing of her "vigorous opposition to any idea which would suggest separation of the state and God. . . . Any such idea would be in conflict with the framers of our Constitution and would distort the spirit of the Constitution." Reverend Bruce Caldwell of the Bible Presbyterian Church of Temple City declared similarly unequivocally: "The facts of the history of American government advocate a definite Biblical morality."[90]

This popular yen for a more explicit godliness clearly energized the developing "patriotic morality." A Los Angeles father, Walter Blount, based his support for the Klotz version on precisely this notion: "As our fathers discovered in 1776, our liberties and blessings depend first of all on our Creator, and then upon sound biblical principles of eternal truth."[91] One San Jose woman fluidly fused the two, imploring Rafferty to start the school day "with an inspirational quote. . . . I can envision national heroes of the past being cited; Lincoln for concern and honesty." This approach, she continued, "would *assure all children* would be exposed to moral laws such as the Ten Commandments and the Golden Rule." In a footnote to this suggestion, indicated with two handwritten stars, she wrote, "Who would object???"[92] To at least some Californians, Biblical teachings and the glories of American history were of a piece. Even the liberal Dr. Todd of San Francisco, who emphasized the need to "respect the separation of church and state," declared before the board, "The most important set of guidelines I believe is needed are . . . for the mandated teaching of morality and morals in all grades and all subjects." However, Todd acknowledged, this morality must "be acceptable to the majority of the organized religious faiths represented in our population," a condition that would become difficult, and perhaps impossible, to satisfy, even as a discourse of tolerant pluralism came to predominate such debates.[93]

Ironically, as the MGIC more readily embraced a nominally secular Americanism as a proxy for godliness, the committee began fielding concerns about the moral questions raised specifically in classes on religion. A few parents, including Eleanor Howe, one of Anaheim's leading sex education opponents, articulated the forthrightly Christian agenda they wished to see propounded in such courses. Commensurately, some parents took particular exception to the "values clarification" approach to teaching morality, which educational progressives were introducing into courses that addressed religious belief systems. First expounded in the late 1960s, values clarification emphasized the capacity of each child to arrive at his or her personal value system individually, steered only by a teacher's guiding questions.[94] The polar opposite of San Diego's sex education program, which ascribed to teachers a monopoly on a singular set of "true values," this values clarification pedagogy echoed central aspects of the sex education programs that had stirred controversy. Rather than deeming one set of morals infallible, this pedagogy argued, "From the many conflicting values in our society . . . students can make rewarding choices."[95] This issue in particular showcases the fluidity between discussions about morality and those about Americanism. Proponents of values clarification tolerated a plurality of moral systems, just as the shifting California demographics were making it clear that tolerance, or at least acknowledgment, of an ethnically heterogeneous populace would be unavoidable. This trend would only gain momentum. By the late 1970s, values clarification was the most "popularized and widely discussed" moral pedagogy, and by the 1990s, pluralism had become such a fact of American life that sociologist Nathan Glazer declared, "We are all multiculturalists now."[96]

To many, an embrace of "difference"—moral, linguistic, or ethnic—appeared pernicious to the American polity. To others, such heterogeneity defined national culture. Increasingly, Americans of all stripes could hardly ignore the diversification of all aspects of their society; the question they faced was whether the schools would countenance or contain this shift. The civil rights movement already filtered into California's public school curricula primarily through nominally bilingual and "multicultural" programs that variegated "whitestream curricula" with selections from Asian, Hispanic, and black literature and history.[97] These curricular changes, even when modest if not tokenistic, reverberated with particular impact at a moment in which the arrival of a so-called new morality, defined by an analogous relativism, irked cultural and social traditionalists. At the April 1969 state hearing, W. B. Woodward, the general secretary of the American Council of Christian Churches of California, had criticized the California Teachers Association's position that "we need to help youth understand that values change, under what conditions they change, and how change can be implemented in the direction that is judged desirable."

Woodward was nonplussed at the union's belief that "the way this change is to occur . . . is acceptance of a pluralistic viewpoint of ethics: all views coexisting side by side without the stabilizing influence of moral absolutes."[98] Diversity was of a piece not only with ethno-racial but also ethical questions.

The impasse became so intransigent that two consultants were hired in 1972 to help the embattled committee. Liberals believed their precious principles of tolerance and critical thinking were in jeopardy. At the same time, values clarification pedagogy, in challenging the idea of a fixed truth, was anathema to those on the committee who insisted the Declaration of Independence decreed God as "the superior judge of the world."[99] The MGIC intended to dissolve in December 1972, but legal advisors warned that ascribing religious authority to the Declaration of Independence, and thus to the state educational establishment, was actionable, and proceedings dragged on for more than another year. MGIC member Laurel Martin supplanted Klotz as the MGIC's most visible conservative, largely for writing a minority report summing up her crusade against the Moomaw guidelines. In direct tension with the state education code, Martin contended, the guidelines "create conflict between theistic and atheistic beliefs." The report acknowledged that the insidious "method of introducing all points of view into the classroom for the purpose of 'value' conflict is being used by teachers" in California, but prior to the board adopting the MGC guidelines, "the ruling body of California's public schools had not purposely promoted this method of teacher training."[100] Rather than leading the state to a higher moral ground, Martin argued, the MGC's prescriptions had a "history of recommending (without any information) the 'value process' method of teacher training which requires free choice by children among moral and immoral alternatives . . . used to promote courses in homosexuality and compromise."[101]

The "law-and-order politics" Reagan and Nixon made famous both in their terms as governors of California and their presidencies found powerful expression in the minority report and among its supporters.[102] Despite Reagan's intention that the MGC restore moral authority to wayward California, the minority report maintained that the committee's five-year tenure had actually set back the state's moral progress. Martin and the faction she represented argued the handbook's reference to "respect for differences" should be revised to "respect for differences within the law," and "respect for opinions" narrowed to "respect for just and moral opinions." Without these modifications, the report contended, "immoral, illegal opinions will be a part of their studies." "Nothing in the education code directs a child to be 'sensitive' to alternatives of morality and justice, nor to play a 'role' which puts him in that situation. The child does not have to approach conflicting religious or ethical views with an open mind, as the handbook recommends. The child should be taught at home, in church, and in school that *principles have no alternatives.*"[103] The MGC conducted business as the counterculture flourished, and Martin and her supporters unapologetically perceived the committee's project to act as a bulwark against it.[104]

The gravity of the MGC's project intensified the sense among Californians that their tax dollars were being squandered on morally suspect programming. Martin framed her pleas "as a member of the MGIC, personally financed by the people of California, and in [her] role as their servant."[105] Echoing Martin's dissatisfaction, especially her complaint about the apparent secrecy of the MGIC's proceedings, the conservative California Federation of Republican Women issued a press release on January 9, 1973, demanding the public release of the teacher handbooks, even before their official approval—calling for a break in the "consensus of silence" infringing upon "the public's right to know."[106] Curiously, the group threatened "to put on demonstrations in order to have the public heard before the State Department of Education," precisely the sort of radical activism the conservative advocates of the guidelines and Reagan and Rafferty had originally sought to contain.[107] The Martin report was fruitless in effecting any changes to the official MGC document. Yet this contention highlights the persistence and profundity of the cultural rift and indicates conservatives' rising discontent with the public schools they perceived as dominated by progressive mores.

Despite the intense acrimony of the MGC/MGIC's tenure, voices across the political spectrum joined to claim Americanism—a concept so protean as to allow wildly divergent interpretations—as the foundation of the moral code by which their children should abide. An increasingly seamless integration of godliness and patriotism among committee members and many Californians was particularly apparent throughout a January 1973 hearing. Conservative speakers such as Margaret Scott, who joined forces with the United Parents Under God, a more overtly religious group than her own Citizens for Parental Responsibility, repeatedly invoked explicitly religious arguments for a robustly patriotic set of guidelines. Even to those who agreed with the liberal psychiatrist from Orange County who proposed a brand of morality based in psychological analysis, a creed "celebrating plural society" was, and should be, distinctly American.[108] The pluralism that these liberal and moderate voices enshrined as "moral" diverged greatly from what jingoistic, often Bible-toting, conservatives envisioned. After spending years deliberating the philosophical foundation of the guidelines, the committee moved forward from this impasse uneasily, settling on a definition of morality that privileged patriotism and the ascendancy of parental rights.

Capacious notions connecting morality to country and family rapidly subsumed other percolating concerns. Comments from the San Francisco Conference on Religion, Race, and Social Concerns revealed an emerging consensus around the primacy of family authority. Speaking in favor of the Moomaw report, the conference's representative perhaps predictably lauded the report's ecumenicalism and "appreciation of the significant contributions made by Americans of all races and religions," but he also celebrated with equal enthusiasm its recognition of "the importance of the home and religious institutions" in raising good citizens.[109] Similarly, the Los Angeles Tenth District PTA espoused the Moomaw version but suggested parent education classes to shore up the home as the protector of "principles of morality, truth, justice, and patriotism."[110] An account of a Stanford University dropout who told a committee member, "I can't think of one reason why I owe my parents or this country anything," inspired concern among board and committee members and also spoke to the conflation between family authority and national allegiance, even among those who disdained it.[111] The consensual valorization that emerged regarding the primacy of parental prerogative and patriotism both reflected and shaped the cultural and political climate.

## Losing Faith in the Public Schools

If parental authority was gaining credibility among all parties, that of teachers continued to fall in the public esteem. One parent who wrote that he liked the Moomaw code because it "lifted up the importance of the teacher" found that many Californians reviled those same teachers as instigators of the troublesome "new morality." The burgeoning and increasingly young, and by many accounts liberal, teaching force had been highly controversial in the sex education debates that first inspired the MGC. Alan Sieroty, a defender of sex education and abortion rights, had emphasized to the MGC, "The question about teachers is fundamental. I think that this is perhaps the greatest area of need, teaching teachers to be able to teach well and to be able to teach in a relaxed and easy manner in this area."[112] Similarly, teachers of new programs such as bilingual education were suspiciously viewed as untrained at best or subversive at worst, a sentiment amplified by vocal conservatives. Implementation of the amorphous guidelines was particularly challenging, especially when the teaching force inspired little confidence among the taxpaying public.

The process of designing a teacher's manual vividly underscored this mounting suspicion of teachers. One student at Menlo-Atherton High School, who pleaded with Rafferty for more stringent guidelines than the board had adopted, called the "faculty members in the Social Studies department on the whole very dangerous and instilling some very wrong . . . leftist, radical ideas . . . in their students." The problems with these teachers were both that they had free rein to "assign only the material THEY want students exposed to," and that they taught "the bad points in American history, such as pollution and race relations."[113] From 1970 to 1971, the MGIC worked on the practical matter of designing a teacher's handbook to the guidelines. As committee member John T. Kehoe pointed out, this approach was deliberate. Designing specific classroom curricula risked generating more controversy, while creating explicit instructions for teachers whose moral proclivities were by 1970 reflexively called into question by frustrated and skeptical parents was potentially a less explosive tack. Even some students scorned their teachers' politics and pedagogy.

The MGIC explored college programs intended to train educators more expansively in moral education and to give them greater legitimacy. This emphasis on concrete teacher training was a definite strategy to "get the teachers under control," according to California Federation of Teachers (CFT) president Raoul Teilhet. Along with the state PTA, the CFT supported the philosophy undergirding the Moomaw guidelines but bemoaned the lack of teacher and student involvement in the implementation plan. "The reason for this is self-evident," Teilhet declared, "Public school teachers live on the firing line of education. . . . There is an abstract world of glittering rhetoric and a real world of human involvement."[114] Ultimately, as adoption of the guidelines would be voluntary, the actual role of teachers would become less central. Teilhet's metaphor was apt; teachers were not only responsible for putting these tenets into action, but they were also first to be attacked when parents disagreed with a new program. As the MGIC struggled to evade controversy and devise a workable framework, the place of pedagogues was paramount.

Teachers were the easiest targets for parents anxious about a free-floating immorality corrupting the schools. Martin, for example, encapsulated her problems with the perspective of the MGC and the schools in her criticism that "ALL SUBJECTS are being taught as 'problems' in conflict," rather than as a finite body of absolute knowledge. To Martin and the curricula's detractors, teaching about protean concepts could only shake children's "love and loyalty" in "parents, house, church, country, dog . . . individuals and institutions . . . that are not relative concepts."[115] By the early 1970s, the perceived failure of the teaching force to inspire confidence among disenchanted parents led the committee to dispense completely with narrowly discussing sex education and to take up concerns over both textbook adoption in multiple disciplines and statewide science standards.[116]

However broad the MGC/MGIC's scope over its six-year tenure, the ideological rifts that spawned its creation were perhaps most pronounced as proceedings wound down, but the balance of power had perceptibly shifted. Reagan and Rafferty—who had been replaced in office by liberal Democrats—had initially handpicked a committee intended to counteract noxious educational progressivism. By 1973, educational progressives only seemed to be gaining more ground, as the committee and society at large was embroiled in deeper conflict. The intense contention among members of the MGIC paradoxically prolonged deliberations and made the committee appear on the verge of dissolution. Surveying the MGIC's progress in October 1972 (the original committee had planned to finalize the guidelines in late 1969), external consultant Ruth French wrote that "conflicting philosophies have split the Committee into two opposing factions" and that "persistent disagreement between these two factions has seriously eroded the effectiveness, the productiveness, and output of this Committee."[117] The final version of the guidelines and implementation guide that the conservatives, led by Klotz and then Martin, found so incendiary was finalized on September 20, 1972. It was revised minimally in December, and again revised and ultimately adopted in January 1973. The minority report Martin and Barbara Taylor filed in 1973 to some press attention excoriated the persistence of moral relativism in the adopted guidelines, as well as the generally debased direction in which teachers were leading the nation.[118] Martin positioned herself as a lone voice defending the common interest:

> As a minority of this committee it should be understood that I am challenging the mass movement in education today. I have been a visitor in a foreign camp as layman in this committee dominated by educators. Six of eleven members are educators, the power of the chairmanship is in the hands of an educator, and all of the proposals in the majority report were written by educators. This minority report and its proposals are those of a layman who finds irreconcilable differences between the goals of state educators and the goals of state citizens.[119]

This bitterness was arguably in vain, for when the handbook, bearing the ambitious title "Moral and Civic Education and Teaching About Religion," was finally released to school districts in mid-June of 1973, it was only as advisory material. A year later it was confirmed that no state funds would be made available for implementation.[120] Victoria Miltenberger, who had been contracted by the MGC to craft a state implementation plan, wrote to the Napa County school system about what she perceived as an abortive errand: "Enforcement [is] going out of vogue because of money and culture, etc." The implementation plan ultimately adopted in December 1974 enacted the guidelines as voluntary and left to the districts the decision on adoption.[121] For all the vividness of Senator Kehoe's recollections of the committee's proceedings, he had little idea of what became of the guidelines after "quite a few thousand" were distributed in "very nice booklet form." He recalled, "I don't know how it's been used or whether it was used at all."[122] Kehoe's recollections, offered to an interviewer fewer than ten years after the MGC adjourned for the last time, underscore that the committee's historical importance lay far more in its proceedings than in its practical impact.

The tide had clearly turned away from statewide implementation by January 1974, when the consultancy that had written the prospectus for the statewide project rescinded its plan to produce a film to train teachers statewide. By 1974, producing such a film was not only "disproportionately costly," but it had become clear that "there is no way in which one can present teachers and administrators with a display of 'what can be done' without incurring resistance. . . . The manner in which we had thought to go ahead seems to us now extremely arbitrary and directive."[123] Instead, consultant Wallace T. Homitz and his colleagues found it "infinitely more prudent" to pursue a bottom-up approach to implementation, a "low-cost" and "quick" survey of teachers, students, and school personnel "to determine the several different approaches and directions in which a program of this type might go."[124]

Though the MGC had commenced with the capacious goal of standardizing moral instruction statewide, after a half decade of deliberation, cost and culture demanded a more constrained approach. Still, the reach and tenor of the debate was reflective of and impactful on the educational and cultural climate, even if it did not create a usable policy. Furthermore, the fact that despite the victory of the liberal guidelines, local control of schools prevailed and the defense of family and nation became more entrenched suggests the continued negotiation between Right and Left characterizing the 1970s. Though the MGIC's proceedings endured the close scrutiny of Klotz and his supporters—Kehoe chuckled that at a hearing in conservative San Diego "there were [so many] tape recorders in the room . . . you could almost feel the electricity generated from the batteries"—the committee finalized a workable set of guidelines, which were adopted by the board and distributed statewide. [125] The final document abided by *Schempp* and *Vitale*, but still "motivated the classes to recognition of a higher being" and "instilled patriotic fervor." Kehoe recalled three shared "fundamental concerns" across the fractious committee: that the moral guidelines include "a respect for one's country and its laws . . ., to respect the religious views whether it's the Buddhists or the Catholics or other denominations . . . even those that did not care to associate," and that "parents should not be provoked" on the question of sex education, which should be respected as "a fundamental right of the family, and not the classroom."[126] These were the tenets upon which the fractured committee could agree.

By 1974, when the MGC/MGIC dissolved, committee members and Californians generally agreed that the children coming of age amid the dizzying changes reshaping society demanded direction and that such guidance should derive from a definition of morality enshrining the nation and parental authority—a "patriotic morality." Beyond that, however, citizens were no more unanimous about the proper version of morality educators should instill in the state's children than they had been six years earlier. One parent still could not fathom "who would object" to biblically based moral instruction in schools, while another humanist minister's suggestion that morality be imparted by making "every student the center" of a humanities-based curriculum revealed a similar myopia.[127]

A group of school administrators from the San Ysidro school district near the Mexican border perhaps presaged a rising dissatisfaction with public schools as a site for negotiating society's largest questions. The president of the town's school board and several members expressed forthrightly to Sacramento that "it is our belief that religion should be taught by the church and parents. God entrusted parents with youngsters and parents should have the total responsibility to bring their children along in the faith they choose." The problem with the challenge facing the MGC, and with the proposed solutions embodied in its guidelines, again hinged on the nation's growing pluralism. To them, "under the State Board's concept a diluted mixture of all faiths would probably only succeed in undoing the work of religious leaders and parents." The nation's diversity thus rendered the MGC's universalist aims futile. "How can *you* . . . put this burden (religion) on the public schools and expect people of all faiths to remain happy with the results?"[128]

Citizens and policymakers operated in a landscape in which curricular questions around race, ethnicity, religion, sexuality, and morality converged, suffusing the nuclear family with patriotic significance. Couching moral questions in a patriotic frame was not dissembling but rather represented the development of an organic Americanism among citizens struggling to find solid, common ground on a rapidly shifting foundation. Still, the San Ysidro board's sense that the polity's burgeoning diversity obviated even tenuous consensus in the schoolhouse portended an age in which Americans would find such universalism in the public sphere increasingly elusive, even as the MGC wrought a patriotic morality that valorized parental authority and national identity in a way that was tentatively embraced across the political spectrum.[129]

# "THIS THING IS SPREADING ALL OVER CALIFORNIA"

## SEX EDUCATION IN THE SEVENTIES

Wearing the sculpted bouffant hairdo and primly tied scarf favored by respectable ladies of the age, first lady Betty Ford appeared on *60 Minutes* in the summer of 1975 and sparked national controversy for her nonchalant comment that she "wouldn't be surprised" if her eighteen-year-old daughter was having an affair, as she was "like all young girls."[1] Ford's remark showcased not only the much-remarked upon "independent streak" that led her to support abortion rights and the Equal Rights Amendment, but also major changes afoot in American attitudes toward sex, youth, and popular culture. Conservatives immediately attacked Ford, but the "bravos" came just as loudly. SIECUS founder Mary Steichen Calderone, often dubbed "the first lady of sex education," praised Ford for obviously understanding "the most important thing . . . not closing any doors to communication with her daughter."[2] Former first daughter Lynda Byrd Johnson Robb chimed in to dismiss the notion that Ford's attitude was "shocking" or "advocated promiscuity" and insisted that it instead reflected an understanding of "young people as individuals and their opinions and needs."[3] Everyday Americans praised Ford's candor with similar enthusiasm.[4]

That the wife of the president of the United States could make such comments at all and that it did not amount to political suicide—in fact, just the opposite—revealed that, even in an era characterized as "rightward bound," progressive attitudes and discursive openness actually thrived.[5] The story of school-based sex education in the 1970s, over which conservatives had declared victory at the close of the 1960s, suggests the need for a revised interpretation of the era. While sustained attacks on sex education reveal how the politics of family became a rallying cry for conservatives in the late twentieth century, the programs themselves—and their quieter successes—speak to the persistent power of progressivism in the K–12 schoolhouse and society. The same summer that Betty Ford so publicly acknowledged her daughter's identity as a sexual being, Calderone, speaking before a Brandeis University audience, praised an apparent paradigm shift in popular attitudes about sex: "Until just the last decade our sexual selves were held in thrall to the age-old fear and suspicion of that force known as eroticism. . . . Yet the news is good about sex; for more and more of us are being emancipated from that crippling and useless fear."[6] Such optimism—from the woman whose advocacy of sex education had earned her the epithets "dirty old lady" and "Misfit Prostitute from Hell"—challenges the notion that conservative backlash was the prevailing spirit of the 1970s.[7] Moderate and conservative Californians' victory over sex education and bilingual education and the cultural trends they symbolized was hardly assured in an era characterized by an embrace of cultural and moral diversity.

Even in the wake of the vitriolic battles over sex education that had proved so damaging to programs nationwide, Calderone correctly perceived a loosening of discursive mores in classrooms and beyond during the 1970s, a shift that was welcomed by many. In 1971, the Boston Women's Health Book Collective published *Our Bodies, Ourselves*, which celebrated a feminist approach to sex education; by 1975, sex educators had access to a wide range of curricular materials, including those addressing the sexual identities of the mentally disabled.[8] (See figure 8.1.) Many church community leaders, once reliably resistant to sex education, even expressed the need to supplant didactic moralism with "a dialogue approach which is a discussion of goals and values." One 1969 survey of fifty Southern California clergy revealed that the "ostrich-like attitude" of believing "the less talk about sex, the better" was eroding as churches eagerly sought to expand their sex education offerings.[9] By the end of the 1970s, one San Francisco mother responded enthusiastically to an article on teaching children about sex in *Family Circle*, hardly a radical publication: "I have been a reader of your magazine for many, many years and do not recall seeing the word *homosexual* appear in print. So when I saw it used two times, I wanted to applaud you."[10] Reflecting this sentiment, sex education programs in California and the country actually multiplied in the 1970s, fueled by the mounting energy of the gay rights, feminist, and sexual liberation movements. In openly discussing topics such as homosexuality and abortion, sex education in this era was far more progressive than that motivated by the sexual liberalism of the 1960s, which tended to eschew talk of nonprocreative sexuality and steered students exclusively toward heterosexual marriage.

FIGURE 8.1 The original cover of the Boston Women's Health Collective's 1971 "Our Bodies, Ourselves," a pioneering text in feminist-influenced sex education. Reprinted with copyright and permission of Our Bodies, Ourselves, and by courtesy of the Schlesinger Library on the History of Women in America, The Radcliffe Institute for Advanced Study.

Conservatives who surveyed this cultural landscape in the 1970s were chagrined. Even in the realm of sex education, where they had successfully dismantled curricula and rallied support among previously moderate Californians to defend the family and traditional morality, they felt uneasy. Journalist John Steinbacher, whose vituperative attacks on sex education in numerous columns and books were often credited with engineering these victories, lamented that the myopia of conservatives in analyzing "each word" in offensive sex educational curricula had distracted them from a greater danger. Sex education, he argued—alluding to the cosmopolitanism of emerging multicultural pedagogies—should be seen as part of "a much larger problem through which educationists or one-worlders are SUCCEEDING at taking over kids and minds."[11] In San Mateo County, opponents of sex education had waged a battle so fierce and well organized it became the standard for community organizers. During the 1970s, however, parents, teachers, and the general public overwhelmingly supported sex education and volunteered to pilot Planned Parenthood-designed programs.[12] Similarly, even in Anaheim, where the Right ostensibly enjoyed its greatest triumph over sex education, dismantling a nationally acclaimed program and sending Paul Cook, a popular local superintendent into early retirement, a local mother wrote plaintively to conservative state superintendent Max Rafferty in 1970. She lamented the "dismal situation" for local conservatives who attempted to combat the grander educational strategies of educational progressives, of which sex education had been a mere facet.[13] Her sense of participating in a movement with waning support was prescient; when two Democrats took Orange County in 1974 for the first time since the New Deal, the *New York Times* reported that the region's identity "as the right-wing capital of the West may be fading."[14]

Indeed, this sense that the victory over sex education was incomplete and that a far broader cultural dissipation was at work was in important ways affirmed in the 1970s. One conservative group, People of America Responding to Educational Needs of Today's Society (PARENTS), reflected disdainfully on the power the "antifamily forces" had gained in the preceding decade for an agenda promoting " 'gay rights,' women's lib, kiddie lib, and increased government bureaucracy to . . . break down traditional American values."[15] While the 1970s saw Anita Bryant's antigay organization Save Our Children gain national attention, and the Briggs Initiative (an ultimately failed effort to ban homosexual teachers) make it to the ballot box in California, this decade was arguably just as powerfully defined by advances in gender and sexuality rights in California and the nation at large. The US Supreme Court's landmark *Roe v. Wade* decision declared abortion legal in 1973 (a year after California), Title IX generated new opportunities for women's athletics, and the Equal Rights Amendment found unprecedented support. Gay rights advocates also built on the advances of the sexual revolution and feminist movement, achieving new visibility in the wake of the Stonewall riots.[16] To some, sex education seemed to be of a piece with these disturbing developments, which were infiltrating the schools. When conservative legislator Gordon John Humphrey expressed horror before Congress at President Carter's 1977 appointment of a "militant lesbian" as an advisor, he cited her authorship of "Lesbians and the Schools," which argued for a curriculum acknowledging that "the struggle for the equality of women must be extended to included control over our entire lives, especially our sexuality," as evidence of how far astray liberals were leading American youth and how besieged their tax-supported classrooms had become.[17]

The threat was not imagined. Sex education programs were multiplying in California and nationwide. A 1978 study showed that in the previous four years the presence of sex education in American schools grew from 10 to 37 percent, and the US Department of Health, Education and Welfare remarked that the presence of extracurricular and informal offerings meant that "there might be more sex education taking place than hitherto believed."[18] This expansion was hardly the project of an out-of-touch cultural elite filled with "permissive pedagogues" and "the leftist college professors who throughout the past decade have lip-smackingly encouraged the violent to become thugs, the unpatriotic to become treasonable, and the obscene to become unspeakable" all by "promoting the philosophy of John Dewey, singing the praise of permissiveness, assiduously massaging each other's ego," as notoriously strident state superintendent Max Rafferty suggested.[19] Rather, the "Moms and Pops" Rafferty championed actually came to show growing acceptance of sex education programs during the 1970s nationwide.[20] A Gallup poll showed that support for teaching about contraception in schools jumped from 35 to 70 percent from 1970 to 1977, while a 1975 survey of superintendents surprisingly revealed that only 5 percent of local battles over sex education resulted in the termination of programs; "more than 50% were *expanded* following controversy."[21]

Sex education programs and the fraught conversations they inspired also engaged a far broader swath of the population than they had just a few years earlier. Even amid the cultural transformations of the late 1960s, sex education programs had been conceived for and rolled out in mostly white districts. Similarly, the parents who organized to combat these curricula were most likely to be suburban Anglo homemakers. In the 1970s, however, greater numbers of children from more diverse backgrounds were studying sexuality; the communities examined by the most comprehensive study of California sex education programs at the time were comprised of almost half minority students, about 30 percent of whom identified as Hispanic, and ultimately recognized that "additional research on the most appropriate methods and approaches for students of different cultural and ethnic backgrounds is clearly needed."[22] The sex education programs launched in this era, many of them by Planned Parenthood, also deliberately targeted the full socioeconomic spectrum; the same study of twelve California districts revealed only 8 percent of parents holding an advanced or professional degree, and over 20 percent not holding a high school diploma.[23] The 1970s saw sex education programs engage more schoolchildren in more hours of instruction and across a broader and more diverse range of communities.

In California, this trend was even more pronounced. The decision of the MGC to empower local districts to make all final decisions regarding sex education curricular materials "differed completely from previous practice in which districts had a mandate to use state-adopted materials and receive pre-approval." Less a victory for small-government conservatives than it may have seemed, this policy provided flexibility in sex education pedagogy throughout the 1970s, often enabling the introduction of programs that engaged topics far more salacious than the mechanical descriptions of masturbation and intercourse that first inspired opposition.[24] For instance, one state Department of Education official failed to console a San Francisco mother worried about the homosexual guest speaker who had visited her child's class, writing that, lamentably, the state lacked power to veto the speakers chosen by her local district. The state followed up weakly on this parent's complaint over a year later with a perfunctory interview of district officials.[25] Over the next decade, San Francisco's efforts in sex education only became more expansive. Other citizens spoke out to defend gay rights, demanding the recognition afforded to "minority groups" and dismissing concerns about classroom discussions of homosexuality as "grotesque hypocrisy," especially when "this country has been killing people in Southeast Asia as long as most young people can remember . . . and the only thing that makes them different . . . is that they have a different kind of LOVING."[26] One homosexual rights advocacy group felt so emboldened as to demand their organizational literature be "listed on all resource lists in this field."[27] Conservatives perhaps won the battle to limit government oversight of schools, but this diffusion of responsibility and reduced supervision permitted the development and implementation of many diverse and adventurous programs shaped by local prerogatives and broader cultural shifts to occur out of the public spotlight.

If local districts were invested with new energy, so too did the state deliberately elaborate an apparatus to support such programs and policy. A 1969 state resolution had been mostly reactive, banning "outside resources" from schools and mandating that parents opt in to family life and sex education programs rather than opt out, lessening the number of students exposed to such instruction. However, a growing group of advocacy organizations ranging from the American Medical Association to the National Education Association articulated "support for sound sex education," and by 1971, the State Board drafted and successfully passed a resolution that secured sex education as part of the state's educational policy.[28] The resolution explicitly called for the state university system to cooperate with the Department of Education and local districts "to develop and expand programs in family life education as part of their secondary and elementary teacher education curriculum."[29] Beyond this commitment to institutionalize family life and sex education in both the K–12 and higher education systems, the resolution pledged to use "all federal funds which may be available therefor [sic]."[30] In spite of the emergent Right's success in targeting sex education as a threat to the American family, the programs only seemed to gain popular and institutional support in the ensuing years.

Perhaps just as important as this decentralization and institutionalization to the growth of new programs was the explicit decision by SIECUS to focus its energies away from sex education. Calderone declared publicly that SIECUS was more interested in educating adults than children and in the 1970s devoted much of her time to exploring sexuality in middle and old age.[31] Especially in California, where the Right had in 1969 secured legislation banning the "communistic and perverse" SIECUS from classrooms, and routinely vilified founder Calderone as "Mary Stinken' Calderone, tool of Satan and the Zionists," the organization had come to symbolize the most pernicious social ills some argued sex education perpetuated.[32] Although SIECUS had never provided more than consultations to districts interested in launching sex education, Calderone recounted, "We've been accused of being communists, perverts, rapers and seducers of children. Wherever there's a local community that would like to contact us to consider sex education in the schools, the clouds of fear and suspicion are raised."[33] Indeed, California's 1972 guidelines for sex education deliberately excised all references to SIECUS, while also removing the explicit ban that conservatives had fought to include three years before.[34]

Hyperbole aside, Calderone's vision for sex education unapologetically faulted parents for cultivating a "long, damaging chain of associations in the child's mind that will later interfere with his or her adult sexual life." She saw sex education as a necessary counterweight to parents, "who surely act most destructively when they impart their own negative attitudes about body image and eroticism."[35] This clarity of purpose enabled SIECUS to help launch and support hundreds of local sex education programs, but also enraged defenders of parental authority, whose ranks grew as the threat of social revolution intensified during the late 1960s. While sex educator Sol Gordon wrote comic books poking fun at parents' ineptness at educating their children about sexuality, many programs launched in the 1970s actively advertised parental involvement in their initiatives.[36] Calderone's shift in interest actually enabled the development of new curricula free from the stigma that had become inseparable from the organization.

Ironically, into this gap stepped sex educators who promoted bolder programs that reflected the greater permissiveness of the larger culture and far exceeded the measured sexual liberalism Calderone and SIECUS espoused.[37] Planned Parenthood, where Calderone had once served as medical director, was better known for its advocacy of abortion and reproductive rights and emerged as California's most inspired and energetic architect of sex education. In the midst of the battles of 1969, Planned Parenthood had proactively reached out to the embattled communities of Anaheim and San Mateo to share with administrators the "scurrilous leaflets" and "exposes" of their programs being circulated statewide, and sometimes even nationally.[38] Planned Parenthood soon assumed a more central role in creating and implementing school-based sex education, between 1974 and 1978 piloting curricula reaching thousands of students. Planned Parenthood trained hundreds of teachers across the state in initiatives funded by state and district monies, largely, according to one independent researcher, due to "teacher requests for Planned Parenthood guest speakers" and "positive student and teacher response."[39] Described by the organization's director of the Western Regions as "zealous" about their errand, some Planned Parenthood educators responded so quickly to provide materials and lectures to interested schools that they "may have gotten some teachers into trouble" by presenting lessons without parental approval.[40] Such challenges were no match for the momentum propelling Planned Parenthood's commitment to sex education. In 1978, the Department of Health, Education, and Welfare actually funded Planned Parenthood to continue assisting local districts.

On the ground and from recently established organizations, there existed considerable support for sex education provided by an operation just as, if not more, controversial than SIECUS. During the 1970s, as such (newly self-identified) "pro-choice" organizations worked to destigmatize

and provide access to safe abortions, Calderone vocally defined sex education as a way to prevent the "medical immorality that is abortion."[41] While
her opponents had depicted her as a debauched libertine, Calderone maintained even at the height of the controversies that "SIECUS is not trying to
change conventional attitudes toward sex."[42] This moderation was upheld
by the broad support she enjoyed from mainline Christian churches; a
letter from one Chicago Unitarian minister was only unique in request-
ing copies of Calderone's *Playboy* interview to distribute to the congregation.[43] As transgressive (or innovative, depending on the perspective) as
Calderone's ideas seemed to some in the late 1960s, in the 1970s many sex
educators and everyday citizens embraced sexual ideologies that ventured
far beyond SIECUS's vision, yet which curiously met far less resistance
than SIECUS had.

The content of sex education classes also shifted markedly in the 1970s,
reflecting the spirit of the times. Extensive letters to the state Department
of Education revealed that local curricula were employing techniques only
imagined in the "depravity narratives" of the preceding decade.[44] One 1979
study showed that "attitudes toward premarital intercourse have changed significantly . . . most younger males and females accept the idea of intercourse
before marriage as permissible," and new sex education programs took
for granted this "new morality"[45] the MGC had portended so ambivalently.
Democratic assemblywoman March Fong, who would successfully carry
Orange County to become California's secretary of state in 1974, effectively
advocated for more honest sex education programs reflecting "realistic attitudes," which had come to mean casting "women as more than procreating
machines" and ceasing "to equate virility with multiple paternity."[46] In Placer
County, located in the sparsely populated Sierra foothills, teachers organized
a Planned Parenthood speaker exchange to foster frank discussion of contraception and abortion. Throughout the state, even in notoriously conservative
Orange County, teachers invited homosexual speakers to "demystify" gay life,
and students at one Berkeley school conducted a critical analysis of a pornography film.[47] Major change was clearly underway, if quietly and locally, in the
wake of the battles of the late 1960s.

Like the family life programs of the postwar era, these expanding curricula had a broad pedagogical purview, covering topics including "contraception, numerous sexual activities, the emotional and social aspects of sexual
activity, values, and decision-making and communication skills." Rather than
confining acceptable forms of sexual expression to marriage, newer programs

echoed the embrace of pluralism usually associated with the era's ethnic rights movements, striving to "make students more tolerant of the sexual practices of others."[48] Significantly, HEW, better known for its pioneering role in desegregation and bilingual education, issued a national report on sex education in 1979 unapologetically advocating for programs that created a "less judgmental atmosphere" and naming an important reason to involve parents as merely "to provide a buffer to opposition."[49] A social psychology professor openly articulated in his course description that the class would "study some alternatives to marriage such as the single life and communal living."[50] This shift was transpiring nationally. In New York City, the Board of Education in 1976 developed the "Changing Sex Roles in a Changing Society" curriculum, which in response to feminist critiques integrated progressive sex education into social studies classes.[51] Sex education programs only multiplied in the United States thanks to popular support and a greater collective willingness to openly acknowledge, and even celebrate, sexuality for pleasure rather than for procreation.

Unlike many offerings in the 1950s and 1960s, which advocated open discussion of sexuality in the service of the nuclear family, these new programs endeavored to facilitate "a positive and fulfilling sexuality" among young people, echoing the growing fascination with "self-actualization" associated with the era's New Age movement.[52] These expanding offerings built upon the sort of capacious definition of sexuality SIECUS espoused, "broadening the concept of sex to include . . . gender-role behavior, which in the long run are more important than physical sex."[53] Yet they were also about enabling youth to develop "personal values that guide their own behavior" in realms beyond sexuality.[54] The programs that found expanding support in the 1970s exhibited a new emphasis on self-esteem, frankness, and autonomous decision-making, "encouraging self-acceptance and self-awareness" and "communication in activities focusing on the family."[55] One thirteen-year-old girl described the main lesson she learned as needing "to make my own decisions and not to let anyone push me into anything."[56] On explicitly sexual matters, these newer curricula also eschewed the moralism that had characterized many earlier programs and accepted that students might be sexually active and that they should "explore the increasing range of sex role options available to young people . . . and define their own concepts of masculinity and femininity."[57] Even at the junior high school level, curricula provided "basic information" on pregnancy and birth, as well as on "alternatives to unplanned pregnancy," and explored the harmful effects of "sex-role stereotyping."[58] Cultivating an independent sense of self was core to the offerings that gained the most traction in the 1970s.

Astonishingly, considering the fervor of debates over sex education a decade earlier, in nine pilot districts selected for their political and cultural diversity, less than 2 percent of parents resisted the curriculum in 1979.[59] This reception had come to be unremarkable: the Tamalpais Unified School District in Northern California introduced a comprehensive program in 1974, and as early as 1972 a state Department of Education report commented, "Even in conservative Orange County, there is significant support for sex education."[60] In the same year, the special assistant to the State Board of Education reported so few incidents (eight) around sex education that he was able to address all but one with personal visits to districts all over the state, though notably none in Orange County, once wracked by sex education controversy.[61] Social movements championing sexual liberation and self-determination gained traction far beyond the college campuses and radical circles in which they first emerged in the 1960s, as the erosion of cultural and bureaucratic barriers permitted the expression of such ideas in once safeguarded classrooms.

Furthermore, the argument that sex educators lacked professional credibility held less merit as certification and degree programs proliferated. Upon founding SIECUS in 1964, Calderone commented that only three medical schools in the country "barely mentioned sex education" in their curricula. In 1972, when the State Board's Policies and Programs Committee turned to address sex education, their first qualitative recommendation was a general "requirement that teachers presenting material and teaching units in the area of family life education receive special preparation that would assure and maintain the highest possible quality of instruction in this area."[62] By 1976, educational institutions had heeded the demands for more, and better trained, sex educators. "All of the medical schools offer such courses and any town in American wanting a program in sex education can get one; more than 90 university workshops annually offer training," Calderone reported enthusiastically in one speech.[63] Nationally, the movement was achieving formal recognition as well. The American Association of Sex Educators and Counselors announced a certification plan for sex educators in 1974, and one week in October 1975 was declared National Family Sex Education Week by the federal Department of Education. In Anaheim, of all places, the National Association of Secondary School Principals convened a forum in 1978 to discuss "Developing an Effective Sex Education Curriculum."[64]

The formal criteria for sex educators that emerged reflected a dramatic shift from the informal standards that had in 1969 made one San Diego educator an "ideal" sex education teacher based on her longstanding heterosexual marriage and motherhood of two children.[65] Instead, embracing the pluralistic attitude embodied by the declaration "I respect different cultural values and mores which exist in my community" made teachers best suited to lead family life and sex education programs, according to authorities.[66] The "competency model" developed by Planned Parenthood over the course of the 1970s defined fitness to teach by moral and philosophical flexibility, by a commitment foremost to recognizing that "acceptance/comfort with one's sexuality is necessary for healthy personal adjustment" and being "open minded and accepting of different values, attitudes, and behaviors in others." Secondarily, the model acknowledged, "parents have a right to be actively involved in the sex education of their own children."[67] Sex educators had learned to tread lightly on the question of parental authority due to the fervor with which this question rallied the Right, though throughout the 1970s they more decisively prized the independence of youth over unquestioning deference to parental prerogative.

More sex education taught by more credentialed (or psychologically well adjusted) educators did not in itself ensure a more liberalized sexual discourse, especially in a nation that "quivered" at the reported one million teenage pregnancies annually.[68] Some sex educators continued to see such programs primarily as bulwarks against pervasive profligacy and adolescent promiscuity, even as innovative tactics such as distributing contraceptives shocked some parents.[69] Historian Rickie Solinger comments that the 1970s saw a particular panic over illegitimacy as "the crux symbol of what was wrong with these overlapping liberation movements," and many perceived sex education primarily as a tool to redress this troubling trend.[70] Even Calderone struck this chord, cautioning that while cultural progress and the passage of a California law requiring doctors and social workers to study human sexuality indicated significant strides, the battle for adequate sex education was hardly won. "There's an impression that there is 'all that sex education' in the schools," she wrote, "but if it were there, we would not have the high venereal disease and pregnancy rates we have today."[71] Similarly, one survey of California programs in the 1970s showed that the more daring topics (specifically sex roles and teen parenting) received the least attention, while pregnancy and birth, always major areas of focus even in very conservative programs, consistently garnered the most.[72]

For all of Calderone's optimism that the 1970s represented the birth of newly enlightened attitudes about sexuality, even she in 1974 posed the question of whether human sexuality represented "battleground or peaceground" as opposition persisted.[73] Some parents continued to link moral dissipation to the growth of sex education programs and levied complaints as many curricula became more adventurous. Just the name "Planned Parenthood" raised hackles, as conservative groups associated the organization with "liberal anti-family forces" such as the national Gay Task Force, the National Alliance for Optional Parenthood, the Zero Population Growth, and Women's Action Alliance, Inc.[74] In 1981, a mother from Lodi, California, claimed that with the help of a few "pro-family people," she and nine thousand irate parents had finally obtained her district's "secret syllabi" and were enraged at the activities suggested by the PTA and Planned Parenthood, who had jointly designed the curriculum. The "radical" programs being "shoved down [their] throats again" over the 1970s were most outrageous for the class assignments of "checking on costs of contraceptives in drug stores" and "making lists of telephone numbers and mapping routes to contraceptive-abortion clinics." Consistent with the claims of earlier opponents, however, was this mother's concern that "all this was available without parental knowledge or consent!," reflecting the persistent and powerful notion that the family was under unremitting attack by sexual progressives.[75] In a Congressional hearing on the upcoming White House Conference on the Family, a conservative senator decried the focus on "personal satisfaction" in existing family life programs as "just about [summing] up the value system of many professional social service activists these days . . . another reason why profamily Americans are mobilizing to protect their homes."[76]

The fracas over California's failed Proposition 6, or the "Briggs Initiative," perhaps best showcases the continued volatility of questions of sexual propriety and education. It also demonstrates how progressive mores were becoming entrenched in school and society. Attempting to build on the successful campaign of popular singer and Florida Citrus Commission spokeswoman Anita Bryant to uphold discriminatory legislation against homosexuals, Orange County state senator John Briggs crafted an initiative to ban homosexuals from teaching in public schools.[77] "This thing is spreading all over California," Briggs told an audience of 250 in a Sherman Oaks Hilton, "and the Bible is very clear that homosexuality is anti-life and anti-family." Bryant and Briggs reacted to the rising power and visibility of the national gay liberation movement, but the most immediate provocation for Briggs was the championing of the "gay lifestyle" as an alternative to "family life" in courses he described as required by the San Francisco Board of Education. The district denied mandating such courses, pointing out that homosexuality was often mentioned along with "threats to optimal growth and development . . . along with illegitimate parentage, dependence on drugs, venereal disease, and marriage before economic competence and emotional maturity."[78] Briggs likely overstated not only the enthusiasm of Bay Area liberals for promoting homosexuality in local classrooms but also the zeal of conservative opposition. The initiative overwhelmingly failed, and Ronald Reagan, by then contemplating a run for the presidency, strongly opposed Briggs, writing in Los Angeles's conservative *Herald-Examiner*, "Whatever it is, homosexuality is not a contagious disease like the measles . . . a child's teachers do not really influence this."[79] Sex at school continued to inspire classroom wars in the 1970s, but sexual progressives were newly able to hold their ground against conservative attack.

California's most significant controversy over sex education in the 1970s was about state approval of the textbook *Human Sexuality*, one of thirty texts recommended by the board for local use.[80] Originally a college textbook, *Human Sexuality* was adopted by the State Board of Education in January 1972, pending revisions for its intended younger public, California's seventh- and eighth-grade students.[81] The debate reflects the evolving issues at stake in sex education: complaints about the textbook were articulated in far more measured rhetoric than those in the battles that transpired only a few years prior, even as the material at stake was substantially more explicit. While any mention of masturbation had ignited controversy in the late 1960s, the board insisted only that the sentence, "Masturbation is a normal sexual activity," be edited to read, "Masturbation is a frequent sexual activity." Similarly, while all discussion of premarital sex, especially that acknowledging female desire, had so recently been forbidden, the editors were requested only to change the figure estimating how many women had engaged in sexual intercourse before marriage from "almost 50 %" to "some or all." The *Los Angeles Times* education reporter remarked on the unprecedented extent of the board's revisions, but virtually none of the items critics demanded be redacted—frigidity, impotency, nymphomania, incest, and parthenogenesis—had even entered into the discourse of the earlier battles.[82] Echoing preceding fights, however, the board demanded an entire chapter removed that blamed teenage promiscuity on "uninformed" and repressed parents. This move emphasized the continued power of parental authority on educational questions.

Though some ardent opponents of sex education continued to depict the burgeoning programs as evidence of vast plots to pervert children and enact a world revolution—the pamphlet "Is the Schoolhouse the Place to Teach Raw Sex?" entered its fourth print run in 1974—by 1972 the rhetoric of opponents to *Human Sexuality* had cooled considerably.[83] Critics of the textbook addressed the board from cities as far-flung as Mountain View, Visalia, Sacramento, and San Diego, but took exception primarily to the text's language and explicitness rather than to its connection to any larger moral or geopolitical implications.[84] While one parent mentioned the "moral disaster" represented by the text's imminent adoption, the majority of letters contained anodyne criticisms such as the comment of a Downey parent, who noted that the board should adopt "good, appropriate texts," or another who questioned the need for such "unnecessary detail."[85] Reflecting a broader concern about the social implications of the rising teenage pregnancy rate, this parent commented that the adoption of the text would only encourage runaway population growth, but among the hundreds of letters received by the board, virtually none connected sex education to social cataclysm. When the text came before the board for approval for the second time, a staff member remarked that the book would most likely fail to be adopted due to insufficient demand. When the revised text was ultimately approved for use in September 1974, upon request of "local school districts wishing to order it," the decision inspired virtually no backlash.[86]

Opposition to sex education hardly vanished in the 1970s. Certain cases were idiosyncratic—Santa Cruz County suspended its classes in 1976 when a teacher allegedly boasted of decorating his Christmas tree with inflated condoms and used another as a balloon in the classroom.[87] In certain districts, sex educators described a state of "fear and confusion" that inhibited the development of any new programs, even as, one Compton teacher described under the shield of anonymity, "my 12th graders already have kids who are two and three years old. It's too late."[88] California's programs continued to draw national opposition. As late as 1980, the national Moral Majority specifically identified a textbook, *Life and Health*, in use in Los Angeles schools as pernicious for acknowledging that only in "societies that condemn [premarital sex] there are possible negative consequences." To critics, such relativism amounted to teachers de-privileging American exceptionalism. Curiously, a health educator in Pasadena's public schools framed the inclusion of sex education as a distinctly American project, insisting that "hesitation" felt by "newly arrived immigrants from Spanish-speaking countries and the Near East" should be set aside as sex education was "part of their new country's ways."[89]

If conservatives could claim one major victory from the sex education battles of the late 1960s, it was that parental perspectives became paramount in the development of sex education curricula thereafter. No community wanted to find itself as the next Anaheim or San Mateo, and seeking parental engagement—even explicit approval—on sex education curricula appealed to educators and policymakers across the political spectrum as the most reliable way to avoid controversy. The most comprehensive report on program implementation showed that throughout the 1970s parent committees were overwhelmingly involved in the development of the new curricula (most of them run by Planned Parenthood). Fittingly, the popular family life education curriculum guide included five tenets of a "responsible program," the first three of which deemed parents as the primary party to consult in curriculum design (before professionals) and noted the importance of "[promoting] respect for parental values" and "helping students clarify and appreciate their values related to the family and sexuality."[90] Sex education, even in the more liberal 1970s, was an important crucible for forging the "family values" sensibility that has become so integral to modern political culture.

Ironically, once incorporating parental perspectives became indispensable to designing and implementing sex education programs, many parents apparently became less unnerved by sex education offerings, even as programs became bolder. While parents who spoke out against sex education had once advocated silent acceptance of traditional values on such matters, many parents celebrated the new programs specifically for encouraging discussion of sexuality and "responded most positively to the programs' . . . emphasis on decision-making, self-esteem and clarification of personal values," literally using the language of "values clarification" that had earned such opprobrium in social studies and sex education debates.[91] As opposed to the clash between students loudly advocating for sex education and parents attempting to silence them evidenced in the Anaheim and San Mateo controversies, by the late 1970s, parents were almost as enthusiastic about expanding such programs as were students: 87 percent and 90 percent, respectively.[92]

Teenagers only spoke up louder over the course of the 1970s to praise and shape sex education programs, often in chorus with their parents. Unlike the young people in this era who perhaps found a new closeness with their parents' generation by distancing themselves from 1960s radicalism, the case of sex education suggests that some parents and young people were together embracing more relaxed sexual attitudes.[93] Even as sex education continued to bear the influence the burgeoning family values movement, these programs also revealed subtle challenges to family authority. Beyond the nuclear family,

sex education programs continued the work of the 1960s social justice movements in questioning power relationships writ large. An impact study showed
that girls overall not only liked the programs best, but consistently credited
sex education curricula with empowering them as decision makers. Race
and class only heightened these effects. Hispanic girls were most likely to
feel a boost in their self-esteem thanks to the classes, while students of lower
socioeconomic backgrounds most consistently reported that their concepts
of conventional sex roles had been altered.[94] The report acknowledged that
most programs were too modest—occupying from just seven to sixty hours of
class time per school year—to be credited with effecting these shifts, but their
significance is perhaps greater in reflecting larger cultural transformations at
work.[95] While the report described the programs existing in a society defining
"women's highest value in terms of childbearing and childrearing, which continue to promulgate a 'double standard,'" hindsight suggests this worldview
truly was coming apart. The almost uncontested presence of sex education in
many communities in the 1970s symbolizes this unremarked revolution, even
if it did not cause it.[96]

Overall, sex education was no longer the most controversial educational
question of the day in this decade. As a supportive Berkeley mother wrote to
Calderone in late 1970, "busing seems to have displaced sex ed as the number one educational issue."[97] Similarly, when Calderone visited a school in
Marietta, Georgia, in 1975 to lecture on sex education, a local journalist commented that her appearance "was far different from her 1968 visit. Thursday
there were no pickets, no demonstrations. . . . Instead, an opening night
crowd of eight hundred was enthusiastically receptive to the remarks by the
pioneer in sex education."[98] Calderone, "the stately grandmother," argued to
the supportive crowd that "we won't have civil rights until we have human
sexual rights," boldly making the sort of connection to broader social context
that once had made her and sex education programs so controversial.[99] This
audience clearly evinced a greater openness to sexual discourse than the many
Calderone had encountered just several years earlier, though a journalist still
noted "slight uncomfortable shifting by the audience when Dr. Calderone
touched on masturbation and on sex for the mentally retarded"— topics she
almost certainly would never have publicly broached before.[100]

Focusing on defeating sex education alone—even as the programs themselves and society at large came to resemble the dystopia against which opponents had raged with great success in the late 1960s—had begun to seem like
attempting to beat back an inexorable rising tide. Not only were sex education programs taking up the ever more capacious questions of gender and

sexuality preoccupying the nation, but they were integrated across the curriculum, making the threat even harder to root out. Calderone began to appear moderate in the face of the radicalizing social climate. By 1975, Calderone felt her public resistance to the militant feminists who "want other women to see and practice life as she does," meant she "got it from all sides—from the conservatives to the feminists."[101] She unapologetically embraced the kind of essentialist interpretation of gender that was losing favor among many women who might have supported her just a few years earlier. "It is women alone," she argued, "who can give men the courage to become gentle and loving and fostering human beings, but the militancy and hardness that I deplore can only drive men further back into their hardened attitudes in self-defense."[102] Calderone had been the symbol of sex education during the classroom wars of the 1960s; over the course of the 1970s, her distance from the programs represented just as vividly the bold new directions of both sex education and society.

Sex educators had for years advocated integrating the study of sexuality into the broader curriculum, inspiring fury that they were attempting to "sneak" lascivious content past parents. During the 1970s, educators began to achieve this ambitious goal, and one definitive study showed that most family life and sex education programs were integrated into existing social science, health education, or physical education courses.[103] While less than one-half of one percent of parents of high school students questioned these programs, those who did take exception found the changes especially pernicious since their target became more difficult to identify. In 1972, only eight California communities received complaints about sex education programs, but parents in San Mateo were especially concerned that speakers from Planned Parenthood and United for Life were included in programming for Earth Day. In Placer County, parents took exception that a summer school course opaquely entitled "State Requirements" included lectures on human reproduction, the distribution of contraceptive and abortion information, and reportedly "ridiculed sexual abstinence as a primary method of avoiding unwanted pregnancies and VD."[104] The homosexual speakers about which some parents complained were just as likely to visit world history or minority studies classrooms, while new offerings in social psychology propounded the values clarification philosophy MGC conservatives had so reviled.[105] Sex education had become a moving target.

This marked an important change in focus and implementation, for during the classroom wars of the late 1960s, sex educators—SIECUS foremost among them—had defended their programs primarily as bulwarks against the social revolutions and sexual temptations children would inevitably encounter on their own. During the 1970s, greater numbers of parents and citizens wrote in favor of sex education programs in their children's schools, but they also articulated this support in the context of defending homosexual and ethnic rights and critiquing the Vietnam War. Schools were in important ways becoming more progressive, even in the face of intensified and well-organized conservative critiques. Despite parents vocally disagreeing about the place of sex education at school, in general parental authority burgeoned. In 1980, Superintendent Riles conceded that he had been mistaken in thinking "that we know the answers [about sex education] up here. We don't." Instead, he planned to turn "the whole problem over" to local PTAs and reflected that the most important lesson he gleaned from California's sex education classroom wars was "to tiptoe around controversial issues."[106]

In the classroom and beyond, growing numbers of Californians and Americans were apparently aligning sexual openness and tolerance with a broader agenda for social and personal change. Mary Steichen Calderone lamented in 1975 that attacks on her and sex education had been "based on bigotry and prejudice," reflecting how this pedagogy was becoming tied up in the public mind with the struggles for self-determination that defined the era.[107] The 1970s were thus a fertile, if forgotten, moment in the history of sex education. Students and teachers engaged broadly with family, gender, and social issues as the 1950s developers of family life education had intended, yet the discursive openness and social progressivism of the era infused these curricula with new foci and energy. To many, this evolution merited little cause for alarm; social mores were also shifting among citizens more likely to visit a suburban coffee klatch than a campus coffee house. At the same time, some continued to see sex education as a threat to family values and American patriotism. Yet its messages had become so thoroughly integrated into the curriculum and the shifting social fabric that the emergent political Right largely ceased to construct sex education as a unique threat but rather cast it as of a piece with declining morality and rising tax bills. Even one father who had protested the 1971 state resolution expanding sex education—"it's my tax money as much as it is any other parents'," and such instruction was "clearly a matter of individual parental rights"—relented that he and his wife "both fully support *voluntary* sex education in public schools."[108] If sex education opponents of the late 1960s had railed against sex educators like the debauched "Candy Love," by the late 1970s, targeting specific teachers, or even sex education programs, as a unique threat seemed ineffectual when these courses were simply part of broader—and to many, not all that troubling—transformations taking place and spreading across California.

# CONCLUSION

## PROPOSITION 13, PUBLIC SCHOOLS, AND NEW ARENAS IN THE CLASSROOM WARS

By the mid-1970s, two curricular innovations that might have seemed wildly different a decade earlier—one federally funded, linked to antipoverty initiatives, and advocated for by ethnic minorities; the other locally financed, concentrated in affluent districts, and supported by white sexual liberals—had become meaningfully intertwined in a transformed political culture. While programs styled as "bilingual education" and "sex education" had come to encompass varied pedagogical approaches with just as many philosophical orientations, they also symbolized a progressive educational agenda that recognized diversity and questioned cultural and ethical absolutes. The proliferation of these programs, as well as the impassioned opposition they inspired, during the 1960s and 1970s helped give rise to a capacious "patriotic morality" among liberals and conservatives alike. Citizens embracing divergent political agendas increasingly, if uneasily, agreed that family, nation, and morality were tightly enmeshed, and that the embattled public schools bore the responsibility to recognize and respect this relationship.

Some historians, echoing a refrain now familiar on the political left, argue that the era and the issues this book explores bore a conservative groundswell that has exerted the most powerful influence on our modern political culture. Indeed, *Classroom Wars* concurs that the "rise of the Right" has been a signal development of the late twentieth century. The newly volatile curricular questions of bilingual and sexuality education illuminate how concerns about changing demographics, sexual mores, and America's place in the world rallied conservatives to unprecedented activism.

At the same time, the schoolhouse legacies of these traditionalist passions have been less clear. The anti-sex education movement, for example, undoubtedly maintained a national profile into the 1980s. However, the portrait opponents of sex education themselves painted was as increasingly aggrieved by the enduring strength of secularism, educational progressivism, and attendant moral dissolution. Tim LaHaye, a vocal critic of sex education in the early 1970s and today best known for his bestselling *Left Behind* novels, made national headlines in 1981—at the dawn of the Reagan era—declaring that "we are being controlled by a small but very influential cadre of committed humanists, who are determined to turn traditionally moral-minded America into an amoral humanist country."[1] Similarly, when sex educator Sol Gordon embarked on a book tour in 1987, he laughed off the occasional protestors he encountered as reflective of "the irrational elements in society" and impactful mostly in generating welcome publicity.[2]

The same year, in politically conservative San Diego County, held up as a model of traditionalist moral pedagogy in the 1960s and 1970s, the Grossmont district piloted a program showcasing how thoroughly the "new morality" of the 1970s clearly pervaded. Principal Art Pegas wrote that "teachers are in no way told, or encouraged, to come right out and 'tell' students which is morally correct or incorrect." He elaborated, "There is a difference between propaganda and education. Propaganda means, 'this is the truth, this one side,' whereas education means bringing in as many different sides of possible.'"[3] In San Diego and beyond, educators only knit questions of morality and nation together more intimately in the 1970s and 1980s, though often to promote tolerance and critical inquiry rather than absolute parental authority or blind patriotism. By the late 1980s, Grossmont's character education curriculum asked students to grapple with such things as the ethical transgressions of Republican appointee Colonel Oliver North. These debates were present in economics, civics, and history courses. In one class featuring the kind of controversial conversation that would have been reviled during the height of the Cold War two decades earlier, the board read, "BONUS: Define socialism."

Significantly, these worldviews coexisted with little apparent philosophical dissonance by the late 1980s, as advocates of the San Diego program actually celebrated it for reviving "old-time values."[4] Sol Gordon, the sex educator, shared in this outlook that blended respect for nation and family with a celebration of discursive openness and diversity. Gordon's *Raising Children Conservatively in a Sexually Permissive World* (first published in 1983 and in its third printing by 1987) defined "conservative families" as those "who love their country, who respect its Constitution and its laws . . . who believe in God (while worshipping Him in different ways) and who believe that the family is the central constituent of society." At the same time, core to his approach was building students' self-esteem and developing "askable parents" who reject simple "don't, stop, no" answers to their children's questions about sex. Gordon described himself as "a missionary" committed "to get across the message nationwide that knowledge is not harmful."[5] As early as 1970, Wilson Riles declared that the polarization that had characterized Rafferty's seven-year tenure marked the cultural politics of a bygone era: "If my election proves anything, it is that the people are tired of these confrontations. They want solutions to educational problems—not talk and divisiveness."[6] Riles presciently observed changes afoot: the classroom wars over sex and bilingual education that so divided Californians during the 1960s and much of the 1970s would find new foci in the 1980s and beyond.

As many Californians across the political spectrum came to embrace the interconnectedness of school, family, and nation with new energy, they also came to agree that both the archconservative Rafferty and the liberal Riles were failing to govern the increasingly diverse public schools effectively. This dissatisfaction began to manifest itself as early as 1970, in growing attention to what the *Los Angeles Times* named "Dr. Riles's most onerous task . . . the area of school financing."[7] Riles acknowledged that "the state's property-tax basis is entirely inequitable," presaging a spreading skepticism about educational spending usually associated uniquely with an ascendant conservatism. These concerns about the rising costs and dubious payoffs of public schools crystallized in Proposition 13, the famous 1978 tax revolt that inspired similar measures nationwide and transformed the nature of California's classroom wars for decades to come.

## Education, Economic Citizenship, and the Making of Proposition 13

In 1987, former California state controller and assemblyman Kenneth F. Cory reflected on how "the seeds of tax revolt were sown," recalling that "what they did politically was take to the streets telling people their property taxes were too high," thus "fanning the flames" of popular discontent successfully enough to send "millions of signatures" to lawmakers in Sacramento and laying the foundation for the state's infamous 1978 tax revolt.[8] This language recalls a familiar historical narrative describing a populist conservative groundswell among fiscal conservatives that caused the June 1978 passage of Proposition 13, the draconian tax cut which reduced the ceiling on property taxes to 1 percent of assessed value, representing a savings to many homeowners of over

50 percent. Scholarly interpretations of the tax cut diverge, but the measure inarguably had an immense impact, as eighteen states passed tax limitation measures "with astonishing speed" in the wake of Proposition 13.[9] Political scientist Jack Citrin, who offered one of the first scholarly accounts of the revolt, solemnly observed thirty years later, "They say nothing is forever. Except, perhaps, Proposition 13."[10]

Other scholars echoed this fateful tone, crediting the measure with "firing the first shot of a national tax revolt," signifying a "fiscal earthquake," and training the eyes of Washington legislators on Sacramento as "the question on everyone's mind was 'What does it mean for us?'"[11] One *New York Times* journalist argued that legislators were so affected by the mood of Proposition 13 that they were making cuts to the foreign aid budget despite escalating Cold War concerns.[12] The outcome of the overwhelmingly popular initiative (also known as Jarvis-Gann, for its two sponsors, Howard Jarvis and Paul Gann) is remembered not only as ushering in a national climate of fiscal austerity so widespread that Jimmy Carter's press secretary credited the Democratic president's victory to his embrace of "the spirit of Proposition 13," but also as eviscerating financial support for the state's public schools.[13]

Cory, however, was not recalling the efforts of frustrated small-business owners or right-wing organizers in the early months of 1978. The grass roots Cory described mobilizing for tax relief in the streets were gathered by the California Teachers Association, the state teachers' union, which in the late 1960s and early 1970s had rallied to oppose what they perceived was a disproportionate tax burden on counties for education. Cory's recollection of this largely forgotten moment suggests that educational questions were crucial to the making of the tax revolt, that it originated deep in the dramatic events of the preceding two decades, and that much of its success lay in its appeal beyond the ranks of the putative supporters of conservative fiscal policy, including even teachers, who would later define themselves as the chief opponents and victims of the measure.[14]

Four months after the passage of Proposition 13, Charlie Knight, the state associate superintendent for elementary education, declared, "We do not accept the theory that people do not want quality education in California simply because they voted for Proposition 13."[15] On the contrary, definitions of "quality education" were becoming increasingly divergent. The 1960s and 1970s witnessed an extraordinary expansion of the California public school system, both demographically and pedagogically, and anti-tax fervor was in important ways a reaction to those shifts. Citizens' deeply felt identities as both parents and taxpayers intersected in the realm of schoolhouse politics, and the heated controversies that transpired in this arena reveal that the origins of cultural and fiscal conservatism were intimately intertwined.

Scholars of the 1970s and of American economic history have acknowledged an important connection between Proposition 13 and education, but have been concerned almost exclusively with the measure's impact. This impact was real, as schools bore the brunt of the fallout of Proposition 13 and came to depend on the state for 80 percent of their funding.[16] That "education that took most of the loss" caused by the Jarvis initiative was felt acutely; according to one report, "intensified austerity was apparent, with across-the-board cuts in certain educational appropriations ensuing almost immediately."[17] However, a significant budget surplus ($11 billion) prioritized protecting for about two years many of the programs initiated during the preceding decade, most of them designated to support historically underserved student populations. Once that surplus was exhausted, however, California's inability to fulfill federal requirements for local contributions substantially limited funding to the state's schools, intensifying Proposition 13's collateral damage. Particularly hard hit were elective offerings ranging from sociology to international relations, the fine and performing arts, and "life skills" such as home economics and the industrial arts—all of which California had pioneered during the 1960s and 1970s.[18] Offerings for disabled students, for American Indian students, and in vocational education all required "maintenance-of-effort" commitments at the state and local level from previous years in order to secure federal monies.[19] All three, among others, were cut or eliminated in districts unable to raise necessary funds.[20]

Countless media accounts nationally attest to how the schools were sent reeling from Proposition 13. Newspapers were filled with stories of districts declaring bankruptcy, shortening the school day, and laying off teachers by the hundreds: Los Angeles, the nation's second largest school district, "killed" summer school programming intended to serve 260,000 youth and 80,000 adults.[21] One single mother who had worked her way through school "with a baby on her back" was told in June—three days after Proposition 13 passed—that her job as a summer school teacher no longer existed.[22] Similarly, education journals advised teachers not to "postpone seeking solutions . . . until staff reductions are required"; conventional wisdom became that teachers' job security was irreversibly diminished, as was their academic freedom to teach a range of curricula.[23] A new mood of fiscal retrenchment fused with an emergent "back-to-basics" curricular sensibility to extinguish the sense of possibility and innovation that had made California schools a "liberal showcase" and that had once inspired a "smugly held opinion" in education circles that "the

elapsed time between the appearance of an idea in a national education journal and its legislation into the California State Education Code averaged about
three months."[24] By 2009, the performance of California public school students had fallen to forty-ninth in the nation in terms of student-teacher ratio,
and per-pupil spending continues to rank significantly below the national
average. Scholarly and media commentators accept that Proposition 13 bears
important responsibility for this sea change.[25]

"So there is no great mystery about a primary cause of the tax revolt," Jack
Citrin stated matter-of-factly, "It was higher taxes."[26] On the contrary, California's
schools were not merely a secondary casualty of the Jarvis-Gann initiative; concerns about education were central to generating the measure's widespread
popularity. Historians have probed the origins of Proposition 13 debate as to
whether it constituted genuine populism or whether it was merely a "revolt of
the haves," and if it invigorated or ruined state and national economic policy,
but have not seriously considered the role of education in effecting its overwhelming passage.[27] Concerns about educational practice, however, helped
propel Californians to vote to slash the taxes funding many public services.
Schools, which undergirded the ideal of universal Californian prosperity that
had drawn so many to the Golden State throughout the twentieth century,
were foremost among these targets. Contemporaries realized how much the
dramatic changes afoot in public schools amplified concerns about fiscal
wastefulness. One Palo Alto high school teacher felt that "the penny-pinching
pragmatism of Jarvis" overwhelming her wealthy, progressive district was a
backlash to the "powder keg" the schools became when they began reshaping their cultures and curricula in response to radical new ideas about race,
gender, and politics.[28] Michael Kirst, president of the California Board of
Education and Stanford University education policy professor, argued that dramatic changes afoot in California's social fabric "shocked" and "overloaded" its
schools during the 1970s. He doubted public education could withstand the
resultant loss of public esteem.[29] The widespread embrace of Proposition 13
and its damning impact on public schools suggests it could not.

In a fight song entitled "Embattled Taxpayers of the Republic," organizers
for Proposition 13 lamented, "We pay for education, fire, and police too / And
we place these three priority one and not priority two / Like those bureaucrats who hide the truth and use scare tactics too."[30] Significantly, the citizens who rallied in support of the tax revolt perceived education as one of
the most costly, but important, social goods. They took issue specifically with
the type of education untrustworthy government bureaucrats and academics
advocated. Jarvis himself was unapologetic about his belief that "13 must and

should force a total reevaluation of the public school system in California."[31] He dismissed the warnings of the California Teachers Association—by 1978 staunchly opposed to the proposed tax measure—that Proposition 13 would cut meals for needy children, child development centers, summer school, enrichment programs, and other "totally worthless" endeavors such as "driver education, finger-painting, and ethnic studies," asking with undisguised condescension, "What do any of those things have to do with educating children anyway?"[32] As *Classroom Wars* has shown, concerns about education are inextricably intertwined with concerns about the family, and Jarvis skillfully linked the two, expressing the hope that cutting extracurricular programs would prompt more involved child-rearing from "parents who don't want to do their own baby-sitting" and instead were "forcing taxpayers to pay for the huge bill."[33] Exploiting the distrust of government that perceptions of Great Society excess and the Watergate scandals had exacerbated, Jarvis's rhetoric suggests that concerns about education and the family were central to Proposition 13's appeal.

The public schoolhouse of 1960s and 1970s California came to represent the transformations in California's demographics and culture that many citizens found deeply troubling. Programs that questioned normative ideas about nation and family in acknowledging the right of "outsiders" to participate in the public schools and civic society, such as bilingual-bicultural and sex education, proved especially inflammatory.[34] Citizens came to articulate this dissatisfaction—even disgust—primarily through an exceptionally resonant discourse that pinpointed the villains as both the fiscally wasteful government and the vocal interest groups making excessive demands upon it. Locating a fertile portion of the seedbeds of Proposition 13 in the schoolhouse not only expands the discussion of the origins of Proposition 13 beyond the realm of tax policy, but also shows how powerful contemporary fiscal and cultural politics are intertwined. The idea that many unsuspecting Americans consistently voted against their best interests because they were blinded by the "cultural anger" Republican strategists inflamed via the "forgettable skirmishes of the never-ending culture wars" in service of enacting "pro-business economic policies" does not hold.[35] Rather, advocating for tax relief was for an overwhelming number of Californians consonant with stemming the disturbing cultural displacements they felt were disfiguring two of their most honored social institutions—the family and the school—and on their dime, no less.

The breadth of the reforms that inspired reaction cannot be underestimated. Social liberals and political moderates had joined forces to support diverse educational policy and pedagogical reforms intended to address the intellectual and social demands of an increasingly plural society throughout the 1960s and 1970s. Support for innovation, especially to meet the needs of the dramatic influx of Spanish-speaking immigrants—the percentage of Latinos in California public schools doubled between 1967 and 1968—had at one point inspired such enthusiasm that even avowed conservatives such as Max Rafferty and Eugene Gonzales rallied to pioneer bilingual-bicultural programs to help redress egregious rates of academic failure among Mexican American students.[36] Supplementing federal Great Society directives and resources, sexual liberals devised and implemented progressive family life education programs that promoted more frank discussions of sexuality than the schoolhouse had ever witnessed.

As bitterly contested as they became, these programs were met with acclaim nationwide and even in some of the state's most conservative regions. Team teaching, flexible scheduling, and educational television were eagerly embraced. Educators in the late 1970s considered the previous two decades a time characterized by a reformist spirit sustained by a fiscal largesse that in the Proposition 13 era was quickly becoming untenable; Michael Kirst described over fifty reform initiatives undertaken in this era, despite declining enrollments during the 1970s.[37] An English teacher remarked that in "the pursuit of relevance and equality" her district had replaced dress codes and classics "simultaneously and indiscriminately" with "elective programs in black history and a rash of new multicultural holidays for Martin Luther King and Rosh Hashonah."[38] Change seemed so rapid, and often so politicized, that she often wondered, as she entered her classroom each morning, "if the class might explode in her face."[39]

Opposition to progressive educational impulses "exploded," in the English teacher's eyes, or evolved into a powerful anti-tax rhetoric that contributed importantly to the passage of Proposition 13 and to a national resistance to federal initiative. As this book has argued, these progressive educational programs, though disparate in their origins, funding sources, and execution, were thematically linked and inspired criticism that they were academically unserious, immoral, unpatriotic, and above all, expensive. Especially as these curricula grew, and at times even flourished, they inspired even louder criticism for inappropriately employing tax dollars to finance allegedly intellectually dubious programs that assaulted a distinctly American patriotic morality. The anti-tax rhetoric that opponents marshaled to attack a wide range of educational programs is remarkable, both in its convergence and in how collectively, and thus effectively, it derided such curricula as mere "frills." Over the course of the decade, discontented citizens invoked fiscal misappropriation as much as curricular philosophy to undergird their complaints. These activists formed a powerful, but overlooked, source of support for Proposition 13.

The concerned, and increasingly irate, entreaties of many citizens to the State Board and Department of Education and to countless newspapers and radio stations conformed to a similar structure: a critique of a particular curriculum or educational philosophy followed by a statement of outrage that such a practice would be financed with public funds. For example, one teacher from the San Fernando Valley of Los Angeles wrote to Rafferty to complain about the impact of bilingual education on her "rather choice" district. The inconvenience of the new programming was made far more "frustrating" by the "the siphoning off of the tax funds . . . to fill pockets in an unearned manner at the expense of our children's schools." She beseeched Rafferty to "put a spotlight on this kind of a thing when speaking to the tax-paying public."[40] Another mother, Laurel Martin, reserved special bitterness for the state's MGC for its alleged withholding of the proposed statewide moral guidelines, because they were "financed by Californian tax dollars."[41] Nearly a decade later, the power of this argument had multiplied: a Lodi mother impugned "the state" for not releasing "copies of their federally and state tax funded syllabus" until a noble group of "pro-family" people wrested it from them.[42] Frustration with high taxes to finance morally questionable curricula clearly fired up many Californians in this era.[43]

Most remarkably, Californians across the political spectrum embraced this sensibility. Cory, reflecting on his career in the California state bureaucracy, recalled how quickly economic concerns had apparently trumped ideological ferment during his tenure. In formulating education policy, he remembered, the government and the state superintendent rarely heeded calls for reform from either the radical left or "the right-wing nuts. . . . [They] only wanted to know how much money was available. No other question was relevant. All they cared about was the money."[44] Cory's comment sheds light on the unifying embrace among diverse political actors of fiscal belt-tightening. This anti-tax discourse gained power because it tapped into a spreading suspicion of government among liberals and conservatives alike; it thus quickly became the dominant idiom for debating educational questions, even among Democrats and avowed liberals. Legislative campaigns in both parties "became a matter of who could be the most fiscally conservative candidate and who could return the most taxes to the public."[45] Barraged with criticism for the failures of the state's bilingual program in 1976, Wilson Riles turned this rhetorical tactic on his conservative attackers, decrying the critical report as "a self-serving exercise in how to waste taxpayer dollars."[46] In San Jose, rival bilingual education activists Ernesto Galarza and Olivia Martinez, both of whose programs owed much to tax-supported state and federal initiatives, privately and publicly traded accusations about which one was duping taxpayers by squandering public funds on poor pedagogy.[47] Ultimately neither program prevailed, and Galarza recalled in the early 1980s, "Funds have been cut back drastically and staff has been reduced . . . mostly by reason of Prop 13."[48] Demonstrating perhaps most extremely how much fiscal retrenchment had suffused the rhetoric of the day, a thirteen-year-old girl from La Habra led her argument against busing with the declaration, "I feel that this is totally unnecessary and a waste of money." She only secondarily mentioned that busing was unnecessary at her school because "no matter what color or creed, every student does receive equal respect."[49] The impact of this shared discourse was real and impactful.

Of course, a significant "anti-13" movement existed. Many teachers, disabused of the idea the more conservative union had held in the late 1960s that county-level tax cuts would benefit schools, organized passionately against Jarvis-Gann. (See Figure 9.1.) Ninety-percent unionization among teachers in the 1970s helped empower this opposition, but even with the support of the larger organized labor movement, the opponents lacked the lingua franca

NOT US—Teachers and city and county employes from around the state assemble in Sacramento to protest Proposition 13 layoff plans.
Times photo by Andy Hayt

FIGURE 9.1 Los Angeles teachers and city and county employees protest Proposition 13 two weeks after its passage. Photograph by Andy Hayt. "Teachers and city and county employees from around the state assemble in Sacramento to protest Proposition 13 layoff plans," June 20, 1978. Reprinted with copyright and permission of the *Los Angeles Times*.

that sustained the popular groundswell Jarvis-Gann was able to exploit. In the wake of the measure's passage, the California Committee on the Status of Women lamented the insufficient organization of their resistance and emphasized the need to fight to restore funds to public education and to empower women who were overrepresented among teachers and poorer women who had relied on skills centers and outreach centers for economic opportunities.[50] Nonetheless, Peter Schrag writes that nearly every ethnic minority voted for Proposition 13, a remarkable fact considering electoral patterns.[51]

Certain putative champions of small government and tax relief resisted the measure as well. Large corporations such as Southern California Edison, Bank of America, and Standard Oil allied with the AFL-CIO and the state teachers' union to resist Proposition 13, largely because they feared the state would compensate for lost property-tax revenues through higher taxes on big business.[52] Surprisingly, Rafferty, so often held up as an archconservative icon for his embrace of the traditionalist pedagogies and moral didacticism of the "little red schoolhouse," opposed the measure. It was true, he argued in countless syndicated columns and radio broadcasts, that big government and long-haired "com-symps" were trying to destroy America. Voting against school funding, however, was as "dunderheaded" as trying "to get rid of an alleged louse by starving its host."[53] Rafferty's overt resistance to this particular measure is noteworthy, but the bulk of materials he produced during his prolific career served to bolster the anti-tax movement, especially his fulminations about state-funded curricula designed to address linguistic, sexual, and ethnic diversity.

Celebrated Harvard economist John Kenneth Galbraith had railed against Proposition 13 as "a disguised attack on the poor" and prophesied a severe backlash within a year.[54] The backlash never came. One feminist organizer commented, "There is the most enormous political disaffection I've seen since I became active . . . people are so cynical and disappointed with the system that people are not voting—we don't even have to talk about activism."[55] A complementary celebratory sentiment of the private sphere—including the family, private enterprise, and independent and parochial schools—was burgeoning. Declining public school enrollments among white students only intensified this devaluation of education as a public good, and some Californians began to pin their hopes for developing their children into moral Americans elsewhere. Howard Jarvis, for one, trumpeted the relative "efficiency" and moral pedagogy of private and parochial schools in comparison to the "monumental waste that takes place in public schools."[56] The anti-tax movement had provided a shared language to express deeply held reservations about the direction of the school and of the society it was creating through a diverse range of progressive curricula and policies conceived, financed, and enacted over the previous decade and a half.

Proposition 13 was thus driven in important ways by a profound skepticism about educational programs perceived to be aligned with an immoral, antipatriotic, and fiscally improvident counterculture. By the late 1970s, the expansion and adventurousness of progressive educational programs rendered them similarly threatening to a broadening conservative sensibility, which constituted these curricular approaches as an unbearable tax burden upon citizens increasingly dubious of the civic and moral purpose of the public schools. Amid the societal centrality of markets, conservatives and liberals alike realized that a loss of faith in public schools signified a deep social malaise. The Pasadena school board president bemoaned this loss of direction in 1978: "Who can question that our school system in a shambles?" His final claim would resonate broadly with the Californian populace, even as the rifts among them had deepened perhaps irreparably in the preceding decade: "As our schools go, so goes our nation."[57]

## New Arenas in the Classroom Wars

The passage of Proposition 13 vividly showcases how Americans with utterly divergent worldviews about morality, nation, and diversity could find consensus about the failure of ever more expensive public schools to address these themes with pedagogical and political propriety. Educational questions, it turns out, were not just casualties of the Jarvis-Gann initiative but also causes of its popularity. Employing the lens of educational politics to consider the world that Proposition 13 helped make reveals another surprising legacy of this era: notwithstanding the presumption of a "rightward turn" defining the last three decades of the twentieth century, public schools also exhibited a persistent progressivism.

The uniqueness of the historical moment *Classroom Wars* explores is due in part to Americans of all political stripes believing the public schools were worth a fight. In the 1960s and 1970s, militant Chicanos in East Los Angeles, suburban housewives in Anaheim, and political aspirants as varied as Max Rafferty and Julian Nava all pinned their hopes on the public schools as the primary institution for cultivating an ethical, informed, moral next generation. Once public schools suffered both a loss of public esteem and an attendant loss of funding, a range of dispirited reformers channeled their efforts elsewhere. Several of the most successful school reform efforts of the late twentieth and early twenty-first century—vouchers, homeschooling, and charters—all offer alternatives to the shared school experience taken for granted for most of American educational history.

The capacious curricular ambitions of sexuality and bilingual education, which had become so linked in the problems and the promises they represented to Californians grappling with the intense social changes of the 1960s and 1970s, contracted meaningfully in the 1980s. Even as the tenor of the attacks on sex education cooled significantly in the 1970s, the persistent rise of unmarried teen pregnancy limited support for such programs.[58] Sex educators made impassioned efforts to enact more comprehensive sex education programs to check this "epidemic of childbearing by children," but to little avail.[59] Known informally as "the chastity act," the federal Adolescent and Family Life Act (1981) specifically funded abstinence-only "reproductive-health" education that condemned or remained silent on abortion and contraception. The discovery of the AIDS virus in Los Angeles in 1981, however, most drastically reduced the scope of sex education programs. In 1982, *The Journal of School Health* first acknowledged the need to address HIV/AIDS. Suddenly, many sex educators, who had grappled with grand questions of gender, family, and ethics, privileged AIDS education at the expense of these broader pedagogical goals. The traditionalists whose fulminations against "Satan and the sex educators" had already begun to seem quaint in the early 1970s exploited a climate of fear to loudly blame sex education for encouraging the moral dissipation that invited this "gay plague" on America. Until the turn of the twentieth century, the AIDS epidemic constrained sex education to a version of its incarnation during the world wars, a philosophically modest curriculum fundamentally dedicated to the regulation of youth sexuality and disease prevention, often through fear-based tactics. By 1990, while forty-one states mandated some sort of sex education, all fifty mandated AIDS education.[60]

Similarly, the 1970s were clearly most strongly defined by the extension of bilingual education programs from timid ESL classes to full-fledged multicultural curricula promoted by Latino community advocates and upheld by a strengthening policy framework. By the passage of Proposition 13, however, reversals were already emerging. The American Institutes for Research's 1978 "AIR Report," commissioned by the federal government, cast serious doubt on the efficacy of bilingual programs. Advocates fruitlessly argued that the report's methodologies were flawed, and that its findings indicated a need for more bilingual programming.[61] The report's public release only amplified approval of California's recently enacted Assembly Bill 2931, which allowed schools to waive the requirement for bilingual classes to contain at

least one-third English-proficient students, when insufficient Anglo enrollment prevented compliance. The bill also specified that such classes should
never be intended to teach foreign language to Anglo pupils.[62] By 1983,
Hayakawa had founded US English, an organization devoted to establishing
English as the United States' official language in the name of cultural unity.
It is still informally known as America's leading antibilingual education organization. A series of federal policies and California ballot initiatives hostile
to Latinos won public support during the 1980s and 1990s. The Immigration
and Reform Control Act of 1986, which thanks to its tightened controls on
agricultural employers especially intensified restrictions on Latinos, soured
much of the sense of possibility generated by the 1960s and 1970s. In 1994,
California's Proposition 187, known by the alarmist name "Save Our State,"
prohibited undocumented immigrants from accessing public services, including schools. Four years later, Proposition 227 (1998) brought national attention to California for its bilingual education politics, this time for the popular
initiative's promise to "end bilingual education in California" and to provide
"English for the Children."[63] Perhaps most tellingly, Eugene Gonzales, who
had overseen the first state-level bilingual education initiatives in the 1960s,
unflinchingly committed his support to 227.[64]

It was in the 1990s that America's broader "culture wars" entered forcefully
into common parlance. The classroom wars this book explores were just a few
of the battles waged over incendiary questions such as the literary canon, rap
music, abortion, modern art, and race in what conservative presidential hopeful Pat Buchanan called "a war for the soul of America."[65] While Democratic
president Bill Clinton governed, Lynne Cheney issued hand-wringing jeremiads that "the end of history" had arrived in the form of multiculturalism and
the censure of explicit artists such as rap group 2LiveCrew and the openly
gay photographer Robert Mapplethorpe. Yet the passions of conservative culture warriors such as Buchanan, Cheney, and Rush Limbaugh were so fervent
because the gains progressives made since 1960s and 1970s had so thoroughly
transformed American culture, perhaps most visibly in the public schools.

Bilingual and sexuality education, for all the challenges they encountered,
were prime examples. By the 1990s, it was clear that these programs that had
appeared so halting in the early 1960s helped engender a pedagogical and cultural paradigm shift in American public schools. Sexual speech expanded, and
bilingual-bicultural programs were integral in supplanting an assimilationist
educational paradigm with a pluralistic model attuned not only to ethnicity
but also to linguistic and cultural difference. For all the enthusiasm for reactionary "back-to-basics" curricula a la Rafferty in the 1980s, within a decade

"multicultural education" had become so entrenched that New Left activist Todd Gitlin lamented that the most pernicious risk to educational progress was the "twilight of common dreams" within the left, manifest in struggles over the most appropriate approach to pluralist pedagogy, rather than over whether it should exist at all.[66] Back in San Diego, still a traditionalist stronghold, a self-described conservative school board hopeful, Lynette Williams, perceived candidacy as a "long shot," gesturing to "the whole Planned Parenthood concept" and the poor reception of her call to "de-emphasize the bilingual and emphasize English immersion" as evidence of her uphill battle.[67]

Across the country, in New York City, a 1992 classroom war over the *Children of the Rainbow* curriculum showcased similar progressive gains, as a Queens school board viciously opposed *Rainbow* for its including homosexuals as deserving of tolerance. Tellingly, opponents took issue almost exclusively with the three pages dealing with gays and lesbians, not the over four hundred urging racial tolerance; one Bayside demonstrator explained to the *New York Times*, "It's not multicultural . . . it's gay rights and it's wrong."[68] Notably, throughout the 1990s, these and other conservative activists came to frame their entreaties in terms of "minority rights."[69] In Newton, Massachusetts, closeted history teacher Robert Parlin used the opportunity of growing ethnic tolerance among educators to advance gay rights. At a 1991 faculty meeting of the Committee on Human Differences, a colleague commented that he had never encountered a gay student—"this isn't California, after all," he explained—spurring Parlin to come out and then to launch the first gay-straight alliance at an American public school.[70] Though germinated in their modern form in distant California three decades earlier, sexuality and bilingual-bicultural education were instrumental in helping—albeit slowly—to institutionalize a tolerance which infused the schoolhouse and reflected and reshaped the political culture beyond.

The intense conflicts bilingual and sex education innovation raised in the 1960s remain with us today, even if the contours of these classroom wars have transformed. In 2014 San Jose, in a situation that would have seemed inconceivable to Ernesto Galarza when he fought for the most basic institutional recognition of Latino culture forty years earlier, a federal court upheld the district's prohibition on Anglo students wearing American flag tee shirts on Cinco de Mayo for fear of angering their Latino classmates.[71] At the same time, when the BEA was passed in the hopeful atmosphere of early 1968, few activists would have foreseen the federal Office of Bilingual Education being renamed the Office of English Language Acquisition in 2001. When Mary Calderone confidently predicted in 1978 "a greater acceptance of sexuality because of greater understanding of it, along with an increased sense of responsibility about the way we use it and teach about it," she likely did not envision a controversy like that in Pine Valley in 2014, inspired by a sex educator who showed students a bloody-faced man with the caption, "A Real Man Loves His Woman Every Day of the Month," generating international outrage.[72] Similarly inconceivable would have been the preponderance of abstinence-only curricula, or the fact that sex education activists working fifty years after the founding of SIECUS would still have to fight against programs such as a Mississippi curriculum that likened sexually active young women to an unwrapped chocolate passed around the class—"to show a girl is no longer clean or valuable after she's had sex."[73]

In 1980, the year before conservative journalist Tom Bethell raged about the presence of Spanish-language signs at the White House Conference on the Family, Hayakawa, best known for his strident attacks on bilingual education and founding of US English, lamented in the *Sex Education and Mental Health Report* about the general degradation of public education: "The public schools have gotten confused about what they should be teaching."[74] It was not the public schools that had become "confused," however; Hayakawa and Bethell were simply bearing witness to the seismic transformations in educational and cultural politics that had transpired over the preceding two decades. At the dawn of the twenty-first century, the range of issues at stake in the classroom wars still includes bilingual and sex education, but has expanded to encompass high-stakes testing, guns, prescription drug abuse, school lunch, and even yoga. The fights over these concerns raise persistent questions about the relationship among family, morality, nation, and school. They reveal that neither the right nor left can claim victory over the fraught arena of education: the classroom wars continue to evolve, ever shaped by and shaping our schools, our society, and ourselves.

APPENDIX

MAPS

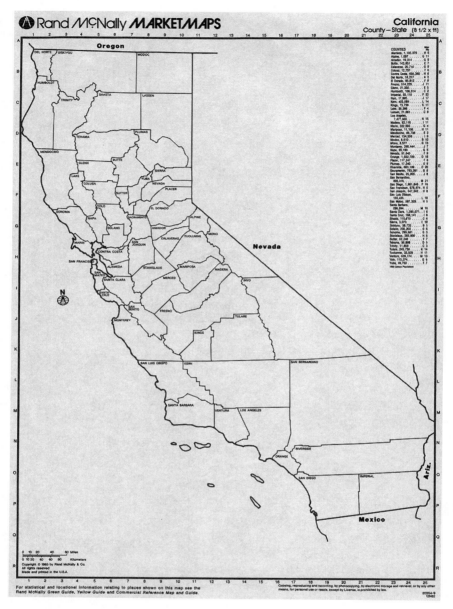

MAP 1 California's county boundaries, 1963. "Rand-McNally market Map of California." © RM Acquisition, LLC d/b/a Rand McNally. Reproduced with permission. License No. R-L. 14-S-021. All Rights Reserved. Courtesy of the Map Division, New York Public Library.

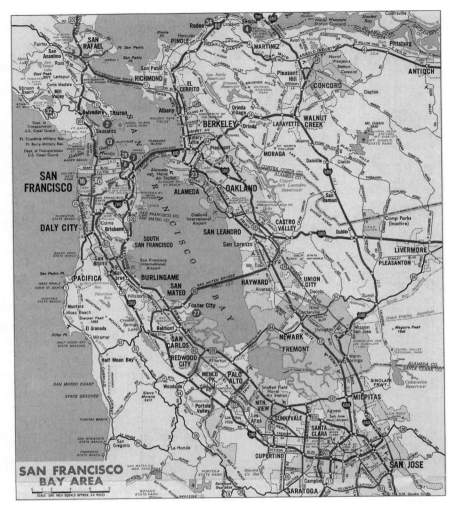

MAP 2 California's Bay Area. "California Official Highway Map." © RM Acquisition, LLC d/b/a Rand McNally. Reproduced with permission. License No. R-L. 14-S-021. All Rights Reserved. Courtesy of the Map Division, New York Public Library.

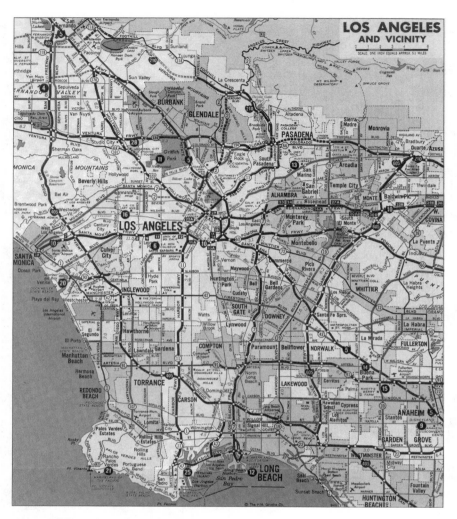

MAP 3 California's Los Angeles and Orange Counties. "California Official Highway Map." © RM Acquisition, LLC d/b/a Rand McNally. Reproduced with permission. License No. R-L. 14-S-021. All Rights Reserved. Courtesy of the Map Division, New York Public Library.

# NOTES

## INTRODUCTION

1. Tom Bethell, "The Family Conference," *Human Life Review* 6, no. 3 (Summer 1980).
2. Ibid.
3. Tom Bethell, "Why Johnny Can't Speak English," *Harper's Magazine*, February 1979, 31.
4. Bethell, "The Family Conference."
5. Edward Wyatt, "Cain Proposes Electrified Border Fence," *New York Times*, October 15, 2011.
6. 2012 State Republican Party Platform, 10–11. Accessed via http://www.tfn.org/site/DocServer/2012-Platform-Final.pdf?docID=3201.
7. Ibid., 12.
8. "Yes on Prop 8" advertisement, paid for by www.protectmarriage.com, Knights of Columbus, National Organization for Marriage: California Committee, and Focus on the Family. Accessed via: http://www.youtube.com/watch?v=0PgjcgqFYP4 on April 7, 2009.
9. Ibid.
10. George Packer, "The Fall of Conservatism," *The New Yorker*, May 26, 2008, 47–48. See also Corey Robin, "Out of Place," *The Nation*, June 23, 2008; James Davison Hunter, *Culture Wars and the Struggle to Define America* (New York: Basic Books, 1991); Andrew Hartman, *A War for the Soul of America: A History of the Culture Wars, From the 1960s to the Present* (Chicago: University of Chicago Press, 2015).
11. Rick Santorum, Q&A, "The Press and People of Faith in Politics," Oxford Centre for Religion and Public Life, August 1, 2008. Accessed via: http://www.ocrpl.org/?p=99, March 8, 2012.
12. Mark J. Hetherington and Jonathan D. Weiler, *Authoritarianism and Polarization in American Politics* (New York: Cambridge, 2009); David Leonhardt, "Old vs. Young," *The New York Times*, June 22, 2012; see blog www.iloveyoubutyouregoingtohell.org, "An Outsider's Guide to Fundamentalist America," accessed July 23, 2012.
13. Matthew Lassiter, "Inventing Family Values: The Crisis of the American Dream in the Seventies," in Bruce Schulman and Julian Zelizer, eds., *Rightward Bound: Making America Conservative in the 1970s* (Cambridge, MA: Harvard,

2008); Natasha Zaretsky, *No Direction Home: The American Family and Fear of National Decline, 1968–1980* (Chapel Hill: University of North Carolina Press, 2007); Robert O. Self, *All in the Family: The Realignment of American Democracy Since the 1960s* (New York: Farrar, Straus, and Giroux, 2012). Though bilingual education throughout American history has engaged groups as diverse as the Germans, French-Canadians, and many Asian and Eastern European groups, I focus on Spanish for two reasons. First, during the period I study, it was the academic crisis in which Latino students found themselves that prompted state and federal legislators to begin thinking seriously about bilingual education programming. The Spanish-speaking minority was the largest community served by the programs and suffered from the lowest levels of academic achievement, thus inspiring the richest discourse on the limits and benefits of bilingual education. Second, a central, and unstudied, aspect of the culture wars has been "the Hispanic Challenge," determining the effect of Spanish-speaking immigrants on American culture since 1965. See Samuel P. Huntington, "The Hispanic Challenge," *Foreign Policy*, March–April 2004; David M. Kennedy, "Can We Still Afford to Be a Nation of Immigrants?" *Atlantic Monthly* 278, no. 5 (November 1996): 52–68.

14. Beth Bailey, *Sex in the Heartland* (Cambridge, MA: Harvard, 1999).

15. Eugene Hopp, Physicians for Good Government, Report of Hearings on Sex Education, State Board of Education, Sacramento, April 10, 1969, 32, California State Archives, Department of Education—State Board of Education (CSA-DOE), Box F3752:9, Folder: 1968–1969.

16. Contemporary scholars of bilingual education define three general pedagogical models: English as a Second Language (ESL), in which the primary goal is to teach English, with little regard for the native tongue; the transitional approach, which employs the native language to ease English instruction; and the maintenance model, which endeavors to teach both the native and English languages, usually by including cultural components of the home language.

17. Steinbacher, *American Educator*, 1972, 10. Columbia University Rare Books and Manuscripts Library (CU-RBML), Group Research Collection (GRC), Box 297, Folder: American Educator, 1969–.

18. Ibid.

19. "What is Sensitivity Training?" Anonymous, n.d., 6. CU-RBML, GRC, Box 297, Folder: "What is Sensitivity Training?"

20. Ibid., 9.

21. Richard Rodriguez, *Hunger of Memory: The Education of Richard Rodriguez* (New York: Bantam Books, 1982).

22. I use the "white" interchangeably with the more regionally specific "Anglo." I use "Latino" and "Mexican American" fluidly, since in California the overwhelming proportion of Latinos were of Mexican origin. "Chicano" is a self-conscious political denotation, and I only use it to discuss historical actors

who so described themselves. "Hispanic" is a term created by the US Census Bureau, and I use it only as contextually appropriate. See Jeffrey S. Passel, "Hispanic/Latino Identity and Identifiers," *Encyclopedia of the U.S. Census* (Washington, DC: Congressional Quarterly Press, 2012).

23. Alan Brinkley, "The Problem of American Conservatism," *The American Historical Review* 99, 2 (1994): 409–29; David Farber and Peter Roche, eds., *The Conservative Sixties* (New York: Peter Lang, 2003); Kim Phillips-Fein et al., "Conservatism: A State of the Field," *Journal of American History* 98, no. 3 (December 2011): 723–773.

24. Mark Rudd, *Underground: My Life with SDS and the Weathermen* (New York: HarperCollins, 2009); Neila Van Dyke, "Hotbeds of Activism: Locations of Student Protest," *Social Problems* 45, no. 2 (1998): 205–220; William H. Orrick, Jr., *Shut it Down! A College in Crisis San Francisco State College, October, 1968–April, 1969* (Honolulu: University Press of the Pacific, 1969); A Report to the National Commission on the Causes and Prevention of Violence" (Washington, DC: Government Printing Office, 1969). Exceptions include Bailey, *Sex in the Heartland*; Paula Fass, *Outside In: Minorities and the Transformation of American Education* (New York: Oxford, 1989); Gael Graham, *Young Activists: American High Schools in an Age of Turmoil* (DeKalb: Northern Illinois University Press, 2006); Robert Cohen, *Freedom's Orator: Mario Savio and the Radical Legacy of the 1960s* (New York: Oxford University Press, 2009).

25. Mae M. Ngai, "The Unlovely Residue of Outworn Prejudices: The Hart-Celler Act and the Politics of Immigration Reform, 1945–65," in Michael Kazin and Joseph A. McCartin, eds., *Americanism: New Perspectives on the History of An Ideal* (Chapel Hill: University of North Carolina Press, 2006), 108–127.

26. James S. Catterall and Emily Brizendine, "Proposition 13: Effects of High School Curricula, 1978–1983," *American Journal of Education* 93, no. 3 (May 1985), 331.

27. "What is Sensitivity Training," 5.

28. J. Russell Kent, Report of Hearings on Sex Education, State Board of Education, Sacramento, April 10, 1969, 55. CSA-DOE, Box F3752:9, Folder: Henry Heydt Jr. papers, 1968–1969.

29. Robert O. Self, "Prelude to the Tax Revolt: The Politic of the 'Tax Dollar' in Postwar California," in Kevin M. Kruse and Thomas J. Sugrue, eds., *The New Suburban History* (Chicago: University of Chicago Press, 2006), 144. Scholars of American and Californian politics have yet to fully engage with the history of education; a notable exception is Adam Laats, *The Other School Reformers: Conservative Activism in American Education* (Cambridge, MA: Harvard University Press, 2014).

30. Ronald Formisano, *Boston Against Busing: Race, Class, and Ethnicity in the 1960s and 70s* (Chapel Hill: University of North Carolina Press, 1991).

31. Synthetic work on desegregation includes James T. Patterson's *Brown v. Board of Education: A Civil Rights Milestone and Its Troubled Legacy* (New York: Oxford,

2001), and special fiftieth-anniversary editions of both the *Journal of American History* 91, 1 (June 2004), and the *History of Education Quarterly* 44, 1 (March 2004). Local studies are too numerous to list, but include cases in the north (Clarence Taylor, *Knocking at Our Own Door: Milton A. Galamison and the Struggle to Integrate New York City Schools* [New York: Columbia University Press, 1997]; Jeanne Theoharris, "'I'd Rather Go to School in the South': How Boston's School Desegregation Complicates the Civil Rights Paradigm," in Komozi Woodward, ed., *Freedom North: Black Freedom Struggles Outside the South, 1940–1980* (Gordonsville, VA: Palgrave Macmillan, 2003), 125–151. Studies on southern cases include Davidson Douglas, *Reading, Writing and Race: The Desegregation of the Charlotte Schools* (Chapel Hill: University of North Carolina Press, 1995); Matthew Lassiter and Andrew Lewis, eds., *The Moderate's Dilemma: Massive Resistance to School Desegregation in Virginia* (Charlottesville: University of Virginia Press, 1998). On border states, see Brett Gadsden, "Victory Without Triumph: The Ironies of School Desegregation in Delaware, 1948–1978," Ph.D. dissertation, Northwestern University, 2006; Elizabeth Jacoway, *Turn Away Thy Son: Little Rock, The Crisis that Shocked the Nation* (New York: Simon and Schuster, 2007). Zevi Gutfreund, a Ph.D. candidate at the University of California, Los Angeles, is currently working on a local study of desegregation in Los Angeles, California.

32. Mary Breasted, *Oh! Sex Education!* (New York: Praeger Books, 1970), 69.

33. Mark Brilliant, *The Color of America Has Changed: How Racial Diversity Shaped Civil Rights Reform in California,1941–1978* (New York: Oxford University Press, 2010).

34. Ibid; Mary L. Dudziak, *Cold War Civil Rights: Race and the Image of American Democracy* (Princeton, NJ: Princeton, 2000); Heather B. Lewis, "Protest, Place and Pedagogy: New York City's Community Control Movement and its Aftermath, 1966–1996," Ph.D. dissertation, New York University, 2006; Adam Nelson, *The Elusive Ideal: Equal Educational Opportunity and the Federal Role in Boston's Public Schools, 1950–1985* (Chicago: University of Chicago Press, 2005); Amy J. Binder, *Contentious Curricula: Afrocentrism and Creationism in American Public Schools* (Princeton, NJ: Princeton University Press, 2002); Timothy Hacsi, *Children as Pawns: The Politics of Educational Reform* (Cambridge, MA: Harvard University Press, 2002); Daryl M. Scott, "Postwar Pluralism, *Brown v. Board of Education* and the Origins of Multiculturalism," *Journal of American History*, June 2004.

35. Carlos Kevin Blanton, *The Strange Career of Bilingual Education in Texas, 1836–1981* (College Station, TX: Texas A & M University Press, 2007); Jeffrey Moran, *Teaching Sex: The Shaping of Adolescence in the Twentieth Century* (Cambridge, MA: Harvard University Press, 2000); Kristin Luker, *When Sex Goes to School: Warring Views on Sex—and Sex Education—since the Sixties* (New York: W. W. Norton and Company, 2006); Ruben Donato, *The*

*Other Struggle for Equal Schools: Mexican Americans in the Civil Rights Era* (Albany: State University of New York Press, 1997); Janice M. Irvine, *Talk About Sex: The Battles Over Sex Education in the United States* (Berkeley: University of California Press, 2002); Guadelupe San Miguel, *Contested Policy: The Rise and Fall of Federal Bilingual Education in the United States, 1960–2001* (Denton, TX: University of North Denton Press, 2004); Jonathan Zimmerman, *Whose America?: Culture Wars in the Public Schools* (Cambridge, MA: Harvard University Press, 2002); Stephen J. Pitti, *The Devil in Silicon Valley: Northern California, Race, and Mexican Americans* (Princeton, NJ: Princeton University Press, 2003).

36. John Steinbacher, *Bitter Harvest* (Whittier, CA: Orange Tree Press, 1970).

37. Interview with Edwin Klotz, December 17, 1968, CU-RBML, GRC, Box 297, Folder: SIECUS 2. "Educator Klotz Dies in Calif.," *The Evening News*, September 5, 1978.

38. Max Rafferty, pamphlet, "Progressive Education: The Lively Corpse," August 1966, University of Iowa Special Collections, Max Rafferty Papers (UI-MR), Box 1, Folder: Printed Materials.

39. Testimony, Lloyd Morain of American Humanist Association, January 8, 1970, public hearing, 1–2, CSA-DOE, Box F3752:439. Folder: Moral Guidelines Committee, 1968–1970.

40. Thomas Frank, *What's the Matter With Kansas? How Conservatives Won the Heart of America* (New York: Henry Holt and Co., 2004); see also Michael Cooper, "Concern in State G.O.P. Over State Focus on Social Issues," *New York Times*, April 22, 2012.

41. Bethany Moreton, *To Serve God and Wal-Mart: The Making of Christian Free Enterprise* (Cambridge, MA: Harvard University Press, 2009).

42. Lisa McGirr, *Suburban Warriors: The Origins of the New American Right* (Princeton, NJ: Princeton University Press, 2001); Jonathan Schoenwald, *A Time for Choosing: The Rise of Modern American Conservatism* (New York: Oxford University Press, 2002); Darren Dochuk, *From Bible Belt to Sunbelt: Plain-Folk Religion, Grassroots Politics, and the Rise of Evangelical Conservatism* (New York: W. W. Norton and Company, 2011).

43. See McGirr, *Suburban Warriors*; Becky M. Nicolaides, *My Blue Heaven: Life and Politics in the Working-Class Suburbs of Los Angeles* (Chicago: University of Chicago Press, 2002); Michelle Nickerson, *Mothers of Conservatism* (Princeton: Princeton University Press, 2014).; Nickerson, "Moral Mothers and Goldwater Girls," in David Farber and Peter Roche, eds., *The Conservative Sixties* (New York: Peter Lang, 2003).

44. Geoffrey Kabaservice, *Rule and Ruin: The Downfall of Moderation and the Destruction of the Republican Party, from Eisenhower to the Tea Party* (New York: Oxford University Press, 2011); Peter N. Carroll, *It Seemed Like Nothing Happened: America in the 1970s* (New Brunswick, NJ: Rutgers

University Press, 1982). Bruce J. Schulman has challenged this idea most energetically. See *The Seventies: The Great Shift in American Culture, Society and Politics* (New York: The Free Press, 2001) and Edward D. Berkowitz, *Something Happened: A Political and Cultural Overview of the Seventies* (New York: Columbia University Press, 2006).

45. Homitz, Allen, and Associates, "Prospectus: Project to Develop Approaches, Methods and Materials for Implementation of Guidelines for Moral and Civic Education and Teaching about Religion," submitted to Mr. Henry Heydt, Special Assistant to the California State Board of Education, 1, n.d., CSA-DOE, Box F3752:445, Folder: Moral Guidelines Committee, 1970–1974.

46. Letter, Herbert Wells Barton to Max Rafferty, February 3, 1970, CSA-DOE, Box F3752:747, Folder: General Correspondence File XIXI.

47. Dominic Sandbrook, *Mad as Hell: The Crisis of the 1970s and the Rise of the Populist Right* (New York: Knopf, 2011).

48. Hopp, April 10, 1969 Hearing, 31.

49. Howard Jarvis, *I'm Mad as Hell* (New York: Times Books, 1979), 262.

50. David Tyack, *Seeking Common Ground: Public Schools in a Diverse Society* (Cambridge, MA: Harvard University Press, 2004); Daniel K. Williams, *God's Own Party: The Making of the Christian Right* (New York: Oxford, 2010); Milton Gaither, *Homeschool: An American History* (New York: Palgrave Macmillan, 2008).

PART I

1. Mitt Romney radio ad, "Hechos," South Florida, 2012. http://electad.com/video/mitt-romney-radio-ad-hechos-espanol/.

2. "Newt Spanish Apology," March 31, 2007, https://www.youtube.com/watch?v=sg-0aB7jf_c.

3. Farley Grubb, *German Immigration and Servitude in America, 1709–1920* (New York: Routledge, 2011).

4. Carlos Kevin Blanton, *The Strange Career of Bilingual Education in Texas, 1836–1981* (College Station: Texas A & M University Press, 2004).

5. Kathleen Newland, "Circular Migration and Human Development," United Nations Development Programme Human Development Reports, October 2009.

6. Jeffrey E. Mirel, *Patriotic Pluralism: Americanization Education and European Immigrants* (Cambridge, MA: Harvard University Press, 2010); David R. Roediger and Elizabeth D. Esch, *The Production of Difference: Race and the Management of Labor in U.S. History* (New York: Oxford University Press, 2012).

7. Mary Antin, *The Promised Land* (Boston: Houghton Mifflin, 1912), accessed via http://digital.library.upenn.edu/women/antin/land/land.html#11.

8. Jon Zimmerman, "Ethnics Against Ethnicity: European Immigrants and Foreign-Language Instruction, 1890–1940," *Journal of American History* 88, no. 4 (March 2002): 1383–1404.

9. Matthew Frye Jacobson, *Whiteness of a Different Color: European Immigrants and the Alchemy of Race* (Cambridge, MA: Harvard University Press, 1999).

10. Lorrin Thomas, *Puerto Rican Citizen: History and Political Identity in Twentieth Century New York City* (Chicago: University of Chicago Press, 2010).

11. Maria Cristina Garcia, *Havana USA: Cuban Exiles and Cuban Americans in South Florida, 1959–1994* (Berkeley: University of California Press, 1994).

12. James Crawford, *Bilingual Education: History, Theory, Politics and Practice.* Trenton, NJ: Crane Books, 1989; Richard Delgado and Jean Stefancic, eds. *A Critical Reader: The Latino Condition.* New York: New York University Press, 1998.

13. David G. Gutierrez, *The Columbia History of Latinos in the United States Since 1960* (New York: Columbia University Press, 2004).

14. Ruben Donato, *The Other Struggle for Equal Schools: Mexican Americans in the Civil Rights Era* (Albany: SUNY Press, 1997).

15. Colin Baker, *Foundations of Bilingual Education and Bilingualism* (Tonawanda, NY: Multilingual Matters, 2011).

16. On opposition to bilingual education, see James Crawford, ed., *Language Loyalties: A Source Book on the Official English Controversy* (Chicago: University of Chicago Press, 1992).

17. D. B. Rawitch and Samuel P. Huntington, "The Hispanic Challenge," *Foreign Policy*, March–April 2004; David M. Kennedy, "Can We Still Afford to Be a Nation of Immigrants?" *Atlantic Monthly* 278, no. 5 (November 1996): 52–68.

18. Elias Lopez, "Major Demographic Shifts Occurring in California," California Research Bureau, 1999, 8.

CHAPTER 1

1. Gilbert Sanchez, "An Analysis of the Bilingual Education Act" (Ph.D. dissertation, University of Massachusetts, 1973), 45–46.

2. Bob Rawitch, "Murphy Hits Lack of Bilingual Education at Senate Hearing," *Los Angeles Times*, June 25, 1967, DB.

3. Guadelupe San Miguel, *Contested Policy: The Rise and Fall of Federal Bilingual Education in the United States, 1960–2001* (Denton, TX: University of North Denton Press, 2004); Gareth Davies, "The Great Society after Johnson: The Case of Bilingual Education," *Journal of American History*, March 2002, http://www.historycooperative.org/journals/jah/88.4/davies.html; James J. Lyons, "The Past and Future Directions of Federal Bilingual Education Policy," *The Annals of the American Academy of Political and Social Science* 508,

no. 1 (March 1990): 66–80; Anne Marie Wiese and Eugene E. Garcia, "The Bilingual Education Act: Language Minority Students and Equal Educational Opportunity," *Bilingual Research Journal* 22, no. 1, (1998): 1–18.

4. Of course, bilingual education has an extensive and largely undocumented history that began long before the passage of the Bilingual Education Act. See Kevin Carlos Blanton, *The Strange Career of Bilingual Education in Texas, 1836–1981* (College Station: Texas A & M University Press, 2004); Jonathan Zimmerman, "Ethnics Against Ethnicity: European Immigrants and Foreign Language Instruction, 1890–1940," *Journal of American History*, March 2002, http://www.historycooperative.org/journals/jah/88.4/zimmerman.html.

5. Elizabeth Bates, "100 Years of Public Education: A Study of the Development of Elementary Education in the City of Los Angeles" (Master's thesis, University of Southern California School of Education, 1928).

6. Sections 71 and 12154, State of California Education Code, 1959.

7. "Mexican-Americans in California's Teaching Profession," Mexican-American Study Project, Graduate School of Business Administration, University of California, Los Angeles. Prepared for First Annual Issues Conference, Association of Mexican-American Educators, December 3–4, 1965. Stanford University Special Collections, Galarza Papers, Box 56, Folder 1. This report in itself caused quite a stir. Gilbert Sanchez wrote that "not until 1965 when the UCLA Mexican-American Study Project . . . started to delve into the educational needs and characteristics of the second largest minority group in the country did people realize what was happening to one of our country's largest resources." Sanchez, "An Analysis of the Bilingual Education Act," 7. Conservative journalist John Steinbacher, however, decried the study as "merely a propaganda vehicle" staffed by "some of the most radical personalities in the state." Steinbacher, *Bitter Harvest*, 47.

8. "Mexican-Americans in California's Teaching Profession," 2.

9. "Mexican-Americans in California's Teaching Profession," 3.

10. Richard I. Miller, "An Appraisal of ESEA Title III," *Theory into Practice* (New York: Lawrence Erlbaum Associates, Inc., 1967), 116–119; "English as a Second Language Newsletter: From these Programs Emerge the Bilingual, Bicultural Citizen of Tomorrow," Vol. 1, No. 2, October 1967, 1, Box 55, Folder 6, Series 4, Ernesto Galarza papers, Stanford University Special Collections.

11. "English as a Second Language Newsletter: From these Programs Emerge the Bilingual, Bicultural Citizen of Tomorrow," 3.

12. Ibid.

13. Natalia Mehlman Petrzela, "Revisiting the Rightward Turn: Max Rafferty, Education, and Modern American Politics," *The Sixties: A Journal of History, Politics and Culture* 6, no. 2 (December 2013): 143–171.

14. Notes, "Meeting with Gene Gonzales in Los Angeles Office, State Department of Education, Subject: "Use of Texts from Mexico for Teaching Foreign Language

and Social Science in California Schools," February 23, 1966, California State DOE: DOI Office Files, General Correspondence and Memos, 1966–1970.

15. Katherine L. Belcher, "Bordering on Success: A Portrait of the Calexico Unified School District since Bilingual Education, 1963–2000" (Ph.D. dissertation, University of Pennsylvania, 2006), chapter 2.

16. Ibid.

17. Richard A. Navarro, "Identity and Consensus in the Politics of Bilingual Education: The Case of California, 1967–1980" (Ph.D. dissertation, Stanford University, 1984), 31; Senate Bill 53, Short, Chapter 200, Statutes of 1967.

18. Eugene Gonzales, chairman, Interdepartmental Committee on Bilingual Instruction, to Dr. Max Rafferty and cabinet members, "Suggested Guidelines for the Implementation of Senate Bill 53," January 5, 1968, 1–2.

19. "English as a Second Language Newsletter: From these Programs Emerge the Bilingual, Bicultural Citizen of Tomorrow," Vol. 1, No. 2, October 1967, 1.

20. Ibid.

21. Eugene Gonzales to Francisco Bravo, M.D., president, Pan American National Bank of East Los Angeles, October 24, 1967.

22. Julia Gonsalves, consultant, Foreign Language Programs, to Eugene Gonzales, assistant to the superintendent of public instruction, April 26, 1966, Sacramento State DOE: DOI Office Files, General Correspondence and Memos, 1966–1970.

23. Soledad Coronel, consultant, to Eugene Gonzales and John Plakos, "Progress Report on Activities: Santa Barbara County, Guadelupe School District, Bonita School District," December 9, 1966, DOE: DOI Office Files, General Correspondence and Memos, 1966–1970.

24. Ibid.

25. Bilingual Education Act, Public Law 90-247, Title VII, Enacted January 2, 1968.

26. Ibid.

27. Susan Gilbert Schneider, *Revolution, Reaction or Reform: The 1974 Bilingual Education Act* (New York: Las Americas Publishing Company, 1976), 26.

28. Joshua Fishman, *Language Loyalty in the United States* (The Hague: Mouton, 1966) and "The Status and Prospects of Bilingualism in the U.S.," *Modern Language Journal* 49 (March 1965); Nathan Glazer and Daniel Moynihan, *Beyond the Melting Pot: The Negroes, Puerto Ricans, Jews, and Italians of New York City* (Cambridge: Massachusetts Institute of Technology Press, 1963).

29. San Miguel, *Contested Policy*, 19.

30. Adam Nelson, *The Elusive Ideal: Equal Educational Opportunity and the Federal Role in Boston's Public Schools, 1950–1985* (Chicago: University of Chicago Press, 2005), xvi.

31. San Miguel, *Contested Policy*, 12–19; Susan Gilbert Schneider, *Revolution, Reaction, or Reform? The 1974 Bilingual Education Act* (New York: Las Americas Publishing Company), 22.

32. Schneider, *Revolution, Reaction, or Reform?*, 20.

33. Ibid., 21.

34. Ibid, 22.

35. Ibid.

36. Ralph Yarborough, "Two Proposals for a Better Way of Life for Mexican-Americans in the Southwest," *Congressional Record*, January 17, 1967, 599–600.

37. Three out of four state conferences held in 1967 to address the question of bilingual education and its prospects were held in California cities: Fresno, Bakersfield, and Los Angeles. All conferences emerged in strong support of robust bilingual education funding. Sanchez, "An Analysis of the Bilingual Education Act," 52–58.

38. Sanchez, "An Analysis of the Bilingual Education Act," 61.

39. Ibid., 75.

40. Ibid., 69.

41. Ibid., 70.

42. Ibid., 36, 152.

43. Schneider, *Revolution, Reaction, or Reform?*, 22. Those coffers amounted to an $85 million authorization, to be spent over three years.

44. Ibid., 71.

45. Ibid., 24.

46. Ibid., 33.

47. Elementary and Secondary Education Act, Statutes at Large 79, sec. 2, 27, 1965. Title I was backed by one billion dollars to fund programs for disabled and impoverished children.

48. San Miguel, *Contested Policy*, 18.

49. Manuel Ceja to James Nelson, 1973. Sacramento Department of Education Archives, Administrative Files 1965–1973; F3752:2947; Administrative Files, Bilingual-Bicultural Task Force.

50. San Miguel, *Contested Policy*, 18; Sanchez, "An Analysis of the Bilingual Education Act," 40.

51. California Free Enterprise Association, "Big Business and Our American Way of Life," pamphlet, n.d., GRC papers, CU-RBML, Folder: California Free Enterprise Association, Box 49.

52. Because of such meager budget allocations, in 1969, advocates already wondered if bilingual education was merely a token program. Schneider, *Revolution, Reaction, or Reform?*, 27.

53. Davies, "The Great Society after Johnson," 26.

54. Sanchez, "An Analysis of the Bilingual Education Act," 55.

55. Lou Cannon, "At Murphy Behest: Bi-Lingual Study Funds Increased," *San Jose Mercury News*, December 17, 1969.

56. Davies, "The Great Society after Johnson"; San Miguel, *Contested Policy*.

57. Davies, "The Great Society after Johnson," 30.

58. Bob Rawitch, "Murphy Hits Lack of Bilingual Education at Senate Hearing," *Los Angeles Times*, June 25, 1967; Sanchez, "An Analysis of the Bilingual Education Act," 76.

59. Rawitch, "Murphy Hits Lack of Bilingual Education at Senate Hearing." Murphy was also a co-sponsor of the original bill. The outspoken commitment of these Republican legislators to serving Latinos was invested with a measure of instrumentalism; see Sanchez, "An Analysis of the Bilingual Education Act" and Davies, "The Great Society after Johnson."

60. For example, HEW appointed Armando Rodriguez, a San Diego school administrator and chief of the State Bureau of Intergroup Relations, to head the newly established Mexican-American Education Unit created to "help insure a balanced program of educational activities for Mexican-Americans;" he went on to become the director of the Office for Spanish Speaking Affairs. (HEW press release, August 18, 1967, Galarza Papers, Box 55, Series 4, Folder 6.)

61. Project Frontier, ESEA, Title VII newsletter, Chula Vista, CA, n.d., 1 Ernesto Galarza papers, Box 55, Folder 6.

62. Ibid., 4.

63. Ibid., 6–7.

64. Project Frontier, ESEA, Title VII grant proposal, January 12, 1970, 2.

65. Ibid.

66. Title VII newsletter, 5.

67. Grant proposal, 3.

68. Title VII newsletter, 3.

69. Nelson, *The Elusive Ideal*, 123; OCR study, cited in Schneider, 9.

70. Ernesto Galarza, "Compensatory Education: Society's Real Threat for Mexican-Americans?" Unpublished paper, n.d., 2, Stanford University Special Collections, Ernesto Galarza Papers, Series 4, Box 55, Folder 6.

71. Davies, "The Great Society after Johnson," 32.

72. "An Investigation of Spanish-Speaking Pupils Placed in Classes for the Educable Mentally Retarded," prepared by John Plakos and John Chandler, Department of Instruction, California State Department of Education, 1969. F3752-1777, DOE-DOI, Office Files-General Correspondence and Memos, 1966–1970, Sacramento State Archives.

73. Alton Safford, coordinator of special education, Santa Barbara County Schools, to Eugene Gonzales, associate superintendent of public instruction, California State Department of Education, June 17, 1969, 1–3, F3752-1777, DOE-DOI, Office Files-General Correspondence and Memos, 1966–1970, Sacramento State Archives. Safford's comments reflect a long tradition of IQ examinations being employed to rationalize the subjugation of minority populations. See Stephen Jay Gould, *The Mismeasure of Man* (New York: Norton, 1981).

74. Gonzales to Safford, July 9, 1969, 1–2.

75. Minutes, first meeting of Mexican-American California School Board Members, International Hotel, Los Angeles, October 19, 1969, 4, Stanford University Special Collections, Ernesto Galarza Papers, Box 55, Folder 6.
76. Diana Walsh, "New York Educator chosen to head SF schools," *San Francisco Examiner*, March 10, 1992; Nanette Asimov, "Report Card for New Superintendent," *San Francisco Chronicle*, April 4, 1992.
77. San Miguel, *Contested Policy*, 30; "Financial Assistance for Bilingual Education Programs," *Federal Register* 34, no 4 (January 7, 1969): 201–205.
78. Galarza, "Compensatory Education," 1.
79. Ibid.
80. Schneider, *Revolution, Reaction or Reform?*, 6, 21. These figures do not include students receiving remedial ESL instruction.
81. Bruce Gaarder, "The Federal Role in the Education of Bilingual Children," conference paper at Symposium of the Spanish-speaking child in the Schools of the Southwest, Tucson, Arizona, September 22, 1966; as cited in Schneider, *Revolution, Reaction or Reform?*, 21.
82. U.S. Congress, Senate, *Elementary and Secondary Education Act Amendments of 1967*, Senate Report 726 to accompany H.R. 7819, 90th Congress, 1st session, 1967, 50.
83. Navarro, "Identity and Consensus," 38.
84. OCR memorandum, "School Districts with more than Five Percent Minority Group Children," May 25, 1970.
85. Davies, "The Great Society after Johnson," 50.
86. San Miguel, *Contested Policy*; Navarro, "Identity and Consensus."
87. Zoe Burkholder, *Color in the Classroom: How Americans Taught Race, 1900–1954* (New York: Oxford University Press, 2011); Frances Fitzgerald, *America Revised, History Schoolbooks in the Twentieth Century* (Boston: Little, Brown and Company, 1979); Joseph Moreau, *Schoolbook Nation: Conflicts over American History Textbooks from the Civil War to the Present* (Ann Arbor: University of Michigan Press, 2004); Jonathan Zimmerman, *Whose America? Culture Wars in the Public Schools* (Cambridge, MA: Harvard University Press, 2002).

CHAPTER 2

1. "Classes Boycotted by Student Groups at 2 High Schools," *Los Angeles Times*, March 6, 1968, 3; Jack McCurdy, "Student Disorders Erupt at 4 High Schools; Policeman Hurt," *Los Angeles Times*, March 7, 1968, 3.
2. Dial Torgerson, "Start of a Revolution? 'Brown Power' Unity Seen Behind School Disorders," *Los Angeles Times*, March 17, 1968, B1.
3. Ibid.
4. Minority enrollment had doubled over the preceding years from 17.4 to 34.4 percent in the Los Angeles city schools, the state's largest district; "Schools Gear to Meet Community Changes," *Los Angeles Times*, March 11, 1968, OC8.

5. Max Rafferty, *Classroom Countdown: Education at the Crossroads* (New York: Hawthorn Books, 1970), xiii.

6. Max Rafferty, *Suffer, Little Children* (New York: Signet Books, 1963), vii–viii.

7. Dolores Delgado Bernal, "Chicana School Resistance and Grassroots Leadership: Providing an Alternative History of the 1968 East Los Angeles Blowouts" (Ph.D. dissertation, University of California, Los Angeles, 1997), 76; Ernesto Chávez, *"¡Mi Raza Primero!" Nationalism, Identity, and Insurgency in the Chicano Movement in Los Angeles, 1966–1978* (Berkeley: University of California Press, 2002); Juan Gómez-Quiñones, *Mexican Students por La Raza: The Chicano Student Movement in Southern California, 1967–77* (Santa Barbara: Editorial La Causa, 1978); Carlos Muñoz Jr., *Youth, Identity, Power: The Chicano Movement* (New York: Verso Books, 1989).

8. Bernal, "Chicana School Resistance," 78.

9. Juan Javier Inda, *"La Comunidad en Lucha*: The Development of the East Los Angeles High School Blowouts," Stanford Center for Chicano Research, Stanford University, Working Papers Series, No. 29, March 1990, 4.

10. Ibid.

11. Marvin E. Elsedal, "Task Force Aims to Motivate Youth," *Los Angeles Times*, March 5, 1968, D14.

12. Cited in Inda, *La Comunidad en Lucha*, 3; Bernal, "Chicana School Resistance," 78.

13. Inda, 5.

14. *Chicano Student News: Mano a Mano*, April 25, 1968, cited in Inda, *La Comunidad en Lucha*, 12.

15. "Classes Boycotted by Student Groups at 2 High Schools," *Los Angeles Times*, March 6, 1968, 3.

16. Jack McCurdy, "1,000 Walk Out in School Boycott," *Los Angeles Times*, March 9, 1968, B1.

17. Ibid., 86.

18. *Chicano Student News*, March 15, 1968, cited in Inda, *La Comunidad en Lucha*, 15.

19. Inda, *La Comunidad en Lucha*, 12–13.

20. Dial Torgerson, "'Brown Power' Unity Seen Behind School Disorders," *Los Angeles Times*, March 17, 1968, B1.

21. Jack McCurdy, "School Board Yields to Some Student Points in Boycotts," *Los Angeles Times*, March 12, 1968, 1.

22. "Classes Boycotted by Student Groups at 2 High Schools," *Los Angeles Times*, March 6, 1968, 3.

23. Paul Coates, "Here, Dr. Rafferty, Are Some REAL Urgencies," *Los Angeles Times*, March 18, 1968.

24. Paul Houston, "3 Negro Officials Take Over at Jefferson High," *Los Angeles Times*, March 14, 1968, 3.

25. Inda, *La Comunidad en Lucha*, 9.

26. Jack McCurdy, "Demands Made by East Side High School Students Listed," *Los Angeles Times*, March 17, 1968, 1; *Chicano Student News: Mano a Mano*, March

15, 1968, cited in Inda, *La Comunidad en Lucha*, 12. "*Gabacho*" is a pejorative term for whites.

27. *Chicano Student News: Mano a Mano*, April 25, 1968, cited in Inda, *La Comunidad en Lucha*, 15.

28. Dial Torgerson, "'Brown Power' Unity Seen Behind School Disorders," *Los Angeles Times*, March 17, 1968, B1.

29. "Student Disorders Erupt at 4 High Schools; Policeman Hurt," *Los Angeles Times*, March 7, 1968.

30. John Kendall, "Venice High Principal Suspends 40 Students," *Los Angeles Times*, March 15, 1968, 3.

31. "Riot Report Meant to Spur Reforms," *Los Angeles Times*, March 12, 1968.

32. "School Boycotts Not the Answer," *Los Angeles Times*, March 15, 1968.

33. "'Bigness' and the School Board," *Los Angeles Times*, March 8, 1968, A4.

34. Jack McCurdy, "1,000 Walk Out in School Boycott," *Los Angeles Times*, March 9, 1968, B1.

35. Ibid.

36. Eugene Gonzales, "Presentation to First General Session: Second Annual Nuevas Vistas Conference—¡*Adelante, Amigos!*," Friday, May 10, 1968, 10:00 a.m., 4. CSA-DOE, Box F3752:1782, Folder: Office Files, Speeches, Eugene Gonzales, 1968–1970.

37. *Chicano Student News: Mano a Mano*, March 15, 1968, 5, cited in Inda, *La Comunidad en Lucha*, 15.

38. Jack McCurdy, "School Board Yields to Some Student Points in Boycotts," *Los Angeles Times*, March 12, 1968, 1; Jack McCurdy, "Demands Made by East Side High School Students Listed," *Los Angeles Times*, March 17, 1968, 1.

39. Throughout the week of March 11, 1968, absenteeism dropped sharply, though protests spread to an African-American junior high school and arrests continued at Venice High School. Jack McCurdy, "Venice High Youths, Police Clash," *Los Angeles Times*, March 13, 1968, 1.

40. LAUSD Board Minutes, March 14, 1968, 4:00 p.m. meeting, LAUSD Board Minutes Files, Box 470, March 14, 1968–June 26, 1975; Mario T. Garcia, *Blowout! Sal Castro and the Struggle for Chicano Educational Justice* (Chapel Hill: University of North Carolina Press, 2011).

41. Ibid.

42. LAUSD Board Minutes, April 1, 1968, 4:00 p.m. meeting, LAUSD Board Minutes Files, Box 470, March 14, 1968–June 26, 1975.

43. Emily Straus, *Death of a Suburban Dream: Race and Schools in Compton, California* (Philadelphia: University of Pennsylvania Press, 2014).

44. Inda, *La Comunidad en Lucha*, 19–20.

45. "School Gears to Meet Community Changes," *Los Angeles Times*, OC8.

46. Research Organizing Cooperative of San Francisco, *Basta Ya! The Story of Los Siete de la Raza*, pamphlet, 1970, 9, San Francisco Public Library, San Francisco History Center (SFHC).

47. Ibid., 2–4.

48. Ibid., 10.

49. "Teacher Labels Minority-Group Administrative Intern Plan Unfair," *Los Angeles Times*, March 31, 1968.

50. The most well-known national example of this dynamic is the reaction of white ethnic New Yorkers to the calls for "community control" of schools by African-Americans in the late 1960s. The California case evokes important parallels and differences with this case. On the New York City case, see Jerold E. Podair, *The Strike that Changed New York: Blacks, Whites, and the Ocean Hill-Brownsville Case* (New Haven, CT: Yale University Press, 2002); Daniel H. Perlstein, *Justice, Justice: School Politics and the Eclipse of Liberalism* (New York: Peter Lang, 2004); Jonathan Rieder, *Canarsie: The Jews and Italians of Brooklyn Against Liberalism* (Cambridge, MA: Harvard University Press, 1985).

51. Rafferty, *Suffer, Little Children*, 65; Paul Coates, "Here, Dr. Rafferty, Are Some REAL Urgencies," *Los Angeles Times*, March 18, 1968, A6.

52. Max Rafferty, *The Education of the Mexican-American: A Summary of the Procedures of the Lake Arrowhead and Anaheim Conferences* (Sacramento: California State Department of Education, 1969), 1.

53. Eugene Gonzales, speech given at Testimonial Dinner, Century Plaza Hotel, April 19, 1968, 2, CSA-DOE, Box F3752:1782, Folder: Office Files, Speeches, Eugene Gonzales, 1968–1970.

54. Ibid.

55. Rafferty, *Classroom Countdown*, xiii.

56. Lisa McGirr, *Suburban Warriors: The Origins of the New American Right* (Princeton, NJ: Princeton University Press, 2001).

57. American Free Enterprise Association pamphlet; John Steinbacher, foreword, in Joseph M. Bean, M.D., "The Source - of the River Pollution" (Fullerton, CA: Educator Publications, 1972), CU-RBML, GRC, Box 119, Folder: The Educator.

58. "YAF + SPARTAN DAILY = RACISM," *El Ojo*, April 1, 1971, Stanford University Special Collections, Ernesto Galarza Papers (SUSC-EGP), Box 55, Folder 6.

59. Ibid.

60. Ibid.

61. Steinbacher, *Bitter Harvest*, 29, 30. Emphasis in original.

62. Ibid., 36.

63. Ibid.

64. "Reagan Vetoes Bill to Require Bilingual Courses," *Los Angeles Times*, October 30, 1971; "The March: San Jo to Sacramento," ¿*Que Tal?*, April 1, 1971, SUSC-EGP, Box 55, Folder 6.

65. "WHAT DOES IT MEAN?," ¿*Que Tal?*, April 1, 1971.

66. Ibid.

67. Eugene Gonzales, speech at Testimonial Dinner, Century Plaza Hotel, April 19, 1968, 4–5, CSA-DOE, Box F3752:1782, Folder: Office Files, Speeches, Eugene Gonzales, 1968–1970.

68. Eugene Gonzales, speech to Annual Division of Instruction Staff Meeting, September 25, 1968, 2, CSA-DOE, Box F3752:1782, Folder: Office Files, Speeches, Eugene Gonzales, 1968–1970.

69. Ibid., 3.

70. Eugene Gonzales, "Presentation to the First General Session: Second Annual Nuevas Vistas Conference—*Adelante, Amigos!*," May 10, 1968, 1–3, CSA-DOE, Box F3752:1782, Folder: Office Files, Speeches, Eugene Gonzales, 1968–1970.

71. Eugene Gonzales, "Speech to the Mexican-American Youth Association, Tri-County Student Conference: 'How to Understand the Mexican—Without Really Trying,'" May 25, 1968, 2, 4, CSA-DOE, Box F3752:1782, Folder: Office Files, Speeches, Eugene Gonzales, 1968–1970.

72. Ibid., 7.

73. Ibid., 3.

74. Ibid., 8.

75. Ibid., 2–3.

76. Ibid., 11.

77. "Passing of the Patriot," original draft, UI-MR, Box 1, Folder: Passing of the Patriot.

78. McGirr, *Suburban Warriors*.

79. Eugene Gonzales, speech at Testimonial Dinner, April 19, 1968, 2, CSA-DOE, Box F3752:1782, Folder: Office Files, Speeches, Eugene Gonzales, 1968–1970.

80. Vahac Mardirosian to Sr. Eugenio Gonzales, May 8, 1969, CSA-DOE, Box F3752-1777, Folder: Office Files-General Correspondence and Memos, 1966–1970. Mardirosian was born in Syria to Armenian parents, who moved to Tijuana, Mexico, when he was two. Mardirosian emigrated to the United States at age 19 and became a naturalized US citizen. Mardirosian first became involved with Latino politics in the aftermath of the blowouts and has remained dedicated to creating educational opportunities for Latinos. He is the founder and president of the Parent Institute for Quality Education, which endeavors to expand college opportunities for Latino youth in San Diego County.

81. Ramirez to Reagan, December 12, 1966; Gonzales to Ramirez, telegram, May 15, 1967. Both CSA-DOE, Box F3752-1777, Folder: Office Files-General Correspondence and Memos, 1966–1970.

82. Ibid.

83. Ibid.

84. Alicia Davila Luff to Gonzales, February 2, 1969, CSA-DOE, Box F3752-1777, Folder: Office Files-General Correspondence and Memos, 1966–1970.

85. Ibid.

86. Gonzales to Luff, March 24, 1969, CSA-DOE, Box F3752-1777, Folder: Office Files-General Correspondence and Memos, 1966–1970.

87. Ibid.

88. Ibid.

89. Dan Reyes to Gonzales, February 27, 1969, CSA-DOE, Box F3752-1777, Folder: Office Files-General Correspondence and Memos, 1966–1970.

90. Ibid.

91. Ibid.

92. Minutes, "First Meeting of Mexican-American California School Board Members," International Hotel, Sunday, October 19, 1969, Los Angeles, California, 3, SUSC-EGP, Box 56, Folder 1.

93. Ibid.

94. Ibid., 2.

95. Ibid.

96. Eddie Hanson to Mr. Eugene Gonzales, memorandum Re: Mr. Herb Ibarra's Presentation at the 1968 TESOL Convention in San Antonio," May 28, 1968, CSA-DOE, Box F3752-1777, Folder: General Correspondence and Memos, 1966–1970.

97. Herb Ibarra, "A Commitment for a Foundation for the Spanish-Speaking Child," attachment to memo, 1, CSA-DOE, Box F3752-1777, Folder: General Correspondence and Memos, 1966–1970.

98. Max Rafferty, "Greetings," Program, Third Annual Nuevas Vistas Conference of the California State Department of Education, April 24–26, 1969, 3, CSA-DOE, Box F3752-1777, Folder: General Correspondence and Memos, 1966–1970.

99. Eugene Gonzales, "The Challenge," Welcome Speech, Third Annual Nuevas Vistas Conference, April 24–26, 1968, 1–2, CSA-DOE, Box F3752-1782, Folder: Speeches-Eugene Gonzales, 1968–1970.

100. Gonzales, "Presentation to First General Session," 2.

101. Gonzales, "The Challenge," 2.

102. Cost estimates of the damage caused to the Biltmore Hotel run from $30,000 to $100,000, all reported in the *Los Angeles Times*.

103. Ruben Salazar, "Reagan Seeks Suggestions from Latins," *Los Angeles Times*, April 25, 1969, D3.

104. Tom Newton, "Seven Fires Set: BILTMORE ARSON," *Los Angeles Times*, April 25, 1969, 1.

105. Ruben Salazar, "Hotel Manager, Nava Differ on Arrests During Reagan Talk," *Los Angeles Times*, April 26, 1969, C1.

106. Ibid., C10.

107. Ron Einstoss, "Hotel Fire Indictments Reveal Heroism of Rookie Policeman," *Los Angeles Times*, June 7, 1969.

108. Manuel Banda Jr., to Eugene Gonzales, May 2, 1969, 2, CSA-DOE, Box F3752-1777, Folder: General Correspondence and Memos, 1966–1970.

109. Mardirosian letter, 1.

110. Ron Einstoss, "Hotel Fire Indictments Reveal Heroism of Rookie Policeman," *Los Angeles Times*, June 7, 1969.

111. Scholars usually locate such perspectives in the more robust backlash of the 1970s and 1980s. See San Miguel, *Contested Policy*, 41–70.

112. Steinbacher, *Bitter Harvest*, 66.

113. Ibid., 67.

114. Alfred Ramirez, "THEY'RE PLAYING FOR KEEPS," pamphlet, American Education Service for Spanish-Surnamed Citizens, La Mirada, California, 1967, CSA-DOE, Box F3752-1777, Folder: General Correspondence and Memos, 1966–1970.

115. Steinbacher, *Bitter Harvest*, 19, 81.

116. Paul Houston, "East L.A. Fete Cancelled 1st Time in 35 Years," *Los Angeles Times*, September 5, 1970.

117. Ibid., 24.

118. Mrs. E. R. Aguerrebere to Dr. Max Rafferty, July 2, 1968, CSA-DOE, Box F3752:744, Folder: General Correspondence, July 1968–1969.

119. Ibid.

120. Ibid.

121. *Que Tal?* No. 6, April 1, 1971, 5.

122. According to several scholars, the tendency of Latinos to claim whiteness transcends this historical moment. Some historians and sociologists have defined Latinos as an ethnoracial "in-between group," defined either as white or as minority depending on circumstance. Latinos have thus enjoyed more fluidity within American racial categories than blacks, perpetually cast one pole of the "black-white dyad" which has proved an enduring part of the American racial ideology. James Barrett and David Roediger, "In-between People: Race, Nationality, and the 'New Immigrant' Working Class," *Journal of American Ethnic History* 16, no. 3 (Spring 1997): 3–44; Matthew Frye Jacobson, *Whiteness of A Different Color: European Immigrants and the Alchemy of Race* (Cambridge, MA: Harvard University Press, 1998); Neil Foley, "Becoming White: Mexican

Americans and their Faustian Pact with Whiteness," *Reflexiones 1997: New Directions in Mexican American Studies 53* (Austin: University of Texas Press, 1997). See also Vicki L. Ruiz, "Moreno/a, Blanco/a y Café con Leche: Racial Constructions in Chicano/a Historiography," *Mexican Studies/Estudios Mexicanos* 20, no. 2 (Summer 2004): 343–359; Ian Haney Lopez, "White Latinos," *Harvard Latino Law Review* 6 (2003): 1–7, accessed via http://www.law.harvard.edu/students/orgs/llr/vol6/lopez.pdf.

123. Philip D. Ortego, "School for the Mexican-American: Between Two Cultures," *Saturday Review*, April 17, 1971, 62.

124. Steinbacher, *Bitter Harvest*, 57.

125. Ibid., 30.

126. Ibid., 58.

127. Ibid., 51.

128. Ibid., 49.

129. Rafferty, *Classroom Countdown*, 22.

130. Ibid.

131. Ibid., 32.

132. Davies, "The Great Society after Johnson," 23.

133. Davies, "The Great Society after Johnson," 15.

134. Steinbacher, *Bitter Harvest*, 54.

135. San Miguel, *Contested Policy*, 2.


CHAPTER 3

1. Richard Chabran, "Activism and Intellectual Struggle in the Life of Ernesto Galarza, 1905–1984," *Hispanic Journal of Behavioral Sciences* 7, no. 2 (1985): 135–152.

2. Ernesto Galarza, "The Burning Light: Action and Organizing in the Mexican Community in California," Oral History, 1977, 1978, 1981, Regional Oral History Office, The Bancroft Library, University of California, Berkeley, 1982, 118.

3. Helen Robinson et al., *Dick and Jane: Fun with Our Friends* (New York: Scott, Foresman, and Company, 1965).

4. Galarza, "The Burning Light," 117–118.

5. Roberto M. DeAnda, "Ernesto Galarza and Mexican Children's Literature in the United States," *Camino Real* 4, no. 7 (2012): 11–28.

6. Ibid., 15.

7. Peter Carroll, *It Seemed Like Nothing Happened: America in the 1970s* (New York: Holt, Rinehart, 1982).

8. See many editorial mentions in the 1940s and 1950s, including: "U.S. INQUIRY URGED ON MEXICAN LABOR: Farm Union Asserts Import Program Abuses," *New York Times*, June 1, 1958; "Dr. Galarza to Speak," *The Washington Post*, October 22, 1940; "Marked Trend Toward Nationalism Noted in Latin-American Education: By Ernesto Galarza," *Washington Post*, October 3,

1937; "COAST WALKOUT DENIED: Boycott Aimed at Only Certain Growers, Farm Union Says," *New York Times*, June 7, 1952.

9. Samuel P. Huntington, "The Hispanic Challenge," *Foreign Policy*, March 1, 2004; Stephen V. Roberts, "5 % in U.S. Cite Spanish Origins," *New York Times*, April 18, 1971.

10. Bill Moore, "Plight of the Spanish-Speaking: The Terrible Barrier," *San Francisco Chronicle*, February 18, 1969; Bill Moore, "The Spanish Minority: Ex-Cuban Executive's Life in S.F.," *San Francisco Chronicle*, February 19, 1969; Ken Overaker, "Bilingual Ballots to be Used First Time Tuesday," *Los Angeles Times*, November 3, 1975.

11. Lau v. Nichols, 414 U.S. 563 (1974).

12. *Equal Educational Opportunity Act: Hearings Before the Select Committee on Educational Opportunity of the United States Senate*, 91st Congress (1971) (statement of David Sanchez); Adam Nelson, *The Elusive Ideal: Equal Educational Opportunity and the Federal Role in Boston's Public Schools, 1950–1985* (Chicago: University of Chicago Press, 2005); Susan Gilbert Schneider, *Revolution, Reaction or Reform: The 1974 Bilingual Education Act* (New York: Las Americas, 1976).

13. Nathan Glazer, *We Are All Multiculturalists Now* (Cambridge, MA: Harvard University Press, 1997).

14. Ibid.; *Hearings Before the Select Committee on Educational Opportunity of the United States Senate* (statement of David Sanchez).

15. "Bilingual Funds for State at Issue: Education Chief Says U.S. Favors Other Regions," *New York Times*, January 31, 1971.

16. "Bilingual Studies Termed Lagging," *New York Times*, May 7, 1971.

17. Stephen V. Roberts, "5 % in U.S. Cite Spanish Origins," *New York Times*, April 18, 1971.

18. "Rights Agency Assails Schools for Southwest Minority Pupils," *New York Times*, December 8, 1971.

19. Letter, multiple signers, to Department of Education, Bilingual-Bicultural Task Force, April 13, 1973, CSA-DOE, Box F3752:3271, Folder: Bilingual-Bicultural Task Force, Consolidated Applications; " 'Token Participation': Chicano Groups Urge Probe of US-Funded School Programs," *Fresno Bee*, May 8, 1973.

20. Richard E. Hughes, O.D., to Honorable Governor Brown, March 12, 1975, CSA-DOE, Box F3752: 3274, Folder: Bilingual-Bicultural Task Force, General Files, 1971–1974.

21. Ibid.

22. William E. Webster to Dr. Xavier Del Buono and Dr. Gilbert Martinez, Memorandum, March 5, 1975, CSA-DOE, Box F3752:3274, Folder: Bilingual-Bicultural Task Force, General Files, 1971–1974.

23. William E. Webster to Dr. Xavier Del Buono, Memorandum, October 21, 1974, CSA-DOE, Box F3752:3274, Folder: Bilingual-Bicultural Task Force, General Files, 1971–1974.

24. Jack McCurdy, "Failures in Bilingual School Plan Alleged," *Los Angeles Times*, July 20, 1976.

25. Jack Jones, "Increasing Friction of Minority Groups Told," *Los Angeles Times*, March 1, 1970; "Mexican-Black Feud Spur Fight-Report," *Chicago Daily Defender*, March 1970.

26. Guadalupe San Miguel Jr., *Contested Policy*: The Rise and Fall of Federal Bilingual Education in the United States, 1960–2002 (Denton: University of North Texas Press, 2004); Richard Navarro, "Identity and Consensus in the Politics of Bilingual Education: the Case of California, 1967–1980," Ph.D. dissertation, Stanford University, 1984.

27. J. Stanley Pottinger to School Districts with more than Five Percent Minority Group Children, Office of Civil Rights Memorandum, Re: Identification of Discrimination and Denial of Services on the Basis of National Origin, May 25, 1970, accessed via http://www.ed.gov/about/offices/list/ocr/ell/may25.html.

28. *San Francisco Chronicle*, June 1, 1974.

29. James J. Lyons, "The Past and Future Directions of Federal Bilingual-Education Policy," Annals of the American Academy of Political and Social Science 508 (March 1990): 69.

30. Lau v. Nichols.

31. Nelson, *The Elusive Ideal.*

32. "California Poll: Majority is Anti-Busing," *San Francisco Chronicle*, September 21, 1979; "Parents Fear Injury to Bilingual Plan," see photo June 11, 1974; Jim Wood, "S.F.'s Bilingual Students Exempted from Busing," *San Francisco Examiner*, June 12, 1974; Ron Moskowitz, "School Board Argues Busing Plan Exceptions," *San Francisco Chronicle*, June 12, 1974. See Mark Brilliant, *The Color of America has Changed: How Racial Diversity Shaped Civil Rights Reform in California 1941–1978* (New York: Oxford University Press, 2010); E. Cahill Mahoney, "School Integration Hits Bilingual Snag," *San Francisco Progress*, June 15, 1974.

33. Of immigration to California in the 1970s, Mexicans had the lowest level of instruction, 72 percent not having completed eighth grade, and only 2 percent possessing an advanced degree. Non-Mexican Hispanics had the second lowest level of education, though 11.4 percent had advanced degrees: significantly more than the Mexicans, but less than half the nearly 25 percent of the Asians who also flooded California in this era. The Asian immigrant population in this era actually had a higher percentage of advanced-degree holders than the white population at large. Thomas Muller, *La Cuarta Ola: Los Inmigrantes Más Recientes de California* (Washington, DC: The Urban Institute Press, 1984), 7; William Petersen, "Success Story, Japanese-American Style," *New York Times*, January 1966.

34. Mark Brilliant, "Color Lines: Civil Rights Struggles on America's Racial Frontier 1945–1975," Ph.D. dissertation, Stanford University, 2000, 345–346;

Ellen D. Wu, *The Color of Success: Asian Americans and the Origins of the Model Minority* (Princeton, NJ: Princeton University Press, 2013).

35. Testimony of Edward Steinman before Committee on Ways and Means of California State Assembly, December 10, 1974, 15, University of California, Los Angeles, Helene V. Smookler Papers (UCLA-HVS), Box 1, Folder 2, Bilingual Education- LAU.

36. "The Big Hassle: Bilingual Teaching for Hispanics," *San Francisco Examiner*, July 31, 1979; "'One-a-day' English is a bitter pill to swallow," *San Francisco Examiner*, May 29, 1974; Dexter Waugh, "Chinese tell schools to comply," *San Francisco Examiner*, January 22, 1974; "Unfair Demands on City Schools," *San Francisco Examiner*, January 25, 1974. Reports: Integration, 1973–1974, Selected Data, 1972–1973, "Study of the extent of primary foreign languages other than English used in the homes of the SFUSD students as of December 1972."

37. "The Big Hassle,"; Bruce Koon, "San Francisco's Role in Planning Bilingual Study," *San Francisco Examiner*, May 27, 1974.

38. Dexter Waugh, "Why Chicanos Drop Out," *San Francisco Examiner*, May 28, 1974.

39. "A Hard Look/Black Language: What's said . . . vs. What's Learned," *San Francisco Examiner*, August 14, 1979.

40. Nancy Dooley, "Hiring Freeze Haunts Schools," *San Francisco Examiner*, September 4, 1974.

41. Lyons, "The Past and Future Directions of Federal Bilingual-Education Policy," 72; "Schools Get US Aid Offer," *Los Angeles Times*, October 13, 1975.

42. "Brown OKs Bilingual Teaching Measure," *Los Angeles Times*, September 19, 1976.

43. Lyons, "The Past and Future Directions of Federal Bilingual-Education Policy," 66. Ernesto Galarza wrote at length about this inherent problem in bilingual education legislation.

44. Jack McCurdy, "Failures in Bilingual School Plan Alleged," *Los Angeles Times*, July 20, 1976.

45. "Unfair Demands on City Schools," *San Francisco Examiner*, January 25, 1974; Big Hassle: Bilingual Teaching for Hispanics," *San Francisco Examiner*, July 31, 1979.

46. Dan Borsuk, "SF School Board Race Heats Up," *San Francisco Progress*, October 29, 1980.

47. Serena Chen, "Appointee Rod McLeod Vows to be an Independent Voice on SF School Board," *East/West*, May 28, 1987.

48. "Bilingual Education Bills Amended," *San Francisco Chronicle*, August 24, 1979.

49. John R. Edwards, "Critics and Criticisms of Bilingual Education," *Modern Language Journal* 64, no. 4 (Winter 1980): 409–416.

50. Noel Epstein, *Language, Ethnicity, and the Schools: Policy Alternatives for Bilingual-Bicultural Education* (Washington, DC: Institute for Educational Leadership, 1977).

51. William Trombley, "BITTER FIGHT: Can Bilingual Education Do Its Job?," *Los Angeles Times*, September 4, 1980.

52. Malcolm N. Danoff et al., *Evaluation of the Impact of ESEA Title VII Spanish-English Bilingual Education Programs, Volume III: Year Two Impact Data, Educational Process, and In-Depth Analysis* (Palo Alto, CA: American Institute of Research, 1978).

53. Edwards, "Critics and Criticisms," 410.

54. Interview conducted by author, September 2004. In 1976, the Supreme Court and the SFUSD jointly signed the "Lau Consent Decree" mandating compliance with the original decision to provide students with "bilingual bicultural" education.

55. Stephen Pitti, *The Devil in Silicon Valley: Northern California, Race, and Mexican Americans* (Princeton, NJ: Princeton University Press, 2004), 4.

56. US Census Bureau. *American Community Survey, 2011*, American Community Survey 5-Year Estimates, Table B03003.

57. Conference talk, Center for the Study of Democratic Institutions, Santa Barbara, recorded 1959–1960, 1, reproduced in Galarza, "The Burning Light."

58. Galarza, "The Burning Light," 93.

59. Mr. Raushenbush, Whitney Foundation to Ernesto Galarza, June 4, 1973, SUSC-EGP, Box 64, Folder 2.

60. Ibid., 77–79. The Studio Lab was funded for its first two years of existence by the Whitney Foundation, and in smaller measure by the federal Model Cities Program. Galarza and his team was then hired on a consultant basis by the SJUSD.

61. Ibid., 87, 72–73.

62. Ibid., 63.

63. Archibald Gillies to Ernesto Galarza, October 7, 1971, SUSC-EGP, Box 64, Folder 2.

64. San Jose Unified School District application for AB2284 state funds, 1973, SUSC-EGP, Box 64, Folder 2.

65. Ernesto Galarza to Commissioner of Education Edward Boyer, February 4, 1978, SUSC-EGP, Box 63, Folder 2.

66. Galarza, "The Burning Light," 63. Emphasis in original.

67. Ibid., 66. Emphasis in original.

68. Ibid., 81, 113.

69. Ernesto Galarza v. Robert Kelley Acosta, civil No. C-77-1081-GBH, original filing July 22, 1977, 2, SUSC-EGP, Box 63, Folder 2, Administrative Complaint, August 1977–July 1978.

70. Ernesto Galarza to Dean, San Jose State University, June 15, 1976, SUSC-EGP, Box 63, Folder 11, SJACBE, Title VII proposal, 1974–1977.

71. Olivia Martinez, public letter, October 7, 1977, SUSC-EGP, Box 62, Folder 2, Administrative Complaint, Aug 1977–July 1978. The fund was meant to assist residents of the town of Alviso, who were threatened by the expanding city of San Jose. Galarza had organized the struggle and was managing the fund.

72. Galarza, "The Burning Light," 63.

73. Rodolfo Acuña, *Occupied America: A History of Chicanos* (New York: Harper and Row, 1981), 398.

74. Ibid., 82.

75. Ibid., 98–99.

76. Ibid.

77. Ibid., 76.

78. Ernesto Galarza, "Students' Responsibilities to the Chicano Community," talk to University of California, Berkeley Chicano Studies students, recorded April 20, 1977, 43. Reproduced in Galarza, "The Burning Light."

79. Galarza, "The Burning Light," 61–62.

80. Ibid., 60. This description resonates with the founding of the myriad conservative groups who opposed sex education as well.

81. Ibid., 67.

82. Ibid.

83. Ernesto Galarza v. Robert Kelley Acosta.

84. COME administrative complaint to Office of Bilingual Education, filed August 8, 1977; Deposition, Olivia Martinez, October 2, 1977, both SUSC-EGP, Box 63, Folder 2, Administrative Complaint, August 1977–July 1978. Galarza, "The Burning Light," 61.

85. January 1978, several articles and press releases, SUSC-EGP, Box 63, Folder 2, Administrative Complaint, August 1977–July 1978.

86. Program, California Association of Bilingual Educators, February 6–9, 1978, SUSC-EGP, Box 63, Folder 2, Administrative Complaint, August 1977–July 1978.

87. William Trombley, "BITTER FIGHT: Can Bilingual Education Do Its Job?," *Los Angeles Times*, September 4, 1980.

88. Kay Mills, "Ernesto Galarza: Activist Historian," *Los Angeles Times*, September 26, 1982, page D3.

89. Galarza, "The Burning Light," 89.

90. Ibid., 89.

91. Ibid., 86.

92. Ibid., 94–95.

CHAPTER 4

1. "Letters to the *Times*: Bilingual Phone Service," *Los Angeles Times*, February 23, 1976.

2. Vernon E. Lattin, Rolando Hinojosa, and Gary D. Keller, eds., *Tomás Rivera, 1935–1984: The Man and His Work* (Tempe, AZ: Bilingual Review, 1988).

3. James J. Lyons, "The Past and Future Directions of Federal Bilingual-Education Policy," *Annals of the American Academy of Political and Social Science* 508 (March 1990).

4. Arthur M. Schlesinger Jr., *The Disuniting of America: Reflections on a Multicultural Society* (New York: Norton, 1991); Charles Taylor, *Multiculturalism: Examining the Politics of Recognition* (Princeton, NJ: Princeton University Press, 1994); Elizabeth Lasch-Quinn, *Race Experts: How Racial Etiquette, Sensitivity Training, and the New Age Hijacked the Civil Rights Revolution* (New York: Norton, 2001).

5. Daryl Michael Scott, "Postwar Pluralism, *Brown v. Board of Education*, and the Origins of Multicultural Education," *Journal of American History* (June 2004): 69–82; Jonathan Zimmerman, "*Brown*-ing the American Textbook: History, Psychology, and the Origins of Modern Multiculturalism," *History of Education Quarterly* 44, no. 1, A Special Issue on the Fiftieth Anniversary of the *Brown v. Board of Education* Decision (Spring 2004): 46–69.

6. Dexter Waugh, "Why Chicanos Drop Out," *San Francisco Examiner*, May 28, 1974.

7. "The State of the City, 1976: Youth Priorities," City of Los Angeles, Office of the Mayor, Community Analysis Bureau, June 1976, 2, University of Los Angeles Special Collections, Helene V. Smookler Collection (UCLA-HVS), Box 1, Folder 8. The Los Angeles Unified School District spanned 714 square miles, the largest in the nation. Zevi Gutfreund, "Language, Education, Race, and the Remaking of American Citizenship in Los Angeles, 1900-1968," Dissertation, University of California, Los Angeles, 2013.; Albert Camarillo, "Cities of Color: The *New Racial Frontier* in California's Minority-Majority Cities," *Pacific Historical Review* 76, no. 1 (2007): 1–28.

8. Raul Arreola, Board of Education, City of Los Angeles to Dr. Max Rafferty, September 25, 1970, CSA-DOE, Box F3752:743, Folder: General Correspondence, July 1969–November 1970.

9. Zevi Gutfreund, "Should Bilingual Education Board the Bus Too?: Spanish Speakers, School Desegregation, and the Challenge of Liberalism in Los Angeles," unpublished paper presented at the University of Pennsylvania conference, "Schools and the New Inequality," April 2008.

10. Albert Camarillo, *Chicanos in a Changing Society: From Mexican Pueblos to American Barrios in Southern California, 1848–1930* (Cambridge, MA: Harvard University Press, 1979).

11. Neil Foley, "Over the Rainbow: *Hernandez v Texas, Brown v Board of Education*, and Black v Brown," in *"Colored Men" and "Hombres Aquí": Hernandez v. Texas and the Emergence of Mexican-American Lawyering*, edited by Michael Olivas (Houston: Arte Publico Press, 2006), 116–117.

12. "Court Case to Test Right of School Board to Bar Girl," *Afro-American*, May 31, 1947.

13. "Mexican-Black Feud Spur Fight-Report," *Chicago Daily Defender*, March 7, 1970.

14. "Desegregation and Education Concerns of the Hispanic Community," Conference Report June 26–28, 1977, National Institute of Education, United States Department of Health, Education, and Welfare, UCLA-HVS, Box 1, Folder 8, Hispanic Community.

15. Jose Cardenas, "Bilingual Education, Segregation, and a Third Alternative," in *Inequality in Education* (Cambridge, MA: Harvard Center for Law and Education, 1975).

16. Camarillo, "Cities of Color"; Patt Morrison and Gerald Farris, "Year-Round School Sessions—A Crisis for the L.A. Board: Overcrowding Dilemma Called a Latino Issue as Explosive as Busing Became for White Parents," *Los Angeles Times*, June 29, 1981.

17. Mr. and Mrs. R. W. Bird to Max Rafferty, April 27, 1970, CSA-DOE, Box 3752:746, Folder: Max Rafferty Papers, General Correspondence, December 1969–March 1970.

18. Orville E. Boylam to Max Rafferty, January 14, 1970, CSA-DOE, Box 3752:746, Folder: Max Rafferty Papers, General Correspondence, December 1969–March 1970.

19. Harry Bernstein, "2 Rival Teacher Groups Finish Plan for Merger," *Los Angeles Times*, January 6, 1970; "New National Teachers Organization Formed," *The Educator*, December 1971, CU-RBML, GRC, Box 119, Folder: *The Educator*.

20. Dorothy Townsend, "Suit Challenging Teacher Integration Program Filed," *Los Angeles Times*, November 7, 1975. Of the state recommendation to hire 10–13,000 bilingual-bicultural certificated teachers to serve over 250,000 NES and LES children, LAUSD had the highest need for the mere 3,000 certificated teachers in 1978–1979. The district thus began granting waivers to new hires, and adopted an evaluation system of "A": can speak, write, and read foreign language, or "B": can converse but not read or write. M. Beatriz Arias, "The Desegregation Plan's Impact on Services to Limited and non-English Speaking Students and Hispanic Students," November 6, 1978, 21–24, UCLA-HVS, Box 30, Folder 2.

21. Letter file, UCLA-HVS, Box 14, Folder 1, Bilingual Education, 1979–1980; Pat B. Anderson, "L.A. Schools Make Exceptions in Bilingual Instructors Search," *Los Angeles Times*, August 20, 1978.

22. Donna Schiebe, "Teachers Bitter, Frustrated Over 'Displacement' Plan," *Los Angeles Times*, September 18, 1975.

23. Ibid.

24. Among others, see "Jump in Minority Reading Scores Reported," *Los Angeles Times*, March 12, 1974; "A School Says Si to Bilingual Education," *Los Angeles Times*, March 31, 1974.

25. Daryl Lembke, "'Hard-Nosed' S.F. School Superintendent Sworn In," *Los Angeles Times*, August 12, 1975.

26. Ibid. By 1970, Latinos had become "the most concentrated of any major racial or ethnic group in San Francisco." See Brian J. Godfrey, *Neighborhoods in Transition: The Making of San Francisco's Ethnic and Nonconformist Communities* (Berkeley: University of California Press, 1988).

27. Louis Freedberg, "LATINO POWER!," *San Francisco Chronicle*, October 19, 1986.

28. Margo Freistadt, "Another View on the Unz Initiative," *San Francisco Chronicle*, May 6, 1998.

29. Ibid.

30. Ibid.

31. Stanford Center for Chicano Research, Demographic Profile on the Latino Population of San Francisco County (Stanford: Stanford Center for Chicano Research, 1984). The 1980 census counted 83,373 Spanish-surnamed individuals living in San Francisco; 140,000 is an estimate by community groups. Estimates are notoriously inaccurate due to the large undocumented community. Mary Jo McConahay, "Hispanics: Fastest Growing Minority," *Sunday Examiner* and *San Francisco Chronicle*, May 16, 1982; Bruce Pettit, "The Pettit Report: Analyzing the Latino Vote," *San Francisco Examiner*, July 6, 1983.

32. Daryl Lembke, "Riles Moves Into Fight to Overhaul S.F. Schools," *Los Angeles Times*, May 4, 1975.

33. Ibid.

34. Mark Brilliant, "Intellectual Affirmative Action: How Multiculturalism Became Mandatory in Higher Education," in *Living in the Eighties*, edited by Gil Troy and Vincent J. Cannato (New York: Oxford University Press, 2009), 100; Benmayor, Rina, and William V. Flores, eds. *Latino Cultural Citizenship: Claiming Identity, Space and Rights.* (Boston: Beacon Press, 1997).

35. Ron Moskowitz, "Low Marks for the SF Schools," *San Francisco Chronicle*, March 15, 1974.

36. Ibid.

37. Felix M. Padilla, *Latino Ethnic Consciousness: The Case of Mexican-Americans and Puerto Ricans in Chicago* (South Bend, IN: University of Notre Dame Press, 1985).
38. "Celebrating a Decade in Style," *El Tecolote* 11, no. 4 (December 1980).
39. "La disciplina en las escuelas es un problema nacional," *Tiempo Latino*, February 29, 1984.
40. Carlos Barón, "From the Belly of the Beast," *El Tecolote*, September 22, 1984. The news reporting throughout the Spanish-speaking world suggested the far reach of this cosmopolitan sensibility. Stories about Argentina, Bolivia, or Uruguay—nations from which few San Franciscans hailed—were as common as pieces on Nicaragua, El Salvador, or Mexico.
41. Natalia Mehlman Petrzela, "Multiculturalism," in *Encyclopedia of Human Global Migration*, edited by Immanuel Ness (New York: Blackwell Publishing, 2013).
42. Ray del Portillo was San Francisco's first director of bilingual education. Carlota del Portillo is currently the dean of the Mission District Campus of the City College of San Francisco, and served on the San Francisco School Board and the San Francisco Civil Service Commission, among many other municipal organizations.
43. Laurie Kay Sommers, "Inventing Latinismo: The Creation of a Hispanic Panethnicity in the United States," *The Journal of American Folklore* 104 (Winter 1991): 32–53.
44. Interview with author, September 2004.
45. Marjorie Leland, "A Day in the Life of a New School Chief," *San Francisco Progress*, September 23, 1970.
46. Nathan Glazer, *Ethnic Dilemmas: 1964–1982* (Cambridge, MA: Harvard University Press, 1983); David Hollinger, *Postethnic America: Beyond Multiculturalism* (New York: Basic Books, 1995); Will Kymlicka, *Multicultural Citizenship* (New York: Oxford University Press, 1991); Taylor, *Multiculturalism*.
47. "The San Francisco Story: Administration, Program, Plant," *American School and University* 37, no. 2 (October 1964).
48. Ibid., 10.
49. Arlene Van Breems, "Mexican Heritage Added to Classroom," *Los Angeles Times*, August 10, 1969.
50. "Improving Instructional Programs," February 1969–1971, Instructional Development and Services, SFUSD, 1971, 21, Curriculum Reports, 1960–1978.
51. "Day in Sacramento," *Los Angeles Times*, December 2, 1972; Noel Greenwood, "Bilingual Education: It's Beginning to Pay Off," *Los Angeles Times*, June 25, 1972.
52. "An Educational Redesign for the SFUSD," Policies [v.2], 3 of 3, November 17, 1976, Article 6, 1–2, 6104, 6105, 1–3.
53. San Francisco Unified School District, "Implementation Plan for 1978–1979, Educational Redesign Plan 1978–1979," February 22, 1978, 6123.
54. Ibid., High School Graduation Requirements, Classes of 1978–1981.

55. Estelle B. Freedman, *No Turning Back: The History of Feminism and the Future of Women* (New York: Ballantine Books, 2002); Linda Gordon, "U.S. Women's History," in *The New American History*, edited by Eric Froner (Philadelphia: Temple University Press, 1997).

56. Implementation Plan, Philosophy of Materials Selection, Article 6, Instruction, 6110; An Educational Redesign for the SFUSD," Policies [v.2], 3 of 3, November 17, 1976, 6100.

57. Annie Nakao, "Mission High: The City's oldest high school comes to life again," *San Francisco Examiner*, December 7, 1977.

58. Ibid.

59. Gene Prat, candidate for sheriff of San Francisco, quoted in "The Mystique of Mission High," n.d., Box: Mission High, 1970–1986, Folder 2, SFPL-SFHC.

60. Bianca J. Hirsch, "Ed Center Helps Language Adjustment," *San Francisco Progress*, July 26, 1978; Nella Reed, chairman—PR Committee, Mission High School Career Development Center, December 1, 1970.

61. Nancy Dooley, "New School Chief Takes the Oath, Vows cooperation," *San Francisco Examiner*, August 12, 1975; Katherine Seligman, "New Superintendent Cortines: Man with a Mission," *San Francisco Examiner*, May 12, 1986.

62. Barbara Nanney, "Mission Impossible?," *The Independent*, June 1, 1996.

63. Mission High School Catalog, 1970–1972, San Francisco Public Library, San Francisco History Center (SFPL-SFHC), Box Mission High School, Folder 2, 1925–1996.

64. Bianca J. Hirsch, "Ed Center Helps Language Adjustment," *San Francisco Progress*, July 26, 1978.

65. Mildred Hamilton, "Mission High Goes Creative," *San Francisco Examiner*, May 21, 1974; "Brilliant and Subtle," *San Francisco Progress*, June 4, 1974.

66. "SFUSD Spotlight on Schools," SFUSD newsletter, Spring 1987.

67. Interview with the author, San Francisco, September 2004.

68. Interview with the author, September 2004.

69. Ibid.

70. Annie Nakao, "Educators Oppose a back-to-basics move," *San Francisco Examiner*, November 23, 1979.

71. Frank O. Sotomayor, "Bilingual Classes Aid Chicano Pupils," *Los Angeles Times*, May 4, 1975.

72. "El Rancho District Plans Major Bilingual Program," *Los Angeles Times*, July 31, 1975.

73. Leroy F. Aarons, "Ex-POW: Re-entering a New World," *The Washington Post*, February 18, 1973.

74. J. T. Holmes, letter to the editor, *Los Angeles Times*, n.d., Stanford University Special Collections, Papers of the Mexican American Legal Defense Fund (SUSC-MLDF), Box 54, Folder 28: Bilingual Education, Newspaper Articles, Los Angeles.

75. Craig Miller, letter to the editor, *Los Angeles Times*, n.d., SUSC-MLDF, Box 54, Folder 28: Bilingual Education, Newspaper Articles, Los Angeles.

76. Guadalupe San Miguel Jr., *Contested Policy: The Rise and Fall of Federal Bilingual Education in the United States, 1960–2001* (Denton, TX: University of North Denton Press, 2004); Carlos Kevin Blanton, *The Strange Career of Bilingual Education in Texas, 1836–1981* (College Station: Texas A & M University Press, 2004); James Crawford, ed., *Language Loyalties: A Source Book on the Official English Controversy* (Chicago: University of Chicago Press, 1992; Ruben Donato, *The Other Struggle for Equal Schools: Mexican Americans in the Civil Rights Era* (Albany: State University of New York Press, 1997).

77. Bruce Koon, "San Francisco's Role in Planning Bilingual Study," *San Francisco Examiner*, May 27, 1974; Malcolm N. Danoff et al., *Evaluation of the Impact of ESEA Title VII Spanish-English Bilingual Education Programs, Volume III: Year Two Impact Data, Educational Process, and In-Depth Analysis* (Palo Alto, CA: American Institute of Research, 1978).

PART II

1. Gordon V. Drake, "Is the Schoolhouse the Proper Place to Teach Raw Sex?" (Tulsa: Christian Crusade Publications, 1968).

2. Jeffrey Moran, *Teaching Sex: The Shaping of Adolescence in the 20th Century.* (Cambridge, MA: Harvard University Press, 2000), 24–29.

3. "Keeping Fit," American Social Hygiene Association/YMCA/United States Public Health Service, 1919, The Social History Welfare Project, http://www.socialwelfarehistory.com/organizations/american-social-hygiene-association-keeping-fit-posters-i 1919/.

4. Moran, 115.

5. See various Coronet Films, including *Are You Popular?* (1947); *Control Your Emotions* (1950); and Sid Davis Productions, *Boys Beware* (1961).

6. *Report of Hearings on Sex Education*, San Diego Unified School District, testimony of Persida Drakulich, February 12, 1969, 6.

7. John D'Emilio and Estelle Freedman, *Intimate Matters: A History of Sexuality in America* (Chicago: University of Chicago Press, 1997).

8. Janice Irvine, *Talk About Sex: Battles Over Sex Education in the United States* (Berkeley: University of California Press, 2004).

9. Kristin Luker, *When Sex Goes to School: Warring Views on Sex—and Sex Education—Since the Sixties* (New York: Norton, 2006).

CHAPTER 5

1. Linda Mathews, "Battle Lines Being Drawn Over Sex Education," *Los Angeles Times*, December 23, 1968, A1.

2. "Sex Education Programs in California Schools: Second Progress Report of the California State Department of Education," Educational Programs Committee of the California State Board of Education, March 13, 1969, 2.

3. Newsletter, National Council of Christian Families Opposed to Sex Education in Public Schools, Tulsa, OK, 74102, January 19, 1971, SL-MSC, Box 14, Folder 233, sex education, printed attacks, 1970–1971; Internal memo, "List of Opponents," SL-MSC, Box 14, Folder 235, SIECUS, sex education controversies, list of opponents, 1969.

4. Minutes, Educational Programs Committee of the California State Board of Education, February 12, 1969, CSA-DOE, Box F3752:9, Folder: Records of Henry J. Heydt Jr., 1968–1969.

5. Matthew Lassiter, "Inventing Family Values: The Crisis of the American Dream in the Seventies," in *Rightward Bound: Making America Conservative in the 1970s*, edited by Bruce Schulman and Julian Zelizer (Cambridge, MA: Harvard), 2008; Natasha Zaretsky, *No Direction Home: The American Family and Fear of National Decline, 1968–1980* (Chapel Hill: University of North Carolina Press, 2007).

6. Elaine Tyler May, *Homeward Bound: American Families in the Cold War Era* (New York: Basic Books, 1999).

7. Citizens for Parental Rights v. San Mateo County Board of Education, 51 Cal. App. 3d (1975), *dismissed*, 425 U.S. 908 (1976). Associated Press, "Suit Filed in Sex Study Controversy," *Berkeley Gazette*, September 11, 1968.

8. Neil Ulman, "A Delicate Subject: Sex Education Courses Are Suddenly Assailed By Many Parent Groups," *Wall Street Journal*, April 11, 1969.

9. Thomas Frank, *What's the Matter with Kansas? How Conservatives Won The Heart of America* (New York: Henry Holt and Co., 2004).

10. "Summary of Actions of the Supreme Court Announced Yesterday," *The New York Times*, April 6, 1976.

11. Clayton Howard, "Building a Family-Friendly Metropolis: Sexuality, the State, and Postwar Housing Policy," *Journal of Urban History*, September 2013, 18.

12. Evelyn Mills Duvall, *When You Marry* (New York: D.C. Heath and Co., 1947); Neil Ulman, "A Delicate Subject: Sex Education Courses Are Suddenly Assailed By Many Parent Groups," April 11, 1969.

13. "How San Mateo Implemented 'Time of your life,'" CSA-DOE, Box F3752:9, Folder: Henry Heydt Jr. papers, 1968–1969; San Mateo County Superintendent J. Russell Kent, in Report of Hearings on Sex Education, State Board of Education, Sacramento, April 10, 1969, 54.

14. In 2007, William Ayres was charged with sexual molestation of a number of his underage male patients. From the1960s until these charges emerged, Ayres was widely considered "a beacon of reason, accuracy and science" and as an innovative sex educator. In 2011, he was remanded to a state mental institution for dementia. Mike Aidax, "William Ayres to be Sent to Mental Hospital Instead of Jail," *San Francisco Examiner*, August 22, 2011, http://www.sfexaminer.com/local/

peninsula/2011/08/william-ayres-sent-mental-hospital-instead-jail. In 2013, at age 81, he was convicted and sentenced to serve eight years in prison for crimes committed against children during the 1980s and 1990s. His children insist he is the victim of another witch hunt. Joshua Melvin, "Peninsula Child Psychiatrist William Ayres sentenced to eight years for molesting patients," *San Jose Mercury News*, August 27, 2013. Ayres is not the only participant in the sex education battles surrounded by personal scandal. Donn Moomaw, a Reagan appointee to the state Moral Guidelines Committee (though he later emerged as its leading liberal voice) faced a similar situation. The pastor of Reagan's Bel Air Presbyterian Congregation and speaker at the 1981 presidential inauguration, Moomaw resigned from his clergyship in 1993 for "unspecified indiscretions" later revealed to be "sexual misconduct" with five female congregants. John Dart, "Church will Report on Moomaw Episode," *Los Angeles Times*, March 13, 1995. Though several of the anti-sex education activists were involved with sex scandals later in their career—Reverend Billie James Hargis was found to be consorting with his male congregants and Congressman John Schmitz is father to the infamous pedophile Mary Kay Letourneau, who ultimately married one of her former sixth-grade students—Ayres is the only sex educator who apparently lived up to the allegations of perversion that the opponents heaped upon him. "Child Psychiatrist Charged with Molesting Patients," *San Francisco Examiner*, April 6, 2007.

15. Forum "Sex Education in the Public Schools," July 25, 1968, 2, CSA-DOE, Box F3752:9, Folder: Henry Heydt Jr. papers, 1968–1969.

16. Ibid.

17. *Sex Education USA*, Williams/MSC movie shown at February 12, 1969, Educational Program Committee meeting, 23; Resolution 68-5, BOE, County of San Mateo, State of California, adopted June 5, 1968. CSA-DOE, Box F3752:9, Folder: Henry Heydt Jr. papers, 1968–1969.

18. Ibid; Forum "Sex Education in the Public Schools," 6.

19. Educational Programs Committee of the California State Board of Education, " 'Sex Education' Programs in Public Schools, Second Progress Report of the California State Department of Education," March 13, 1969, 3, CSA-DOE, Box F3752:9, Folder: Henry Heydt Jr. papers, 1968–1969.

20. Ibid., 4.

21. Child Psychiatrist Charged with Molesting Patients," *San Francisco Examiner*, April 6, 2007.

22. William H. Ayres and Marilyn McCurdy, *Time of Your Life: Family Life and Health Education for Intermediate Grades, Preliminary Teachers Guide Programs 10–15*, prepared by Bay Region Instructional Television for Education for KQED, n.d., 30–31.

23. Ibid.

24. Ibid., 36. Other programs statewide reflected this broad focus in sex education programs as well. Dr. Frances Todd of San Francisco described her expansive vision of such programming: "Human maturation and reproduction are inextricably allied with reason rather than instinct, with rational decision, self control, love, personal and social responsibility, and moral and spiritual values, rather than animal-like impulse and compulsion." Report of Hearings on Sex Education, 42. CSA-DOE, Box F3752:9, Folder: Henry Heydt Jr. papers, 1968–1969.

25. Ayres and McCurdy, viii.

26. Thomas W. Laqueur, *Solitary Sex: A Cultural History of Masturbation* (New York: Zone Books, 2004).

27. Leroy P. Aarons, "The Reagan Regime in Retrospect," *The Washington Post*, December 23, 1974, A2, CU-RBML, GRC, Box 400, Folder: Ronald Reagan, 1969–1975.

28. Educational Programs Committee of the California State Board of Education, "'Sex Education' Programs in Public Schools, Second Progress Report of the California State Department of Education," March 13, 1969, 23.

29. Ibid., 24.

30. Forum "Sex Education in the Public Schools," 7.

31. Michel Foucault, *Abnormal: Lectures at the Collège de France, 1974–75* (New York: Verso Books, 2003), passim.

32. William H. Ayres and Marilyn McCurdy, *Time of Your Life: Family Life and Health Education for Intermediate Grades, Preliminary Teachers Guide Programs 10–15*, prepared by Bay Region Instructional Television for Education for KQED, n.d., ix.

33. "How San Mateo Implemented 'Time of Your Life,'" June 5, 1968, CSA-DOE, Box F3752:9, Folder: Henry Heydt, Jr. papers, 1968–1969.

34. Ibid.

35. Forum "Sex Education in the Public Schools," July 25, 1968

36. Ibid., 2.

37. Ibid., 4.

38. Report of Hearings on Sex Education, 54.

39. "Mother Attacks SIECUS Programs," *News Bulletin*, March 30, 1969.

40. Ulman.

41. Ibid., 31.

42. Ibid.

43. "Mother Attacks SIECUS Programs," *News Bulletin*, March 30, 1969.

44. "Group Vows to Fight Sex Education, Hears it Called Communist Conspiracy," *Sacramento Bee*, November 12, 1968.

45. Marjorie Lemlow, Mothers Support Neighborhood Schools, Inc., San Francisco, at Report of Hearings on Sex Education, State Board of Education, Sacramento,

April 10, 1969, CSA-DOE, Box F3752:9, Folder: Henry J. Heydt, Jr. papers, 1968–1969.

46. Janice M. Irvine, *Talk About Sex: The Battles Over Sex Education in the United States* (Berkeley: University of California Press, 2002).

47. Forum, "Sex Education in the Public Schools," 6.

48. Ibid.

49. Ibid., 4.

50. Ibid., 6.

51. Ibid., 4.

52. Report of Hearings on Sex Education, State Board of Education, Sacramento, April 10, 1969, CSA-DOE, Box F3752:9, Folder: Henry Heydt Jr. papers, 1968–1969.

53. John D'Emilio and Estelle B. Freedman, *Intimate Matters: A History of Sexuality in America* (New York: Harper and Row, 1988), Chapter 14.

54. Educational Programs Committee of the California State Board of Education, "Sex Education Programs in Public Schools," 6.

55. *Sex Education U.S.A.* film shown at state board and staff meeting, Minutes, Educational Programs Committee of the California State Board of Education, February 12, 1969, 25.

56. Ibid., 26.

57. Kent, at Report of Hearings on Sex Education, 54.

58. Forum, "Sex Education in the Public Schools," 5.

59. Ibid., 4.

60. Ibid., 4–5.

61. Ibid., 6.

62. *Sex Education U.S.A.* film, Minutes, 26.

63. Linda Mathews, "Battle Lines Being Drawn All Over the State," *Los Angeles Times*, December 23, 1968, A1.

64. Beth Bailey, "Prescribing the Pill: Politics, Culture, and the Sexual Revolution in America's Heartland," *Journal of Social History* 30, no. 4 (Summer, 1997): 827–856; Elaine Tyler May, *America and The Pill: a History of Peril, Promise, and Liberation* (New York: Basic Books, 2010).

65. Ayres and McCurdy, 34.

66. Ibid., 18

67. Ibid.

68. Ibid.

69. Forum, "Sex Education Programs in Public Schools," 6.

70. Ibid., 5.

71. Ibid., 5.

72. Minutes, Educational Programs Committee of the California State Board of Education, February 12, 1969, 6.

73. Ibid.

74. Testimony of Persida Drakulich of San Diego Unified School District, Report of Hearings on Sex Education, State Board of Education, Sacramento, April 10, 1969, 76.

75. Ibid., 79.

76. Ibid., 77.

77. Julian Carter, "Birds, Bees, and Venereal Disease: Toward an Intellectual History of Sex Education," *Journal of the History of Sexuality* 10, no. 2 (2001): 213–249; Jeffrey Moran, *Teaching Sex: The Shaping of Adolescence in the Twentieth Century* (Cambridge, MA: Harvard University Press, 2000).

78. Ayres and McCurdy, ix.

79. Report of Hearings on Sex Education, State Board of Education, Sacramento, April 10, 1969, 7.

80. Ibid., 9.

81. Mrs. Joseph J. Crawford to Rafferty, July 9, 1969, CSA-DOE, Box F3752:351, Folder: Max Rafferty General Correspondence, July–September, 1969.

82. Forum "'Sex Education' Programs in Public Schools," 1–8. Eugene Gonzales, who was in charge of this review, reported that the standards and practices for sex education were so unclear that the five reviewers assigned to the task "did not completely agree along them regarding those districts that were violating the code." This exploration primarily served to show that concerns about challenges to family authority were shared among opponents to sex education statewide, but reached no conclusion except to resolve that the state Senate Committee on Rules would set up yet another committee to study "the objections and charges made against current sex education programs in elementary and secondary schools in California" to be presented eight months later.

83. John Willson, "Parents Thrash Out Sex Education Dilemma, *Star Free Press*, September 11, 1969, A-6; Public Letter from Ventura Concerned Parents, signed David C. Bartlett, Chairman, n.d., (c. summer 1969), CSA-DOE, Box F3752:747, Folder: Max Rafferty, General Correspondence, July 1969–November 1969.

84. Ibid.; David L. Bartlett to Max Rafferty, November 4, 1969, CSA-DOE, Box F3752:747, Folder: Max Rafferty, General Correspondence, July 1969–November 1969.

85. Mrs. Shirley Cabral of Concord, California, to Max Rafferty, May 1, 1970, CSA-DOE, Box F3752:749, Folder: Max Rafferty, General Correspondence, April–July 1970.

86. TOYL, iv.

87. Ibid.

88. Ibid, emphasis added.

89. Educational Programs Committee of the California State Board of Education, "'Sex Education' Programs in Public Schools," Second Progress Report of the California State Department of Education, March 13, 1969, 8.

90. "'Sex Education' Programs in Public Schools," 7.

91. Forum, "Sex Education in the Public Schools," 4.

92. Minutes, Educational Programs Committee of the California State Board of Education, February 12, 1969, 6.

93. Ibid., 6–7. The six points were: 1) avoid invasion of privacy of home; 2) avoid discussion of sex techniques and abnormal sex acts; 3) examine thoroughly any discussion of methods of contraception, because this invades religious training of students and parents; 4) examine Judeo-Christian ethics regarding premarital intercourse, adultery, and masturbation; 5) emphasize importance of the family unit; and 6) educate parents along with students.

94. Georgetta R. Rust, "A Study of Factors Impeding Proposed Family Life and Sex Education Program Adoption in Sacramento County, California" (Master's thesis, Sacramento State College, 1969), 56.

95. Minutes, Educational Programs Committee of the California State Board of Education, March, 1969; " 'Sex Education' Programs in Public Schools."

96. Minutes, 3,7.

97. Ibid., 4.

98. Ibid., 7.

99. Ibid., 4.

100. "World History Homework Sheet," addendum to Mrs. Edward Bittancourt to Dr. Max Rafferty, November 17, 1969, CSA-DOE, Box F3752:747, Folder: Max Rafferty, General Correspondence, July 1969–November 1969.

101. Ibid.

102. Report of Hearings on Sex Education, State Board of Education, Sacramento, April 10, 1969, 104.

103. Ibid., 105.

104. Ibid.

105. Diane S. Calmis of Santa Clara, California, to Max Rafferty, September 24, 1969, CSA-DOE, Box F3752:751, Folder: Henry J. Heydt Jr., July–September 1969.

106. Anonymous letter to Rafferty from Cypress, California, July 1968, CSA-DOE, Box F3752:744, Folder: Max Rafferty, General Correspondence, July 1968–1969.

107. Ibid.

108. Ibid.

109. Ibid.

110. Anonymous Santa Ana mother, Report of Hearings on Sex Education, State Board of Education, Sacramento, April 10, 1969.

111. J. Russell Kent, ibid., 56; " 'Sex Education' Programs in Public Schools," 3.

112. " 'Sex Education' Programs in the Public Schools, 3.

113. Ibid.

114. Excerpt from Sex Education U.S.A. film, 25.

115. Cf. Irvine, Talk About Sex.

116. Larry J. Connor, Capitola, California, to Max Rafferty, October 26, 1970, CSA-DOE, Box F3752:748, Folder: Max Rafferty, General Correspondence, August–December 1970.

117. Ibid.

118. Ibid.

119. Dr. Howard Busching, Report of Hearings on Sex Education, State Board of Education, Sacramento, April 10, 1969, 84.

120. Ibid.

121. Ibid., 87.

122. Ibid., 86.

123. Ibid., 87.

124. Ibid.

125. Mrs. Frances Crooke and Mrs. Irma McCrahe to Max Rafferty, October 2, 1970, CSA-DOE, Box F3752:748, Folder: Max Rafferty, General Correspondence, August–December 1970.

126. Ibid.

127. Larry "Bing" Crosby to Max Rafferty, July 6, 1970, CSA-DOE, Box F3752:749, Folder: Max Rafferty, General Correspondence, April–July 1970.

128. Ibid.; Max Rafferty to Larry "Bing" Crosby, July 15, 1970, CSA-DOE, Box F3752:749, Folder: Max Rafferty, General Correspondence, April–July 1970.

129. Report of Hearings on Sex Education, State Board of Education, Sacramento, April 10, 1969, 9.

130. Ibid.

131. Mr. and Mrs. Duane Blum to Max Rafferty, May 5, 1970; Max Rafferty to Mr. and Mrs. Duane Blum, May 11, 1970, both CSA-DOE, Box F3752:746, Folder: Max Rafferty, General Correspondence, December 1969–March 1970.

132. William J. Cardinal to Max Rafferty, October 13, 1969, CSA-DOE, Box F3752: 751, Folder: Max Rafferty, General Correspondence, July–September, 1969.

133. Alcyone Bass to Max Rafferty, May 4, 1970, CSA-DOE, Box F3752:746, Folder: Max Rafferty, General Correspondence, April 1970–June 1970.

134. Mary F. Brill to Max Rafferty, April 25, 1970, CSA-DOE, Box F3752:746, Folder: Max Rafferty, General Correspondence, April 1970–June 1970.

135. Mr. and Mrs. R. W. Bird to Max Rafferty, April 27, 1970, CSA-DOE, Box F3752:746, Folder: Max Rafferty, General Correspondence, April 1970–June 1970.

136. *Report of Hearings on Sex Education*, State Board of Education, closing comments by Dr. Ford, April 10, 1969, 112.

137. Ibid.

138. Minutes, Educational Programs Committee of the California State Board of Education, February 12, 1969.

139. Ronald Conway of Atherton, California, to Max Rafferty, July 15, 1970, CSA-DOE, Box F3752:749, Folder: Max Rafferty, General Correspondence, April–July 1970.

140. See Georgetta R. Rust, "A Study of Factors Impeding Proposed Family Life" Rust performed a unique study asking adults and teenagers to rank the reasons they believed sex education had failed to be implemented in the Sacramento City Unified District, and responses of "communism" were barely statistically significant. Teenage respondents overwhelmingly commented on their parents' tenacious belief that "sex is something dirty" to be hidden from children, and only mentioned communism dismissively: "Someone [has been] saying a Communist plot or whatever. Every time someone smells a rat it has to be only one thing, Communist . . . what else?" When asked why parents rejected family life and sex education programs, only three adult respondents credited a belief that the programs were "communist-inspired." By contrast, nineteen respondents answered "due to lack of understanding," fifteen the very similar "for failure to understand the scope of the program," fourteen credited an "infringement on rights of parents by the school's assumption of too much responsibility," and ten pointed simply to "fear." Interestingly, talk of conspiracy in Sacramento's sex education controversy was hardly absent, but it was among sex education *advocates* who doubted that the bulk of opposition stemmed from local parents. Rather, they blamed "a most vociferous minority group with the John Birch philosophy," and the Mormons, "a certain religious organization in Utah." Though the researcher did find in preparing her questionnaire for mailing that "some of the people opposing the program were non-residents of the school district, listed false addresses, or gave names which could not be traced in the Sacramento area," it is clear that conspiracy theories were not uniquely the province of paranoid Orange County conservatives. Rather, the shrill anticommunism that shaped the debate in Anaheim appears to have been a regionally specific idiom for expressing concerns shared statewide.

141. Forum, "Sex Education in the Public Schools," July 25, 1968, 7.

142. *Report of Hearings on Sex Education*, State Board of Education, April 10, 1969, 65.

143. Ibid.

144. Mothers Organized for Responsible Education, Report of Hearings on Sex Education, State Board of Education, Sacramento, April 10, 1969, 92.

145. Ibid., 62.

146. Ibid., 62.

147. Ibid., 64.

148. D'Emilio and Freedman, *Intimate Matters*, passim.

149. Lassiter, "Inventing Family Values: The Crisis of the American Dream in the 1970s."

150. Citizens for Parental Rights v. San Mateo County Board of Education, U.S., 1976, No. 75-1024, 425 U.S. 1000, 96 S.Ct 2217, 48 L.Ed.2d 825, May 24, 1976, Petition for Rehearing Denied.

151. Steven V. Roberts, "Teaching of Sex Fought on Coast: Conservatives' Effort Fails as Board Votes Program," *New York Times*, April 13, 1969, 48.

152. Rafferty, *Classroom Countdown: Education at the Crossroads* (New York: Hawthorn Books, 1970), xiii.

153. Mrs. Margaret Christiansen to Dr. Max Rafferty, December 1, 1970, CSA-DOE, Box F3752:748, Folder: Max Rafferty, General Correspondence, August–December, 1970.

CHAPTER 6

1. Kenneth G. Gehret, "Anaheim Citizens Divided Over Sex Education," *The Christian Science Monitor*, May 7, 1970.

2. Educational Programs Committee of the California State Board of Education, discussion of "'Sex Education' Programs in Public Schools," Second Progress Report of the California State Department of Education, March 13, 1969, 6, CSA-DOE, Box F3752:9, Folder 1968–1969.

3. Ibid.

4. *Report of Hearings on Sex Education*, State Board of Education, April 10, 1969, 102, CSA-DOE, Box F3752:9, Folder 1968–1969.

5. Ibid.

6. Ibid.

7. Ibid.

8. Ibid., 104.

9. Ibid.

10. Ibid.

11. Esther D. Schulz and Sally D. Williams, *Family Life and Sex Education: Curriculum and Instruction* (New York: Harcourt, Brace, and World, Inc., 1968), 42.

12. Several historians have examined the Anaheim battle of 1968–1969 to consider why sex education, which had often enforced sexual restraint rather than liberation, raised the ire of conservatives in many communities in the late 1960s and allowed them to portray liberal educators as morally dissolute. The Anaheim controversy serves both as an example of a more open discourse on sexuality and of the emerging conservative Right's targeting sex education as symbolic of this disturbing pattern. Lisa McGirr's influential Orange County study suggests Anaheim's regional significance, but her contention that by the late 1960s religious evangelicalism supplanted anticommunism as conservatism's animating force cannot explain the persistent anticommunism and only vague appeals to "godliness" in the 1968 sex education fracas. The absence of analysis through the lens of state politics or educational policy has failed to fully consider the historical context of the Anaheim example. See Jeffrey Moran, *Teaching Sex: The Shaping of Adolescence in the Twentieth Century* (Cambridge, MA: Harvard University Press, 2000); Janice M. Irvine, *Talk About Sex: The Battles Over Sex Education in the United States* (Berkeley: University of California Press, 2002); Lisa McGirr, *Suburban Warriors: The Origins of*

*the New American Right* (Princeton, NJ: Princeton University Press, 2001); William Martin, *With God on Our Side: The Rise of the Religious Right in America* (New York: Broadway Books, 1996); James Hottois, and Neal A. Milner, *The Sex Education Controversy: a Study of Politics, Education, and Morality* (Lexington, MA: Lexington Books, 1975.

13. Clayton Howard, *The Closet and the Cul de Sac: Sex, Politics, and Suburbanization in Postwar California* (Philadelphia: University of Pennsylvania Press, forthcoming).

14. "School Sex Education Under Attack," *Los Angeles Times*, January 6, 1969.

15. Alice Lupiano [pseud.] to Superintendent Paul Cook, phone message, December 9, 1968, Anaheim Union High School District Board of Trustees papers (AUHSD-BOT), uncatalogued correspondence file. Except public figures, all names are pseudonyms; this secretary signed "A.L."

16. Association for Decency in California to Paul Cook, 1969, AUHSD-BOT, uncatalogued correspondence file.

17. Ibid.

18. For a journalistic overview of the Anaheim case, see Mary Breasted, *Oh! Sex Education!* (New York: Praeger Books, 1970).

19. "Watered down" is how the curriculum's fate was widely described. See "Mrs. Pippenger Takes a Stand on a Major Issue," *Los Alamitos Crusader*, February 13, 1970; Paul Cook, interview by Michael Jackson, KABC, January 17, 1970, AUHSD-BOT, uncatalogued correspondence file.

20. *FLSE Course Outline*, Fifth Revision, June 1968, Anaheim Public Library, Local History Room (APL-LHR), Box: FLSE.

21. Schulz and Williams, *Family Life and Sex Education: Curriculum and Instruction.* Foreword by Mary Calderone.

22. Northrop Nortronics, North American Aviation, and Kwikset Locks followed General Electric in relocating to Anaheim.

23. Booth, interview with author, 2004.

24. John Findlay, *Magic Lands: Western Cityscapes and American Culture after 1940* (Berkeley: University of California Press, 1992), 92; *Anaheim Bulletin*, "Survey Shows Big Business Gain in Anaheim Since Disneyland Opening," August 17, 1955. John Westcott, a local historian, described the union between Disney and Anaheim as "a happy marriage." *Anaheim: City of Dreams: An Illustrated History* (Chatsworth, CA: Windsor Publications, 1990), 72.

25. "GOP Women to meet at Knott's Berry Farm Tuesday," *Anaheim Gazette*, February 23, 1961; American Free Enterprise Association, headquartered at Knott's Berry Farm, "The American Way" pamphlet, n.d., Knott's Berry Farm file, APL-AHC.

26. "Queen of Halloween to be Chosen," *Anaheim Gazette*, September 15, 1955.

27. Westcott, *City of Dreams*, 52.

28. "City's Halloween Festival Opens Saturday: Event Opens with Kickoff Breakfast in Downtown Area," *Anaheim Gazette*, October 29, 1961.

29. Waldo Hunter, "Oblong Views From an Egg-Shaped Head," *Anaheim Gazette*, July 7, 1955.

30. "Kwikset Announces Public School Week," *Anaheim Gazette*, April 21, 1955.

31. Advertisement, "Kwikset Salutes the Community," *Anaheim Gazette*, May 5, 1955. Among whites, between 1950 and 1970, the number of American women joining the civilian labor market jumped by more than 10 percent, whereas the percentage of white men dropped by 8 percent. In the same twenty-year span, the number of white women "keeping house" dropped from 61 percent of all women to less than half (47 percent). US Department of Commerce and Bureau of the Census, *Statistical Abstract of the United States: 1970, 91st Annual Edition*, Table No. 316, "Employment Status of the Non-institutional Population, by Sex and Race: 1950–1970," Department of Labor, Monthly Labor Report, US Census, 213. Accessed via http://www2.census.gov/prod2/stat-comp/documents/1970-01.pdf.

32. "Anaheim to Pay Homage to Industry; 'Industrial Queen' to Be Selected," *Anaheim Gazette*, March 24, 1955.

33. "AH Boys State Opinions on Short Skirts, Hairdos," *ANORANCO*, February 17, 1961.

34. "Anaheim's Dress Board Presents Year's Rules," *ANORANCO*, September 21, 1962.

35. Louise Booth, *One to Twenty-Eight: A History of the Anaheim Union High School District* (Anaheim: Anaheim Union High School District, 1980), 106–112, 197.

36. Ibid., 153; "Polite Connies Honor Boys at Sadie Hawkins," *ANORANCO*, May 3, 1963.

37. "Second Beatnik Ball Scheduled," *ANORANCO*, March 9, 1960.

38. "Want After Game Dances?," *ANORANCO*, November 4, 1960; "Are you an Interdigitator?," *ANORANCO*, December 2, 1960; "Munching in Class Regarded as Downfall of AH Grades," *ANORANCO*, January 3, 1961.

39. "Retraction," *ANORANCO*, January 3, 1961.

40. "Anti-Red Program Planned by School," *Anaheim Gazette*, March 23, 1961.

41. McGirr, *Suburban Warriors*, 54.

42. "Attitudes Toward Communism Outlined to Committee of 150," *Anaheim Gazette*, February 9, 1961; "Youth Target of Reds, Claim," *Anaheim Bulletin*, February 28, 1961; "Anti-Red Rally Slated," *Anaheim Gazette*, August 24, 1961. Disneyland itself continued to nurture considerable links with the AUHSD, hosting school drama and choral performances. Tellingly, the student body of one school voted to change its name to "Walt Disney," and Disney continued to hire teachers and coaches as security staff rather than police officers, continuing to blur the boundaries between park and community.

43. McGirr, *Suburban Warriors*, 44.

44. Jessica Wendell [pseud.], email interview with author, January 14, 2004.

45. Susan Penton [pseud.], blog entry on OCThen: Memories of Orange County California (www.octhen.com), December 8, 2007. Accessed via http://www. octhen.com/labels/Racism.htm on September 5, 2008.

46. In *Cold War Civil Rights*, Mary Dudziak argued that *Brown* must be considered within the context of Cold War propaganda, which exported an image of progressive race relations to counter Soviet claims of the persistence of American racial castes.

47. "Local Women Mark World Community Day at Church," *Anaheim Gazette*, November 19, 1955; "Keynote Talk Will be Given by Dr. Imhoff," *Anaheim Gazette*, March 2, 1961.

48. Unsigned editorial, *Anaheim Gazette*, February 16, 1956.

49. "This Day of Labels," *Anaheim Gazette*, April 27, 1961.

50. David Wells [pseud.], email interview with author, January 2004. Wells also wrote a short story about this years later.

51. Lowell B. Jones, director of curriculum, to Paul W. Cook, superintendent, Memorandum Re: Sex Education—A Brief Survey of What Is Being Taught in Orange County High Schools, December 28, 1962, APL-LHR, Box: FLSE. In 1962, no surrounding communities had comprehensive programs. Moreover, it is important to note that Superintendent Cook had introduced other progressive curricular reforms to the AUHSD: multimedia foreign language instruction and a creative writing program met little opposition, though did elsewhere.

52. Public memorandum by Superintendent Paul W. Cook, "Family Life and Sex Education Program in the Anaheim Union High School District," n.d., APL-LHR, Box: FLSE.

53. He emphasized the breadth of this endorsement in a later memorandum: "THIS OVERWHELMING SUPPORT HAS BEEN THE FOUNDATION OF THE SUCCESS OF OUR [FLSE] PROGRAM" (emphasis in original). Survey, "Public Opinion Study Concerning Sex Education in Junior and Senior High Schools of Anaheim Union High School District," November, 1963, APL-LHR, Box: FLSE, Folder: Mrs. Harold J. McAferty.

54. Kenneth G. Gehret, "Anaheim Citizens are Divided Over Sex Education," *The Christian Science Monitor*, March 7, 1970; Jack McCurdy, "Birch Society Leads Opposition to Sex Education, Board Told: Heavy Mail Protesting Study Projects in State Schools Called Concentrated Effort of Right-Wing Organizations," *Los Angeles Times*, March 15, 1969.

55. David Shaw, "County School Friction Laid to Political Stress," *Los Angeles Times*, March 16, 1969; Elaine Lewinnek, "Social Studies Controversies in 1960s California: The Fight for Public Memory and the Rise of the New Right," *Pacific Historical Review*, forthcoming 2015.

56. Jack McCurdy, "Sex Education Inquiry Enters Its Final Phase," *Los Angeles Times*, April 6, 1969.

57. Martin, *With God on Our Side*, 112–115.

58. Course evaluations, Senior Problems class, 1965, APL-LHR, Box: FLSE.

59. Ibid.

60. Calter, email interview, January 2004.

61. Breasted, *Oh! Sex Education!*, 25.

62. "Silly Season in Sex Education Fight," *Los Angeles Times*, January 30, 1969.

63. Westcott, *City of Dreams*, 77.

64. AUHSD and City of Anaheim, "Amendment to Lease of Facilities," May 28, 1964, AUHSD-BOT.

65. Westcott, *City of Dreams*, 78.

66. Ibid.; John Steinbacher, "The Child Seducers Revisited," *American Mercury* (Fall 1970): 5–8.

67. Anaheim Police Officers Association, *A History of the Anaheim Police Department* (Dallas: Taylor Publishing Company, 1992).

68. Booth, *One to Twenty-Eight*, 122, 220.

69. Ibid., 106.

70. Ibid., 222.

71. Ibid.

72. "School Board Recognizes ASTA as 'Official' Group," *Anaheim Bulletin*, September 25, 1965; Booth, 276.

73. "High School Supt. Cook Reported Leaving Post," *Anaheim Bulletin*, September 23, 1969.

74. Anonymous, email to Classmates.com Los Alamitos High School Alumni message board, 2003, www.classmates.com. Los Alamitos, where flexible scheduling remained in place until 1977, also supported FLSE strongly.

75. Louise Booth, *Fulfilling A Dream: The History of Chapman University* (Villa Park, CA: Donald R. Booth and Associates, 2001), 189; Booth, interview with author, 2004; "Girls Join All-Male 4-H Club," *Anaheim Bulletin*, October 8, 1962.

76. Mark Wigginton, "Do You Want Johnny to Do Dirty Things? Heaven Forbid!" *Los Alamitos Crusader*, November 7, 1969.

77. Priscilla Feld [pseud.], email interview with author, January 2004.

78. Booth, *One to Twenty-Eight*, 221.

79. See, all from the *Anaheim Bulletin*: "Glue Sale Jails Fullerton Youth," September 25, 1962; "Multiple Charges Jail Two Youths," September 25, 1962; "BP Girl Charged with Lewd Life," October 5, 1962; "VD Epidemic Amongst Us," September 24, 1965; "Birth Control Issue Lurks Behind Scenes at Council," September 25, 1965.

80. "Hoover Hits Rising Teenage Crime," *Anaheim Bulletin*, September 2, 1965; "It's Up to the Parents," *Anaheim Bulletin*, September 8, 1965.

81. "Anaheim Drive-In Rowdyism Studied," *Anaheim Bulletin*, September 24, 1965.

82. "Fischetti" cartoon, *Anaheim Bulletin*, September 8, 1965.

83. Mary Bryson, "Points for Parents," *Anaheim Bulletin*, January 3, 1969.

84. Feld, email interview with author, 2004.

85. Melissa Finch [pseud.], email interview with author, February 2004.

86. "Jump in Unmarried Pregnant Girls in OC," *Anaheim Bulletin*, October 25, 1968; Mrs. Raymond L. Burns, letter to the editor, *Anaheim Bulletin*, November 11, 1969; "First OC Home for Unmarried Moms Delayed," *Anaheim Bulletin*, January 3, 1969. Stephanie J. Ventura, T. J. Matthews, and Brady Hamilton, "Births to Teenagers in the United States, 1940–2000," *National Vital Statistics Report* 49, no. 10 (2001).

87. Martin, *With God on Our Side*, 106.

88. "Kuchel Family Receives Honors," *Anaheim Gazette*, April 20, 1961.

89. "Committee Urges Kuchel to be Demo," *Anaheim Bulletin*, September 3, 1965.

90. Capitol News Service, "Newsman Tells How: Officials Rigged Senator Kuchel 'Whitewashing'," news release, September 1965, APL-LHR, Thomas Kuchel biographical file. Interestingly, I can find no other mention of this alleged incident involving Kuchel.

91. The State Department in 1950 authorized a formal inquiry into "homosexuals and other moral perverts in government." These investigations, one of which allegedly apprehended Senator Kuchel, operated on the premise that homosexuals, already "morally enfeebled by sexual indulgence . . . would readily succumb to the blandishments of the spy" and betray the United States. See John D'Emilio and Estelle B. Freedman, *Intimate Matters: A History of Sexuality in America* (New York: Harper and Row, 1988), 292–293; David K. Johnson, *The Lavender Scare: The Cold War Persecution of Gays and Lesbians in the Federal Government* (Chicago: University of Chicago Press, 2004).

92. Estelle B. Freedman, "Uncontrolled Desires: The Response to the Sexual Psychopath, 1920–1960," in *Feminism, Sexuality, and Politics* (Chapel Hill: University of North Carolina Press, 2006), 128.

93. By 1968, most workers on the Convention Center payroll were not from Anaheim, nor were nearly half of attendees to Stadium events. *Anaheim Stadium and Convention Center, One-Year Update*, Table 1, "Geographic Origin of Baseball Fans as Indicated by Mail Order and Season Ticket Purchases and Requests, 1968 Season, Table 11, "Convention Center Payroll," APL-LHR, Anaheim Stadium and Convention Center file.

94. See Terry H. Anderson, *The Movement and the Sixties: Protest in America from Greensboro to Wounded Knee* (New York: Oxford University Press, 1995); George Lipsitz, "Youth Culture and Social Crises," in David Farber, ed., *The Sixties: From Memory to History* (Chapel Hill: University of North Carolina Press, 1994); Todd Gitlin, *The Sixties: Years of Hope, Days of Rage.* (New York: Bantam Books, 1987).

95. McGirr, *Suburban Warriors*, 88; Findlay, *Magic Lands*, 64.

96. Advertisement, Union Oil Company of California, *Anaheim Gazette*, repeated through 1955.

97. McGirr, *Suburban Warriors*; Bart Barnes, "Barry Goldwater, GOP Hero, Dies at 89, " *Washington Post*, May 30, 1998.

98. David Allyn, *Make Love, Not War, The Sexual Revolution: An Unfettered History*, (New York: Little, Brown and Company, 2000), 48.

99. D'Emilio and Freedman, *Intimate Matters*, 279, 287; Booth, discussion; Booth, *One to Twenty-Eight*; Booth interview with author, 2003.

100. D'Emilio and Freedman, *Intimate Matters*, 303–305.

101. James Patterson, *Grand Expectations: The United States, 1945–1974* (New York: Oxford University Press, 1996), 443. See US Bureau of the Census, Urban Atlas, Tract Data for Standard Metropolitan Statistical Areas: Anaheim - Santa Ana - Garden Grove, CA (Washington, DC: Government Print Office, 1974).

102. Wendell, email interview, January 2004.

103. Feld, email interview, January 2004.

104. Wells, email interview, January 2004.

105. See email interviews, Wendell and Finch.

106. Breasted, *Oh! Sex Education!*, 24.

107. Ibid.

108. See, for example, Americans for Civil Harmony, "Violence or Reason?" pamphlet, San Jose, September 3, 1966, SUSC-Margaret Meier Collection of Extreme Right Ephemeral Materials, 1930–1980, Box 5, Folder 11.

109. Anonymous letter to Max Rafferty, February 25, 1969, CSA-DOE, Box F3752:744, Folder: Rafferty, General Correspondence, July 1968–1969.

110. Breasted, *Oh! Sex Education!*, 69.

111. Ibid., 68.

112. Ibid., 66.

113. Irvine, *Talk About Sex*, 54.

114. Martin, *With God on Our Side*, 111.

115. John Steinbacher, *The Child Seducers* (Fullerton, CA: Educator Publishers, 1970).

116. Breasted, *Oh! Sex Education!*, 136.

117. Ibid., 137.

118. Sally Williams, quoted in Martin, *With God on Our Side*, 110.

119. Jim Townsend, untitled editorial, *Long Beach/Dixon Town-Line Reason*, January 24, 1969, CU-RBML, GRC, Box 297, Folder: Sex Education.

120. Gordon Drake, "Is the Schoolhouse the Proper Place to Teach Raw Sex?" (Tulsa: Christian Crusade, 1968). This influential pamphlet was in its fourth printing by 1974.

121. Opponents of curricular reform often linked controversial curricula to outside intruders, frequently pointing to the federal government or other externally funded entities as threats to community and parental control of local schools.

Whereas programs such as the inflammatory "Man: A Course of Study" curriculum did indeed benefit from federal funding, the traction such criticism of
FLSE gained is notable, since the program was entirely homegrown.

122. Mary S. Calderone, "Sex Education and the Roles of School and Church," *Annals
     of the American Academy of Political and Social Science* (March 1968): 53–60.

123. Ibid., 60; Breasted, *Oh! Sex Education!*, 227.

124. Breasted, 206.

125. Esther D. Schulz and Sally R. Williams, *Family Life and Sex Education: Curriculum
     and Instruction* (New York: Harcourt, Brace and World, 1968), vi.

126. Max Rafferty, "Who Needs More Sex Education?," *Anaheim Bulletin*, December 28,
     1964.

127. Breasted, *Oh! Sex Education!*, 114–115.

128. "State Board Warns on Use, Ruling Deals Staggering Blow to New York
     Publishing Houses," *Anaheim Bulletin*, April 11, 1969. Indeed, the headline of
     the *Bulletin's* article on the SIECUS ban in California speaks to the organiza-
     tion's symbolism for the "Eastern money power."

129. Mary Calderone to James Morrow, March 26, 1970, Schlesinger Library, Mary
     Steichen Calderone Papers, 1904–1971 (SL-MSC), Box 14, Folder 230.

130. Transcript, Board of Trustees AUHSD Workshop Meeting, AUHSD-BOT,
     October 17, 1968, 23–25.

131. Ibid., 20.

132. Rafferty to Mr. Ronald Conway, July 20, 1970, CSA-DOE, Box F3752:749,
     Folder: Max Rafferty, General Correspondence, April–July, 1970.

133. Natalia Mehlman Petrzela, "Revisiting the Rightward Turn: Max Rafferty,
     Education, and Modern American Politics," *The Sixties: A Journal of History,
     Politics, and Culture*, May 2014.

134. Breasted, *Oh! Sex Education!*, 34.

135. Jack Boettner, "Revised Sex Class Program Delayed by Anaheim Schools," *Los
     Angeles Times*, October 24, 1969.

136. Jack Boettner, "Anaheim Schools Revise Sex Studies," *Los Angeles Times*,
     September 26, 1969.

137. Jack Boettner, "Sex Education Leader's Fear of Firing Proves Groundless,"
     *Los Angeles Times*, September 25, 1969; Joseph N. Bell, "Speaking Out on Sex
     Education," *Los Angeles Times*, November 20, 1987.

138. "Sex Class Foes Take Fight to Washington," *Anaheim Bulletin*, September 16,
     1969; Steve Emmons, "Foes of Sex Education Aim at Social Studies," *Los Angeles
     Times*, April 11, 1970.

139. Transcript, workshop meeting, 8, APL-LHR, Box FLSE; Martin, *With God on
     Our Side*, 104.

140. Richard Parlour, quoted in Larry Schulz, "Call zit What You Want—It Leads to
     'Trouble,'" *Arcadia News Post*, November 19, 1969.

141. "Cook Deplores FLI Conflict," *Anaheim Bulletin*, December 4, 1969.

142. Family Life and Sex Education Course Outline, Grades Seven through Twelve, Fifth Revision, June 1968, ii, APL-LHR, Box FLSE.

143. "Consultant Defends Sex Classes, Hits Right-Wingers," *Santa Ana Register*, March 13, 1969.

144. FLSE Course Outline, 240.

145. Ibid., 240.

146. Ibid., 215.

147. Course evaluations, Senior Problems class, 1965, APL-LHR, Box: FLSE.

148. Ibid.

149. Feld, email interview.

150. Transcript, workshop meeting, 1.

151. Michel Foucault, *The History of Sexuality, Part One: An Introduction* (New York: Random House, 1978), 8.

152. Breasted, *Oh! Sex Education!*, 74.

153. Lynette Mayer, letter to the editor, *Anaheim Bulletin*, December 6, 1969; Anonymous, letter to the editor, *Anaheim Bulletin*, September 6, 1969.

154. Transcript, workshop meeting, 22.

155. "Trustees Under Fire From Citizen Group," *Anaheim Bulletin*, October 18, 1968.

156. "Silent Majority Should Stand Up And Be Counted Before It's Too Late," *Los Alamitos Crusader*, November 7, 1969; "Mrs. Pippenger Takes a Stand on Major Issue," *Los Alamitos Crusader*, February 13, 1970; "Premarital Sex Discussed Openly," *Los Alamitos Crusader*, April 10, 1970.

157. "Mrs. Pippenger Takes a Stand on Major Issue," *Los Alamitos Crusader*, February 13, 1970.

158. "Sex Education Foe Confronts Students," *Los Angeles Times*, May 12, 1970.

CHAPTER 7

1. Minutes, State Board of Education, July 11, 1968, CSA-DOE, Box F3752:437, Folder: Moral Guidelines Committee, 1968–1969.

2. Ibid.

3. Jack McCurdy, "Morality Code for Schools Goes to State Board," *Los Angeles Times*, January 5, 1970.

4. Minutes, State Board of Education, July 11, 1968.

5. Open letter from Governor Ronald Reagan to Moral Guidelines Committee members, April 25, 1969, CSA-DOE, Box F3752:437, Folder: Moral Guidelines Committee, 1968–1969.

6. Homitz, Allen, and Associates, "Prospectus: Project to Develop Approaches, Methods, and Materials for Implementation of Guidelines for Moral and Civic Education and Teaching About Religion," submitted to Mr. Henry Heydt, Special Assistant to the California State Board of Education, 1, n.d., CSA-DOE, Box F3752:445, Folder, Moral Guidelines Committee, 1970–1974; Klotz to Board,

Memorandum on survey to schools and teacher training institutions, September 4, 1968, CSA-DOE, Box F3752:439, Folder: Moral Guidelines Committee, 1968–1970.

7. Todd, Report of Hearings on Sex Education, State Board of Education, Sacramento, April 10, 1969, 94, CSA-DOE, Box F3752:9, Folder: Henry Heydt Jr., 1968–1969.

8. "The Men Who Gave the Board Its Moral Guidelines," *San Francisco Chronicle*, May 10, 1969, 6.

9. Bill Boyarsky, "Three in Bitter Fights for State Schools Post," *Los Angeles Times*, May 27, 1970.

10. Reverend Pierre E. Lachance, Fall River, Massachusetts, to Henry J. Heydt Jr., November 28, 1972, CSA-DOE, Box F3752:445, Folder: Moral Guidelines Committee, 1970–1974.

11. "Guidelines For Moral Instruction in California Schools," iii, May 9, 1969, CSA-DOE Box F3752:438, Folder: Moral Guidelines Committee, 1969–1970.

12. J. Russell Kent, Report of Hearings on Sex Education, State Board of Education, Sacramento, April 10, 1969, 55.

13. Gordon V. Drake, *Blackboard Power: NEA Threat to America* (Tulsa: Christian Crusade Publications, 1968); Interview with Klotz, December 17, 1968, 1, CSA-DOE, Box F3752:440, Folder: Moral Guidelines Committee, 1968.

14. Barry Hankins, *American Evangelicals: A Contemporary History of a Mainstream Religious Movement* (New York: Rowman and Littlefield Publishers, 2009), 141.

15. Mrs. Dorothy Spivey to Max Rafferty, July 19, 1968, CSA-DOE, Box F3752:439, Folder: Moral Guidelines Committee, 1968–1970.

16. Robert F. Williams to Howard Day, board president, April 29, 1969, CSA-DOE, Box F3752:439, Moral Guidelines Committee, 1968–1969.

17. California Education Code, Section 13556.5, amended by Stats. 1963, Ch. 251, and by Stats. 1965, Ch. 1970. Added by Stats. 1968, Ch. 182.

18. Allen Homitz and Associates, "Prospectus: Project to Develop Approaches, Methods and Materials for Implementation of Guidelines for Moral and Civic Education and Teaching about Religion," submitted to Mr. Henry Heydt, Special Assistant to the California State Board of Education, 1, n.d., CSA-DOE, Box F3752:445, Folder: Moral Guidelines Committee, 1970–1974.

19. Schmitz's political views were considered so far to the right that he allegedly said that he joined the John Birch Society to appease the left wing of his base.

20. California State Senate Bill 413, CSA-DOE, Box F3752:9, Folder: Henry Heydt Jr., 1968–1969.

21. Of course, conservatives have a long history of invoking state power selectively. For a long historical view, see Leigh Ann Wheeler, *Against Obscenity: Reform and the Politics of Womanhood in America, 1973–1935* (Baltimore: Johns Hopkins University Press, 2004).

22. Minutes, May 9, 1969, meeting, CSA-DOE, Box F3752:439, Folder: Moral Guidelines Committee, 1968–1969.

23. Ron Moskowitz, "A State Plan for Morality Lessons," *San Francisco Chronicle*, May 9, 1969, 1.

24. Jack McCurdy, "Morality Code for Schools Goes to State Board," *Los Angeles Times*, January 5, 1970, A1.

25. Interview with Klotz, December 17, 1968, 2.

26. "The Men Who Gave the Board Its Morality Guidelines," *San Francisco Chronicle*, 6.

27. John T. Kehoe, an oral history conducted 1981 by Sarah Sharp, in "Legislative Issue Management and Advocacy, 1961–1974," Regional Oral History Office, The Bancroft Library, University of California, Berkeley, 1983, 24, CSA-DOE, Box F3752:449, Folder: Moral Guidelines Committee, 1974.

28. Ron Moskowitz, "A State Plan for Morality Lessons," *San Francisco Chronicle*, May 9, 1969, 1.

29. Mrs. Doris Caldwell to Rafferty, April 21, 1970, CSA-DOE, Box F3752:749, Folder: General Correspondence, April–July 1970.

30. Interview with Klotz, December 17, 1968, 1.

31. Assorted responses to August 9, 1968, letter from Klotz, CSA-DOE, Box F3752:440, Folder: Moral Guidelines Committee, 1968.

32. Ibid.

33. Memorandum on survey to schools and teacher training institutions, to Board from Klotz, September 4, 1968, CSA-DOE, Box F3752:439, Folder: Moral Guidelines Committee, 1968–1970.

34. Tom Yonker, "The Teaching of Morality in the Public Schools," Modesto Teachers' Association, n.d., 3, CSA-DOE, Box F3752:445, Folder: Moral Guidelines Committee, 1970–1974.

35. Ibid., 7–8.

36. "Philosophy of Education," Sierra-Plumas Joint Unified School District, Adopted March 4, 1959, revised October 18, 1967, CSA-DOE, Box F3752:440, Folder: Moral Guidelines Committee, 1968.

37. Douglas C. Campbell, Director Secondary Curriculum, Santa Rosa City Schools, to Dr. Edwin F. Klotz, October 16, 1968, CSA-DOE, Box F3752:440, Folder: Moral Guidelines Committee, 1968.

38. "Citizenship and Discipline: Kindergarten," Dr. A. Bruce Hawk, Superintendent of Schools, Fresno, CA, n.d.; "Citizenship Education Guidelines," Orinda Union School District, n.d., CSA-DOE, Box F3752:440, Folder: Moral Guidelines Committee, 1968.

39. "Scan Profile: Joseph Forcinelli, A Passion for Human Values in H.S. Education," *Progress Bulletin*, Pomona, California, January 8, 1972, CSA-DOE, Box F3752:445, Folder: Moral Guidelines Committee, 1970–1974.

40. Testimony, Mrs. R. M. Evans, La Mesa Republican Women's Club, Federated, January 8, 1970, 2.

41. Transcript, November 15, 1969, public hearing, CSA-DOE, Box F3752:437, Folder: Moral Guidelines Committee, 1968–1969.

42. Minutes, April 25, 1969, meeting, CSA-DOE, Box F3752:437, Folder: Moral Guidelines Committee, 1968–1969.

43. Minutes, May 9, 1969, meeting CSA-DOE, Box F3752:437, Folder: Moral Guidelines Committee, 1968–1969.

44. Minutes of California State Board of Education, May 1969, Volume 2, CSA-DOE, Box F3844:189, Folder: Minutes, May meetings.

45. Letter exchange among Kathleen Bresnahan, Henry Heydt, and Patricia Hill (Health Consultant), CSA-DOE, Box F3752:445, Folder: Moral Guidelines Committee, Correspondence, 1970–1974.

46. Ibid.

47. Ibid.

48. Minutes, Educational Programs Committee of the California State Board of Education, February 12, 1969, CSA-DOE, Box F3752:9, Folder: Henry J. Heydt Jr., 1968–1969.

49. John T. Kehoe interview, 27. Legislative Issue Management and Advocacy, 1961–1974: oral history transcript and related material, 1981–1983, Bancroft Library, Regional Oral History Office.

50. Ron Moskowitz, "Teaching Morality—Navy Style," *San Francisco Chronicle*, May 9, 1969, 1.

51. Jack McCurdy, "State Board Hears Proposal for Moral Teaching in Schools," *Los Angeles Times*, May 10, 1969.

52. "Guidelines for the Education of Responsible Citizens in the Public Schools of California: A Report Presented to the California State Board of Education," December 11, 1969, CSA-DOE, Box F3752:437, Folder: Moral Guidelines Committee, 1968–1969.

53. John Dart, "Reagans Regulars at Church but Can't Join," *Los Angeles Times*, February 6, 1971.

54. Moomaw had been appointed to the State Board of Education by Reagan in January 1968. "Moomaw Choice Delights Parents," *Los Angeles Times*, January 26, 1968. The pastor of Reagan's Bel Air Presbyterian Congregation, and speaker at the 1981 presidential inauguration, Moomaw stepped down from his clergyship in 1993 for "unspecified indiscretions" later revealed to be "sexual misconduct" with five female congregants. John Dart, "Church will Report on Moomaw Episode," *Los Angeles Times*, March 13, 1995; Kehoe interview with Kehoe, 26.

55. John Patrick Diggins, "How Ronald Reagan Reinvented Religion," *History News Network*, June 6, 2007, accessed via http://hnn.us/articles/38958.html. See also

Diggins, *Ronald Reagan: Fate, Freedom, and the Making of History* (New York W. W. Norton, 2007).

56. Interview with Kehoe, 25.

57. Alan Sieroty, Report of Hearings on Sex Education, State Board of Education, Sacramento, April 10, 1969, 11.

58. "The Men Who Gave Board Its Morality Guidelines," *San Francisco Chronicle*, May 10, 1969, 6.

59. Interview with Kehoe, 25.

60. Various letters, CSA-DOE, Box F3752:437, Folder: Moral Guidelines Committee, 1968–1969; Interview with Klotz, 2, CSA-DOE, Box F3752:440, Folder: Moral Guidelines Committee, 1968.

61. John Oglesby to Max Rafferty, CSA-DOE, Box F3752:438, Folder: Moral Guidelines Committee, 1969–1970.

62. Ron Moskowitz, "Board OKs Morality Guidelines," *San Francisco Chronicle*, May 10, 1969, 1.

63. Ron Moskowitz, "Guidelines Analysis: The Reagan Majority's Great Leap Backward," *San Francisco Chronicle*, May 13, 1969.

64. Ibid.

65. Ibid.

66. Jack McCurdy, "State Board Hears Proposal for Moral Teaching in Schools," *Los Angeles Times*, May 10, 1969.

67. Howard Day to Donn Moomaw, November 12, 1969, enclosed in "Guidelines for the Education of Responsible Citizens in the Public Schools of California: A Report Presented to the California State Board of Education," December 11, 1969, CSA-DOE, Box F3752:437, Folder: Moral Guidelines Committee, 1968–1969.

68. "Guidelines for the Education of Responsible Citizens in the Public Schools of California: A Report Presented to the California State Board of Education," 1–2.

69. Ibid., 7.

70. Ibid., 1, 4–5.

71. Ibid.

72. Jack McCurdy, "Morality Code for Schools Goes to State Board," *Los Angeles Times*, January 5, 1970.

73. Kenneth F. Cory, an oral history conducted 1981 by Sarah Sharp in "Legislative Issue Management and Advocacy, 1961–1974," Regional Oral History Office, The Bancroft Library, University of California, Berkeley, 1983, CSA-DOE, Box F3752:449, Folder: Moral Guidelines Committee, 1974.

74. Jack McCurdy, "First Moral Guidelines for State Schools OKd," *Los Angeles Times*, January 9, 1970.

75. Klotz speech, transcript, CSA-DOE, Box F3752:438, Folder: Moral Guidelines Committee, 1969–1970.

76. Ron Moskowitz, "Board OKs Morality Guidelines," *San Francisco Chronicle*, May 10, 1969, 1.

77. "Guidelines for the Education of Responsible Citizens in the Public Schools of California: A Report Presented to the California State Board of Education," 21.

78. Ibid.

79. Ibid., 9.

80. Jack McCurdy, "Morality Code for Schools Goes to State Board," *Los Angeles Times*, January 5, 1970.

81. Ken Fanucchi, "Curriculum in Morals May Take 6 Years," *Los Angeles Times*, November 30, 1972.

82. Marilyn Angle, public hearing, January 8, 1970, 2, CSA-DOE, Box F3752:441, Folder: Moral Guidelines Committee, 1969–1970.

83. Ibid., 4.

84. League of Men Voters, January 8, 1970, public hearing, 2.

85. Margaret Scott, January 8, 1970, public hearing, 3.

86. Lloyd Morain of American Humanist Association, January 8, 1970, public hearing, 1–2.

87. Henrietta Pankhauser, January 8, 1970, public hearing, 2.

88. Ibid.

89. California State Board of Education, MGIC Minutes of Meeting, October 15, 1970, 2, CSA-DOE, Box F3752:442, Folder: Moral Guidelines Committee, 1970–1971.

90. January 8, 1970, hearing, 3–6.

91. Mr. Walter Blount, January 8, 1970, public hearing, 7.

92. Miss Helen Dillon to Max Rafferty, August 22, 1970, CSA-DOE, Box F3752:445, Folder: Moral Guidelines Committee, 1970–1974.

93. Frances Todd, Report of Hearings on Sex Education, State Board of Education, Sacramento, April 10, 1969, 94.

94. Merrill Harmin, Louis E. Raths, and Sidney Simon, *Values and Teaching: Working with Values in the Classroom* (Columbus, OH: Merrill Books, 1966); Leland Howe, Richard Kirschenbaum, and Sidney Simon, *Values Clarification: A Practical, Action-Directed Workbook* (New York: Hart Publishing Company, 1972).

95. Gordon M. Hart, *Values Clarification for Counselors* (Springfield, IL: Charles C. Thomas, 1978), 23.

96. John Dart, "Classroom Trend: Back to Moral Values," *Los Angeles Times*, May 15, 1976; Nathan Glazer, *We Are all Multiculturalists Now* (Cambridge, MA: Harvard University Press, 1997).

97. Luis Urrieta Jr., "Dis-connections in 'American' Citizenship and the Post/neo-colonial: People of Mexican Descent and Whitestream Pedagogy and Curriculum," *Theory and Research in Social Education* 32, no. 4 (Fall 2004): 433–458; Zoe Burkholder, *Color in the Classroom: How American Schools*

*Taught Race, 1900–1954* (New York: Oxford University Press, 2011); Frances Fitzgerald, *America Revised, History Schoolbooks in the Twentieth Century* (Boston: Little, Brown and Company, 1979); Joseph Moreau, *Schoolbook Nation: Conflicts over American History Textbooks from the Civil War to the Present* (Ann Arbor: University of Michigan Press, 2004); Jonathan Zimmerman, *Whose America? Culture Wars in the Public Schools* (Cambridge, MA: Harvard University Press, 2002).

98. Report of Hearings on Sex Education, State Board of Education, Sacramento, April 10, 1969, 94.

99. Letter exchange among Kathleen Bresnahan, Henry Heydt, and Patricia Hill (Health Consultant), CSA-DOE, Box F3752: 445, Folder: Moral Guidelines Committee Correspondence, 1970–1974.

100. Mrs. Laurel Martin to Mr. Newton Stewart, president, California State Board of Education, January 25, 1973, CSA-DOE, Box F3752:445, Folder: Moral Guidelines Committee, 1970–1974.

101. Ibid.

102. David Greenberg, *Nixon's Shadow: The History of an Image* (New York: W. W. Norton and Co., 2003); Jonathan Schoenwald, *A Time for Choosing: The Rise of Modern American Conservatism* (New York: Oxford, 2002).

103. Martin to Stewart, 1973.

104. Theodore Roszak, *The Making of a Counterculture: Reflections on the Technocratic Society and its Youthful Opposition* (Berkeley: University of California Press, 1995).

105. Martin to Stewart, 1973.

106. California Federation of Republican Women, Southern Division, January 9, 1973, Press Release, CSA-DOE, Box F3752:444, Folder: Moral Guidelines Committee, September 1972–January 1973.

107. Ibid.

108. Public hearing, January 8, 1970, 2, CSA-DOE, Box F3752:441, Folder: Moral Guidelines Committee, 1969–1970.

109. San Francisco Conference on Religion, Race, and Social Concerns, January 8, 1970, public hearing, 9.

110. Mrs. Phil H. Jackson, vice president, Los Angeles Tenth District PTA, January 8, 1970, public hearing, 8.

111. "The Men Who Gave the Board Its Morality Guidelines," *San Francisco Chronicle*, May 10, 1969, 6.

112. Sieroty, Report of Hearings on Sex Education, State Board of Education, Sacramento, April 10, 1969, 13.

113. Ronald Conway to Max Rafferty, July 16, 1970, CSA-DOE, Box F3752:749, Folder: General Correspondence, April–July 1970.

114. Raoul Teilhet, president, California Federation of Teachers, January 8, 1970, public hearing, 2.

115. "A Model of a Way of Investigation Using Certain Methods of Intelligence," excerpted from state-adopted textbook, *Concepts and Values: Grade 5, Teachers Edition* (New York: Harcourt, Brace—Merrill Publishing Company, 1970), T-37, adopted 1972, CSA-DOE, Box F3752:445, Folder: Moral Guidelines Committee, 1970–1974.

116. Assorted letters, minutes. See CSA-DOE, Box F3752:446, Folder: Moral Guidelines Committee, 1972, and Box F3752:449, Folder: Moral Guidelines Committee, 1974.

117. Ruth French to Wilson Riles, Thomas Shellhammer, Henry Heydt Jr., and Mitchell Voydat, Subject: My Personal Evaluation of the Progress of the Moral Guidelines Committee in Implementing the Guidelines for the Education of Responsible Citizens in the Public Schools of California, October 10, 1972, CSA-DOE, Box F3752:445, Folder: Moral Guidelines Committee, 1970–1974.

118. Laurel Martin and Barbara Taylor, "Minority Report of the Moral Guidelines Implementation Committee," submitted to the California State Board of Education, January 25,1973, CSA-DOE, Box F3752:448, Folder: Moral Guidelines Committee, 1973.

119. Ibid., 2.

120. Donald A. McCune to Victoria Miltenberger, June 21, 1974, CSA-DOE, Box F3752:445, Folder: Moral Guidelines Committee, 1970–1974.

121. Ibid.

122. Interview with Kehoe, 26.

123. Wallace T. Homitz of Homitz, Allen and Associates to Henry J. Heydt Jr., special assistant, State Board of Education, January 15, 1974, Box F3752:445, Folder: Moral Guidelines Committee, 1970–1974.

124. Ibid.

125. Interview with Kehoe, 26.

126. Ibid., 27.

127. Mrs. Helen Dillon to Max Rafferty, August 22, 1970, CSA-DOE, Box F3752:445, Folder: Moral Guidelines Committee, 1970–1974; "A Passion for Human Values in H.S. Education," *Progress-Bulletin*, January 8, 1972, Pomona, California.

128. Letter, San Ysidro School District to State Board of Education Members, February 14, 1973, CSA-DOE, Box F3752:445, Folder: Moral Guidelines Committee, 1970–1974.

129. Todd Gitlin, *The Twilight of Common Dreams: Why America is Wracked by Culture Wars* (New York: Henry Holt, 1995); David Tyack, *Seeking Common Ground: Public Schools in a Diverse Society* (Cambridge, MA: Harvard University Press, 2004).

CHAPTER 8

1. Betty Ford interview, *60 Minutes*, taped July 21, 1975, aired August 10, 1975.

2. Judith Serrin, "Mary Calderone: 'Behavior Catching Up,'" *Detroit Free Press,* August 24, 1975.

3. "Betty's Blockbuster brings boos, bravos," *Daily News,* August 15, 1975.

4. Catherine Rymph, *Republican Women: Feminism and Conservatism from Suffrage through the Rise of the New Right* (Chapel Hill: University of North Carolina Press, 2006); Maryanne Borrelli, "Competing Conceptions of the First Ladyship: Public Responses to Betty Ford's *60 Minutes* Interview," *Presidential Studies Quarterly* 31, no. 3 (September 2001): 397–414.

5. Bruce Schulman and Julian Zelizer, eds., *Rightward Bound: Making America Conservative in the 1970s* (Cambridge, MA: Harvard University Press, 2008).

6. Mary Steichen Calderone, Speech at Brandeis University, Waltham, MA, June 1, 1975, SL-MSC, Box 2, Folder 54, 1975 articles about MSC.

7. Assorted correspondence, 1966–1969, SL-MSC, Box 1, Folder 12, Crank Correspondence. Books such as Gloria Lentz, *Raping our Children: The Sex Education Scandal* (New Rochelle, NY: Arlington House, 1972), show that some anti-sex education activists sustained the fever pitch of the 1960s battles.

8. Boston Women's Health Book Collective, *Our Bodies Ourselves,* 1971; "The ABCs of Sex Education for Trainables," Hallmark Films, 1975.

9. James Carberry, "More Churches Facing Sexuality as a Fact of Life," *Press-Enterprise,* December, 1969.

10. Mother, San Francisco, CA, letter, March 11, 1980, SL-MSC, Box 82-M129, Folder 6, letters in response to *Family Circle* interview: "The Right Way to teach Children About Sex," by Margaret Jaworski.

11. John Steinbacher, foreword, pamphlet, Joseph P. Bean, M.D., "The Source of the River Pollution" (Fullerton, CA: Educator Publications, 1972), CU-RBML, GRC, Box 119, Folder: The Educator.

12. Lynne Cooper, "The Effectiveness of Family Life Education Programs in 12 California School Districts," (Hunt Valley, MD: Network Publications, 1982), 14.

13. Mrs. Roger D. Axworthy to Max Rafferty, April 6, 1970, CSA-DOE, Box F3752:743, Folder: Max Rafferty, General Correspondence, July 1969–November 1970.

14. "Voting Shift Seen in Orange County," *New York Times,* November 10, 1974.

15. PARENTS Newsletter, "The White House Conference on Families," January 19, 1980, 3, CU-RBML, Group Research Collection, Box 274, unsorted papers.

16. Estelle Freedman, *No Turning Back: The History of Feminism and the Future of Women* (New York: Ballantine, 2002).

17. Sen. Humphrey, "The White House Conference on the Family," *Congressional Record,* May 9, 1980, S5032.

18. Douglas Kirby, Judith Alper, and Peter Scales, "An Analysis of U.S. Sex Education Programs and Evaluation Methods," prepared for US Department of Health, Education, and Welfare (Bethesda, MD: Mathtech Inc., 1979), 5, 11.

19. Max Rafferty, *Classroom Countdown: Education at the Crossroads* (New York: Hawthorn Books, 1970), 184.

20. Bill Boyarsky, "Three in Bitter Fight for State Schools Post," *Los Angeles Times*, May 27, 1970.

21. Kirby et al., "An Analysis of U.S. Sex Education Programs and Evaluation Methods," 14. Emphasis in original.

22. Cooper, "The Effectiveness of Family Life Education Programs," 18, 31, 155.

23. Ibid., 31.

24. Patricia Hill, consultant in health education, to Kathleen M. Bresnahan, January 31, 1973, Box 3752:445, Folder: Moral Guidelines Committee, 1970–1974.

25. Henry J. Heydt Jr., special assistant to the State Board of Education, memorandum, July 13, 1972, CSA-DOE, Box F3752:10, Folder: Records of Henry J. Heydt Jr., 1972–1973.

26. Pat Pomerleace to Novato Board of Education, June 13, 1972, CSA-DOE, Box F3752:10, Folder: Records of Henry J. Heydt Jr., 1972–1973.

27. "Letters Received as of July 5 Concerning Sex Education in Public Schools," quoting William Edward Glover, Homosexual Information Center, Hollywood, CA, July 5, 1972, CSA-DOE, Box F3752:10, Folder: Records of Henry J. Heydt Jr., 1972–1973.

28. Resolution adopted by the Joint Committee on Health Problems in Education of the National Education Association and the American Medical Association: SUPPORT FOR SOUND SEX EDUCATION," February 9–11, 1969, CSA-DOE, Box F3752:10, Folder: Records of Henry J. Heydt Jr., 1972–1973; James Wrightson, "Medical Unit Favors Sex Education in Schools," *The Sacramento Bee*, March 20, 1969; Assembly Bill No. 2770, Chapter 12.5: Family Education Programs," Approved by governor November 30, 1971.

29. Assembly Bill No. 2770, 7361.5.

30. Ibid.

31. Among other articles, "Sex and the Senior Citizen," "Sex Education for the Retarded?," *Boston Globe*, January 21, 1974; "Middle-Age Sex: Myths and Misconceptions," *Dynamic Maturity*, November 1974, 40–42, SL-MSC, Box 2, Folders: 50–53, Articles about Calderone, 1972–1974.

32. Assorted correspondence, 1966–1969, SL-MSC, Box 1, Folder 12, Crank Correspondence.

33. Associated Press, "Planned Parenthood Director Unrelenting Advocate," *The Montgomery Advertiser*, July 7, 1977, SL-MSC, Box 2, Folder 58, Articles by or about MSC, 1977.

34. California Department of Education, "Framework for Health Instruction in Public Schools, Resolution," December, 1972; Letter, Henry J. Heydt Jr., special assistant to State Board of Education, to Mary S. Calderone, executive director, SIECUS, December 6, 1972, CSA-DOE, Box F3752:10, Folder: Records of Henry J. Heydt Jr., 1972–1973.

35. International Medical News Service, "Negative Parental Attitudes on Body, Eroticism Scored," *Clinical Psychiatry News*, November, 1976, SL-MSC, Box 2, Folder 56.

36. Jean Douglas Murphy, "Sex Education Comes to the Comic Book," *Los Angeles Times*, March 27, 1973; "Sex Education Class for Fathers, Sons Due," *Los Angeles Times*, April 15, 1973; Robin Heffler, "Sex Education Film Becomes Parental Option," *Los Angeles Times*, March 1, 1979.

37. Jeffrey Moran, *Teaching Sex: The Shaping of Adolescence in the Twentieth Century* (Cambridge, MA: Harvard University Press, 2000), passim.

38. J. Russell Kent, Superintendent of Schools, San Mateo County Board of Education, to Mr. Willard Johnson, Executive Director, Planned Parenthood Association, San Diego County, March 13, 1969; letter, Paul W. Cook, Superintendent of Schools, Anaheim Union High School District, March 13, 1969, to Johnson, SL-MSC, Box 14, Folder 231.

39. Cooper, "The Effectiveness of Family Life Education Programs," 2.

40. Robert L. Webber, Director, Western Regions, Planned Parenthood, to California PP Affiliates, September 29, 1972, CSA-DOE, Box F3752:10, Folder: Records of Henry J. Heydt Jr., 1972–1973.

41. "Profile," *The Hour*, Norwalk, CT, n.d., in 1977 folder, SL-MSC, Box 2, Folder 28.

42. *Journal of the American Medical Association*, November 17, 1969, Volume 210, no. 7, SL-MSC: Box 17, Folder 291, Articles on sex education, pro and con, 1965–1970.

43. Minister Charles Stevens to Mary Calderone, March 19, 1970. See also Pastor Ted Steenblock to Mary Calderone, May 26, 1968, SL-MSC, Box 14, Folder 231; Mrs. Bernadette Spoerl to Mary Calderone, September 19, 1968, SL-MSC, Box 14, Folder 230.

44. Irvine, *Talk About Sex*, passim.

45. Morton Hunt, *Sexual Behavior in the 1970s* (New York: Playboy Press, 1974).

46. "Ignorance About Sexuality Assailed," *Los Angeles Times*, October 11, 1972; "Voting Shift Seen in Orange County," *New York Times*, November 10, 1974.

47. Various letters, 1972–1973, CSA-DOE, Box F3752:10, Folder: Records of Henry J. Heydt Jr., 1972–1973.

48. Cooper, "The Effectiveness of Family Life Education Programs," 5; Elizabeth Lasch-Quinn, *Race Experts: How Racial Etiquette, Sensitivity Training and New Age Therapy Hijacked the Civil Rights Revolution* (New York: Norton, 2001).

49. Cooper, 5.

50. Mrs. R. Taylor to Gentlemen of the Board, July 1, 1972, CSA-DOE, Box F3752:10, Folder: Records of Henry J. Heydt Jr., 1972–1973.

51. Moran, *Teaching Sex*, 197.

52. Ibid., 12. Robert Wuthnow, *After Heaven: Spirituality in America since the 1950s* (Berkeley: University of California Press, 1998); Jeffrey Kripal, *Esalen: America and the Religion of No Religion* (Berkeley: University of California Press, 2007).

53. Letter to *Journal of American Medicine*, November 17, 1969, Volume 210, Number 7, SL-MSC, Box 17, Folder 291, Articles on sex education, pro and con, 1965–1970.

54. Cooper, "The Effectiveness of Family Life Education Programs," 5.

55. Ibid., 26.

56. Ibid., 55.

57. Ibid., 69.

58. Ibid., 55.

59. Ibid., 27.

60. Family Life and Sex Education Curriculum Plan, Tamalpais Unified School District, 1974, CSA-DOE, Box F3752:10, Folder: Records of Henry J. Heydt Jr., 1972–1973; California Department of Education, "Framework for Health Instruction in Public Schools, Resolution," December 1972, CSA-DOE, Box F3752:10, Folder: Records of Henry J. Heydt Jr., 1972–1973.

61. Memorandum, Henry J. Heydt Jr. to Members, State Board of Education, Subject: Summary of complaints and general findings re districts conducting courses in the area of Family Life and Sex Education," October 31, 1972, CSA-DOE, Box F3752:10, Folder: Records of Henry J. Heydt Jr., 1972–1973.

62. Memorandum, Henry J. Heydt Jr. to Policies and Programs Committee, Subject: Staff Recommendations for Possible Action by the Committee in the Area of Family Life and Sex Education, July 13, 1972, October 31, 1972, CSA-DOE, Box F3752:10, Folder: Records of Henry J. Heydt Jr., 1972–1973.

63. Sandra Mathers, "Sex and the 72-year-old Grandmother," *Sentinel Star, Florida Magazine,* November 7, 1976, SL-MSC, Box 2, Folder 56.

64. Conference Proceedings, 62nd Annual Meeting, National Association of Secondary School Principals, Anaheim, CA, 1978.

65. Cooper, "The Effectiveness of Family Life Education Programs," 156. Testimony, Persida Drakulich of San Diego Unified School District, Report of Hearings on Sex Education, State Board of Education, April 10, 1969, 76,

66. Cooper, "The Effectiveness of Family Life Education Programs," 118.

67. Ibid.

68. Editorial "The Wanted Child," *IMPACT,* special issue on teen pregnancy, 1978, SL-MSC, Box 2, Folder 59.

69. Cooper, "The Effectiveness of Family Life Education Programs," 9–10.

70. Rickie Solinger, *Wake Up Little Susie: Single Pregnancy and Race before Roe v. Wade* (New York: Routledge, 1992), 233.

71. Associated Press, "Planned Parenthood Director Unrelenting Advocate," *The Montgomery Advertiser,* July 7, 1977, SL-MSC, Box 2, Folder 58, Articles by or about MSC, 1977.

72. Cooper, "The Effectiveness of Family Life Education Programs," 70.

73. Mary Steichen Calderone, "Human Sexuality- Battleground or Peaceground?," Address to Brearley graduating class, Spring 1974.

74. PARENTS Newsletter, 3.

75. Mary C. Kaehler to *60 Minutes,* October 28, 1981, SL-MSC, Box 82-M129, Folder 3, Cons re: Mike Wallace segment.

76. Sen. Humphrey, "What We Can Expect from the White House Conference on Families," *Congressional Record,* May 9, 1980, S5033.

77. Clayton Howard, "Culture War: Gay Rights, the Religious Right, and a Moderate Right to Privacy," *The Closet and the Cul de Sac: Sex, Politics, and Suburbanization in Postwar California* (Philadelphia: University of Pennsylvania Press, forthcoming); Gillian Frank, "The Civil Rights of Parents: Race and Conservative Parents in Anita Bryant's campaign Against Gay Rights in 1970s Florida," *Journal of the History of Sexuality* 22, no. 1 (January 2013): 126–160; William Overend, "Gay Rights: Is a Backlash Forming?," *Los Angeles Times*, July 29, 1977.

78. Overend.

79. Ronald Reagan, "Editorial: Two Ill-Advised California Trends," *Los Angeles Herald Examiner*, November 1, 1978.

80. James L. McCary, *Human Sexuality: A Course for Young Adults* (New York: Van Nostrand, 1972). See "Letters Received as of July 5 Concerning Sex Education in California Public Schools," July 5, 1972, CSA-DOE, Box F3752:10, Folder: Records of Henry J. Heydt Jr., 1972–1973.

81. Letter exchange among Kathleen Bresnahan, Henry Heydt, and Patricia Hill (Health Consultant), CSA-DOE, Box F3752:445, Folder: Moral Guidelines Committee, Correspondence, 1970–1974.

82. Jack McCurdy, "State Board Refuses to Adopt Textbook on 'Human Sexuality,'" *Los Angeles Times*, May 11, 1973.

83. Lawrence Mass, "A Nation of Sexual Stutterers: A Conversation with Mary Calderone," *Christopher Street*, September/October 1981, SL-MSC, Box 82-M129, Folder 11.

84. Various letters, CSA-DOE, Box F3752:10, Folder: Records of Henry J. Heydt Jr., 1972–1973.

85. Phyllis A. Gibson to State Board of Education, July 13, 1973; Boyd R. Benson to Governor Reagan, June 13, 1973; Richard Seymour to State Board of Education, July 9, 1973, all CSA-DOE, Box F3752:10, Folder: Records of Henry J. Heydt Jr., 1972–1973.

86. Henry Heydt Jr., Special Assistant to State Board of Education, Memorandum, July 24, 1973, CSA-DOE, Box F3752:10, Folder: Records of Henry J. Heydt Jr., 1972–1973 (emphasis in original). Districts were also mandated by the education code to "notify parents or guardians if classes are offered in which human reproductive organs and their functions and processes are described, illustrated or discussed and that each parent or guardian shall be provided an opportunity that his child not attend such a class." See California Department of Education, "Facts Relating to Adoption and Availability of the Book Entitled *Human Sexuality – A Course for Young Adults*," June 26, 1973.

87. "Charges Made Against Teacher; Sex Class Ends," *Los Angeles Times*, January 20, 1976.

88. Lynn Lilliston, "Sex Education Crisis in the Public Schools," *Los Angeles Times*, June 12, 1972.

89. Jack Birkinshaw, "Moral Majority Letter Assails L.A. Sex Education Text," *Los Angeles Times*, December 28, 1980.

90. Ibid., 23.

91. Cooper, "The Effectiveness of Family Life Education Programs," 67.

92. Ibid., 87.

93. Bethany Moreton, "Make Payroll, Not War: Business Culture as Youth Culture," in *Rightward Bound: Making America Conservative in the 1970s*, edited by Bruce Schulman and Julian Zelizer (Cambridge, MA: Harvard University Press, 2008).

94. Cooper, "The Effectiveness of Family Life Education Programs," 63–68.

95. Ibid., 107.

96. Ibid., 109.

97. Mrs. Richard A. Meier to Mary Steichen Calderone, October 18, 1970, SL-MSC, Box 1, Folder 13.

98. Dee Bryant, "Access to Sex Facts Urged," *The Marietta Daily Journal*, April 11, 1975, SL-MSC, Box 2, Folder 54, 1975 articles about MSC.

99. Ibid.

100. Ibid.

101. "Daily Closeup: Grandmother Courage," *New York Post*, November 12, 1975, SL-MSC, Box 2, Folder 54, 1975 articles about MSC.

102. Mary Steichen Calderone to Anne Brady, August 8, 1970, SL-MSC, Box 14, Folder 230, SIECUS, general correspondence, 1964–1971.

103. Cooper, "The Effectiveness of Family Life Education Programs," 70.

104. Henry J. Heydt Jr. to Members, State Board of Education, Memorandum, Subject: Summary of complaints and general findings re districts conducting courses in the area of Family Life and Sex Education," 2, October 31, 1972, CSA-DOE, Box F3752:10, Folder: Records of Henry J. Heydt Jr., 1972–1973.

105. Mrs. R. Taylor to Gentlemen of the Board, July 1, 1972, CSA-DOE, Box F3752:10, Folder: Records of Henry J. Heydt Jr., 1972–1973.

106. Associated Press, "Sex Education Approach A Failure, Riles Admits," *Los Angeles Times*, October 10, 1980.

107. Speech before the American Group Psychotherapy Association, February 8, 1975, San Antonio, TX SL-MSC, Box 2, Folder 54.

108. Robert L. Williams, to Donald J. Kreps, principal, Redwood High, June 12, 1972, CSA-DOE, Box F3752:10, Folder: Records of Henry J. Heydt Jr., 1972–1973.

CONCLUSION 9

1. Russell Chandler, "Humanists: Target of the Moral Right," *Los Angeles Times*, July 16, 1981.

2. Susan Perry, "Sol Gordon's Crusade: Sex Education for Young People," *Los Angeles Times*, January 9, 1987.

3. David Smollar, "Adding a Slice of Life to the Three Rs," *Los Angeles Times*, October 12, 1987.

4. Ibid.

5. Susan Perry, "Sol Gordon's Crusade: Sex Education for Young People," *Los Angeles Times*, January 9, 1987.

6. Curtis J. Sitomer, "California School Chief Vows to Unify, Upgrade," *Christian Science Monitor*, December 20, 1970.

7. Ibid.

8. Oral History with Kenneth F. Cory, 1987–1988, California State Oral History Program, Regional Oral History Office, the Bancroft Library, 6–7.

9. Lee Sigelman, David Lowery, and Roland Smith, "The Tax Revolt: A Comparative State Analysis," *Western Political Quarterly* 36, no. 1 (March 1983): 30.

10. Jack Citrin and David O. Sears, *Tax Revolt: Something for Nothing in California* (Cambridge, MA: Harvard University Press, 1982); Citrin, "Proposition 13 and the Transformation of California Government," *The California Journal of Politics and Policy* 1, no. 1 (2009): 1.

11. Joel S. Berke, "Federal Educational Policy on School Finance After Proposition 13: Short and Long Run Implication," *Educational Evaluation and Policy Analysis* 1, no. 9 (1979): 19; Richard P. Nathan, "The Nationalization of Proposition 13," *PS* 14, no. 4 (Autumn 1981): 752; Jerome L. Himmelstein, "The Road to Proposition 13," *Contemporary Sociology* 20, no. 1 (January 1991): 60.

12. James Reston, "California and the World," *New York Times*, June 18, 1978, E19.

13. Berke, "Federal Educational Policy on School Finance," 19. See also Kevin M. Kruse, "The Politics of Race and Public Space: Desegregation, Privatization, and the Tax Revolt in Atlanta," *Journal of Urban History* 31, no. 5 (July 2005). Notably, thirty years after the passage of Proposition 13, a poll indicated that 57 percent of voters would vote for the measure, more than double the 23 percent who would vote against it. Among homeowners, 64 percent still supported the measure, as did 79 percent who had purchased their homes before the passage of Proposition 13. California Opinion Index, "Proposition 13 Thirty Years After its Passage," Field Research Corporation, June 2008.

14. William T. Phelan, "Staffing Policies in Times of Retrenchment: Teacher Opinions," *Peabody Journal of Education* 6, no. 2 (Winter 1983).

15. Committee on the Status of Women, "Sacramento Summit: Hearing on Proposition 13," October 16, 1978, 123. Accessed through Women and Social Movements database, www.alexanderstreetpress.com.

16. James S. Catterall and Emily Brizendine, "Proposition 13: Effects of High School Curricula, 1978–1983," *American Journal of Education* Vol. 93, no. 3 (May, 1985): 332.

17. Oral History with Kenneth F. Cory, conducted by Sarah Sharp, 1981, in "Legislative Issue Management and Advocacy, 1961–1974," Regional Oral

History Office, The Bancroft Library, University of California, Berkeley, 1983, 42.

18. Catterall and Brizendine, "Proposition 13: Effects of High School Curricula," 343.

19. Berke, "Federal Educational Policy on School Finance," 20.

20. Ibid.; Catterall and Brizendine, "Proposition 13: Effects of High School Curricula," 343.

21. Among many other media accounts in California and nationally, see Bennett Karmin, "California's Bankrupt Schools," *New York Times*, July 17, 1983, E21; Robert Lindsey, "Los Angeles Schools Kill Summer Classes," *New York Times*, June 14, 1978.

22. Committee on the Status of Women, "Sacramento Summit: Hearing on Proposition 13," October 16, 1978, 31. Accessed through Women and Social Movements database, www.alexanderstreetpress.com.

23. Phelan, "Staffing Policies in Times of Retrenchment," 47; Catterall and Brizendine, "Proposition 13: Effects of High School Curricula," 327.

24. Kevin O'Leary, "The Legacy of Proposition 13," *Time*, June 27, 2009; Catterall and Brizendine, "Proposition 13: Effects of High School Curricula," 331.

25. National Center for Education Statistics (NCES): Common Core of Data (CCD), "National Public Education Financial Survey (State Fiscal)," 2007–2008 (FY 2008) v.1a Common Core of Data (CCD), "State Nonfiscal Survey of Public Elementary/Secondary Education," 2007–2008 v.1a

26. Jack Citrin, "Proposition 13 and the Transformation of California Government," *California Journal of Politics and Policy* 1, no. 1 (2009): 3.

27. Among others cited throughout, also see Robert O. Self, "Prelude to the Tax Revolt: The Politic of the 'Tax Dollar' in Postwar California," in *The New Suburban History*, edited by Kevin M. Kruse and Thomas J. Sugrue (Chicago: University of Chicago Press, 2006); Daniel A. Smith, "Howard Jarvis, Populist Entrepreneur: Reevaluating the Causes of Proposition 13," *Social Science History* 23, no. 2, 173–210; Robert Kuttner, *Revolt of the Haves: Tax Rebellions and Hard Times* (New York: Simon and Schuster, 1980); Thomas Byrne and Mary D. Edsall, *Chain Reaction: The Impact of Race, Rights, and Taxes on American Politics* (New York: W. W. Norton and Company, 1991).

28. Mary Lee Glass, "Sputnik to Proposition 13: Exploding the Myths," *The English Journal* 68, no. 6 (September 1979): 25, 27.

29. Michael W. Kirst, "Organizations in Shock and Overload: California's Public Schools 1970–80," *Educational Evaluation and Policy Analysis* 1, no. 4 (July–August 1979): 28.

30. Bob Deisenroth and Linda Hildreth, "Hymn of the Embattled Taxpayer," quoted in Martin, 106.

31. Howard Jarvis, *I'm Mad as Hell* (New York: Times Books, 1979), 262.

32. Ibid., 260–261.

33. Ibid.

34. Paula Fass rightly uses the term "outsiders" rather than "minorities" to enfold groups whose interests have been marginalized in the schoolhouse. Additionally, in California the preponderance of Latinos in the public schools—overtaking whites in many districts throughout the 1970s until today—makes the term useful. See Paula Fass, *Outside In: Minorities and the Transformation of American Education* (New York: Oxford University Press, 1989).

35. Thomas Frank, *What's the Matter with Kansas? How Conservatives Won the Heart of America* (New York: Henry Holt., 2004), 5.

36. Kirst, 27.

37. Ibid.

38. Glass, 25.

39. Ibid.

40. Miss Brill to Max Rafferty, April 25, 1970, CSA-DOE, Box F3752:746, Folder: Max Rafferty, General Correspondence, December 1969–March 1970; Michael B. Katz, *The Undeserving Poor: from the War on Poverty to the War on Welfare* (New York: Pantheon Books, 1990).

41. Mrs. Laurel Martin to Mr. Newton Stewart, president, California State Board of Education, January 25, 1973, CSA-DOE, Box F3752:445, Folder: Moral Guidelines Committee, 1970–1974

42. Mary C. Kaehler to *60 Minutes*, October 28, 1981, SL-MSC, Box 82-M129, Folder 3, Cons re: Mike Wallace segment.

43. Notably, the rapid pace of pedagogical and policy innovation in the 1960s and 1970s meant that there were legitimate concerns with implementation of new programs. Even Kirst, the president of the state board of education, admitted that the state had sometimes "mandated that a measure be adopted before it was adequately tested." Kirst, 28.

44. Kenneth F. Cory, an oral history conducted 1981 by Sarah Sharp in "Legislative Issue Management and Advocacy, 1961–1974," Regional Oral History Office, The Bancroft Library, University of California, Berkeley, 1983, CSA-DOE, Box F3752:449, Folder: Moral Guidelines Committee, 1974, page 42. This privileging of economic exigency figured in educational policymaking nationwide. See *Cintron v. Brentwood Union Free School District* (1978), in which a New York district court rules that a high school teaching cultural and linguistic maintenance with students who have learned English constitutes a "misuse of funds." Teresa Scassa, "Language, Culture, and the Courts: Bilingual Education in the United States," *Canadian Review of American Studies* 26, no. 1 (January 1996).

45. "A Report on the 1978 Federal and State Legislatures and Local Actions Affecting Education," prepared by the Office of Government Relations, LAUSD, UCLA-HVS, Box 1, Folder 5, Education Legislation, 1978.

46. Jack McCurdy, "Failures in Bilingual School Plan Alleged," *Los Angeles Times*, July 20, 1976.

47. Letter exchange, Olivia Martinez and Ernesto Galarza, SUSC-EGP, Box 62, Folder 10, C.O.M.E., correspondence, 1976 –1977.

48. Ernesto Galarza, "The Burning Light: Action and Organizing in the Mexican Community in California," Oral History, 1977, 1978, 1981. Interviews by Gabrielle Morris, Timothy Beard, Regional Oral History Office, the Bancroft Library, University of California, Berkeley, 1982, 83.

49. Lisa Begun to Max Rafferty, January 8, 1970, CSA-DOE, Box F3752:746, Folder: Max Rafferty Papers, General Correspondence, December 1969–March1970.

50. Committee on the Status of Women, "Sacramento Summit: Hearing on Proposition 13," October 16, 1978, 11. Accessed through Women and Social Movements database, www.alexanderstreetpress.com.

51. Peter Schrag, *Paradise Lost: California's Experience, America's Future* (Berkeley: University of California Press, 1998), 22.

52. Dominic Sandbrook, *Mad as Hell: The Crisis of the 1970s and the Rise of the Populist Right* (New York: Alfred A. Knopf, 2011), 283.

53. Max Rafferty, *Max Rafferty on Education* (New York: Devin-Adair, 1968), 131.

54. "Galbraith Calls Tax Vote an 'Attack on the Poor'" *New York Times*, June 29, 1978, B2.

55. Ann Fleischer, "Proposition 13: Setback for Women," *Womenews* 3, no. 3 (September 1978). Accessed via Women and Social Movements Database, www.alexanderstreetpress.com.

56. Jarvis, *I'm Mad as Hell*, 262.

57. Henry S. Myers Jr., "Never-Ending War for the Minds of Our Children: Why Conservatives Should Run for their Local School Boards," *Human Events*, May 6, 1978, SL-MSC, Box 82-M129, Folder 3.

58. Incidence of Unmarried Teenage Pregnancy, United States, 1950–2000. Accessed via http://www.guttmacher.org/pubs/tgr/05/1/gr050107.html.

59. Grace Naismith, "Too Many Pregnancies, Too Early," *Reader's Digest*, November 1977, SL-MSC, Box 2, Folder 57, Articles by/about MSC 1977.

60. Jeffrey Moran, *Teaching Sex: The Shaping of Adolescence in the Twentieth Century* (Cambridge, MA: Harvard University Press, 2000), 208.

61. Ibid., 4.

62. California Assembly Bill 2931, passed March 16, 1978.

63. Proposition 227, also known as the "Unz Initiative," passed June 2, 1998. CITE

64. Eugene Gonzales, "I Support Your Initiative," September 7, 1997. Accessed via http://www.onenation.org/ys/ysgonzales.html.

65. Andrew Hartman, *A Battle for the Soul of America: A History of the Culture Wars, from the Sixties to the Present* (Chicago: University of Chicago Press, 2015).

66. Todd Gitlin, *The Twilight of Common Dreams: Why America is Wracked by Culture Wars* (New York: Holt, 1996).

67. David Smollar, "Views of District B Candidates Deeply Divided," *Los Angeles Times*, October 27, 1990.

68. Steven Lee Myers, "How a Rainbow Curriculum Turned into Fighting Words," *New York Times*, December 13, 1992.

69. Amy J. Binder, *Contentious Curricula: Afrocentrism and Creationism in American Public Schools* (Princeton, NJ: Princeton University Press, 2002).

70. Ann Banks, "Teaching Tolerance: Meet the Teacher Who Started Gay-Straight Alliances," *Edutopia*, February 26, 2010.

71. Paul Elias, "School Can Ban American Flag Shirts Over Safety Concerns, Federal Court Rules," *Huffington Post*, February 27, 2014.

72. FORUM 1978: "Sex in America: The Next 10 Years," n.d., SL-MSC, Box 2, Folder 57, Articles by/about MSC 1977; Leon Watson, "That's Something You Can't 'Unsee'—Parents Outraged by 'Horrific' Sex Education Class," *Daily Mail*, June 9, 2014.

73. Alana Semuels, "Sex Education Stumbles in Mississippi," *Los Angeles Times*, April 2, 2014.

74. "Senator Hayakawa says schools teaching 'heresy,'" *Sex Education & Mental Health Report* 10, no. 1 (Winter 1980): 1, CU-RBML, Box 297, Folder: Sensitivity Training.

# BIBLIOGRAPHY

MANUSCRIPT COLLECTIONS

Anaheim Public Library—Anaheim Heritage Collection (APL-AHC)
Anaheim Union High School District Papers (AUHSD)
Board of Trustees Papers (BOT)
California State Archives (CSA)
Department of Education and State Board of Education Archives (DOE)
Department of Instruction Archives (DOI)
Carlota del Portillo Personal Papers
Columbia University Rare Books and Manuscript Library (CU-RBML)
Group Research Collection, 1955–1996 (GRC)
Carnegie Corporation Papers
Harvard University—Schlesinger Library
Papers of Mary Steichen Calderone, 1904–1971 (SL-MSC)
Los Angeles Unified High School District
Board Minutes Files
New York Public Library
Map Division
San Francisco Public Library, San Francisco History Center (SFPL-SFHC)
Stanford University Special Collections (SUSC)
Margaret Meier Collection of Extreme Right Ephemeral Materials, 1930–1980
Ernesto Galarza Papers, 1973–1988 (EGP)
Mexican American Legal Defense and Educational Fund Collection,
1968–2002 (MLDF)
University of Arkansas, Fayetteville—James D. Bales Library
University of California, Berkeley—Bancroft Library
University of California, Los Angeles (UCLA) Department of Special Collections
Underground, Alternative and Extremist Literature Collection, Helene V. Smookler
    Papers on School Integration, 1965–1981 (HVS), Los Angeles School Monitoring
    Committee Records, 1978–1981
University of Iowa—Special Collections
Max Rafferty Papers (UI-MR)

MAPS

"California, The World Within a State." San Jose: The H. M. Gousha Company, 1975.
"California, County-State." Chicago: Rand McNally, 1963.


PERIODICALS

*The Afro-American*
*Anaheim Bulletin*
*Anaheim Gazette*
*ANORANCO*
*Arcadia News Post*
*Atlantic Monthly*
*Berkeley Gazette*
*The Boston Globe*
*The Christian Science Monitor*
*Christopher Street*
*Chicago Daily Defender*
*Dynamic Maturity*
*East/West*
*El Tecolote*
*Family Circle*
*Foreign Policy*
*Fresno Bee*
*Harper's*
*The Hour*
*Huffington Post*
*Human Events*
*Independent*
*Lingua Franca*
*Long Beach/Dixon Town-Line Reason*
*LOOK Magazine*
*Los Alamitos Crusader*
*Los Angeles Times*
*Marietta Daily Journal*
*The Montgomery Advertiser*
*The Nation*
*The New Yorker*
*New York Post*
*New York Times*
*News Bulletin*
*Orange County Register*

*Pittsburgh Courier*
*Progress-Bulletin*
*¿Que Tal?*
*Reader's Digest*
*Sacramento Bee*
*San Francisco Chronicle*
*San Francisco Examiner*
*San Francisco Progress*
*San Jose Mercury News*
*San Mateo County Times*
*Santa Ana Register*
*Sentinel Star*
*Star Free Press*
*The State*
*St. Louis Post-Dispatch*
*Tiempo Latino*
*Time*
*Wall Street Journal*
*Washington Post*
*Womenews*

PUBLISHED PRIMARY SOURCES

Anaheim Police Officers Association. *A History of the Anaheim Police Department.* Dallas: Taylor Publishing Company, 1992.

Ayres, William H. and McCurdy, Marilyn. *Time of Your Life: Family Life and Health Education for Intermediate Grades, Preliminary Teachers Guide Programs 10–15,* prepared by Bay Region Instructional Television for Education for KQED, n.d.

Bethell, Tom. "The Family Conference." *Human Life Review* 6, no. 3 (Summer 1980).

Booth, Louise. *One to Twenty-Eight: A History of the Anaheim Union High School District.* Anaheim, CA: Anaheim Unifed High School District, 1980.

Booth, Louise. *Fulfilling A Dream: The History of Chapman University.* Villa Park, CA: Donald R. Booth and Associates, 2001.

Calderone, Mary S. "Sex Education and the Roles of School and Church." *Annals of the American Academy of Political and Social Science* 376 (1968): 53–60.

Cardenas, Jose. "Bilingual Education, Segregation, and a Third Alternative." *Inequality in Education.* Cambridge, MA: Harvard Center for Law and Education, 1975.

*Concepts and Values: Grade 5, Teachers Edition.* New York: Harcourt, Brace—Merrill Publishing Company, 1970.

Cooper, Lynne. "The Effectiveness of Family Life Education Programs in 12 California School Districts." Hunt Valley, MD: Network Publications, 1982.

Danoff, Malcolm N. et al., *Evaluation of the Impact of ESEA Title VII Spanish-English Bilingual Education Programs, Volume III: Year Two Impact Data, Educational Process, and In-Depth Analysis*. Palo Alto, CA: American Institute of Research, 1978.

Drake, Gordon V. *Blackboard Power: NEA Threat to America*. Tulsa: Christian Crusade Publications, 1968.

Drake, Gordon V. "Is the Schoolhouse the Proper Place to Teach Raw Sex?" Tulsa: Christian Crusade, 1968.

Duvall, Evelyn Mills. *When You Marry*. New York: D.C. Heath and Co., 1947.

Epstein, Noel. *Language, Ethnicity, and the Schools: Policy Alternatives for Bilingual-Bicultural Education*. Washington, DC: Institute for Educational Leadership, 1977.

Fishman, Joshua. *Language Loyalty in the United States*. The Hague: Mouton, 1966.

Galarza, Ernesto. "The Burning Light: Action and Organizing in the Mexican Community in California." Oral History, 1977, 1978, 1981, Regional Oral History Office, The Bancroft Library, University of California, Berkeley, 1982.

Glass, Mary Lee. "Sputnik to Proposition 13: Exploding the Myths." *The English Journal* 68, no. 6 (September 1979), 23–27.

Harmin, Merrill, Louis E. Raths, and Sidney Simon. *Values and Teaching: Working with Values in the Classroom*. Columbus, OH: Merrill Books, 1966.

Hart, Gordon M. *Values Clarification for Counselors*. Springfield, IL: Charles C. Thomas, 1978.

Homitz, Allen, and Associates, "Prospectus: Project to Develop Approaches, Methods, and Materials for Implementation of Guidelines for Moral and Civic Education and Teaching About Religion," n.d.

Howe, Leland, Richard Kirschenbaum, and Sidney Simon. *Values Clarification: A Practical, Action-Directed Workbook*. New York: Hart Publishing Company, 1972.

Hunt, Morton. *Sexual Behavior in the 1970s*. New York: Playboy Press, 1974.

Jarvis, Howard. *I'm Mad as Hell*. New York: Times Books, 1979.

Kirby, Douglas, Judith Alper, and Peter Scales. "An Analysis of U.S. Sex Education Programs and Evaluation Methods." Prepared for U.S. Department of Health, Education, and Welfare. Bethesda, MD: Mathtech, Inc., 1979.

"Legislative Issue Management and Advocacy, 1961–1974." Regional Oral History Office, The Bancroft Library, University of California, Berkeley, 1983.

Lentz, Gloria. *Raping our Children: The Sex Education Scandal*. New Rochelle, NY: Arlington House, 1972.

McCary, James L. *Human Sexuality: A Course for Young Adults*. New York: Van Nostrand, 1972.

National Council of Christian Families Opposed to Sex Education in Public Schools Newsletter, Tulsa, OK, 74102, January 19, 1971.

Rafferty, Max. *Classroom Countdown: Education at the Crossroads*. New York: Hawthorn Books, 1970.

Rafferty, Max. *The Education of the Mexican-American: A Summary of the Procedures of the Lake Arrowhead and Anaheim Conferences.* Sacramento: California State Department of Education, 1969.

Rafferty, Max. *Suffer, Little Children.* New York: Signet Books, 1963.

Robinson, Helen, et al., *Dick and Jane: Fun with Our Friends.* New York: Scott, Foresman, and Company, 1965.

San Francisco Unified School District, "An Educational Redesign for the SFUSD," Policies [v.2], 3 of 3, November 17, 1976.

San Francisco Unified School District, "Implementation Plan for 1978–1979, Educational Redesign Plan 1978–1979", February 22, 1978.

Schulz, Esther D., and Sally D. Williams. *Family Life and Sex Education: Curriculum and Instruction.* New York: Harcourt, Brace, and World, Inc., 1968.

"Senator Hayakawa Says Schools Teaching 'Heresy,'" *Sex Education and Mental Health Report,* 10, no. 1, Winter 1980.

Stanford Center for Chicano Research. *Demographic Profile on the Latino Population of San Francisco County.* Stanford, CA: Stanford Center for Chicano Research, 1984.

Steinbacher, John. *Bitter Harvest.* Whittier, CA: Orange Tree Press, 1970.

Steinbacher, John. *The Child Seducers.* Fullerton, CA: Educator Publishers, 1970.

Steinbacher, John. "The Child Seducers Revisited." *American Mercury,* Fall 1970, 5–8.

"The San Francisco Story: Administration, Program, Plant." American School and University 37, no. 2 (October 1964).

US Bureau of the Census. Urban Atlas, Tract Data for Standard Metropolitan Statistical Areas: Anaheim - Santa Ana - Garden Grove, CA. Washington, DC: Government Printing Office, 1974.

US Census Bureau. *American Community Survey, 2011,* American Community Survey 5-Year Estimates.

US Congress, Senate, *Elementary and Secondary Education Act Amendments of 1967,* Senate Report 726 to accompany H.R. 7819, 90th Congress, 1st session, 1967.

US Department of Commerce and Bureau of the Census. *Statistical Abstract of the United States: 1970, 91st Annual Edition.* http://www2.census.gov/prod2/statcomp/documents/1970-01.pdf.

Ventura, Stephanie J., T. J. Matthews, and Brady Hamilton. "Births to Teenagers in the United States, 1940–2000." *National Vital Statistics Report* 49, no. 10 (2001).

Yarborough, Ralph. "Two Proposals for a Better Way of Life for Mexican-Americans in the Southwest," *Congressional Record, January 17,* 1967, 599–600.

BOOKS

Acuña, Rodolfo. *Occupied America: A History of Chicanos.* New York: Harper and Row, 1981.

Anderson, Terry H. *The Movement and the Sixties: Protest in America from Greensboro to Wounded Knee.* New York: Oxford University Press, 1995.

Allyn, David. *Make Love, Not War: The Sexual Revolution, an Unfettered History.* Boston: Little, Brown and Company, 2000.

Baker, Colin. *Foundations of Bilingual Education and Bilingualism.* Tonawanda, NY: Multilingual Matters, 2011.

Bailey, Beth. *Sex in the Heartland.* Cambridge, MA: Harvard University Press, 1999.

Benmayor, Rina, and William V. Flores, eds. *Latino Cultural Citizenship: Claiming Identity, Space and Rights.* Boston: Beacon Press, 1997.

Berkowitz, Edward D. *Something Happened: A Political and Cultural Overview of the Seventies.* New York: Columbia University Press, 2006.

Binder, Amy. *Contentious Curricula: Afrocentrism and Creationism in the Public Schools.* Princeton, NJ: Princeton University Press, 2002.

Breasted, Mary. *Oh! Sex Education!* New York: Praeger Books, 1970.

Blanton, Carlos Kevin, *The Strange Career of Bilingual Education in Texas, 1836–1981.* College Station: Texas A & M University Press, 2004.

Brilliant, Mark. *The Color of America Has Changed: How Racial Diversity Shaped Civil Rights Reform in California, 1941–1978.* New York: Oxford, 2010.

Brilliant, Mark. "Intellectual Affirmative Action: How Multiculturalism Became Mandatory in Higher Education." In *Living in the Eighties,* edited by Gil Troy and Vincent J. Cannato. New York: Oxford University Press, 2009.

Burkholder, Zoe. *Color in the Classroom: How American Schools Taught Race, 1900–1954.* New York: Oxford University Press, 2011.

Camarillo, Albert M. *Chicanos in a Changing Society: From Mexican Pueblos to American Barrios in Santa Barbara and Southern California, 1848–1930.* Cambridge, MA: Harvard University Press, 1979.

Carroll, Peter N., *It Seemed Like Nothing Happened: The Tragedy and Promise of America in the 1970s.* New Brunswick, NJ: Rutgers University Press, 1990.

Chávez, Ernesto. "¡Mi Raza Primero!" *Nationalism, Identity, and Insurgency in the Chicano Movement in Losa Angeles, 1966–1978.* Berkeley: University of California Press, 2002.

Citrin, Jack, and David O. Sears. *Tax Revolt: Something for Nothing in California.* Cambridge, MA: Harvard University Press, 1982.

Cohen, Robert. *Freedom's Orator: Mario Savio and the Radical Legacy of the 1960s.* New York: Oxford, 2009.

Crawford, James. *Bilingual Education: History, Theory, Politics and Practice.* Trenton, NJ: Crane Books, 1989.

Crawford, James, ed., *Language Loyalties: A Source Book on the Official English Controversy.* Chicago: University of Chicago Press, 1992.

Cuban, Larry, and David Tyack. *Tinkering Toward Utopia: A Century of Public School Reform.* Cambridge, MA: Harvard University Press, 1997.

Damon, William. *The Moral Child: Nurturing Children's Natural Moral Growth.* New York: The Free Press, 1988.

Davis, Mike. *Magical Urbanism: Latinos Reinvent the U.S. City.* New York: Verso Books, 2000.

De Genova, Nicholas, and Ana Y. Ramos-Zayas. *Latino Crossings: Mexicans, Puerto Ricans and the Politics of Race and Citizenship.* New York: Routledge, 2003.

Delgado, Richard, and Jean Stefancic, eds. *A Critical Reader: The Latino Condition.* New York: New York University Press, 1998.

D'Emilio, John. *The World Turned: Essays on Gay Politics, History and Culture.* Durham, NC: Duke University Press, 2002.

D'Emilio, John, and Estelle B. Freedman. *Intimate Matters: A History of Sexuality in America.* New York: Harper and Row, 1988.

Diggins, John Patrick. *Ronald Reagan: Fate, Freedom, and the Making of History.* New York: W. W. Norton and Company, 2007.

Dillard, Angela. *Guess Who's Coming to Dinner Now? Multicultural Conservatism in America.* New York: New York University Press, 2001.

Dochuk, Darren. *From Bible Belt to Sunbelt: Plain-Folk Religion, Grassroots Politics, and the Rise of Evangelical Conservatism.* New York: W. W. Norton and Company 2011.

Donato, Ruben. *The Other Struggle for Equal Schools: Mexican Americans in the Civil Rights Era.* Albany: State University of New York Press, 1997.

Douglas, Davidson. *Reading, Writing and Race: The Desegregation of the Charlotte Schools.* Chapel Hill: University of North Carolina Press, 1995.

Dudziak, Mary L. *Cold War Civil Rights: Race and the Image of American Democracy.* Princeton, NJ: Princeton University Press, 2000.

Edsall, Thomas Byrne, and Mary D. Edsall. *Chain Reaction: The Impact of Race, Rights, and Taxes on American Politics.* New York: W. W. Norton and Company, 1991.

Farber, David, and Beth Bailey, eds. *America in the Seventies.* Lawrence: University of Kansas Press, 2004.

Farber, David, and Beth Bailey, eds. *The Sixties: From Memory to History.* Chapel Hill: University of North Carolina Press, 1994.

Farber, David, and Peter Roche, eds. *The Conservative Sixties.* New York: Peter Lang, 2003.

Fass, Paula S. *Outside In: Minorities and the Transformation of American Education.* New York: Oxford University Press, 1989.

Findlay, John. *Magic Lands: Western Cityscapes and American Culture after 1940.* Berkeley: University of California Press, 1992.

Fitzgerald, Frances. *America Revised, History Schoolbooks in the Twentieth Century.* Boston: Little, Brown and Company, 1979.

Foley, Neil. "Becoming White: Mexican Americans and their Faustian Pact with Whiteness." *Reflexiones 1997: New Directions in Mexican American Studies* 53. Austin: University of Texas Press, 1997.

Formisano, Ronald. *Boston Against Busing: Race, Class, and Ethnicity in the 1960s and 70s.* Chapel Hill: University of North Carolina Press, 1991.

Foucault, Michel. *Abnormal: Lectures at the Collège de France, 1974–75*. New York: Verso Books, 2003.

Foucault, Michel. *The History of Sexuality, Part One: An Introduction*. New York: Random House, 1978.

Frank, Thomas. *What's the Matter With Kansas? How Conservatives Won the Heart of America*. New York: Henry Holt and Co., 2004.

Freedman, Estelle B. *Feminism, Sexuality, and Politics*. Chapel Hill: University of North Carolina Press, 2006.

Freedman, Estelle B. *No Turning Back: The History of Feminism and the Future of Women*. New York: Ballantine Books, 2002.

Gaither, Milton. *Homeschool: An American History* (New York: Palgrave Macmillan, 2008.

Garcia, Maria Cristina. *Havana USA: Cuban Exiles and Cuban Americans in South Florida, 1959–1994*. Berkeley: University of California Press, 1994.

Garcia, Mario T. *Blowout! Sal Castro and the Struggle for Chicano Educational Justice*. Chapel Hill: University of North Carolina Press, 2011.

Gitlin, Todd. *The Sixties: Years of Hope, Days of Rage*. New York: Bantam Books, 1987.

Gitlin, Todd. *The Twilight of Common Dreams: Why America is Wracked by Culture Wars*. New York: Henry Holt, 1995. Glazer, Nathan. *Ethnic Dilemmas: 1964–1982*. Cambridge, MA: Harvard University Press, 1983.

Glazer, Nathan. *We Are All Multiculturalists Now*. Cambridge, MA: Harvard University Press, 1997.

Glazer, Nathan, and Daniel Patrick Moynihan. *Beyond the Melting Pot: The Negroes, Puerto Ricans, Jews, and Italians of New York City*. Cambridge: Massachusetts Institute of Technology Press, 1963.

Glazer, Nathan, and Reed Ueda. *Ethnic Groups in American History Textbooks*. Washington, DC: Ethics and Public Policy Center, 1983.

Godfrey, Brian J. *Neighborhoods in Transition: The Making of San Francisco's Ethnic and Nonconformist Communities*. Berkeley: University of California Press, 1988.

Gómez-Quiñones, Juan. *Mexican Students por La Raza: The Chicano Student Movement in Southern California, 1967–77*. Santa Barbara, CA: Editorial La Causa, 1978.

Gonzalez, Gilbert G. *Chicano Education in the Era of Segregation*. Cranbury, NJ: Associated University Presses, 1990.

Gordon, Linda. "U.S. Women's History." In *The New American History*, edited by Eric Foner. Philadelphia: Temple University Press, 1997.

Gould, Stephen Jay. *The Mismeasure of Man*. New York: W. W. Norton and Company, 1981.

Graham, Gael. *Young Activists: American High Schools in an Age of Turmoil*. DeKalb: Northern Illinois University Press, 2006.

Greenberg, David. *Nixon's Shadow: The History of an Image*. New York: W. W. Norton and Company, 2003.

Grubb, Farley. *German Immigration and Servitude in America, 1709–1920.* New York: Routledge, 2011.

Gutierrez, David G. *The Columbia History of Latinos in the United States Since 1960.* New York: Columbia University Press, 2004.

Hacsi, Timothy A. *Children as Pawns: The Politics of Educational Reform.* Cambridge, MA: Harvard University Press, 2002.

Hakuta, Kenji. *The Debate on Bilingualism.* New York: Basic Books, 1987.

Hankins, Barry. *American Evangelicals: A Contemporary History of a Mainstream Religious Movement.* New York: Rowman and Littlefield Publishers, 2009.

Hartman, Andrew. *A War for the Soul Of America: A History of the Culture Wars, From the 1960s to the Present.* Chicago: University of Chicago Press, forthcoming 2015.

Hollinger, David. *Postethnic America: Beyond Multiculturalism.* New York: Basic Books, 1995.

Hottois, James, and Milner, Neal A. *The Sex Education Controversy: a Study of Politics, Education, and Morality.* Lexington: Lexington Books, 1975.

Hunter, James Davison. *Culture Wars: The Struggle to Define America.* New York: Basic Books, 1991.

Jacobson, Matthew Frye. *Whiteness of A Different Color: European Immigrants and the Alchemy of Race.* Cambridge, MA: Harvard University Press, 1998.

Jacoway, Elizabeth. *Turn Away Thy Son: Little Rock, The Crisis that Shocked the Nation.* New York: Simon and Schuster, 2007.

Johnson, David K. *The Lavender Scare: The Cold War Persecution of Gays and Lesbians in the Federal Government.* Chicago: University of Chicago Press, 2004.

Kabaservice, Geoffrey. *Rule and Ruin: The Downfall of Moderation and the Destruction of the Republican Party, from Eisenhower to the Tea Party.* New York: Oxford University Press, 2011.

Kalman, Laura. *Right Star Rising: A New Politics, 1974–1980.* New York: W. W. Norton, 2010.

Katz, Michael B. *The Undeserving Poor: From the War on Poverty to the War on Welfare.* New York: Pantheon Books, 1990.

Kazin, Michael, and Joseph McCartin, eds. *Americanism: New Perspectives on the History of an Ideal.* Chapel Hill: University of North Carolina Press, 2006.

Kripal, Jeffrey. *Esalen: America and the Religion of No Religion.* Berkeley: University of California Press, 2007.

Kruse, Kevin M., and Thomas J. Sugrue, eds. *The New Suburban History.* Chicago: University of Chicago Press, 2006.

Kurashige, Scott. *The Shifting Grounds of Race: Black and Japanese Americans in the Making of Multiethnic Los Angeles.* Princeton, NJ: Princeton University Press, 2008.

Kurlansky, Mark. *1968: The Year that Rocked the World.* New York: Ballantine, 2004.

Kuttner, Robert. *Revolt of the Haves: Tax Rebellions and Hard Times.* New York: Simon and Schuster, 1980.

Kymlicka, Will. *Multicultural Citizenship.* New York: Oxford University Press, 1991.

Irvine, Janice M. *Talk About Sex: The Battles Over Sex Education in the United States.* Berkeley: University of California Press, 2002.

Laats, Adam. *The Other School Reformers: The Conservative Tradition in American Education.* Cambridge, MA: Harvard University Press, 2015.

Lasch-Quinn, Elizabeth. *Race Experts: How Racial Etiquette, Sensitivity Training, and the New Age Hijacked the Civil Rights Revolution.* New York: W. W. Norton and Company, 2001.

Laqueur, Thomas W. *Solitary Sex: A Cultural History of Masturbation.* New York: Zone Books, 2004.

Lassiter, Matthew, and Andrew Lewis, eds. *The Moderate's Dilemma: Massive Resistance to School Desegregation in Virginia.* Charlottesville: University of Virginia Press, 1998.

Lassiter, Matthew D. *The Silent Majority: Suburban Politics in the Sunbelt South.* Princeton, NJ: Princeton University Press, 2006.

Lattin, Vernon E., Rolando Hinojosa, Rolando, and Gary D. Keller, eds. *Tomás Rivera, 1935–1984: The Man and His Work.* Tempe, AZ: Bilingual Review, 1988.

Lord, Alexandra. *Condom Nation: The U.S. Government's Sex Education Campaign from World War I to the Internet.* Baltimore: Johns Hopkins University Press, 2009.

Luker, Kristin. *When Sex Goes to School: Warring Views on Sex—and Sex Education Since the Sixties.* New York: W. W. Norton and Company, 2006.

Macedo, Stephen. *Diversity and Distrust.* Cambridge, MA: Harvard University Press, 2000.

Macedo, Stephen, ed. *Reassessing the Sixties: Debating the Political and Cultural Legacy.* New York: W. W. Norton and Company, 1997.

Martin, Isaac William. *The Permanent Tax Revolt: How the Property Tax Transformed American Politics.* Stanford, CA: Stanford University Press, 2008.

Martin, William. *With God on Our Side: The Rise of the Religious Right in America.* New York: Broadway Books, 1996.

May, Elaine Tyler. *Homeward Bound: American Families in the Cold War.* New York: Basic Books, 1988.

McGirr, Lisa. *Suburban Warriors: The Origins of the New American Right.* Princeton, NJ: Princeton University Press, 2001.

May, Elaine Tyler. *America and The Pill: A History of Peril, Promise, and Liberation.* New York: Basic Books, 2010.

Miller, Richard I. "An Appraisal of ESEA Title III." *Theory into Practice.* New York: Lawrence Erlbaum Associates, Inc., 1967.

Mirel, Jeffrey, *Patriotic Pluralism: Americanization Education and European Immigrants.* Cambridge, MA: Harvard University Press, 2010.

Moran, Jeffrey. *Teaching Sex: The Shaping of Adolescence in the Twentieth Century.* Cambridge, MA: Harvard University Press, 2000.

Moreau, Joseph. *Schoolbook Nation: Conflicts over American History Textbooks from the Civil War to the Present.* Ann Arbor: University of Michigan Press, 2004.

Moreton, Bethany. *To Serve God and Wal-Mart: The Making of Christian Free Enterprise.* Cambridge, MA: Harvard University Press, 2009.

Moreton, Bethany. "Make Payroll, Not War: Business Culture as Youth Culture." In *Rightward Bound: Making America Conservative in the 1970s*, edited by Bruce Schulman and Julian Zelizer. Cambridge, MA: Harvard University Press, 2008.

Muller, Thomas. *La Cuarta Ola: Los Inmigrantes Más Recientes de California.* Washington, DC: The Urban Institute Press, 1984.

Muñoz, Carlos. Jr., *Youth, Identity, Power: The Chicano Movement.* New York: Verso Books, 1989.

Nelson, Adam. *The Elusive Ideal: Equal Educational Opportunity and the Federal Role in Boston's Public Schools, 1950–1985.* Chicago: University of Chicago Press, 2005.

Nicolaides, Becky M. *My Blue Heaven: Life and Politics in the Working-Class Suburbs of Los Angeles.* Chicago: University of Chicago Press, 2002.

Nickerson, Michelle. *Mothers of Conservatism: Women and the Postwar Right.* Princeton, NJ: Princeton University Press, 2014.

Orrick William H.Jr., *Shut it Down! A College in Crisis: San Francisco State College, October, 1968–April, 1969.* Honolulu: University Press of the Pacific, 1969.

Padilla, Felix M. *Latino Ethnic Consciousness: The Case of Mexican-Americans and Puerto Ricans in Chicago.* South Bend, IN: University of Notre Dame Press, 1985.

Passel, Jeffrey S. "Hispanic/Latino Identity and Identifiers," *Encyclopedia of the U.S. Census.* Washington, DC: Congressional Quarterly Press, 2012.

Patterson, James T. *Brown v. Board of Education: A Civil Rights Milestone and Its Troubled Legacy.* New York: Oxford University Press, 2001.

Patterson, James T. *Grand Expectations: The United States, 1945–1974.* New York: Oxford University Press, 1996.

Pérez, Gina M. *The Near Northwest Side Story Migration, Displacement, and Puerto Rican Families.* Berkeley: University of California Press, 2004.

Perlstein, Daniel H. *Justice, Justice: School Politics and the Eclipse of Liberalism.* New York: Peter Lang, 2004.

Perlstein, Rick. *Barry Goldwater and the Unmaking of the American Consensus.* New York: Hill and Wang, 2001.

Perlstein, Rick. *Nixonland: The Rise of a President and the Fracturing of America.* New York: Scribner, 2009.

Pitti, Stephen. *The Devil in Silicon Valley: Northern California, Race, and Mexican Americans.* Princeton, NJ: Princeton University Press, 2004.

Podair, Jerold E. *The Strike that Changed New York: Blacks, Whites, and the Ocean Hill-Brownsville Case.* New Haven, CT: Yale University Press, 2002.

Ramos-Zayas, Ana. *National Performances: The Politics of Class, Race, and Space in Puerto Rican Chicago.* Chicago: University of Chicago Press, 2003.

Ribuffo, Leo P. *The Old Christian Right the Protestant Far Right from the Great Depression to the Cold War*. Philadelphia: Temple University Press, 1983.

Ravitch, Diane. *The Troubled Crusade: American Education 1945–1980*. New York: Basic Books, 1983.

Redekop, John Harold. *The American Far Right: A Case Study of Billy James Hargis and Christian Crusade*. Grand Rapids, MI: W. B. Eerdmans Publishing Company, 1968.

Rieder, Jonathan. *Canarsie: The Jews and Italians of Brooklyn Against Liberalism*. Cambridge, MA: Harvard University Press, 1985.

Rodriguez, Richard. *Hunger of Memory: The Education of Richard Rodriguez*. New York: Bantam Books, 1982.

Rosenblum, Nancy. *Membership and Morals: The Personal Uses of Pluralism in America*. Princeton, NJ: Princeton University Press, 1998.

Roszak, Theodore. *The Making of a Counterculture: Reflections on the Technocratic Society and its Youthful Opposition*. Berkeley: University of California Press, 1995.

Rúa, Mérida M. *A Grounded Identidad: Making New Lives in Chicago's Puerto Rican Neighborhoods*. New York: Oxford University Press, 2012.

Rudd, Mark. *Underground: My Life with SDS and the Weathermen*. New York: HarperCollins, 2009.

Rymph, Catherine. *Republican Women: Feminism and Conservatism from Suffrage through the Rise of the New Right*. Chapel Hill: University of North Carolina Press, 2006.

Sanchez, George J. *Becoming Mexican American: Ethnicity, Culture, and Identity in Los Angeles, 1900–1945*. New York: Oxford University Press, 1993.

Sánchez Korrol, Virginia. *From Colonia to Community: The History of Puerto Ricans in New York City, 1917–1948*. Westport, CT: Greenwood Press, 1983.

Sandbrook, Dominic. *Mad as Hell: The Crisis of the 1970s and the Rise of the Populist Right*. New York: Knopf, 2011.

Sandoval, Tomas. *Latinos at the Golden Gate: Creating Community and Identity in San Francisco*. Chapel Hill: University of North Carolina Press, 2013.

San Miguel Guadelupe. Jr., "Let All of Them Take Heed": *Mexican-Americans and the Campaign for Educational Equity in Texas, 1910–1981*. Austin: University of Texas Press, 1987.

San Miguel Guadelupe. Jr., *Contested Policy: The Rise and Fall of Federal Bilingual Education in the United States, 1960–2002*. Denton: University of North Texas Press, 2004.

Schiesl, Martin, and Mark M. Dodge, eds. *City of Promise: Race and Historical Change in Los Angeles*. Claremont, CA: Regina Books, 2006.

Schlesinger Arthur M. Jr., *The Disuniting of America: Reflections on a Multicultural Society*. New York: W. W. Norton and Company, 1991.

Schneider, Susan Gilbert. *Revolution, Reaction or Reform? The 1974 Bilingual Education Act*. New York: Las Americas Publishing Company, 1976.

Schneiderman, David. *Language and the State: The Law and Politics of Identity.* Montreal: Les Editions Yvon Blais Inc., 1991.

Schoenwald, Jonathan. *A Time for Choosing: The Rise of Modern American Conservatism.* New York: Oxford University Press, 2002.

Schrag, Peter. *Paradise Lost: California's Experience, America's Future.* Berkeley: University of California Press, 1998.

Schulman, Bruce. *The Seventies: The Great Shift in American Culture, Society and Politics.* Cambridge, MA: Da Capo Press, 2002.

Schulman, Bruce, and Julian Zelizer, eds. *Rightward Bound: Making America Conservative in the 1970s.* Cambridge, MA: Harvard University Press, 2008.

Sears, James T. *Sexuality and the Curriculum: The Politics and Practices of Sexuality and Freedom.* New York: Teachers College Press, 1992.

Self, Robert O. *American Babylon: Race and the Struggle for Postwar Oakland.* Princeton, NJ: Princeton University Press, 2005.

Self, Robert O., *All in the Family: The Realignment of American Democracy Since the 1960s.* New York: Farrar, Strauss, and Giroux, 2012.

Shor, Ira. *Culture Wars: School and Society in the Conservative Restoration, 1969–1984.* Boston, MA: Routledge and K. Paul, 1986.

Solinger, Rickie. *Wake Up Little Susie: Single Pregnancy and Race before Roe v. Wade.* New York: Routledge, 1992.

Sommer, Doris. *Bilingual Aesthetics: A New Sentimental Education.* Durham, NC: Duke University Press, 2004.

Spring, Joel. *Deculturalization and the Struggle for Equality: A Brief History of the Education of Dominated Cultures in the United States,* 3rd edition. New York: McGraw Hill, 2001.

Stein, Colman Brez. *Sink or Swim: The Politics of Bilingual Education.* New York: Praeger, 1986.

Straus, Emily. *Death of a Suburban Dream: Race and Schools in Compton, California.* Philadelphia: University of Pennsylvania Press, 2014.

Summers-Sandoval, Tomas. *Latinos at the Golden Gate: Creating Community & Identity in San Francisco.* Chapel Hill: University of North Carolina Press, 2013.

Ullman, Sharon. *Sex Seen: The Emergence of Modern Sexuality in America.* Berkeley: University of California Press, 1997.

Taylor, Charles. *Multiculturalism: Examining the Politics of Recognition.* Princeton, NJ: Princeton University Press, 1994.

Taylor, Clarence. *Knocking at Our Own Door: Milton A. Galamison and the Struggle to Integrate New York City Schools.* New York: Columbia University Press, 1997.

Thomas, Lorrin. *Puerto Rican Citizen: History and Political Identity in Twentieth-Century New York City.* Chicago: University of Chicago Press 2013.

Tyack, David. *Seeking Common Ground: Public Schools in a Diverse Society.* Cambridge, MA: Harvard University Press, 2004.

Walzer, Michael. *Spheres of Justice: A Defense of Pluralism and Equality*. New York: Basic Books, 1983.

Westcott, John. *Anaheim: City of Dreams: An Illustrated History*. Chatsworth, CA: Windsor Publications, 1990.

Whalen, Carmen Teresa. *From Puerto Rico to Philadelphia: Puerto Rican Workers and Postwar Economies*. Philadelphia: Temple University Press, 2001.

Wheeler, Leigh Ann. *Against Obscenity: Reform and the Politics of Womanhood in America, 1973–1935*. Baltimore: Johns Hopkins University Press, 2004.

Whitehead, Fred. *Culture Wars: Opposing Viewpoints*. San Diego: Greenhaven Press, 1994.

Williams, Daniel K. *God's Own Party: The Making of the Christian Right*. New York: Oxford, 2010.

Williams, Rhys H. *Culture Wars in American Politics: Critical Reviews of a Popular Myth*. New York: Aldine de Gruyter, 1997.

Wolfe, Alan. *One Nation, After All*. New York: Viking, 1998.

Woodward, Komozi, ed. *Freedom North: Black Freedom Struggles Outside the South, 1940–1980*. Gordonsville, VA: Palgrave Macmillan, 2003.

Wu, Ellen D. *The Color of Success: Asian Americans and the Origins of the Model Minority*. Princeton, NJ: Princeton University Press, 2013.

Wuthnow, Robert. *After Heaven: Spirituality in America since the 1950s*. Berkeley: University of California Press, 1998.

Zaretsky, Natasha. *No Direction Home: The American Family and Fear of National Decline, 1968–1980*. Chapel Hill: University of North Carolina Press, 2007.

Zimmerman, Jonathan. *Whose America? Culture Wars in the Public Schools*. Cambridge, MA: Harvard University Press, 2002.

ARTICLES

Bailey, Beth. "Prescribing the Pill: Politics, Culture, and the Sexual Revolution in America's Heartland." *Journal of Social History* 30, no. 4 (Summer 1997): 827–856.

Barrett, James, and David Roediger. "In-between People: Race, Nationality, and the 'New Immigrant' Working Class." *Journal of American Ethnic History* 16, no. 3 (Spring 1997): 3–44.

Berke, Joel S. "Federal Educational Policy on School Finance After Proposition 13: Short and Long Run Implication." *Educational Evaluation and Policy Analysis* 1, no. 9 (September–October 1979), 19–27.

Borrelli, Maryanne. "Competing Conceptions of the First Ladyship: Public Responses to Betty Ford's 60 Minutes Interview." *Presidential Studies Quarterly* 31, no. 3 (September 2001): 397–414.

Brinkley, Alan. "The Problem of American Conservatism." *The American Historical Review* 99, no. 2 (1994): 409–429.

Camarillo, Albert M. "Cities of Color: The New Racial Frontier in America's Minority-Majority Cities," *Pacific Historical Quarterly* 76, no. 1 (February 2007): 1–28.

Catterall, James S., and Emily Brizendine. "Proposition 13: Effects of High School Curricula, 1978–1983." *American Journal of Education* 93, no. 3 (May 1985), 324–351.

Carter, Julian. "Birds, Bees, and Venereal Disease: Toward an Intellectual History of Sex Education." *Journal of the History of Sexuality* 10, no. 2 (2001): 213–249.

Chabran, Richard. "Activism and Intellectual Struggle in the Life of Ernesto Galarza, 1905–1984." *Hispanic Journal of Behavioral Sciences* 7, no. 2 (1985): 135–152.

Citrin, Jack. "Proposition 13 and the Transformation of California Government." *The California Journal of Politics and Policy* 1, no. 1 (2009).

Cohen, Gaynor. "Alliance and Conflict Among Mexican Americans." *Ethnic and Racial Studies* [Great Britain] 5, no. 2 (1982): 175–195.

Davies, Gareth. "The Great Society After Johnson: The Case of Bilingual Education." *Journal of American History* 88, no. 4 (2002): 1405–1429.

DeAnda, Robert M. "Ernesto Galarza and Mexican Children's Literature in the United States," *Camino Real* 4, no. 7 (2012): 11–28.

del Olmo, Frank. "Hispanic, Latino, or Chicano? A Historical Review." Accessed via http://www.nahj.org/resourceguide/intro2.html. 2001.

Diggins, John Patrick. "How Ronald Reagan Reinvented Religion." *History News Network.* June 6, 2007. Accessed via http://hnn.us/articles/38958.html.

Edwards, John R. "Critics and Criticisms of Bilingual Education," *Modern Language Journal* 64, no. 4 (Winter 1980): 409–416.

Fishman, Joshua. "The Status and Prospects of Bilingualism in the U.S." *Modern Language Journal* 49, (March 1965): 143–155.

Foley, Neil. "Over the Rainbow: Hernandez v Texas, Brown v Board of Education, and Black v Brown." In "Colored Men" and "Hombres Aquí": *Hernandez v. Texas and the Emergence of Mexican-American Lawyering*, edited by Michael Olivas. Houston: Arte Publico Press, 2006, 116–117.

Frank, Gillian. "The Civil Rights of Parents: Race and Conservative Parents in Anita Bryant's Campaign Against Gay Rights in 1970s Florida." *Journal of the History of Sexuality* 22, no. 1 (January 2013): 126–160.

Galston, William. "Two Concepts of Liberalism." *Ethics* 105, no. 3 (April 1995): 516–534.

Gold, Deborah. "Two Languages, One Aim: Two-Way Learning." *Education Week*, January 20, 1988.

Gutmann, Amy. "Civic Education and Social Diversity." *Ethics* 105, no. 3, (April 1995): 557–581.

Higham, John. "Multiculturalism and Universalism: A History and Critique." *American Quarterly* 45, no. 2 (June 1993): 195–219.

Himmelstein, Jerome L. "The Road to Proposition 13." *Contemporary Sociology* 20, no. 1 (January 1991).

Howard, Clayton. "Building a Family-Friendly Metropolis: Sexuality, the State, and Postwar Housing Policy." *Journal of Urban History* (September 2013).

Huntington, Samuel P. "The Hispanic Challenge." *Foreign Policy* (March–April 2004): 1–12.

Inda, Juan Javier. "La Comunidad en Lucha: The Development of the East Los Angeles High School Blowouts," Stanford Center for Chicano Research, Stanford University, Working Papers Series, No. 29, March 1990.

Kirst, Michael W. "Organizations in Shock and Overload: California's Public Schools 1970–80," *Educational Evaluation and Policy Analysis* 1, no. 4, July–August 1979.

Kruse, Kevin M. "The Politics of Race and Public Space: Desegregation, Privatization, and the Tax Revolt in Atlanta." *Journal of Urban History* 31, no. 5 (July 2005), 610-633.

Lau, Estelle Pau-on. "California's Contribution to Bilingual Education: Lau vs. Nichols." *Pacific Historian* 24, no. 1 (1980): 45–54.

LeBars, Sylvie. "Strategies de Participation des Chicanos a la Societe Civile Americaine." *Revue Francaise d'Etudes Americaines.* [France] 17, no. 66 (1995): 543–551.

Lee, N'Tanya, Don Murphy, and Juliet Ucelli. "Whose Kids? Our Kids! Race, Sexuality, and the Right in New York City's Curriculum Battles." *Radical America* 25, no. 1 (1991): 9–21.

Lopez, Ian Haney. "White Latinos." *Harvard Latino Law Review* 6 (2003): 1–7. Accessed via http://www.law.harvard.edu/students/orgs/llr/vol6/lopez.pdf.

Lyons, James J. "The Past and Future Directions of Federal Bilingual-Education Policy." *Annals of the American Academy of Political and Social Science* 508 (March 1990).

Macedo, Stephen. "Liberal Civic Education and Religious Fundamentalism: The Case of God v. John Rawls?" *Ethics* 105, no. 3, 1995, 468–496.

Mackintosh, Douglas R., Kathy L. Glassman, Nancy Picard, and Shelley C. Herman. "Sex Education in New Orleans: The Birchers Win a Victory." *New South* 25, no. 3 (1970): 46–56.

Malfetti, James L., and Arline M. Rubin. "Sex Education: Who is Teaching the Teachers?" *Teachers College Record* 69, no. 3 (1967): 213–222.

Mattingly, Doreen J. "Gender and the Politics of Scale: The Christian Right, Sex Education, and 'Community' in Vista, California, 1990–1994." *Historical Geography* 26 (1998): 65–82.

Mehlman, Natalia. "Sex Ed . . . and the Reds?: Reconsidering the Anaheim Battle Over Sex Education, 1962–69." *History of Education Quarterly* 47, no. 2 (May 2007).

Mehlman Petrzela, Natalia. "Multiculturalism." In Encyclopedia of Human Global Migration, edited by Immanuel Ness. New York: Blackwell Publishing, 2013.

Mehlman Petrzela, Natalia. "Revisiting the Rightward Turn: Max Rafferty, Education, and Modern American Politics." *The Sixties: A Journal of History, Politics, and Culture* 6, no. 2 (December 2013): 143–171.

Miller, Lamar P., and Lisa A. Tanners. "Diversity and the New Immigrants." *Teachers College Record* 96, no. 4 (1995): 671–680.

Nathan, Richard P. "The Nationalization of Proposition 13." PS 14, no. 4 (Autumn 1981).

Newland, Kathleen. "Circular Migration and Human Development." United Nations Development Programme Human Development Reports. October 2009.

Phelan, William T. "Staffing Policies in Times of Retrenchment: Teacher Opinions." *Peabody Journal of Education* 6, no. 2 (Winter 1983).

Ruiz, Vicki L. "Moreno/a, Blanco/a y Café con Leche: Racial Constructions in Chicano/a Historiography." *Mexican Studies/Estudios Mexicanos* 20, no. 2 (Summer 2004): 343–359.

Scassa, Teresa. "Language, Culture, and the Courts: Bilingual Education in the United States." *Canadian Review of American Studies* 26, no. 1 (1996).

Schmidt, Ronald. "Uniformity or Diversity? Recent Language Policy in California Public Education." *California History* 68, no. 4 (1989–1990): 230–239.

Scott, Daryl M. "Postwar Pluralism, Brown v Board of Education and the Origins of Multiculturalism," *Journal of American History.* June 2004.

Sigelman, Lee, David Lowery and Roland Smith, "The Tax Revolt: A Comparative State Analysis." *Western Political Quarterly* 36, no.1, (March 1983), 30–51.

Smith, Daniel A. "Howard Jarvis, Populist Entrepreneur: Reevaluating the Causes of Proposition 13." *Social Science History* 23, no. 2 (1999): 173–210.

Sommers, Laurie Kay. "Inventing Latinismo: The Creation of a Hispanic Panethnicity in the United States." *The Journal of American Folklore* 104 (Winter 1991): 32–53.

Urrieta Luis. Jr., "Dis-connections in 'American' Citizenship and the Post/neo-colonial: People of Mexican Descent and Whitestream Pedagogy and Curriculum." *Theory and Research in Social Education* 32, no. 4 (Fall 2004): 433–458.

Van Dyke, Neila. "Hotbeds of Activism: Locations of Student Protest." *Social Problems* 45, no. 2 (1998): 205–220.

Young, Iris Marion. "Polity and Group Difference: A Critique of the Ideal of Universal Group Citizenship." *Ethics* 99, no. 2 (1989): 250–274.

Zimmerman, Jonathan. "Brown-ing the American Textbook: History, Psychology, and the Origins of Modern Multiculturalism." *History of Education Quarterly* 44, no. 1, A Special Issue on the Fiftieth Anniversary of the "Brown v. Board of Education" Decision (Spring 2004): 46–69.

Zimmerman, Jonathan. "Ethnics Against Ethnicity: European Immigrants and Foreign-Language Instruction, 1890–1940." *Journal of American History.* 2002. http://www.historycooperative.org/journals/jah/88.4/zimmerman.html.

UNPUBLISHED THESES AND DISSERTATIONS

Anderson, Kimberly Susan. "Bilingual Education and the Politics of Cultural Citizenship in California pre- and post-Proposition 227." Ph.D. dissertation, University of Texas, Austin, 2003.

Baez, Luis Antonio. "From Transformative School Goals to Assimilationist and Remedial Bilingual Education: A Critical Review of Key Precedent-Setting

Hispanic Bilingual Litigation Decided by Federal Courts between 1974 and 1983." Ph.D. dissertation, University of Wisconsin, Milwaukee, 1995.

Bates, Elizabeth. "100 Years of Public Education: A Study of the Development of Elementary Education in the City of Los Angeles." Master's thesis, University of Southern California School of Education, 1928.

Belcher, Katherine L. "Bordering on Success: A Portrait of the Calexico Unified School District since Bilingual Education, 1963–2000." Ph.D. dissertation, University of Pennsylvania, 2006.

Bernal, Dolores Delgado. "Chicana School Resistance and Grassroots Leadership: Providing an Alternative History of the 1968 East Los Angeles Blowouts." Ph.D. dissertation, University of California, Los Angeles, 1997.

Brilliant, Mark. "Color Lines: Civil Rights Struggles on America's Racial Frontier, 1945–1975." Ph.D. Dissertation, Stanford University, 2000.

Burkholder, Zoe. "'With Science as His Shield': Teaching Race and Culture in American Schools." Ph.D. dissertation, New York University, 2008.

Carmona, Ralph Chris. "Language and Ethnic Politics: Bilingualism in Los Angeles City Schools, 1975–1980." Ph.D. dissertation, University of California, Santa Barbara, 1984.

Dominguez, Fernando Carlos. "The Relationship of Parental Involvement and Language Dominance to Academic Achievement in a Bilingual Program in a California High School." Ph.D. dissertation, Texas A & M University, 1984.

Gadsden, Brett. "Victory Without Triumph: The Ironies of School Desegregation in Delaware, 1948–1978." Ph.D. dissertation, Northwestern University, 2006.

Gutfreund, Zevi. "Should Bilingual Education Board the Bus Too?: Spanish Speakers, School Desegregation, and the Challenge of Liberalism in Los Angeles," unpublished paper. Presented at the University of Pennsylvania conference, "Schools and the New Inequality," April 2008.

Gutfreund, Zevi. "Language, Education, Race, and the Remaking of American Citizenship in Los Angeles, 1900–1968," Dissertation, University of California, Los Angeles, 2013.

Howard, Clayton. "The Closet and the Cul de Sac: Sex, Politics, and Suburbanization in Postwar California," Ph.D. dissertation, University of Michigan, 2010.

Lewis, Heather B. "Protest, Place and Pedagogy: New York City's Community Control Movement and its Aftermath, 1966–1996." Ph.D. dissertation, New York University, 2006.

Muo, Martin Chuks. "The Passage of the 1968 Bilingual Education Act and Its Aftermath: A Legislative Systems Analysis." Ph.D dissertation, Howard University, 1994.

Navarro, Richard. Identity and Consensus in the Politics of Bilingual Education: The Case of California, 1967–1980." Ph.D. dissertation, Stanford University, 1984.

Rust, Georgetta R. "A Study of Factors Impeding Proposed Family Life and Sex Education Program Adoption in Sacramento County, California, During 1968." Master's thesis, Sacramento State College, 1969.

Sanchez, Gilbert. "An Analysis of the Bilingual Education Act." Ph.D. dissertation, University of Massachusetts, 1973.

Truett, Samuel J. "Neighbors by Nature: The Transformation of Land and Life in the United States-Mexico Borderlands, 1854–1910." Ph.D. dissertation, Yale University, 1997.

# INDEX